CRITICAL INSIGHTS

The Inferno

by Dante

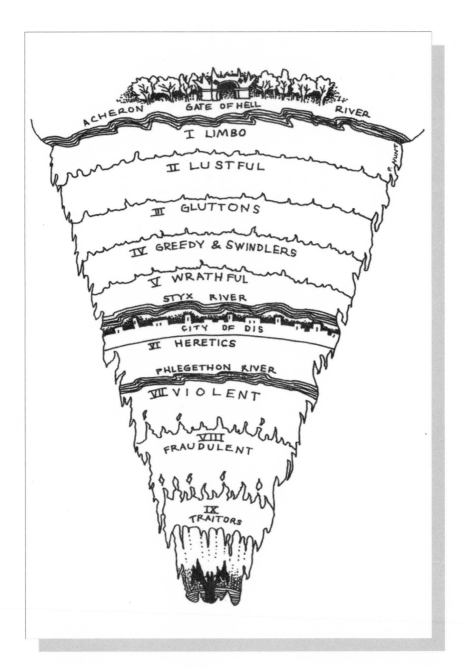

CRITICAL INSIGHTS

The Inferno

by Dante

Editor
Patrick Hunt
Stanford University

Salem Press
Pasadena, California   Hackensack, New Jersey

Cover photo: The Granger Collection, New York

Frontispiece: Patrick Hunt

Copyright © 2012 by Salem Press,
a Division of EBSCO Publishing, Inc.

Editor's text © 2012 by Patrick Hunt
"The *Paris Review* Perspective" © 2012 by Nicole Rudick for *The Paris Review*

∞ The paper used in these volumes conforms to the American National Standard for Permanence of Paper for Printed Library Materials, Z39.48-1992 (R1997).

Library of Congress Cataloging-in-Publication Data
The Inferno, by Dante / editor, Patrick Hunt.
    p. cm. — (Critical insights)
Includes bibliographical references and index.
    ISBN 978-1-58765-838-9 (alk. paper) — ISBN 978-1-58765-821-1 (set, Critical insights : alk. paper)
    1. Dante Alighieri, 1265-1321. Inferno. I. Hunt, Patrick.
PQ4443.I525 2012
851'.1—dc23

                                                                        2011019115

Contents _____

Resources

About This Volume

Patrick Hunt

Dante deserves a new reading with each successive generation, not because his poetry evokes an obsolete Christian world or relict philosophy worthy of being curated in the museum of intellectual history, or because he bridges several influential worlds long gone from view but still deeply rooted in our art, literature, and common figurative language. Dante is immortal because his epic poem *La divina commedia*, or *The Divine Comedy*, distilled more creative genius in the few decades it took to write—indeed it may take place symbolically over only three days—than many cultures preserve of their legacies over millennia. Dante is at the very heart of Western culture.

Dante was for a while underappreciated soon after the Renaissance—although, early on, Giovanni Boccaccio expressly lauded him, and Giotto and Masaccio, for example, posthumously painted him at times with laurels—and it was the great romantic poet Samuel Taylor Coleridge (1772-1834) who helped to restore Dante's reputation by bringing him back into favor in the modern Anglophone world, quoting Dante in his poetry (see Coleridge's 1830 poem "Reason") and even more often in his lectures and his written *Biographia Literaria* (1817). Judging by his own imagination and appreciation of poetic epic and theology (*The Rime of the Ancient Mariner*), Coleridge was a visionary in his own right and was a good judge of poetic genius and a cosmic view of life through a deeply religious or metaphysical lens.

Now on the shelves of every major university and college library in the world, hundreds of volumes of translations of the *Commedia* as well as commentaries and derived scholarship on the work demonstrate that many academic careers have been devoted entirely to Dante. Whole highly regarded journals, conferences, and learned societies still center on or gather frequently around Dante's peerless work. In the preface to his 2007 reader's guide *Danteworlds*, Guy P. Raffa notes, "We are in the midst of a mini renaissance in the cultural appreciation of Dante's poetic masterpiece, the *Divine Comedy*." If one reads the lists of new books published each year across many countries, new Dante studies always manage to turn up in different languages, many far removed from Italian. Symposium conferences such as the one held in late October 2010 on "Galileo in Hell" at the Center for Medieval and Renaissance Studies, University of California, Los Angeles, showcase new awareness of Dante's influence even on the Galilean mathematics and science of measuring "Hell" as scientific scaling laws began in modern thought. This is just one example of the nearly endless possibilities Dante still offers for research so many years after his writing.

This Critical Insights volume is not intended to add to the ever-growing, almost endless number of commentaries on Dante's work; rather, it is intended to make Dante's *Inferno* even more accessible to inquiring students who wonder, like so many of us, at his genius. The contributors to this volume are in the main Dante scholars of great importance, especially in Anglophone circles, whether in new work by current magisterial authorities or reprints of seminal scholarship over decades. Along with Robert Pogue Harrison's new essay offering a close reading of Dante from a standpoint of his choice, Heather Webb provides a new essay that compares and contrasts the *Inferno* with Dante's other writing. In other essays written specifically for this volume, David Lummus discusses the critical reception of Dante, reviewing a history of responses to the poet's work, and Elizabeth Coggeshall addresses the cultural and historical context of the *Inferno*. An excellent contribution by Nicole Rudick (*Paris Review*) muses on various *Inferno* interpretations.

Additionally, those of us who have also sat spellbound by lectures given by the likes of John Freccero or Robert Harrison are privileged to remember how captivatingly they have tracked Dante's path and followed his peerless influence. Acknowledgments are thus made here to Robert Harrison, without whose generous vision and assistance this volume would have been unlikely. Also, to many of my students over the years at Stanford University and elsewhere who have journeyed in Dante's literary footsteps in difficult places, I offer my gratitude for their patience in treading not lightly but nonetheless thoughtfully through Dante's incredibly wrought cosmos. As Archibald Macallister notes in his 1953 preface to John Ciardi's *Inferno* translation and commentary, "In the *Divine Comedy* we must remember that Dante had for his subject the whole world, the entire universe, all of man's history."

THE BOOK
AND
AUTHOR

On the *Inferno*_____

Patrick Hunt

If we consider the subject matter [of the *Commedia*], at the beginning it is horrible and foul, as being Hell . . .

—Dante, *Letter to Cangrande della Scala*

Prologue

Dante Alighieri (1265-1321) is the giant of the Italian medieval world, the very spirit of genius looming not only over his native Florence and Italy but over all of Europe as well. His vision of what could take place beyond this life illumines both the religious and the political life of his time. His vast literary and philosophical imagination fills the richest intellectual and cultural template coloring the age when nobles and prelates clamored for power in the Age of Faith, highlighting beatific inspiration and bitter intrigues alike. Like the soaring and profound music of Johann Sebastian Bach, Dante's creation will outlive many monuments of stone. In Dante, courtly love and heavenly devotion intermingle realistically with venial sin and violence. While generally metaphysical in scope and allegorical in style, Dante's poetry is also graphically physical in its imagery. Dante's profound and profane language surprisingly runs the full range of registers, from the most sublime and elevated to the most vernacular and ribald, and his literary inventiveness remains an amazement to scholars nearly seven hundred years later.

The triple epic poem Dante conceived as the *Commedia* somewhere around 1300 soon spread through and beyond Italy. Quoted by the best minds of the day, his lines in the new vernacular of Italian even appeared in the correspondence of members of learned society and in the margins of civic records outside Florence. Because he championed Italian over Latin when all learning was conveyed in Latin, Dante is often called the father of the Italian language. Another justly deserved epithet of Dante is *Il Sommo Poeta* in Italian—the Supreme Poet. The title of his *Commedia*, a work written mostly during the decades of Dante's exile from Florence after 1302, was soon expanded to the *Commedia divina—Divine Comedy*—by an admiring Giovanni Boccaccio (1313-75), himself one of the three greatest early Italian literary giants, along with Petrarch (1304-74), both of them instrumental figures in the early Italian Renaissance.

The *Inferno*, the first epic of the *Divine Comedy*, is Dante's most famous work, an immense inward journey of a thoughtful, mystical soul attempting to justify the baneful wrath of God against unrepentant sinners. It is fictional but at the same time nonetheless grounded in real events of Dante's life. Thanks to Dante, the Italian loanword *inferno* is now a commonplace metaphor for a raging firestorm. Perhaps more than many thoughtful, educated Christians before him, Augustine included, Dante grappled literarily and philosophically with understanding afterlife judgment and divine reckoning in the *Inferno* as well as with projecting redemption, mercy, and forgiveness in the *Purgatorio* and *Paradiso*.

Dante's *Inferno* owes much to Christian thought but also owes much to classical lore and learning, borrowing from the Underworld of antiquity and filled with its monsters. His many allusions to Virgil, his mentor and guide through the downward spiral, echo not only mythology and poetic precedent but also rhetoric and philosophy, and his liberal use of other poets such as Ovid also shows Dante to be one of the most learned minds of the medieval world. His sources are developed in some detail below.

Dante's vision is not only farsighted in time, as he deals with eternity, but also cosmic, as he considers space in both the earthly sense and beyond, in the vast heavens above and hell below, although his *Paradiso* does not really take place in what we can easily call outer space. If his politics, as gleaned from the *Inferno*, often bear a personal grudge, Dante nonetheless considers well that corrupted human actions on earth have unintended consequences in life and afterlife. His purview of the world may be medieval, but it is also greatly tinged by a trail of scholarship and philosophy that many of his less educated contemporaries would have been unlikely to follow so assiduously. A particular critical lens through which best to view Dante is provided in this volume with Robert Pogue Harrison's new essay "The Love That Moves."

Dante's Sources

The Bible was Dante's most important single source; in the *Inferno* Christian Scriptures are referenced more than any other work, cited at least 575 times, according to Hawkins, more than Aristotle (395 times) or Virgil (192 times).[1] One of the clearest biblical ideas in the *Inferno* beyond the lasting judgment itself is the shuddering notion that painful burning flames pervade the dire atmosphere and heated rock, accompanied by noxious smoke, sulfur (brimstone), and burning pitch. While Dante may not always explicitly quote Christian Scripture in a direct fashion to evoke authoritatively the perpetual burning, the *Inferno*'s overall background is derived from, for example, passages such as the biblical Mark 9:45-48: "hell, where the fire never goes out . . . where their worm does not die, and the fire is not quenched. Everyone will be salted with fire." Here Jesus allegorizes an actual biblical landscape place as Gehenna (in Aramaic), so named after the Hebrew Ge-[Ben]-Hinnom, or Hinnom Valley (Geenna in Koiné New Testament Greek), a place of perpetual stench and physical corruption where Jerusalemites traditionally dumped and burned their refuse so that it was always smoking. Dante must have known of the biblical passage since this ethos is inescapable in his *Inferno*, whose meaning is also connected with Hell's consuming-yet-preserving eternal furnace.

On the other hand, Dante is not as preoccupied with eternal hellfire as are other medieval literary accounts and apocalyptic visions. Thus the context of hellfire and related burning is better represented elsewhere, including in medieval art. For example, somewhat earlier sculpted tympana of Romanesque and Gothic cathedral portals are often more macabre with demons, flames, and serpents (note those of Ghislebertus at the Church of Saint Lazare-Autun, circa 1130, and others at Saint Etienne-Bourges, circa 1195, respectively), although flames are most noticeable in paintings. This fiery ethos is seen in illuminated manuscripts and the considerably later (around 1450) highly detailed Rogier van der Weyden painting *The Last Judgment*, which visualizes the gospel setting of Matthew 25, with its homily on allegorized sheep and goats in "blessing" (*benedictus*) or "cursing" (*maledictus*), now in the Hôtel-Dieu of the Hospice de Beaune. In van der Weyden's visual work of art, red flames lick at and surround the damned in graphic luridness, each doomed sinner with mouth agape in a grim rictus of pain or gnashing of teeth. While anatomically precise in his epic poem, Dante is more interested in philosophical dialogue with sinners who can yet converse with him (as the Pilgrim) even in Hell.

In fact, in startling contrast to hellfire, at the very bottom pit of Hell is the frozen lake of Cocytus in the ninth circle of canto 34, where Lucifer is condemned forever. Why the complete antithesis of ice instead of fire? How can freezing cold be the absolute depth of damnation when biblical unquenchable fire is one of Dante's extended metaphors—the above qualifier notwithstanding—in the *Inferno*? Dante is a master of symbolism, and fire still has warmth—too much so; as a speculative but effective contrasting metaphor, Dante might be suggesting that warmth is still a suggestion of God's far-reaching presence, a living fire himself according to Scripture ("Our God is a consuming fire" in Hebrews 12:29). The absence of heat and light, like the absolute zero cold of outer space in a prescience Dante could not even know, could appropriately symbolize the complete absence of God's presence, the stone-cold lifelessness of being as far from God as possible. Dante even calls this coldness a mystery, but such a symbolic image would be just like him to think through as a superb poet and master of dramatic context. This unique image from canto 34 is examined further below in the discussion of the landscape of the *Inferno*.

Not only was Dante familiar with classical authors such as Virgil and Ovid and many biblical texts, but he also had read and referenced other ancient authors, including Boethius, Cicero, Horace, Lucan, Statius, Augustine, and Averröes, and near-contemporary theologians such as Thomas Aquinas, Bonaventura, and Bernard of Clairvaux, along with certain mystics and even parts of Plato in Latin translation. It has long been noted by scholars that Dante's "Limbo" in the *Inferno*'s canto 2, with the unbaptized souls of infants at the Acheron River, directly references the metaphysical passage of *Aeneid* 6.325-30, where Virgil seems to suggest metempsychosis or transmigration of the soul in rebirth.[2] At times Dante makes his borrowings and influences clear by leaving a literary trail in the *Divine Comedy* and in his other writings, including *La vita nuova*, written circa 1294 (translated into English as *Vita Nuova* in 1861; also known as *The New Life*), *Il convivio* (c. 1307; *The Banquet*, 1887), and *De monarchia* (c. 1313; English translation, 1890; also known as *On World Government*), but at other times it is less obvious where his omnivorous reading took him. Dante often studied ancient and contemporary texts on his own, without official interpreters or schools of thought beyond the constricting Scholasticism of his day. Scholasticism by itself was an inadequate commentary because Dante was both a product of the Middle Ages and a poet looking far beyond his time in both directions, past and present. More than any prior author, Dante created in his *Inferno* that alloy of classical and Christian tradition that would become the literary hallmark of Western civilization. How the *Inferno* can be read in context with contemporary literature and Dante's other writing is addressed in the new essay in this volume by Heather Webb. How the *Inferno* has been perceived since its publication in terms of critical reception is found in the new essay by David Lummus.

Dante's Literary Language

While the plot of the *Inferno* appears simple on the surface—count on the pains and horrors to multiply exponentially in the steeper and steeper descent—the work's internal structure and literary craft are of the highest sophistication. As a poet Dante was well acquainted with devices of classical rhetoric such as *paronomasia* (wordplay and punning based on similar sounds and meanings), *onomatopoeia* (words that sound like or reinforce their own meaning), *extended simile* (where his figurative choices for comparisons beginning with the word "like" or "as" are chillingly evocative and powerful psychologically reinforcing effects), *chiasmus* (where ends of passages or lines somehow mirror or parallel their beginnings,[3] often used in both classical writing and Christian Scripture), *antithesis* (where his poetry amalgamates opposites to brilliant effect), *peripety* (reversal of the expected in upside-down or topsy-turvy twists), and *euphony* (where ripples of word sounds echo everywhere in his Italian verse). These are only a few of the literary devices Dante employs to great effect. He also often hints in *euphemism* (understatement) or wraps his identifications of real persons in layers of subtlety.

Dante's sensory language is among the richest and most intense in all literature, heightening the memorability of his descriptions and exemplary of what later poets such as Samuel Taylor Coleridge called *eidetic* imagery—as found in the lyricism of the ancient Greek poet Sappho, often called the Tenth Muse—where all senses (sight, sound, smell, touch, and taste) are multiplied together to great effect in a *synesthesia* (combined senses) of acute awareness. Even his use of light, including that of stars mostly absent in the *Inferno*, follows scholiastic rules or philosophical tradition and has significance always layered with theological erudition or medieval lore of astrology. In this capacity Dante serves as a mirror for the complexity of the medieval world, and he pours this incredible richness into his great poem.

The *Inferno* also uses much *irony*, as Dante even plays at times with a sense of ludicrous or base humor. Some of Dante's most controversial passages are in the Malebolge (Evil Ditches) of the eighth circle with cantos 20-22, especially canto 21, with its litany of devils' names such as Calcabrina (Brine Crusher[?]), Libicocco ([Evil] Winds or Lust[ful] Winds[?]), Ciriatto (Piggy), Draghignazzo (Leering Dragon[?]), and Graffiacane (Dog Scratcher). These fang-gnashing demons rip and tear at sinners as if they are meals, poking them with pitchforks as they try to escape into the burning pitch. The end of canto 21 is one of the best ironic parodies of Hell, where the departing archdemon Malacoda (Evil Tail) sticks a trumpet to his backside and praises his master with flatulence by design, apropos for such devilry as an acutely deliberate inversion of God being praised by angelic trumpets in Heaven. Dante must have had at least a faint smile as he wrote this particular parody.

Dante's extensive use of symbolism and prolific use of allegory— even in incredible anatomical detail—have been often plumbed as scholars have explored the gamut of his work's classical, biblical, historical, and contemporary political significance. Dante's friends and enemies are rewarded or punished accordingly with famous or infamous antecedents in the *Inferno* as well as the *Purgatorio* and *Paradiso*. His almost countless references to corruption and intrigue in Florence and the Church at large sometimes mask his bitterness and anguish over his exile but just as often strike at the heart with direct invective. While Dante's anger may often be personal, his immense yet intricate architectonic structure for the *Divine Comedy* is so carefully planned as to render his consternation a sublime mechanism for transcendence, ordering not only an immediate literary revenge for Dante between 1302-21 but also a timeless justice as he understood eternity.

Design and Structure in the *Inferno*

The *Inferno* is divided into thirty-four cantos. Because the entire *Divine Comedy* comprises one hundred cantos, the number of cantos is deliberately fixed. *Purgatorio* and *Paradiso* are holistically "perfect" with thirty-three cantos each, whereas *Inferno* is "imperfect" with an added canto, fracturing the symmetry. Numerological consistency of triplicity is repeated throughout the work. Each stanza is a tercet, or three lines, in terza rima, where the rhyming pattern is *aba, bcb, cdc,* and so on. None of this triplicity is accidental. While references to the Trinity (in Christianity the three persons of one God) are as ubiquitous as the actual mention of God is absent, Dante also often makes use of a parallel or infernal triplicity, where his Underworld mocks or mimics heaven upside down, countering it at every step as if his work rests subtly on an infinite balance beam of universal symmetry.

The visual plan of the *Inferno* is organized around a giant downward cone plummeting like a funnel from the surface of this world into the depths of the fallen earth. Sin and its sad effects are the determining forces of its architecture. Its topography is of descending tiers, each terrace lower and more destitute of divine benevolence than its predecessor. Some names in the *Inferno* are clearly derived from classical sources, such as Dis, the City of Hell that encircles all the tiers below the fifth circle of Dante's Inferno. This borrowing is apparent if one reads classical Latin gravestones, which are often dedicated as *Dis Manibus*, "to the Shades of the Departed" in the Underworld. The rivers that border or flow through the classical Underworld are here in the *Inferno*, including the Acheron, Styx, Phlegethon, and Lethe, and some infernal tiers are connected by bridges over flaming rivers filled with damned souls until the lowest abysses are reached only by winged monsters who assist the Pilgrim (Dante) and Virgil, his virtuous pagan guide. Ancient monsters such as Cerberus, Medusa, Geryon, Minotaur, Harpies, and Cacus assist in the punitive functions of the Inferno or guard its thresholds. Dante ascribes his literary vision of the *Inferno* to take place symbolically when he is at "midlife" ("mezzo del cammin di nostra vita"; midway on the journey of our life) at age thirty-five in 1300; he is lost in a dark, tangled wood at "the middle of the journey of life" (canto 1).

Contrapasso and Themes of Sin in the *Inferno*

The themes of the *Inferno* have sinners following their sins in *contrapasso*, which is the resulting punishment fitting the sins. Dante creates an incredibly rational peripety (reversal) for every shade of sin, with each trespass repaid in like fashion but by amazingly clever inversions of symbolic cause and effect, where "each vice brings by its own nature its own torture."[4] For example, Paolo and Francesca in canto 5 are caught in adultery and are thus condemned to swirl together in the hellish whirlwind, forever locked in shame. In his iconic play *No Exit*, Jean-Paul Sartre draws directly on Dante here for his own brand of eternal existential *contrapasso* even while denying a traditional afterlife in ironic satire.

While the deserved woes of the damned intensify with each canto, Dante's *Inferno* deals out justice accordingly. The structure of Hell is also organized by the sins punished therein. First, the *Inferno* starts with the Dark Wood of Error in canto 1, where its leopard, lion, and she-wolf beasts block the lost Pilgrim's path until Virgil appears to serve as his guide downward before he can climb to the now suddenly distant Mount of Joy. Canto 2 is the descent into growing darkness on the "dark and perilous track." Then in canto 3 they pass through the famous Gate of Hell, with its inscription ending in the line "Abandon All Hope, You Who Enter Here." Among the "mysteries" inscribed on the gate are that this is the sad way into Eternal Sorrow leading to the City of Woe. Once inside, suddenly the two poets hear the voices of eternal anguish of those lost in sin.

Landscape of the *Inferno*

Dante's landscape in the *Inferno* is, as mentioned, a peripety or reversal of the living world. Reminding us of Achilles' complaints in the Underworld, that he would gladly return as a servant to a place where he could feel the sun again (*Odyssey* 11.486ff.), Dante's Hell is benighted, dark with divine absence, where all living positives are turned upside down. Its fires do not warm as above but burn nonetheless; these flames do not give light but barely breach the gloom. Its few trees are dead and lifeless, bearing no leaves but only thorns. Its rivers carry no water for the thirsty, only molten tar and magmatic brimstone, flowing with pain or forgetfulness.

After the Acheron River just inside the Gate of Hell, where Charon the Boatman ferries souls across the river, the descending circles of Hell must be traversed. Circle I, which is Limbo, is filled with the souls of virtuous pagans and unbaptized children. Circle II is filled with the souls of the carnal, and in between the second and third circles are Minos and Cerberus. Circle III is filled with gluttons; circle IV, hoarders and wasters; circle V, the wrathful and the sullen. Leaving circle IV en route to circle V, the Pilgrim (Dante) and Virgil encounter the Great Tower, and then running through circle V is the Styx River. Just beyond the Styx are found the Walls of the City of Dis, where Furies harass souls. Circle VI is filled with heretics, and a giant cliff separates circles VI and VII, with the Minotaur near the top of the cliff and centaurs at the base. Circle VII is divided into three rings: its outer is the Phlegethon River, the Wood of Suicides is found in the middle ring, and the Burning Plain is the last ring. After passing through the Burning Plain, the Pilgrim and Virgil reach the Great Waterfall pouring over the Abyss above circle VIII. Here Geryon flies them in long downward spirals by the waterfall to circle VIII, deep in Hell.

Circle VIII is the steep funnel of the Malebolge, comprising ten Bolgia (Ditches) in rings of the Abyss. The First Bolgia traps the seducers and panderers; the Second Bolgia punishes flatterers; the Third Bolgia holds simoniacs, those who tried to buy or sell religious favors or offices; the Fourth Bolgia traps the fortune-tellers and diviners; the Fifth Bolgia punishes the grafters; the Sixth Bolgia holds hypocrites; the Seventh Bolgia traps thieves; the Eighth Bolgia punishes the evil counselors; the Ninth Bolgia holds sowers of discord; and the Tenth Bolgia punishes counterfeiters and alchemists.

In Circle IX, the lowest depths of the Inferno, is the great well of the

Central Pit, guarded by giant Titans, one of whom—Antaeus—sets the Pilgrim and Virgil down into the frozen lake of Cocytus, where the worst and most treacherous betrayers and frauds are doomed in the Inferno's four final descending levels. These four levels are named Caïna (for Cain), Antenora (for the Trojan Antenor, who was perceived as traitorous for sparing the lives of the Greek envoys to Troy and whose house was spared when Troy fell but whom later legend says betrayed Troy), Ptolemea (for Ptolemaeus, who murdered his guests in the apocryphal book I Maccabees 16) and finally Judecca (for Judas Iscariot). In Judecca are the most heinous human traitors, including Brutus, Cassius, and Judas Iscariot in the three mouths of the fallen archangel Satan—the "Great Worm of Evil"—at the very center of the frozen lake fed by the Lethe River.

As mentioned earlier, one of the most original images in all literature is found in the final canto of the *Inferno*: canto 34 portrays Satan caught waist deep in ice in the frozen lake of Cocytus pit, seemingly lifeless except for his batlike beating wings. Dante uses the comparison of the arms almost of a windmill for these dread wings that stir the icy winds, freezing the final pit. It is as if Dante is suggesting that because Satan was made in the image of God, although he is now devoid of even the last mark of redemptive intelligence, his mindless action still bears only a mechanical resemblance to sentience in the endless movement of a windmill. But here his sole movement is the source of cold—he is the "Emperor of the Universe of Pain"—rather than the sails of a windmill merely moved by the effect of wind. Why does the Pilgrim also find himself breathless and analogously dead, his "blood running cold"? Such an icy breath proceeding from Lucifer's horrible wings is a direct antithesis or reversal (literary peripety) of God himself, who in Genesis 1:2 is the animating spirit or wind (*ruach* in Hebrew can mean "spirit," "breath," or "wind") moving across the face of the water in life-giving creation. So is Satan the ultimate cause of death-dealing sin.

To understand some of the *Inferno*'s complex specificity and how carefully Dante planned its every detail, we can also subdivide the eighth and ninth circles very discretely into particular "sins." The original beasts that the Pilgrim first encounters in canto 1 have several allegorical meanings. The leopard, mentioned in a biblical passage in Jeremiah 5:6 and explored in medieval bestiaries, can be symbolic of sins of lust, sensuality, or lack of sexual control; the lion can be symbolic of pride and violence; and the she-wolf may be symbolic of rapacious avarice or feral greed (not all scholars agree that Dante intended these specific allegories, however). Thus several deadly sins can be enumerated through different expressions of bestiality, a reduction of the *imago Dei* (Genesis 1:26-7 says humans are made in the "image of God") in a human being who becomes subjugated to baser instincts.

Dante plots out greater distinctions in less general and more specific channels. The eighth circle's three rings (or rounds) emphasize particular violent or bestial sins. Ring 1 is the Phlegethon River, filled with those who embodied violence against neighbors, specifically murderers and those who made war against neighbors. Ring 2 is the Wood of Suicides, filled with those who embodied violence themselves by destroying their lives given to them by God. Ring 3 is the Burning Plain, filled with those who embodied violence against God, Nature, and the Arts; these include blasphemers, those who perverted Nature, and those who extorted money as usurers.

As Harrison brilliantly notes in his essay in this volume, Dante's Pilgrim cannot turn around and find salvation unless he descends to the depths of the Inferno (canto 34), an about-face that echoes the Gospel in Matthew 5:3: "Blessed are the poor in spirit, for theirs is the kingdom of heaven."[5] That one must "descend" in order to "ascend" is a requisite in Christian salvation repeated through many biblical writers and later commentaries, including those of Augustine and Thomas Aquinas, two of Dante's influences. Thus Dante suggests that one must hit the absolute depth before one can begin to ascend, a gloss on how only those who realize how beggarly poor they are spiritually in life actually reach out for salvation, knowing their spiritual poverty, affirming that salvation is not an automatic guarantee even for clergy. Dante's Pilgrim has to reach the bottom of the abyss before he can climb out toward the stars.

Church Controversy in the *Inferno*

Bold as he must have been to do so, Dante the critic was not afraid to place recent high clergy in the *Inferno* even though he faced some risk of excommunication. His condemnation included then-living popes such as Clement V (in office 1305-14), "the lawless shepherd" (canto 19, 73-82); possibly Celestine V (in office July 5-December 13, 1294) as "he who made the Great Refusal" (canto 3, 59-60), as Dante tradition suggests; Nicholas III (earlier in office 1277-80), guilty of simony, who in nepotism favored his own Orsini family, the "little bears" (as *orso* in Italian is "bear"), over worthier people, and with whom Dante (as the Pilgrim) even has a conversation in the *Inferno* (canto 19, 63-67); and finally his immediate contemporary Boniface VIII (in office 1294-1303), the Church potentate behind Dante's exile, he "who took the Lady [the Church] by deceit," and also often thought to be a possible murderer of Celestine V after imprisoning him for months (canto 19, 49-63). Simon Magus, the legendary biblical sorcerer (Acts 8:9-13, 18-24) after whom simony is named (for his attempting to buy the Holy Spirit from Peter so he could do miracles), is in like company in the *Inferno* in canto 19, not the least because in tradition Simon Magus was also the originator of Gnosticism, trying to keep early Christianity in hermetic secrecy only the cognoscenti could control.[6] Dante's condemnation also included Archbishop Ruggieri (canto 33, 1-15) and infamous priests such as Fra Alberigo of Faenza (canto 33, 113-15), who murdered a kinsman, Manfredo, and Manfredo's son at a banquet in his home.

If Dante's political idealism is as unbending as his vision is idiosyncratic, his portrayal of the Church as a political beast is right on the mark, holding contemporary religious leadership to a higher responsibility because clergy even in the medieval world were supposed to be holier than the average humanity. (Elizabeth Coggeshall explores this contemporary political setting of Florence and Italy in her essay in this volume.) Where others such as Boccaccio and Geoffrey Chaucer (c. 1343-1400) soon made ribald jokes of religious purity or lack thereof, Dante as their antecedent took the high road without apparent moral hypocrisy himself. Regarding egregious sins that were not so obviously physical as heated lust and undisciplined gluttony, Dante treats cold heresy and venial simony almost as harshly as any other sins or even more so when desire becomes perverted and debased (this is why Paolo and Francesca are only in canto 5 and Pope Boniface is "deeper" in canto 19). Nonetheless, all are in Hell. Damnation, according to the New Testament or at least Saint Paul (Epistle to the Romans 3:23ff.), was just deserts for any unrepented error, so Dante still stands on smoking but solid biblical ground and paves the way to Purgatory for those who appear to have repented sinful lives while still breathing. Dante accepted that Christianity's beginnings may have been full of "great sinners" like Peter (who denied Christ), Mary Magdalene or her Gospel composite (who abandoned her voluptuous courtesan life), Paul (who called himself the chief of sinners for torturing early martyrs), and Augustine (whose *Confessions* appear less disingenuous about his wallowing in Carthage's fleshpots), but these became great saints because they ultimately saw themselves in God's eyes and sought mercy. No respecter of office or persons, Dante even places his own philosophic mentor Brunetto Latini (c. 1220-94) in the *Inferno* in canto 15.

John Freccero notes in his foreword to Pinsky's translation of the *Inferno*: "In spite of Dante's reputation as the greatest of Christian poets, there is no sign of Christian forgiveness in the *Inferno*. The dominant theme is not mercy but justice." Forgiveness was not always deeply rooted in Church policy either, as the fourteenth-century persecuted followers of John Wyclif (c. 1328-84) and John Hus (c. 1369-1415) soon found out after Dante's own era as they were labeled heretics in pre-Reformation times. Even though in the *Paradiso* (cantos 10-11) Dante also elevates Thomas Aquinas as well as praises Saint Francis and Saint Dominic, "*due principe*, two princes . . . to guide an errant church" as Steven Botterill puts it, in the *Inferno* Dante excoriates the Church's failures in anything but gentleness. While sinful leaders were highly visible examples most likely known even to his early readers, Dante's fearless censure of the Church display an almost pre-Renaissance mentality in leading the way in excoriating corruption in the Church.

If in some way, as mentioned, Dante's *Inferno* anticipates Sartre in his existential *No Exit*, Harrison also subtly argues that Dante often saw human life itself as hell on earth, full of suffering as he experienced himself, yet with hope for heaven in the successive parts of his *Divine Comedy*.[7] For a religious man—and this is shown even more strongly in his deeply theological-philosophical *Purgatorio* and his mystical *Paradiso*—Dante, in his pioneering expression of the need to purge evil at the heart of Rome as well as in the soul of Florence, was all the braver because he did it in writing at the zenith of medieval Church power.

Epilogue

Dante's imagination is one of the richest in literature, rewarding the reader with a whole cosmos of historical, philosophical, religious, and sensory detail, one that centuries of interpretation have yet to exhaust. The landscape of the *Inferno* is unforgettably complete down to the last thorny dead branch, echo of agony, and boiling bubble of tar. Dante is to religious and philosophically profound poetry what Rembrandt is to the most sublime visual art. As a gauge of how well we know literature, we cannot be considered educated unless we have read and pondered Dante's work. Dante is the very pinnacle from which we can look in all directions and survey the past, present, and future of Italian literature and indeed of Western culture.

Notes

1. Peter S. Hawkins, "Dante and the Bible," in *The Cambridge Companion to Dante*, ed. Rachel Jacoff, 2d ed. (New York: Cambridge University Press, 2007), 125.

2. Robert Hollander, "Dante's Use of *Aeneid* I in *Inferno* I and II." *Comparative Literature* 20, no. 2 (1968): 142-56.

3. Sometimes these literary devices are very subtle, and they may be noticeable only in Dante's Italian. See Patrick Boyde, "*Inferno* XIII," in *Cambridge Readings in Dante's "Comedy,"* ed. Kenelm Foster and Patrick Boyde (New York: Cambridge University Press, 1981), 12.

4. Gianvincenzo Gravina, "From *Della Ragion Poetica* (Book II), § XIII: 'About Dante's Morality and Theology,'" in *Critical Essays on Dante*, ed. Giuseppe Mazzotta (Boston: G. K. Hall, 1991), 50-57.

5. That one must "descend" in order to "ascend" is a requisite in Christian salvation, and this is the cause-effect crux of Matthew 5:3, whereby it is thought that to admit spiritual poverty on earth will bring blessing with heavenly riches in the afterlife. While material and spiritual poverty are by no means synonymous, in *Paradiso* 11.73ff. Dante highlights Saint Francis of Assisi, who is wedded to his love, personified as Lady *Povertà*. This elevation of humility in the spiritual principle of material humility also greatly tempers spiritual humility. Similar equivalences (spiritual and material poverty) and sometimes paradoxical reversals occur in biblical text, as in John 3:14-15, when Christ connects the healing power of gazing on the poisonous viper (symbolic of confessing sin) with a proleptic gazing on him on the cross: "Just as Moses lifted up the serpent [when the Israelites acknowledged their sin by looking at the bronze serpent in the wilderness; see Numbers 21:5-9], so must the Son of Man (Christ) be lifted up." This is also a major biblical principle of vicarious substitution in II Corinthians 5.21a: "God made him who had no sin to be sin for us." Dante was more than likely aware of this familiar scholiastic homily of ascent requiring descent and what is cursed (serpent and Christ) transformed into a blessing through Augustine's *Tractate* 12 (*Tractatus in evangelium Iohannis* 12) on John 3:6-21 as well as Thomas Aquinas, *Commentary on John 3* (see Thomas Aquinas, *Commentary on the Gospel of John, Chapters 1-5*, trans. Fabian Larcher and John Weisheipl [Albany, NY: Magi Books, 1998], lectura 2, §473-75). Also see Steven Botterill, "Aquinas, St. Thomas," in *The Dante Encyclopedia*, ed. Richard Lansing (New York: Garland, 2000), 56-58; and Paget Toynbee, "Povertà," in *A Dictionary of Proper Names and Notable Matters in the Works of Dante*, 1898, revised by Charles S. Singleton (Oxford: Clarendon Press, 1968), 524.

6. V. Stanley Benfell, "Simony," in *The Dante Encyclopedia*, ed. Richard Lansing. (New York: Garland, 2000), 781-82.

7. Robert Pogue Harrison. "Comedy and Modernity: Dante's Hell." *Modern Language Notes* 102, no. 5 (1987): 1043-58.

Bibliography

Auerbach, Erich. *Dante: Poet of the Secular World*. New York: New York Review of Books, 2006.

Becker, Christopher Bennett. "Dante's Motley Cord: Art and Apocalypse in *Inferno* XVI." *Modern Language Notes* 106.1 [Italian issue] (1991): 179-83.

Benfell, V. Stanley. "Simony." *The Dante Encyclopedia*. Ed. Richard Lansing. New York: Garland, 2000. 781-82.

Botterill, Steven. "Aquinas, St. Thomas." *The Dante Encyclopedia*. Ed. Richard Lansing. New York: Garland, 2000. 56-58.

Boyde, Patrick. "*Inferno* XIII." *Cambridge Readings in Dante's "Comedy."* Ed. Kenelm Foster and Patrick Boyde. New York: Cambridge UP, 1981. 1-22.

Curtius, Ernst Robert. "Dante." *European Literature and the Latin Middle Ages*. Trans. W. R. Trask. 1953. Princeton, NJ: Princeton UP, 1990. 348-79.

Dante. *The Divine Comedy*. Trans. Allen Mandelbaum. New York: Everyman's Library, 1995.

_____. *The Divine Comedy: 1. Inferno*. Trans. John D. Sinclair. New York: Oxford UP, 1961.

Frayling, Christopher. *Strange Landscape: A Journey Through the Middle Ages*. London: Penguin Books, 1995.

Freccero, John. Foreword. *The Inferno of Dante*. Trans. Robert Pinsky. New York: Farrar, Straus and Giroux, 1994.

Harrison, Robert P. "Comedy and Modernity: Dante's Hell." *Modern Language Notes* 102.5 (1987) 1043-61.

Hawkins, Peter S. "Dante and the Bible." *The Cambridge Companion to Dante*. 2d ed. Ed. Rachel Jacoff. New York: Cambridge UP, 2007. 125-40.

Hollander, Robert. "Dante's Use of *Aeneid* I in *Inferno* I and II." *Comparative Literature* 20.2 (1968): 142-56.

Kirkpatrick, Robin. *Dante's Inferno: Difficulty and Dead Poetry*. New York: Cambridge UP, 2008.

Kleinhenz, Christopher. "Notes on Dante's Use of Classical Myths and the Mythological Tradition." *Romance Quarterly* 33 (1986): 477-84.

Lewis, R. W. B. *Dante: A Life*. 2001. New York: Penguin, 2009.

Mazzotta, Giuseppe, ed. *Critical Essays on Dante*. Boston: G. K. Hall, 1991.

Raffa, Guy P. *Danteworlds: A Reader's Guide to the "Inferno."* Chicago: U of Chicago P, 2007.

Thomas Aquinas. *Commentary on the Gospel of John, Chapters 1-5*. Trans. Fabian Larcher and James Weisheipl. Washington, DC: Catholic U of America P, 2010.

Toynbee, Paget. *A Dictionary of Proper Names and Notable Matters in the Works of Dante*. 1898. Revised by Charles S. Singleton. Oxford: Clarendon Press, 1968.

Wilkins, Ernest Hatch, and Thomas Goddard Bergin. *A Concordance to the "Divine Comedy" of Dante Alighieri*. Cambridge, MA: Belknap Press of Harvard UP, 1965.

Biography of Dante_____

Patrick Hunt

Dante Alighieri was born in Florence, in what is now Italy, in the early summer of 1265. While not nobility, his family was significant in Florentine life. His father, Alighiero di Bellincione, had status in the city, and his mother, Bella (or Gabriella) degli Abati, also came from a family of modest privilege. The family's prominence continued after the Battle of Montaperti in 1260, when the political party with which Dante's father identified, the Florentine Guelfs, were beaten by the Sienese Ghibellines. Yet Dante's family suffered no loss or reprisals, suggesting some form of higher civil protection, since many Florentine Ghibellines also participated in the rout of the Guelfs. The only known Florentine ancestors of Dante include Cacciaguida degli Eleisei around 1100, whom Dante mentions in *La divina commedia* (*The Divine Comedy*) in *Paradiso*, canto 15.

Dante's mother died in 1274 or 1275, when he was around nine years old, and his father appears to have soon remarried, although this is uncertain only because the father's legal status may have precluded an actual remarriage. Nonetheless, Dante's new stepmother, Lapa di Chiarissimo Cialuffi, bore several children, including Dante's half brother and half sister, Francesco and Gaetana.

At the age of nine Dante met Beatrice (or Bice) Portinari at a May Day celebration at the home of her father, Folco Portinari. Dante was a year older than Beatrice, and he remained smitten by her throughout his life, although his love was sublimated to the highest spiritual esteem even when she would have nothing to do with him. At the age of twelve, around 1278, Dante formally entered a marriage contract with Gemma di Manetto Donati, the daughter of a local aristocrat, Manetto Donati. A formal marriage contract at the edge of adolescence was normal in medieval Florence, and such a prenuptial arrangement with aristocracy also shows Dante's family status. When Dante was eighteen, in 1283, Beatrice Portinari had a brief conversation with him, although it appears she soon removed herself from further contact for various possible reasons, including that her own family was preparing her for marriage to a more suitable wealthy Florentine banker and to avoid rumor.

After having received some Latin education in Florence as expected for young men of his social class, Dante began to meet some members of Florence's literary circle and to emulate the Sicilian School, a community of poets that flourished in the Palermo court of Frederick II (who was called *stupor mundi* or "wonder of the world" for his genius) and held sway for its cosmopolitan clout in the medieval Italian literary world.

Like his Florentine literary associates, the young poet Dante had immersed himself in troubadour verse that espoused courtly loving and its elevation of women. His initial contacts with the Florentine literary circle eventually led after several years to greater immersion within a group of local writers and philosophers, practitioners of the *dolce stil nuovo* (or *novo*), the "sweet new style" or just "new style," whose Tuscan members were called *stilnovisti*. Some of them also wrote in vernacular Italian, a novelty at the time, although Latin remained the language of scholarship. These writers included the poet Guido Cavalcanti and the scholar-philosopher Brunetto Latini, both of whom had a strong influence on Dante. Brunetto Latini was also a Cicero scholar as well as a historian of ideas. While Cavalcanti became a friend of Dante, Brunetto is seen more as an informal teacher because Dante refers to him as *Maestro* in the *Inferno* (canto 15, 82-87).

Fulfilling his prior prenuptial arrangement, Dante married Gemma Donati when he was around twenty years old in 1285, three years after his father's death. In 1287 Beatrice married a Florentine banker, Simone dei Bardi, and disappeared almost entirely from the life of Dante, although she would occupy his and the world's imagination ever after.

Dante in His Prime

In 1289, when Dante was twenty-four, he fought in the famous Battle of Campaldino, apparently as a cavalry officer in the forefront of the fight against the city of Arezzo. This battle won by Florence marked a new period in Florentine civil law, and Dante soon had to join the apothecary guild in order to enter the life of politics, as required by new Florentine law. Because apothecaries needed a modicum of medical learning and also sold books, Dante would not have been out of place in this medieval guild even if he was not much of a medical practitioner.

Beatrice (Portinari) dei Bardi died in 1290 at age twenty-four, and even in grief Dante would thus forever remember her as ageless, an inaccessible spiritual beauty. Almost as intellectual compensation, Dante thereafter devoted himself to philosophy, literature, law, history, and science, even though he now had a family of his own—his four likely children with Gemma were named Jacopo, Pietro, Giovanni, and Antonia—and he would soon also immerse himself in Florentine politics, carving out his own place in the embattled world of Guelfs and Ghibellines. Later, Dante's daughter Antonia ultimately entered a convent, appropriately as Sister Beatrice.

Although it is likely that his formal studies took place in 1291-94, in his later work *Il convivio* (II.12.7) Dante confirmed that he spent nearly three years—"thirty months"—in the Dominican School of Santa Maria Novella in Florence studying Thomas Aquinas and Aristotle. Debate still exists regarding whether and when Dante studied in Bologna,[1] but he certainly knew the extremism of Aristotelian traditions in Bologna. Dante appears to have also studied some Neoplatonic thought in his interpreting the work of Albertus Magnus. If he had been a student at the early University of Bologna, he would have experienced firsthand the weight of ecclesiastical law taught there.

Probably during or after his studies with Dominican scholars at Santa Maria Novella and with Franciscan scholars at Santa Croce, both in Florence, in 1293-94, at age thirty-two, Dante wrote his first major work: *Vita Nuova*, a poetic anthology filled with his musings about love, especially its spiritual dimensions. Beatrice and her inspiration figure largely in this work.

Although his posthumous account is not trustworthy, Boccaccio provides a description of Dante in midlife that is nonetheless useful:

> Our poet was of middle height; and when he had reached maturity he went somewhat bowed, his gait grave and gentle. . . . His face was long, his nose aquiline, his eyes rather large than small; his jaws big, and the under lip protruding beyond the upper. His complexion was dark, his hair and beard thick, black, and curling. And his complexion was ever melancholy and thoughtful.

Boccaccio continues by mentioning Dante in Verona, when women whom he passed noted Dante as the man who goes to Hell and back bringing tidings to the world: "Do you not see how his beard is crisped and his skin darkened by the heat and smoke that are there below." Naturally, Boccaccio's apocryphal account is unverifiable as a bona fide physical description of Dante.

In Florence in 1294, at age twenty-nine, Dante met Charles Martel, heir to the kingdom of Naples and already king of Hungary. The next year, Dante formally entered political life in Florence at age thirty.

The year 1300, when Dante was thirty-five, is an important watershed year for the *Divine Comedy*. Pope Boniface VIII had declared it to be a jubilee year celebrating a milestone of Rome's religious life; Dante mirrored this date as a personal touchstone as he chose Easter of this year as the fictional date of his journey in the *Inferno*. Dante was also selected in 1300 to hold office as one of six priors of Florence for several months.[2]

In 1301 Dante was made an emissary of Florence to Pope Boniface VIII in Rome as the pope's military force advanced on Florence under the punitive leadership of Prince Charles of Valois. In January of 1302, at age thirty-six, Dante was exiled from Florence, and his property and assets were seized; this exile became permanent in spring of 1302. From 1303 onward, Dante began to develop his next works, *De vulgari eloquentia* (on the eloquence of the vernacular), in which he defended his use of Italian, and his poetic allegory and commentary *Il convivio* (translated into English as *The Banquet* in 1887); both were left unfinished. Also in 1303, during his exile, Dante visited Verona as a guest of Bartolomeo della Scala.

In 1310, when Dante was forty-five, Henry VII, prince of Luxembourg and putative Holy Roman Emperor, entered Italy and tried to unite the rival Guelf and Ghibelline factions. That year Dante wrote an epistle to him, fully aware that the papacy had just moved the previous year from Rome to Avignon, an exile many Italians considered the Babylonian Captivity and a hallmark of Rome's corruption. Dante may have begun his *De monarchia* in this year, distilling his political philosophy in an allegorical treatise on ideal global kingship balancing the role of the Church.

Infernal Politics of the City of Man

The political feud dominating Dante's own life also heavily permeates the *Inferno*, where his peers can be counted among the Guelfs—"White" and "Black"—or the Ghibellines or good and bad clergy. The Ghibellines were among or supported the aristocracy and the emperor. The Guelfs, on one hand, belonged to or advocated more democratic constitutional government (essentially communes) rather than aristocracy, or, on the other hand, recognized papal authority in contrast to the tyranny of major noble families. Guelfs were most often from the emerging merchant class or the comfortable middle class, like Dante himself. The Guelfs divided into Black and White in Dante's time. Pope Boniface VIII was supported by the Black Guelfs but not by the White Guelfs, Dante's party, who wanted greater independence from Rome. The White Guelfs initially had the upper hand and expelled the Black Guelfs. In response, Pope Boniface planned a military campaign to subdue the White Guelfs in Florence, and the pope's representative, Prince Charles of Valois, sacked Florence while Dante, as a guild officer and a prior of Florence, and other Florentine White Guelfs were on an embassy to Rome. Dante never returned to Florence after he was exiled in absentia in 1302 by the Black Guelfs who now ruled Florence.

At first, Dante's exile from Florence was for only two years, with a resulting fine assessed against him, which he challenged and never paid on principle because all his property had been seized. No doubt partly because of his visible resistance and at times possibly vitriolic writing, Dante's exile became permanent until his death in Ravenna in 1321. He never forgave or forgot the injustices of his exile from Florence, and his grievances against Black Guelfs and Ghibellines alike are fairly transparent in the *Inferno*. For example, Boniface VIII is embedded upside down in licking flames in canto 19 (in the eighth circle, which is for those who consciously perpetrate sins of fraud and treachery); thus Dante repaid the pope with literary damnation for playing a major role in his exile.

Dante in Later Life

In 1312, at age forty-seven, Dante began a long-term guesthood in Verona in the palazzo of Cangrande della Scala, who became Dante's most important patron in his life, even though della Scala was Ghibelline. Cangrande served Henry VII in trying to unify the Guelfs and Ghibellines in northern Italy. The della Scala family was the ruling family in Verona, and Cangrande himself was both religiously devout and valiant as a warrior. Dante later praised Cangrande della Scala in his *Paradiso* (canto 17, 73-93), stating, "Even his enemies cannot keep silent about him." Making Verona his home, Dante also traveled and wrote for the next seven years, until 1318, during which time Henry VII died and Dante published the *Inferno* in 1314, along with letters to the Italian cardinals.

In a further Florentine indignity, in 1315, when Dante was fifty, the city of Florence offered to end his permanent exile if he would admit prior guilt, but Dante archly rejected the offer, restating his innocence of any crime against Florence. Dante also published the *Purgatorio* at this time. In 1319, at the age of fifty-four, Dante traveled to Ravenna; in this city, which became his final home in exile, he was a guest of Guido II Novello da Polenta, lord of the city from 1316 to 1322. This was also the period of Dante's correspondence with Giovanni del Virgilio in Bologna, and in 1320, at age fifty-five, Dante lectured on the *Quaestio de aqua et terra* in Verona as an exercise in cosmology and geomorphology, stating that the earth is never and nowhere completely swallowed by the sea. Dante fulfilled embassies for Novello to various city-states, including Venice.

Finally, in 1321 Dante completed the *Paradiso* and at age fifty-six died shortly thereafter in Ravenna; he had contracted malaria in the marshes en route back to Ravenna as he returned from a diplomatic mission. His tomb is in Ravenna, despite a later unsuccessful attempt by Florence to secure his remains to be placed in a monument tomb the city built for Dante in the basilica of Santa Croce. The inscription on the alternate tomb in Florence calls him the most exalted poet and quotes a passage from *Inferno* canto 4 but ironically omits the line, "His spirit, having departed from us, returns," since Dante's tomb in Florence is empty.

Although subsequent generations of literary Italians have acknowledged, cherished, and quoted the *Divine Comedy* as a work of genius, in his lifetime Dante did not actually receive anything similar to the Italian status of the ancient poet laureate, as this literary honor was not revived until Petrarch. Consensus would have been likely, and even humanist critics of Dante's use of vernacular Italian, such as Giovanni del Virgilio in Bologna, appeared to have offered him such laurels if he wrote in Latin instead. Famous posthumous portraits of Dante by noted early artists, however, often depict him with a laurel crown, including works by Domenico di Michelino circa 1465, Botticelli in 1495, Luca Signorelli in 1499, and Raphael circa 1500.

Early biographies of Dante include that found in Giovanni Villani's (c. 1276-1348) *Nuova cronica*, written between 1300 and 1346, and Boccaccio's *Vita di Dante*, circa 1347, although both accounts are filled with legend and are thus not always reliable. Perhaps first of many, Guido da Pisa (c. 1250-1327) also wrote an early commentary on Dante's *Inferno* around 1345,[3] and in the fifteenth century Leonardo Bruni (c. 1370-1444) also wrote an account of Dante's life and work, followed by an endless stream of literary studies. Since Bruni's era, myriad books and articles have been written on Dante's life in context with his personal comments in the *Divine Comedy* and his other writing; in fact, an almost endless number of works about Dante have been published, replete with justified admiration for Dante's timeless genius.

Notes

1. Gertrude Leigh, *New Light on the Youth of Dante: The Course of Dante's Life Prior to 1290 Traced in the Inferno, Cantos 3-13* (London: Kenikat Press, 1969), 154-57.

2. George Holmes, *Dante* (New York: Farrar, Straus and Giroux, 1980), 42.

3. Guido da Pisa, *Expositiones et glose super Comediam Dantis*, ed. Vincenzo Cioffari (Albany: State University of New York Press, 1974); Vincenzo Cioffari, "Guido da Pisa's Basic Interpretation," *Dante Studies* 93 (1975): 1-25.

Bibliography

Cioffari, Vincenzo. "Guido da Pisa's Basic Interpretation." *Dante Studies* 93 (1975) 1-25.

"Dante Alighieri." *Stanford Encyclopedia of Philosophy*. Web. http://plato.stanford .edu/entries/dante

Guido da Pisa. *Expositiones et glose super Comediam Dantis*. Ed. Vincenzo Cioffari. Albany: State U of New York P, 1974.

Holmes, George. *Dante*. New York: Farrar, Straus and Giroux, 1980.

Leigh, Gertrude. *New Light on the Youth of Dante: The Course of Dante's Life Prior to 1290 Traced in the Inferno, Cantos 3-13*. London: Kenikat Press, 1969.

Lewis, R. W. B. *Dante: A Life*. 2001. New York: Penguin, 2009.

Mazzotta, Giuseppe. "Life of Dante." *The Cambridge Companion to Dante*. 2d ed. Ed. Rachel Jacoff. New York: Cambridge UP, 2007.

Raffa, Guy P. "Dante's Mocking Poetic Muse." *Dante Studies* 114 (1996): 271-91.

the PARIS
REVIEW

The *Paris Review* Perspective_____
Nicole Rudick for *The Paris Review*

Merciless Harpies, maddening tempests, flaming tombs, enraged centaurs, baptism by fire, a river of blood, pools of excrement, a lake of boiling pitch—no book does Hell and damnation better than the *Inferno*, Dante Alighieri's fourteenth-century epic allegorical poem. The first part of the trilogy (together with the *Purgatorio* and *Paradiso*) that is *The Divine Comedy*, the *Inferno* is literature's quintessential journey through the afterlife, one that does not just describe Hell's torments but weighs the social and moral significance of various sins. In this second role, the poem becomes a record of the mores and attitudes of the medieval world, a cultural construction that has long influenced Western arts—architecture, painting, sculpture, music, literature, poetry, film, and comics—and continues to do so today.

Dante's Inferno the video game, a recent addition to this list, offers a curious reinterpretation of the classic text. Replete with its own take on the poem's untold horrors, it concerns a young warrior named Dante who must blast and slash his way through the multilevel torments of Hell in pursuit of Satan, who has absconded into the bowels of the underworld with Dante's beloved, Beatrice (who serves as the poet's guide in the *Comedy*'s third book). The hero defeats his enemies through a variety of moves, including absolving them of their sins, "judging" them, and the ever-reliable hacking them to bits. In the game, Dante is rewarded when he saves the historical figures he encounters, but the original *Inferno* is far less forgiving: once you're in Hell, you're there for eternity.

Dante created a rigid view of good and evil, showing no mercy for those who did not repent during their lifetimes and sparing no one in his accounting of misdeeds, vice, immorality, and generally inappropriate comportment. His sinners include popes, kings, and Italian political figures; personal enemies; Greek mythological heroes such as Aeneas, Ulysses, and Jason; biblical malefactors such as Pontius Pilate, Judas Iscariot, and Caiaphas; suicides and murderers; and more ordinary thieves, blasphemers, and no-goodniks. Hell's nine concentric circles correspond to the seven deadly sins, with some levels expanded by additional rounds in consideration of a sin's variations. Dante first encounters an antechamber designed to accommodate the souls of those who remained uncommitted toward a cause in life. Here, he is greeted by a gate that bears one of the most oft-repeated epigraphs in literature—"Abandon hope, all ye who enter here"—and a hint of what is to come: "the ancient spirits disconsolate,/ Who cry out each one for the second death."

Hell's minions uniquely dispense a full range of justice, and vice is personified by the punishment: the wrathful attack each other; fortune-tellers spend eternity with their heads twisted backward, doomed only to see where they have been; the gluttonous wallow on their bellies in hail and mud. Dante saves his greatest enmity for traitors, the worst of the fraudulent, who stand imprisoned in a frozen lake at the lowest point of Hell, the furthest point from God—a scene so fearful that the great poet is struck dumb:

> How frozen I became and powerless then,
> > Ask it not, Reader, for I write it not,
> > Because all language would be insufficient.
> I did not die, and I alive remained not;
> > Think for thyself now, hast thou aught of wit,
> > What I became, being of both deprived.

The warden of these souls is Lucifer, a Brobdingnagian bat-winged, hairy, three-faced monster; in his trio of mouths he crunches the bodies of three sinners singled out for their treachery—Judas, Brutus, and Cassius. Dante is unsparing in his description of their gruesome penalty: "To him in front the biting was as naught/ Unto the clawing, for sometimes the spine/ Utterly stripped of all the skin remained."

Dante's vision of justice is harsh even by modern standards. But the *Inferno*, perhaps the most accessible of the *Comedy*'s three books, is, in a sense, instructive. The poem's opening lines find Dante in a state of spiritual despair. Allegorically speaking, he wanders frightened and alone in a "darksome wood," pursued by a leopard, a lion, and a she-wolf, signifying sensual pleasure, pride, and avarice, respectively. Thought to be roughly thirty-five years old while writing the *Inferno*, Dante was already an accomplished poet. His *Vita Nuova*, a series of lyric poems and prose commentary on the subject of courtly love, was published in 1295, five years before he began the *Inferno*, but the interim between these works represents a rift in the poet's life. Dante was actively involved in the turmoil of northern Italian politics, but by the turn of the century, he found himself on the losing side of a heated contest and was exiled from Florence in 1302, never to return (he died in Ravenna in 1321, at age fifty-six). His personal and political identities were adrift, and, struggling, he found his salvation in poetry.

In the context of the *Inferno*, Dante is rescued from this "desert vast" by the Roman poet Virgil, a symbol, in Dante's creation, of human reason. (He is also indebted to his predecessor for his poetic guidance; it is from Virgil's verse that Dante borrows "The beautiful style that has done honour to me.") The unrestrained appetites of human vice that the poet sees in the world—both in the poem and outside it—must be tempered by reason, and those who populate the "red city" possessed, in life, an imbalance of the two qualities. The wayfaring poet's journey, then, becomes an exercise in what not to do in life.

"The way is long," Virgil advises, "and difficult the road." But on the other side of this abyss, Dante's view of the world has improved, and beyond the rocky tomb of Hell, he glimpses "Some of the beauteous things that Heaven doth bear."

Works Consulted

Dante. *The Inferno*. Trans. Robert Hollander and Jean Hollander. New York: Anchor, 2002.

——————. *Inferno*. Trans. Henry Wadsworth Longfellow. 1867. New York:
   Modern Library, 2003.

Contino, Paul J. Introduction. *The Divine Comedy*. By Dante. Trans. Burton Raffel.
   Evanston, IL: Northwestern UP, 2010.

CRITICAL CONTEXTS

The Love That Moves_____

Robert Pogue Harrison

To modern readers the *Divine Comedy* appears as a great Gothic cathedral made not of stone but of verse. The poem's architecture is as sublime, vertical, and vertiginous as the Duomo of Milan or Notre Dame de Paris. Its elaborate construction reflects a world order that Dante took to be absolute, even if nowadays we view it as a historically determined construction of Christian faith, not as an accurate representation of reality. Nevertheless, there is something awesome about the sheer weight and grandeur of the *Comedy*. One has a sense that a thousand or ten thousand years from now, the nine circles of its *Inferno* and the nine spheres of its *Paradiso* will perdure unchanged, while the world of our diminutive modernity, with all its fleeting concerns and anxieties, will have long disappeared.

It seems therefore strange and counterintuitive to claim, as I intend to do in the following pages, that this monumental poem—as solid and immovable as the Alps or the Rockies—has one overriding, all-consuming vocation, namely, to probe, understand, and represent the nature of motion. Just as Shakespeare is the poet of motivation, Dante is the poet of motion in its physical, spiritual, and cosmic manifestations. To advance my claim, I will begin by discussing (1) the crisis that is staged in *Inferno* 1; (2) Dante's choice of Virgil as his guide through Hell and Purgatory; (3) the rhyme scheme of the *Comedy*; (4) Dante's understanding of the nature of sin; and finally (5) his conviction that love is essentially another word for motion.

1. The Prologue Scene

Inferno 1 is a bewildering canto. The reader who approaches it for the first time feels as dazed and confused as the pilgrim in his dark wood. The landscape is hallucinogenic. We go from a forest to a deserted shore to the foot of a mountain, where three beasts confront the terrified pilgrim. The commentary tradition tells us that the landscape is allegorical, as are the three beasts that impede Dante's ascent up the mountain. Yet even after we have consulted our notes—which identify the leopard, the lion, and the she-wolf with lust, violence, and greed, and which tell us that the mountain may in fact be the Mount of Purgatory (which is supposed to be in the southern hemisphere!)—the entire scene remains opaque in meaning. One thing at least is certain. The pilgrim is lost. His way is blocked. Until Virgil arrives on the scene, he is unable to move forward.

To find yourself at a dead end in the midst of life—to discover all of a sudden that all your venues are closed off—is a kind of spiritual death. Anyone who has experienced even mild forms of depression knows what this state of immobilization is all about. Depression brings everything to an oppressive standstill; its objective correlative is a dark room and a bed. Depression debilitates and renders helpless, and there is little doubt that shortly before Dante embarked on his *Comedy* he had succumbed to what we today would call a clinical depression, due to his exile from Florence, his adversities of fortune, and his growing despair over the intractability of human folly. In Dante's day there was no psychoanalysis and no antidepression medication. Dante had to administer his own cure. His treatment—one of the most extraordinary self-therapies in history—took the form of a poem that sent him on an extended journey through Hell, Purgatory, and Paradise. In sum, his cure took the form of self-mobilization.

How does the pilgrim get out of his bind in *Inferno* 1? How does he get moving again? It is not until the next canto that we learn that an act of grace actually saved him from his impasse. All we know in *Inferno* 1 is that the ghost of Virgil—a Roman poet who had been dead for well over a millennium—shows up at Dante's side to unblock the situation. This is a bizarre apparition: a pagan poet coming to the rescue of a lost soul in the most Christian poem ever written. It adds to the weird oneiric (dreamlike) quality of the Prologue Scene, as *Inferno* 1 is often called.

Before we go on to probe more in depth the reasons for Virgil's presence in the *Comedy*, let us remark that, ever since Homer's *Iliad*, classical epic poems traditionally begin *in medias res*, "in the middle" of some kind of action. Dante incorporates and transforms this literary convention by beginning his poem *nel mezzo del cammin di nostra vita*, "in the middle of our life's way." Most editions of the *Comedy* will note that Dante is using the biblical measure of a man's natural life span (seventy years). They also tell us that, according to the temporal coordinates provided by the poem, Dante's journey takes place in the year 1300, hence that Dante, who was born in 1265, was literally halfway through the biblical span when he woke up in the dark wood. (Dante in fact did not live until seventy but died at fifty-six.)

I believe it is misleading to think of Dante's *mezzo del cammin* in literal geometric or chronological terms. The middle here is not a midpoint on a rectilinear trajectory. It can occur at any age, and can occur more than once. The *mezzo del cammin* are those critical moments in a person's life, or even a nation's life (the American Civil War, for example) when a crisis arises, when the path one has been following leads to an impasse or to an inevitable decision. In this sense, the *mezzo del cammin* is not a halfway mark at all but a volatile point at which, in order to move forward, you have to reorient yourself and discover—with the help of others—another way than the one you've been on. As Virgil tells Dante in line 91: "You must hold to another path." The midpoint for Dante is a turning point. If you do not take a turn at the midpoint—if you stay on the same path that led you there—you are lost.

I insist on the importance of turning because in *Inferno* 1 the pilgrim is forced to rethink what it means to be on the *diritta via*, or "straight path." The straight path is not at all straight in the rectilinear sense of the term. This is signaled by the fact that the pilgrim's attempt to climb the mountain of transcendence by moving forward in a straight line ends in failure. Virgil arrives on the scene to tell the pilgrim that if he wants to reach the top of the mountain—if he wants to attain salvation—he must turn himself around. Indeed, he arrives on the scene to tell him that *the way up the mountain actually leads downward*, through the very bowels of the earth. In the topsy-turvy world of *Inferno* 1, the way up is the way down, and vice versa. Descent is ascent, just as God's descent into human personhood through the Incarnation prepared the way for ultimate redemption. The pilgrim must reenact this act of humility whereby God became man. As it pursues the initial descending motion of Christian ascent, the true "straight way" does not follow a straight line but in fact turns.

All this is confirmed by the form of motion that leads Dante and Virgil down through the circles of Hell and up the terraces of the Mount of Purgatory. They move forward in a spiral. The spiral is a form of motion that combines rectilinear and circular motion. It moves forward by turning. I will have more to say about this kind of motion further on.

2. Why Virgil?

We learn from the first words the pilgrim addresses to Virgil, after the latter identifies himself, that Virgil is an authority figure for Dante:

> "O honor and light of other poets, let my long
> study and great love avail me, that has caused me to
> search through your volume [the *Aeneid*].
>   You are my master and my author. . . ."
>
>   (*Inferno* 1, 82-5)

We know from his book *Convivio*, which he abruptly left unfinished, that Dante had been rereading Virgil's *Aeneid* just before embarking on the *Comedy*. The advent of Virgil in *Inferno* 1 surely has something to do with Dante's deep engagement with Virgil's poem around the time the idea of writing an epic of his own came to him (it came to him no doubt *thanks* to his rereading of Virgil). Nonetheless, it is extremely unusual and unorthodox for Dante to have chosen a poet and a pagan—rather than, say, a saint or an angel—to lead him through the Christian afterlife.

Commentators have written extensively about Dante's decision to enlist Virgil as his guide through Hell and Purgatory. They tell us that in the *Comedy* Virgil represents the light of natural reason. This is true enough. Virgil embodies the full extent of pagan wisdom, which did not have the benefit of Christian revelation. They also remind us that Virgil's *Aeneid* is about the prehistory of the city of Rome, which plays such a central role in Dante's theory of history and redemption. This is also true. Dante viewed Rome as the place where the great river of pagan wisdom flows into the sea of Christian truth. Furthermore they point out that Virgil was the so-called poet of empire, writing during the reign of Augustus, and that both Augustus and empire are critical to Dante's vision of providential history. This too is true, for Dante did indeed believe that the institutions of the Roman Empire were essential to bringing about universal peace and justice on earth, even or especially in the Christian era. (See Elizabeth Coggeshall's essay in this volume for an in-depth discussion of Dante's political vision.) Yet the most crucial aspect of Virgil's importance for Dante, in my view, is encapsulated by the last verse of *Inferno* 1: *Allor si mosse, e io li tenni dietro*—"Then he moved, and I followed after him." Let us linger for a moment on this image.

It is an image of filial piety, to be sure, and a beautiful tribute to Dante's " master and author," yet what is most interesting about it, from the point of view of this essay, is that it casts Virgil in the role of the "first mover," as it were. The reason Dante casts Virgil in that role, I believe, is because motion is almost as important in Virgil's *Aeneid* as it is in the *Comedy*. Virgil's poem, in its all-important first half, tells the story of the hero Aeneas, who mobilizes the Trojan refugees after the fall of Troy and leads them across the Mediterranean to a *terra nova*, or new land, where the Trojan legacy—according to the decree of the gods—will one day be reborn in the city of Rome. Like his defeated people, Aeneas is grief-stricken, weary, and prone to depression, yet he is duty-bound to continue moving forward until he accomplishes his mission.

The great temptation for the Trojan wanderers is to put down their oars and settle in some random place along the way before they arrive at their appointed destination. On the island of Sicily, for example, the Trojan women in their weariness of travel set fire to the ships, which are saved thanks to a divinely inspired downpour of rain. Aeneas feels obliged to keep prodding his people onward, yet even he succumbs to the temptation of stasis in Carthage, where, by forming a marriage alliance with Queen Dido, he and his people could live out the rest of their days in comfort and dignity. It takes the visitation of a god to get Aeneas to abandon Dido and depart from Carthage. Aeneas does so reluctantly, for he does not have Odysseus's wanderlust. He has a horror of the open sea, yet he keeps pushing on in the *Aeneid* because the gods have enjoined him to lead his people to Latium and resettle them there.

It is from Virgil that Dante learned what I would call the dynamic imperative—of keeping both the journey and the poem moving forward until it reaches its projected end. We recognize this Virgilian imperative in the way Virgil the character constantly prods the pilgrim along throughout Hell and Purgatory. In the journey's relentless forward drive, where Virgil acts as the prime agent, we should also see the movement of narrative itself. This too is a lesson Dante learned from Virgil. Before embarking on the *Comedy*, Dante had been primarily a lyric poet writing in fixed, self-contained verse forms such as the sonnet and the *canzone*. There was little, if any, narrative dynamism in his poems. It was the *Aeneid* that provided him with the blueprint for an altogether different, more kinetic, more drama-driven kind of poem. One of the reasons Dante calls Virgil his "master and author" is because Virgil taught him what it means to write an epic, that is to say, a poem that unfolds a complex narrative over an extended sequence of scenes, characters, actions, episodes, and parts. It is primarily as the disciple of Virgil's epic art that Dante "follows after him" at the end of *Inferno* 1.

Of course Dante was no humble imitator of Virgil. Throughout the *Comedy* he undermines Virgil's authority as much as he champions it, for Dante authored a distinctly Christian epic, which cannot fully subscribe to the worldview of a pagan poet like Virgil. One of the fascinating aspects of both *Inferno* and *Purgatory* has to do with the ideological and stylistic tensions that obtain between Dante and his guide, or between Virgil's pagan "tragedy" and Dante's Christian "comedy." From Dante's Christian perspective the entire pagan era was tragic, precisely because the possibility of salvation was closed off to it. The relationship between the pagan era and the Christian era in Dante's poem is altogether dynamic, in the sense that Dante is always *moving beyond* Virgil even as he re-inherits Virgil's legacy. This is a crucial, ideological aspect of what I have called the dynamic imperative. Dante's Christian poem must both appropriate and transcend the pagan past.

What this means, for the purposes of this essay, is that in Dante's poem motion has a different structure and endpoint, hence a different meaning, than motion does in Virgil's *Aeneid*. In the *Aeneid* the impetus is for the most part rectilinear as the Trojans move from point A to point Z. In the *Comedy*, by contrast, motion is both rectilinear and circular—which means it is also vertical rather than merely lateral—as the pilgrim moves from the paralyzing darkness of *Inferno* 1 to the blinding light of *Paradiso* 33. To express it otherwise: the *Aeneid* is earthbound, while the *Comedy* is heaven bound. The final endpoint of the *Aeneid* is the founding of the earthly city of Rome. The *Comedy*'s final endpoint is the City of God, or "that Rome where Christ is a Roman," as Dante puts it in *Purgatory* 31.

3. Dante's Rhyme Scheme

I have claimed that the midpoint in Dante is a turning point. I have remarked that the kind of motion that propels Virgil and Dante forward as they descend the various circles of Hell is one that combines rectilinear and circular motion, namely, the spiral. I have also claimed that Dante inherits from Virgil the dynamic imperative, and that this imperative is at work in the way Dante constantly moves beyond Virgil even as he incorporates his predecessor's legacy. All these patterns I have discussed so far are reflected in the *Comedy*'s prosody, especially its rhyme scheme. How so?

To begin with, we should recall that the poem has a triadic structure. There are three canticles (*Inferno*, *Purgatory*, and *Paradiso*), and the verses are grouped in tercets (units of three verses). This triadic pattern, which has any number of other manifestations in the *Comedy*, including the number of circles in Hell and spheres in Heaven, relates analogically to the Christian doctrine of the Trinity. It is not necessary to enter into a discussion of that doctrine here, except to remark that the *Comedy*'s rhyme scheme, which is known as *terza rima* (literally, "third rhyme"), has a Trinitarian structure as well, for in Dante's universe, poetic form is informed by theological principles.

Terza rima is an extraordinary, yet basically simple, pattern that Dante invented for the purposes of this poem alone. It follows a readily discernible pattern: *aba, bcb, cdc, ded*, and so on. This is not a closed but an open pattern that potentially could continue on forever. According to its scheme, once a canto gets under way, every rhyme is repeated three times (except for the first and last tercets of each canto). The middle verse of each tercet contains a new rhyme word that looks forward to the next tercet, where the rhyme is repeated twice. Thus while the middle rhyme looks forward, the other two glance backward to the previous tercet. It has been rightly claimed that it is the most dynamic, forward-moving rhyme pattern in all of Western poetry.

I would remark first of all that terza rima mirrors, in uncanny fashion, the pattern of reappropriation-and-transcendence that marks Dante's Christian relationship to the pagan traditions on which he draws so heavily throughout the *Comedy*. By that I mean that, just as Dante presumes to incorporate the pagan legacy as well as move beyond it, so terza rima circles backward even as it moves forward. This is the most remarkable aspect of his rhyme scheme. By the same token, this is as close as one can get, in the realm of prosody, to integrating linear and circular motion. Terza rima keeps propelling the verses forward even as it keeps them circling back in a self-transcending, dynamic, movement. One could compare it to a bicycle wheel that moves forward as it rotates. In that respect it literally incorporates the spiral motion the pilgrim follows down the circles of Hell.

4. Sin in Motion

For Dante the two main faculties of the soul are will and intellect. While we judge with our intellect, we act through our will. Desire belongs to the will, for it is a force within the self that *moves* a person to act one way or another, to incline in this or that direction, or to pursue this or that object. One of the most fascinating aspects of motion in the *Comedy* is its depiction of the mysterious workings within the inner self, or moral will, of human beings.

Apart from the souls in Limbo, who are guiltless, the sinners in Hell are damned as a result of the choices they made in life. When it comes to salvation or damnation in Dante's universe, the burden falls entirely on the individual's free will. Thus all the sins punished in Hell proper are connected to the will. This holds true even for heresy, which at first blush would seem to be an error of the intellect rather than an act of will, yet a close reading of *Inferno* 10 reveals that both Farinata and Cavalcante are haughty and prideful, and that their heresy was due more to a stubbornness of the will than to clouded judgment.

Each individual who has attained the age of reason (seven years old, according to the Catholic tradition) freely chooses to follow—or not to follow, as the case may be—the inclinations of his or her will. We must always remember when reading the *Inferno* that, despite their wails and lamentations, Dante's damned are exactly where they want to be. It is their desire and will that brought them to their infernal destination. Virgil suggests as much when he informs Dante that the newly arrived shades on the shores of the Acheron river are eager to reach their designated place in Hell: "God's justice so spurs them that fear turns to desire" (*Inferno* 3, 125).

What distinguishes the *Comedy* from earlier medieval representations of Hell—and there were many before Dante composed the *Inferno*—is that Dante's Hell is not merely a torture gallery. It is a place
where the true nature of each particular sin (as Dante conceived it from
his Christian worldview) is revealed by the punishment it receives.
The punishments offer symbolic insights into the transgressions. To
put it boldly, but not inaccurately, the sinners in Dante's Hell *desire*
their punishment, insofar as the punishment lays bare (in a symbolic
way) what the sinners truly desire when they freely commit their sin.

One has a natural tendency to assume, when reading the *Inferno*,
that the sinners regret the choices they made in life now that, in Hell,
they must pay such a heavy price for their past acts. This is not the case.
There are no penitents in the *Inferno*. There is plenty of self-pity and
self-justification, but no genuine contrition. The most compelling evidence for this claim—which some may consider controversial—is that
so many of Dante's sinners *reenact* for Dante (and hence for the
poem's reader) the choices that landed them in Hell in the first place.
Francesca repeats in her speech the errors, self-delusions, and romantic
mystifications that seduced her at the time of her adultery with Paolo.
Her self-exculpations in *Inferno* 5 only serve to re-indict her. Farinata
is as supercilious as ever in the circle of the heretics. Guido da
Montefeltro rehearses for Dante in his ambiguous and duplicitous
speech the willful self-deception that got him damned. Likewise Ulysses restages for us in his sublime oration the heroic but tragic hubris
that brought about disaster for him and his men. Any number of other
examples confirm that, by reembracing their sins before our very eyes
(or ears), the sinners track in their soliloquies the psychological or
moral motions of the will that led them to their present fates.

Given that the inner motions of the sinful will are symbolically represented in the punishments that are on display in this great theater of
moral insight that is Dante's *Inferno*, it is fitting that several of the punishments take the form of various kinds of motion. The lustful are
swept up in an "infernal whirlwind" that buffets them *di qua, di là, di*

giù, di sù—"here, there, down, up." The hypocrites move slowly in a semicircle. The sodomites must keep running around a track under the raining flames, and so on. It would be interesting to chart, classify, and interpret punitive motion in the *Inferno*, yet that is not my intention here.

What I would like to suggest instead is that, while many of the sinners are forced to keep moving around, the moral reality of Hell is without any real dynamism. Or better: Hell is the place where motion is issueless. Or better yet: infernal motion does not lead anywhere. It is a useless kind of displacement, endlessly repetitious, which can't move beyond itself, for it is denied transcendence. In this respect even the most restless and agitated sinners are trapped in a condition of fixity. Hell's occupants are stuck there, the way Satan, who lords over the entire realm, is stuck in his frozen lake at the bottom of Hell, where all gravity is gathered together.

Having read through the whole of *Inferno*, the reader understands in retrospect that there was a hellish quality about the pilgrim's immobilization in *Inferno* 1. The pilgrim's blockage was Satanic—a sign that he was under the threat of damnation, bogged down by the weight of sin. Virgil arrives on the scene to rescue him, yet we should not assume that the crisis of *Inferno* 1 gets resolved once Virgil gets Dante moving again. On the contrary, the crisis of the midpoint is not overcome until Dante passes through the very midpoint of Hell, which is located at the center of Satan's massive body. In order to exit Hell, Virgil and Dante must climb onto Satan's body and use it as a passageway. The mechanics of what takes place on the body are vague, yet we are told that, as Dante and Virgil approach the place where Satan's thighbone turns, Virgil turns himself upside down and, with considerable effort, pulls himself up. For a moment it seems to Dante that they are returning to Hell, yet they are in fact climbing up out toward the shores of the Purgatory in the southern hemisphere (they will exit, appropriately enough, on Easter morning, the day of the Resurrection). This turn on Satan's body marks the moment of Christian conversion (from the

Latin *convertere*, to completely turn around). By virtue of this conversion Dante finally passes beyond the debilitating, deathly midpoint of *Inferno* 1. Thus in retrospect the entire journey between *Inferno* 1 and *Inferno* 34 appears to us an extended turning motion. At the end of his infernal journey, after the turnabout on Satan's body, the pilgrim is finally ready to start climbing.

5. Circles

The kind of motion that leads Virgil and Dante up the Mount of Purgatory is the same as the one that led them down through Hell. It is a spiraling motion. The difference is that in Hell Virgil and Dante move clockwise as they descend, while in Purgatory they move counterclockwise. Technically speaking, however, they do not change the direction of their motion at all. Having passed through the midpoint on Satan's body, the world is now turned upside down, which means it has been turned right-side up, given that from a Christian point of view we live in a topsy-turvy world. Thus the same motion that led them downward in a spiral now leads them up the mountain. Such are the ways of Christian conversion: the way up is the way down. The most humble rise the highest, while the most prideful (Satan) sink the lowest.

The most dramatic difference between the sinners in Hell and the penitents in Purgatory is that the former are going nowhere while the latter are working toward a goal, namely, the purgation of their sins and their eventual assumption into paradise. In Purgatory everyone is on the go, even when a penitent remains confined to one of its terraces for an extended length of time. The main difference between the two realms is that in Purgatory time matters, whereas Hell is a colossal waste of time. Just as time matters in Purgatory, so too does motion. For motion takes place in time. Indeed, time is engendered by motion, so much so that the medieval tradition from which Dante derived his worldview held that "time is the moving image of eternity."

For the Christian cosmological tradition within which Dante operated—a tradition that had its roots in Platonic and Aristotelian theories—the truest image of eternity in the material world is circular motion. This is why the heavens remind us of paradise and eternity. In Dante's cosmos, the heavens revolve in perfect circles around the unmoved Mover who created them, namely, God. Yet Dante makes it clear throughout his *Paradiso* that paradise is NOT located in the heavenly spheres through which he travels with his new guide Beatrice. Paradise is beyond the space-time continuum altogether; it has no "place" in the material universe at all. Hence it cannot be represented or imagined by mortals like Dante. The most Dante can do to give us a moving image of paradise is to take us up through the celestial spheres, whose stable and circular motion is as perfect as the material world will allow for.

What moves the heavens is the same force that moves both sinners and saints alike, namely, love. The sinner is motivated by self-love, the saint by love of God; nevertheless, both sinners and saints "follow their bliss," as it were, for it is their "love" or will that moves them both. What distinguishes the sinner from the saint is that the sinner's love is misdirected, while the saint's is directed rightly. (See Heather Webb's discussion of misdirected love in this volume.) This means that the saint's love is in harmony with the orderly movement of the universe, all of whose bodies are moved by their love of the Creator. The sinner, by contrast, due to the perversions of self-love, is "out of tune" with the cosmos. I use the metaphor of attunement because the first impression Dante receives of the infernal realm is that of *discordant* cries and wails, whereas in Purgatory and Paradise he hears voices singing in choruses and celestial harmonies.

The basic "plot" of the *Comedy* is at once simple and dismaying. It has to do with the pilgrim's efforts to complete a long, self-integrating journey at the end of which his inner being—which, like human history, suffers from the perversion of sin—becomes harmonized with the trans-temporal and trans-spatial love that moves the divinely created universe in circles. Salvation means nothing more, and nothing less, than such harmonization. It is not until the very last lines of *Paradiso* that the *Comedy*'s story comes to its conclusion. In the last tercet we read that, thanks to a special act of grace, the love that moves the sun and other stars "turns" (*volgeva*) the pilgrim's inner self (turns his "desire and will," to be precise) like a wheel. It is impossible for Dante to describe in human words what actually took place in that breakthrough moment, and it is equally impossible to render in English translation the beauty and harmony of the Italian original:

> ma già volgeva il mio disio e l velle,
> sì come rota ch'igualmente è mossa,
> l'amor che move il sole e le altre stelle

The best one can hope to do in English is to convey the literal meaning of Dante's last tercet accurately, as in the following version:

> [my] desire and will were moved already—like
> a wheel revolving uniformly—by
> the Love that moves the sun and other stars.

This final reconciliation of the pilgrim's soul to the orderly motion of the universe at the end of the *Comedy*—a motion sponsored and promoted by love—gains its full weight and meaning only after the reader has undertaken the effort to accompany Dante on his laborious journey from its very inception in the dark wood of *Inferno* 1. "In my beginning is my end," writes T. S. Eliot in the first verse of "East Coker," whose last verse inverts that statement: "In my end is my beginning." So it is with the *Comedy*. Its end circles back to its beginning, as its beginning turns toward its end, through the motion of love. Or as Beatrice puts it when she descends into Limbo to enlist Virgil's help before the action of the poem even begins: *Amor mi mosse, che mi fa parlare*, "Love has moved me and makes me speak."

The *Inferno* from a Purgatorial (and Paradisiacal) Perspective_____

Heather Webb

In the fifth canto of the *Inferno*, Dante and Virgil come upon a realm where souls are tormented by an eternal storm that "never rests, [but] drives on the spirits with its violence: wheeling and pounding, it harasses them" (*Inf.* 5, 31-33). Few episodes in the *Commedia* are as famous as the pilgrim's encounter in canto 5 of the *Inferno* with the souls of Paolo and Francesca, two lovers who come forth from the storm. The episode has often been read as an excerpt, extracted from the rest of the text. As an excerpt, it has been retold in opera, in works of visual art of various kinds, and in numerous later texts. For this reason, Dante scholars have had to remind readers that Paolo and Francesca are textually located in Hell, and that despite this tempting extractability, the duo are meant to be read in an infernal context.

In this essay I will show that, in addition to the necessary infernal context of the Paolo and Francesca episode, two other levels of context must be added if we are to comprehend fully Dante's treatment of the damned lovers. The *Inferno* gives us a visceral experience of sin, but it does little to explain the reasons we fall into sin, or how to remedy such a condition in life. The pilgrim moves through Hell not because he is learning from each experience and leaving different kinds of sin behind, but rather simply because he is dragged along by Virgil, who often needs to urge him to keep moving and sometimes needs to carry him physically. As he speaks with each of the sinners, the pilgrim, like the reader of the *Commedia*, is frequently absorbed into the powerful psychology of the sinners, even to the point of imitating their modes of speech and ways of portraying themselves. It is only in the *Purgatorio* that we are finally given a series of explanations of the causes of sin and provided with notions of the ways in which a person can cure him- or herself of sin. And it is only in *Paradiso* that the pilgrim is able to interact fully with models of sin-free behavior. In order to comprehend properly the sins that we experience and even, in some ways, are brought to *participate* in during our reading of (or journey through) the *Inferno*, we must take into consideration the explanations given in the *Purgatorio* and the positive models presented in *Paradiso*.

This is not always easy to accomplish. We do not find traitors in Purgatory or in Paradise, for example. Sins do not usually match neatly across canticles. Sins are divided differently in *Purgatorio* than they are in *Inferno*. In Purgatory, for example, we find a terrace on which the sin of pride is healed. In the Inferno, there is no particular circle dedicated to pride, but we might say that all the sinners in the Inferno are guilty of the sin of pride as well as that for which they are punished. The heretic Farinata, to give just one example, is clearly prideful in his mode of being. *Purgatorio* shows us what lies beneath each of the conditions we encounter in the *Inferno*, though we must work backward from the explanations there to understand what we have read earlier. *Paradiso* does not show sin, but rather portrays the opposite. There is one clear case in which we do manage to read a single sin across all three canticles, however. The lustful are present as such in both *Inferno* and *Purgatorio*, and in a recovered fashion in the sphere of Venus in *Paradiso*. This essay will show the ways in which comparisons among the three canticles can allow us to achieve better comprehension of the episodes that so involve the reader in the *Inferno*.

The storm in canto 5 is, of course, the *contrapasso* for the lustful, or a revelation of the nature of their sin. If the properly ordered body, governed by a properly ordered soul, walks a straight line toward the divine, these shades instead reveal their willed lack of control over their course through life. While still alive, they did not choose to maintain a course toward the highest good, but rather allowed themselves to follow their passions wherever they led. After their deaths, the storm enacts their mode of being in life, tossing their shades this way and that. The passions to which they allowed themselves to be prey are now externalized in the force of the storm. Through such externalization of an internal psychological state, we are allowed to see in an enhanced way what lust truly looks like.

The pilgrim asks to speak with two souls who are moving through the storm together. Francesca tells her story and gives us further insight into the condition of these shades, trapped forever in the mode of being in which they found themselves at the time of their deaths. As she explains, "Love, that can quickly seize the gentle heart, took hold of him because of the fair body taken from me—how that was done: still wounds me. Love, that releases no beloved from loving took hold of me so strongly through his beauty, that, as you see, it has not left me yet. Love led the two of us unto one death. Caïna waits for him who took our life" (*Inf.* 5, 100-107). Francesca defers all responsibility and agency to other people and forces. Love caused Paolo to fall in love with her; love also obliged her to love him in return. Love led them to death. The triple repetition of the word *Amor* as the personified agent in each of her phrases emphasizes the degree to which Francesca believes that Love has acted upon her, emphasizing her sense of powerlessness in the face of this force. Love, in her description, is something akin to one of the gods of antiquity, toying with human lives. Consequently, this is what she experiences in the Inferno; the storm, like love, is an overwhelming force. What she believed to be true has come to be true for her. The sinners in the *Inferno* live out their expectations eternally. Hell is something they have made for themselves.

The pilgrim is a misleading model for readers here. When Francesca tells her story, he feels great pity for her and allows himself to be convinced by her justification of her actions. We see this as he questions her further, using her terminology and her modes of explanation: "but tell me, in the time of gentle sighs, with what and in what way did Love allow you to recognize your still uncertain longings?" (*Inf.* 5, 118-120). Following Francesca's lead, the pilgrim here imagines that it must be Love that allows her to know her desires. Love is the active force. Just as Francesca describes it, the pilgrim imagines the two lovers to be entirely passive in the face of a force greater than they are. Francesca responds:

> "One day, to pass the time away, we read of Lancelot—how love had overcome him. We were alone, and we suspected nothing. And time and time again that reading led our eyes to meet, and made our faces pale, and yet one point alone defeated us. When we had read how the desired smile was kissed by one who was so true a lover, this one, who shall never be parted from me, while all his body trembled, kissed my mouth. A Gallehaut indeed, that book and he who wrote it, too; that day we read no more." (*Inf.* 5, 127-38)

Here again we see that Francesca describes Lancelot as overcome or seized by love, a passive player just as she has described both Paolo and herself. When the two read of the kiss between Guinevere and Lancelot, they kiss as well, imitating their illustrious literary model. The book and its author are agents here, doing the work of bringing the couple to kiss. As Francesca tells it, she and Paolo are compelled to imitate.

After Francesca tells this story, the pilgrim faints as if dead, having lost control of his body just as the lustful have, and at the same time mimicking the death that Francesca describes. Readers, following the pilgrim's example, have likewise felt pity for Francesca. But this is the experience of the *Inferno*; we come to see sin, but we do not understand it, or see where the individuals with whom we speak went wrong. *Purgatorio* will supply this information.

In *Purgatorio*, sins are both explained comprehensively in philosophical terms and revealed intuitively to the reader by means of opposition; the cure for each sin is unfolded in detail. The cure for sin consists in part in the study of both negative and positive examples, of the worst cases of each sin and of the virtue that opposes each sin. Let us begin with the explanation before passing on to the examples. In canto 16 of the *Purgatorio*, a penitent by the name of Marco Lombardo explains how it is that the soul comes to sin: "issuing from His hands, the soul—on which He thought with love before creating it—is like a child who weeps and laughs in sport; that soul is simple, unaware; but since a joyful Maker gave it motion, it turns willingly to things that bring delight. At first it savors trivial goods; these would beguile the soul, and it runs after them, unless there's guide or rein to rule its love" (*Pur.* 16, 85-93). As God is a joyful, loving creator, the soul is modeled on that mode of being. Loving and joyful itself, the soul finds a world full of beautiful things, takes joy in those things, and moves naively toward them, wherever they may lead. The problem is that not all goods are equal, and the soul cannot at first distinguish between greater and lesser goods. It may run after lesser goods, or follow goods that ought to be pursued only with measured enthusiasm. The soul is thus described as essentially innocent in its natural and divinely created propensity to love, but very prone to distraction. Its love must be governed by some sort of rule or must be curbed in some way.

Virgil explains in canto 17 that sin is caused by certain defects in love, echoing and expanding Marco Lombardo's description of love's primary goodness and its potential dangers. Love may err through the choice of the wrong object or "through too much or too little vigor." The lustful are among those sinners who suffer from "the love that seeks the good distortedly." It is important to note that the lustful are seeking the good but have somehow gone a bit wrong in their modes of doing so. Along with the avaricious and prodigal and the gluttonous, the lustful have yielded excessively to lesser goods: "Each apprehends confusedly a good in which the mind may rest, and desires it; and thus, all strive to reach that good. . . . There is a different good, which does not make men glad; it is not happiness, is not true essence, fruit and root of every good" (*Pur.* 17, 127-135). The love of possessions or of food or of sensual pleasure is, in each case, a striving for something that is *a* good, but is not *the* good that stands at the root of all the others. Excessive movement toward these lesser goods can impede progress toward *the* good that is the ultimate goal of all humans. It is important to note, however, that Virgil describes a "striving" for something. This contradicts Francesca's story in that Virgil makes it clear that lust is not simply passive. Lust, as explained in the purgatorial context, is excessive pursuit of a lesser good. In *Purgatorio*, we learn that every sin is willed action and never a passive "being drawn into" some state.

This leads to a longer discussion in which Virgil explains how it is that love works, and how love can go wrong. He explains how we may first be drawn to something, almost without thought, as Francesca describes, but that this soon leads to willed action on our part:

> "The soul, which is created quick to love, responds to everything that pleases, just as soon as beauty wakens it to act. Your apprehension draws an image from a real object and expands upon that object until the soul has turned toward it; and if, so turned, the soul tends steadfastly, then that propensity is love—it's nature that joins the soul in you, anew, through beauty. Then, just as flames ascend because the form of fire was fashioned to fly upward, toward the stuff of its own sphere, where it lasts longest, so does the soul, when seized, move into longing, a motion of the spirit, never resting till the beloved thing has made it joyous. Now you can see how deeply hidden the truth is from the scrutinists, who would insist that every love is, in itself, praiseworthy; and they are led to error by the matter of love, because it may seem—always—good; but not each seal is fine, although the wax is." (*Pur.* 18, 19-39)

The soul is thus naturally drawn to love because of its creation by a loving maker. The apprehension of beauty leads the soul to turn toward the beautiful and pleasing thing; persistence in that turning is love. The next step in that movement is longing or desire that spurs the soul to striving, or to willful action that seeks to obtain joy from the beloved thing.

It is thus clear that, contrary to what Francesca says, there is always a component of will, of voluntary movement toward the desired object. Though the grammatical constructions she employs, such as "took hold of me" and "took hold of him," suggest passivity, this rhetorical passivity is above all a demonstration of the infernal state of the lustful. These damned are not defined so much by their acts as by their belief that they are powerless to resist love and their denial that it is they who are moving, of their own free will, toward a lesser goal. Becoming fully absorbed in that lesser goal does not permit them salvation.

Each sin in Dante's *Inferno* is defined by a psychological state, or by a means of approaching life, rather than by a specific act. Such a treatment of sin is very different from others of Dante's time, or in texts that he might have read, in which the lustful were considered to be guilty of a specifically sexual crime. Accordingly, the lustful in other visions of Hell were punished in sexual ways—forced, for instance, to have intercourse with demons, or punished by torture inflicted on the genitalia. For Dante, instead, the punishment for a mode of thinking involves allowing that mode of thinking to become reified visibly and sensibly into the mode of being it was in life for all eternity.

Love itself, Virgil reiterates, is a positive thing, but it can take bad forms. It is inchoate matter that can easily be molded into different configurations, just as wax can run into different seals and harden there into many multiple forms. Not all forms are equal, and not all the shapes and goals of love are equal either. The metaphor of wax is useful also for consideration of the problem of misdirection or distraction. Once the wax has been allowed to harden within a certain form, it cannot easily be redirected into another course. The problem of lust is often that of obsession and the sensation of powerlessness that results.

When Virgil and the pilgrim arrive at the terrace where lust is purged, Virgil warns the pilgrim, "On this terrace, it is best to curb your eyes: the least distraction—left or right—can mean a step you will regret" (*Pur.* 25, 118-20). To his left, the penitents walk through flames; to his right, the cliff threatens. Virgil's statement recalls earlier analyses of the ways in which love can err. A curb or rein is exactly what Marco Lombardo says is needed to keep the soul from excessive pursuit of lesser goods. And it is Virgil's explanation of love that makes reference to the role of vision; it is the perception of beauty that leads to love. Francesca notes this same cause of Paolo's love "because of the fair body taken from me." The pilgrim here must go through the purgatorial experience of testing himself against temptation. He must observe what goes on around him without becoming distracted from his ultimate goal of advancing up the mountain of Purgatory toward the Earthly Paradise and eventually to Paradise itself.

The lustful complete their penance in a number of ways. The pilgrim first notes that they sing "*Summae Deus clementiae*" and repeat references to the chastity of the Virgin and the goddess Diana at the hymn's end. Two groups move through the flames in opposite directions. When they meet, they briefly kiss one another in greeting without pausing and move on, each member of each group accusing him- or herself with references to their sin. The kiss is a form of spiritual practice within the therapy of *Purgatorio:* "as ants, in their dark company, will touch their muzzles, each to each, perhaps to seek news of their fortunes and their journeyings. No sooner is their friendly greeting done than each shade tries to outcry all the rest even before he starts to move ahead" (*Pur.* 26, 34-39). If we compare such kisses to the one Francesca describes in *Inferno* 5, we may see the ways in which *Purgatorio* retrains the individual. The kiss between Paolo and Francesca stops their reading, leading them into what they understand to be an unchangeable course of passion that inevitably draws them directly to their deaths. And death, both bodily and spiritual, is the only possibly outcome of desire that understands itself to be beyond control. Francesca links their sin to violence from the very beginning of her speech to the pilgrim, speaking of "our souls, that stained the world with blood" (*Inf.* 5, 90).

Here, the kiss of the lustful penitents is recontextualized within a practice of progression and movement toward a different and higher goal. Unlike Paolo and Francesca, who allowed the direction of their souls to be dictated by the kiss and all that seemed to follow inevitably, the penitents do not pause or linger, or move in the direction of the kiss, but rather continue onward in each individual's movement toward healing and toward the promise of Paradise. The greeting is friendly and understood as good; the souls must recognize the others around them but not allow themselves to be distracted by the presence of these others and thus drawn away from their ultimate goal. They learn to recognize lesser goods on the way to the highest good that awaits them. The highest good does not exclude all others, but rather places those lesser goods in a new and enhanced context in which they are recognized proportionally to a greater goal.

The effects of the group serve to reinforce the individual in this case. First, the presence of the group saves the individual from the dangerous isolation Paolo and Francesca experience. Paolo and Francesca read alone, looking to literary models. In purgatory, souls work together to enforce a number of different models, repeating references to chastity. The group does not allow fixation on a single person or a single model. It does not permit the establishment of couples, but rather creates a dynamic between the group or the many and the individual. Second, each of the penitent souls tries to outcry all the others, to make his or her individual voice heard above the group. This form of healthy competition moves the souls forward as individuals toward a common goal.

Those in the group generally assumed to be the homosexual lustful call out, "Sodom and Gomorrah," while those in the other group, generally assumed to be the heterosexual lustful, call out, "That the bull may hurry toward her lust, Pasiphaë hides in the cow." There has been some debate among scholars about the identification of the groups. The difference between the two groups, as Guido Guinizelli, one of the penitent, explains to the pilgrim, is as follows:

> "The people moving opposite us shared the sin for which once, while in triumph, Caesar heard 'Queen' called out against him; that is why, as they move off from us, they cry out 'Sodom,' reproaching their own selves, as

you have heard, and through their shame abet the fire's work. Our sin was with the other sex; but since we did not keep the bounds of human law, but served our appetites like beasts, when we part from the other ranks, we then repeat, to our disgrace, the name of one who, in the bestial planks, became herself a beast."

Here we find one of the intriguing mysteries of the *Commedia*. In the *Inferno*, Virgil explains that one of the realms in the circle of the violent against nature is related to the city of Sodom. The sin of violence against nature is much graver than the sin of lust; the lustful are in the second circle, while the violent against nature are in the seventh. So why is it that the sin associated with Sodom is classified as violence against nature in the *Inferno*, but as lust in *Purgatorio*?

This is a question that scholars have pondered at length and have not found easy to answer conclusively. Certainly, it reinforces the point made earlier in this essay; sins in the *Inferno* are not categorized according to specific acts, but rather according to ways of thinking and thus ways of being. In *Purgatorio*, it becomes clear that a homosexual act can be understood as lust, or as the excessive pursuit of a lesser good. Here, there is no violence of any kind. In fact, the example of Caesar shows the ways in which violence is mitigated by openness to love. The victorious general is reminded of (or teased about) his vulnerability to the Bithynian king, Nicomedes. Furthermore, there is no suggestion that one group of the two was somehow guilty of acting against nature. Both are described with the same metaphors from the natural world: "just like cranes, of whom a part, to flee the sun, fly north to the Riphean mountains, while the rest, to flee the frost, fly toward the sands, one group moves with—the other opposite—us" (*Pur.* 26, 43-46). The movement of the cranes is natural in both cases.

The shades in *Purgatorio* are defined by their penitence, just as those in the *Inferno* are defined by their unalterable impenitence. Guinizelli notes that the shades reproach themselves, that their shame works to purge them just as the fire does. Both Hell and Purgatory,

Dante suggests, are effectively of our own making. The infernal condition is precisely that of being allowed to continue in the same state of mind in which each sinner died, rendered literal and eternally fixed. By the same token, *Purgatorio* is a realm of self-purification. The flames that surround the shades can only do so much. These souls have attained Purgatory, and continue to move forward toward Paradise, precisely because of their own shame and their own recognition of their fault. Above all, they are distinguished by their desire to change.

The characterization of heterosexual lust in *Purgatorio* presents itself in clear opposition to Francesca's romantic portrayal of her story and of her state. In service to their appetites, Guinizelli explains, these penitent abandoned the limits of human law. As Marco Lombardo points out, the soul will run after lesser goods with abandon if it is not held back by curb or rein. These souls did not remain within the boundaries of the law, but continued their pursuit of those things they found pleasing. Guinizelli explains all of this by giving strong emphasis to the agency of each of the penitent. They chose to abandon those boundaries in pursuit of their desires. Unlike Francesca, he does not attempt to displace blame; it is his acceptance of his responsibility that has allowed him to reach Purgatory. Whereas Francesca claims that she has followed the example of Guinevere and Lancelot, the penitent lustful admit that they have, in reality, followed the example of Pasiphaë. Pasiphaë, a queen like Guinevere, had the inventor Daedalus build her a hollow wooden cow so that she might mate with a bull. In this case, lust is not passively being drawn into love with another person; rather, it is the active decision to find a way to couple with a beast and, in so doing, become a beast. In ceasing to respect the boundaries of human law that would have prohibited Francesca from having an affair with her husband's brother, for instance, the lustful discard their humanity and become bestial. Rather than imagining this transgression in the light of tales of romantic love and poetry, the penitent in Purgatory rethink this transgression by means of reidentifying the sort of example that they have followed. Whereas Francesca identifies with Queen Guinevere, the lustful in Purgatory see themselves as a queen who has utterly debased herself in defiance of human law.

But we must recall that this is the last terrace of Purgatory before souls reach the Earthly Paradise on their way to Paradise proper. In short, it is the least grave of the sins that must be cured to achieve a state of blessedness. It is, therefore, one of the few sins we see redeemed in *Paradiso*. In canto 9 of the *Paradiso*, in fact, we have the opportunity to see what lust redeemed looks like. The blessed in the sphere of Venus were much subject to love in life. The pilgrim speaks with Cunizza, who had five different husbands or companions during her life. She tells her story briefly, as follows:

> "In that part of indecent Italy that lies between Rialto and the springs from which the Brenta and the Piave stream, rises a hill—of no great height— from which a firebrand descended, and it brought much injury to all the land about. Both he and I were born of one same root: Cunizza was my name, and I shine here because this planet's radiance conquered me. But in myself, I pardon happily the reason for my fate; I do not grieve—and vulgar minds may find this hard to see." (*Par.* 9, 25-36)

As we began to note in the purgatorial context, the redeemable part of lust is that openness to love that acts as the virtue that opposes the sin of violence. Cunizza here speaks of her brother, Ezzelino, located among the tyrants in the seventh circle of the *Inferno*. The two siblings, born of the same root, had opposing characters. He conquered the lands around him, bringing injury wherever he went, while Cunizza was conquered by love. In her redeemed state, she is able to joyfully forgive herself her earlier sins. They are of no consequence now. In some ways, we may imagine that her loving nature is what has allowed her to open herself toward love of the highest good.

Love in *Paradiso* is directed first and foremost toward God, but it also embraces the other blessed and even the pilgrim himself. Secure in the fixed portion of their love and alignment with the divine, the blessed find it possible to share love with others without fear of distraction from the ultimate goal (they have arrived) or fear of violating boundaries (this is no longer an issue). Later on in the same canto, the pilgrim speaks with Folco of Marseille, who tells of his lustful past but, like Cunizza, explains that it no longer matters: "One does not repent here; here one smiles—not for the fault, which we do not recall, but for the Power that fashioned and foresaw. For here we contemplate the art adorned by such great love, and we discern the good through which the world above forms that below" (*Par.* 9, 103-8). Once again, like the newborn soul described in *Purgatorio*, souls in Paradise are free to love all that is beautiful. The perspective from Paradise allows the souls continually to contemplate the highest good that forms the world and the greatest love that is the font of creation. They have returned to a state of innocence in which they can joyfully mirror the happiness of the creator.

It is thus only by comparison with the lustful, or the formerly lustful, of *Purgatorio* and *Paradiso* that we may come to see what is wrong with Francesca's deeply seductive story. She herself cannot see her fault, and the pilgrim who has not yet climbed through Purgatory to encounter his own tendency toward lust is equally blind to the problems present in her justifications and misdirections. The *Commedia* challenges us by demanding that we develop a capacity to continually read and interpret multidirectionally. We cannot simply read through the canticles from beginning to end and stop there. We must go back and, like the blessed in *Paradiso*, keep the larger picture, or the "art adorned by such great love" in mind at all times. In an endlessly complex interactive structure, the *Inferno* cannot be understood (although it can be experienced) without knowledge of the *Paradiso*, which in turn cannot be comprehended without the *Purgatorio*, and so on. Entering into the *Commedia* is an endless adventure, and it is my hope that this essay has served as an invitation to do just that.

Works Consulted

Barolini, Teodolinda. *Dante and the Origins of Italian Literary Culture*. New York: Fordham UP, 2006.

_____. *Dante's Poets: Textuality and Truth in the "Comedy."* Princeton, NJ: Princeton UP, 1984.

Boswell, John E. "Dante and the Sodomites." *Dante Studies* 112 (1994): 63-76.

Cestaro, Gary P. *Dante and the Grammar of the Nursing Body*. Notre Dame, IN: U of Notre Dame P, 2003.

Dante. *The Divine Comedy of Dante Alighieri: Inferno*. Trans. Allen Mandelbaum. New York: Bantam Books, 1980.

_____. *The Divine Comedy of Dante Alighieri: Purgatorio*. Trans. Allen Mandelbaum. New York: Bantam Books, 1982.

_____. *The Divine Comedy of Dante Alighieri: Paradiso*. Trans. Allen Mandelbaum. New York: Bantam Books, 1984.

Girard, René. "The Mimetic Desire of Paolo and Francesca." *To Double Business Bound: Essays on Literature, Mimesis, and Anthropology*. Baltimore: Johns Hopkins UP, 1988.

Gragnolati, Manuele. *Experiencing the Afterlife*. Notre Dame, IN: U of Notre Dame P, 2005.

Hollander, Robert. "Dante's Harmonious Homosexuals (*Inferno* 16.7-90)." *Electronic Bulletin of the Dante Society of America* 27 June 1996.

Jacoff, Rachel. "Transgression and Transcendence: Figures of Female Desire in Dante's *Commedia*." *Dante*. Ed. Jeremy Tambling. New York: Longman, 1999. 51-67.

_____. ed. *The Cambridge Companion to Dante*. 2d ed. New York: Cambridge UP, 2007.

Mazzotta, Giuseppe. *Dante, Poet of the Desert: History and Allegory in the "Divine Comedy."* Princeton, NJ: Princeton UP, 1979.

_____. *Dante's Vision and the Circle of Knowledge*. Princeton, NJ: Princeton UP, 1993.

Pequigney, Joseph. "Sodomy in Dante's *Inferno* and *Purgatorio*." *Representations* 36 (Fall 1991): 22-42.

Scott, John A. *Understanding Dante*. Notre Dame, IN: U of Notre Dame P, 2004.

Dante's *Inferno*:
Critical Reception and Influence _____

David Lummus

Dante and the *Divine Comedy* have had a profound influence on the production of literature and the practice of literary criticism across the Western world since the moment the *Comedy* was first read. Although critics and commentators normally address the work as a whole, the first canticle, *Inferno*, is the part that has met with the most fervent critical response. The modern epoch has found in it both a mirror with which it might examine the many vices and perversions that define it and an obscure tapestry of almost fundamentalist punishments that are entirely alien to it. From Ezra Pound, T. S. Eliot, and Osip Mandelstam in the early twentieth century to Seamus Heaney, W. S. Merwin, and Robert Pinsky at century's end, modern poets of every bent have been drawn to the *Inferno* and to the other two canticles of the *Comedy* as an example of poetry's world-creating power and of a single poet's transcendence of his own spiritual, existential, and political exile.[1] To them Dante was and is an example of how a poet can engage with the world and reform it, not just represent it, through the power of the poetic imagination. In order to understand how Dante and his poem have been received by critics and poets in the twentieth and twenty-first centuries, we must glance—however cursorily—at the seven-hundred-year critical tradition that has formed the hallowed academic institution of Dante studies. In this way, we can come to see the networks of understanding that bind Dante criticism across its history.

The story of the critical response to Dante's poem begins with Dante himself (or with someone writing under Dante's name). Upon completing the last canticle of the *Comedy* he wrote a letter to his patron in Verona, Cangrande della Scala, in which he dedicated the *Paradiso* to him and then, as a reader of his own poem, explained its subject and meaning.[2] Although most of the epistle is dedicated to the interpretation of *Paradiso*, for our purposes he introduces several concepts important for the history of criticism of the poem as a whole and for literary criticism in general. The structure of the epistle is modeled on the schema that was used in Dante's time for writing prologues to classical texts (the *accessus ad auctores*), which suggests that his work, though in the vernacular, deserved and demanded the same kind of attention as if it had been written in Latin. Also, Dante importantly illustrates the meaning of the poem by applying the fourfold system of allegory normally reserved for interpretation of the Bible. According to this system texts may have several meanings (Dante uses the word "polysemous"): the literal or historical, the allegorical (regarding the life of Christ), the moral or tropological (regarding the actions of the individual soul in this life), and the anagogical (regarding the life of the soul to come). As an example of this interpretive method, Dante briefly analyzes the first two lines of Psalm 113, "When Israel went out of Egypt,"[3] obliquely opening up the possibility of comparing his own poem and personal experience with these biblical verses and the narrative of transcendence through exile that they recount.

The interpretation of the poem's title and subject, however, is rather unimaginative and does not fully account for the poem's radical novelty. Dante explains that the poem is a comedy because "the subject matter, at the beginning it is horrible and foul, as being Hell; but at the close it is happy, desirable, and pleasing, as being Paradise" and because the "style is unstudied and lowly."[4] The subject, he writes, is literally "the state of souls after death," but allegorically it is "man according as by his merits or demerits in the exercise of his free will he is deserving of reward or punishment by justice."[5] The allegorical subject of the *Inferno*, then, would be those who deserve punishment by exercising poorly their free will. Furthermore, in the tradition of most medieval commentaries on Latin literature, Dante and those who follow him describe the work as belonging to the field of ethics, which gives even its most abstract moments a practical purpose. In sum, whether penned by Dante or not, this epistle establishes the *Comedy* as a work of poetic theology whose truth as a fiction lies somewhere between the Bible and the *Aeneid*.

The first commentaries on the *Comedy* were written in the period immediately following Dante's death, beginning with his own sons, Jacopo and Pietro. These commentaries for the most part sought to redeem the work's unorthodoxy by explaining it allegorically. A generation after Dante, the contributions of Giovanni Boccaccio (1313-75) founded the cult of Dante and created the institution of Dante studies that spans the globe today. The famed author of the *Decameron* wrote the first biography of Dante (the *Trattatello in laude di Dante*, or "treatise in praise of Dante"; translated into English in 1898 as *Life of Dante*) and gave a series of public lectures (the *Esposizioni sopra la Commedia di Dante*, or "expositions on Dante's *Comedy*") meant to elucidate the literal and allegorical meanings of the poem.

Convinced that the poem could have a profound practical effect on the Florentine community, the *comune* of Florence paid Boccaccio to lecture on the poem in the church of Santo Stefano in Badia. The first official *lector Dantis*, Boccaccio was able to speak only about the first seventeen cantos of *Inferno* between October 1373 and January 1374 before falling ill.[6] Boccaccio, like other medieval and Renaissance interpreters of the poem, considered Dante a *poeta theologus*, or poet theologian, whose art was able to probe major philosophical questions as well as treatises on theology or the interpretation of Scripture. Even more, he treated Dante as the heir both to the biblical poets David and Solomon—as a new *scriba Dei*, or "scribe of God"—and to the classical bards Homer and Vergil, creating for Dante a persona that is somewhere between prophet and poet. Whereas most of the early commentators were interested in the allegorical meanings alone, Boccaccio focused in his *Esposizioni* on the literal meaning of the text because he thought that the uneducated would be less likely to misunderstand its allegorical message if they understood it literally first. For Boccaccio, as for Dante before him, the fact that the poem was written in vernacular was key to its fulfilling a practical purpose. By the end of the fifteenth century, after numerous commentaries and lives of Dante had been written, the *Comedy*'s status as a "classic" had been secured, and Dante had become a key figure in the establishment of a Florentine identity.

In Renaissance Florence, Cristoforo Landino (1424-98), the chair of poetry and rhetoric at the University of Florence, wrote a commentary on the *Comedy* that was printed in the first Florentine edition of the poem in 1481, which included illustrations by Sandro Botticelli and a now famous discussion of the physical dimensions of Hell. Landino's commentary is important both for the political role it assigns to the poem and for the philosophical truths it finds therein. If medieval commentators had been interested in establishing the poem's authority, Renaissance critics had a freedom of interpretation that is recognizably modern. In fact, certain similarities might be drawn between Landino's Neoplatonic vision and that of Jungian psychology, both of which make the pilgrim's journey into a flight of the *psyche* toward unity and wholeness. For Landino the journey to Paradise is a metaphor for the return of the soul to its maker, and he casts it in terms of the contrast between movement and quietude, as in the initial note on *del cammin*, or "of the journey," in the first line of the *Inferno*, where he writes that human life is not situated in eternity, "where everything is stable and in eternal peace, but in time, which is nothing but continuous flux and movement."[7] He goes on to interpret Dante's journey as the descent of the soul into the depths of corruption and sin (the "prison" of the earthly body), out of which it then rises toward the incorruptible, disembodied happiness of *Paradiso* after having purged the body of the weight of its vices in *Purgatorio*.

Although Landino's Neoplatonic interpretations were often questionable, he did pay careful attention to Dante's language, making Dante into the ideal heir to the classical epic poets and Florence into a center of culture to rival ancient Athens and Rome. For Landino and the centuries that followed, Dante and his poem were pillars of Florentine civic identity. The connection between language and politics was key to the poetic receptions of the *Inferno* that would emerge in the sixteenth century. The language of Hell, which was criticized by those who wanted to purify the dialects of Italy and make a homogeneous literary language, became the model for satirical poets of the Italian courts. No longer interested in transcending human experience in their poetry, poets began to see the *Inferno* as the mirror of a flawed reality, both in its language and in its landscape. In principle, this is not dissimilar from Sandow Birk and Marcus Sanders's adaptation of the *Inferno* as a mirror for the city of Los Angeles at the end of the twentieth century.[8]

Only in the eighteenth century, with "The Discovery of the True Dante" by Giambattista Vico (1668-1744),[9] did the *Comedy* become analyzed as a cultural product that was definitive of its age. For Vico, Dante was a new Homer for a barbarous age in which the poetic language of the Italians had been born. Through his "high fantasy," Dante was able to fuse the culture of his age rhetorically—from popular customs and language to theological concerns—into a poetic language that drew from all the major dialects of the peninsula. By the middle of the next century, however, Giuseppe Mazzini wrote that the critical tradition on the poem had become so overwhelming that the only valid approaches that remained were "the study of life and works of the poet and the correction of the text."[10] Almost overcome by the weight of the authority that Dante's poem had accumulated over the years, critics of eighteenth-century and nineteenth-century Italy were left with the choice between biography and philology as approaches to the text.

In response to this weight, Italian romantic critic Francesco de Sanctis (1817-83) sought to renew the poem and to translate its beauty into terms that a "new generation" could appreciate. He was captivated by the poetry of the *Inferno*, where the soliloquies of the sinners and Dante's pathetic interaction with them spoke to his romantic sensibilities, and he wrote memorable essays on Francesca da Rimini (canto 5), Farinata degli Uberti (canto 10), and Count Ugolino (canto 33), in which he focused on the existential pathos that emerges from them.

These cantos are so moving, he thought, precisely because they had existed in history. For example, in his 1869 essay on canto 5, de Sanctis juxtaposes Francesca da Rimini with Beatrice, both of whom he understands as personifications of different kinds of love. Beatrice, he says, "is less than a woman . . . pure femininity, the genus or type and not the individual," whereas Francesca is "not the divine, but the human and the earthly; she is a fragile, passionate creature, capable of sin, guilty of sin; her condition therefore is such that all her faculties are stirred to life, resulting in deep-rooted conflicts that stir irresistible emotions: and this is life!"[11] De Sanctis saw characters of the *Inferno* as representative of human imperfections and of the trials and tribulations of human experience. Like many romantics, he tried to engage directly with the poem, its author, and its characters and to leave behind the crippling weight of tradition.

This same process of renewal and translation is what first engaged the critical analysis and the poetic reception of Dante in the Anglo-American tradition. In the nineteenth century Dante and his poem become for the first time a true part of the Western critical canon outside of Italy. Although Dante's poetry had been read and imitated in the English-speaking world since the generation after his death—for Geoffrey Chaucer (c. 1343-1400) Dante was just as much a model as were Boccaccio and Petrarch—the revival of interest in the Middle Ages that came with romanticism made the *Comedy* the figurehead for a new kind of visionary poetry. For English romantic poets like Samuel Taylor Coleridge (1772-1834) and Henry Francis Cary (1772-1844) Dante's poetry was an example of how Art could represent the totality of human experience, and it was their job to *English* that Art. For Cary this meant translating the poem into unrhymed paragraph verses in the style of Milton, and for Coleridge it meant popularizing Dante in his lectures and imitating that poet's "gloomy imagination" in his own poetry. On the other side of the Atlantic, Dante's poem was translated twice by Americans in the nineteenth century—by Henry Wadsworth Longfellow in 1865-67 and by his student Charles Eliot Norton in

1891-92—and the Dante Society of America was founded in 1881 in Longfellow's Cambridge, Massachusetts, home, where American Dante studies as an academic discipline would come into its own in the twentieth century. The early efforts of translators and critics in the American context sought to relate Dante's medievalism to their own rapidly expanding world.

The most significant of the Americans to engage with Dante in the early twentieth century, however, were two expatriates living in Europe, T. S. Eliot (1888-1965) and Ezra Pound (1885-1972), both of whom wrote about the *Comedy* as critics and engaged with it as poets. In his early essay on Dante in *The Spirit of Romance* (1910), Pound presents the *Comedy* according to the terms of the epistle to Cangrande, but then interprets the character of the pilgrim in typically modernist terms: the pilgrim is an "everyman" who strives to leave ignorance behind for the "clear light of philosophy."[12] Pound writes that "Dante conceived the real Hell, Purgatory, and Paradise as states, and not places" and recommends that readers "regard Dante's descriptions of the actions and conditions of the shades as descriptions of men's mental states in life . . . that is to say, men's inner selves stand visibly before the eyes of Dante's intellect."[13] For Pound, then, the theology of the *Comedy* is of little importance; Dante's poem is an example of how poetry can engage with the living world of history by turning the reader's mind toward his or her own moral flaws. For Pound it is the poetic and moral measure of the modern world. In fact, Pound's own long poem, the *Cantos*, engages precisely with the poetry of Hell and Purgatory. It begins with an image of a descent into the underworld patterned on the *Odyssey* but politicized and moralized much like the *Inferno*, and it concludes with the lament that he was never able to raise himself out of the mire of the *Inferno* and write a *Paradiso terrestre*, or earthly paradise, as Dante had.[14]

For T. S. Eliot, writing in 1929, Dante represented the most "universal" poet ever to have written. Dante not only dealt with "what is universally human," as did Molière and Shakespeare, but he also did so in a language and with a lucidity that was less localized in language and style. His vernacular poem comprehended all of European culture up until his time and bequeathed that culture universally to the Europeans who followed. When faced with interpreting the first canto of the *Inferno* Eliot took the novel approach of recommending that readers not worry "about the identity of the Leopard, the Lion, and the She-Wolf," since "it is really better . . . not to know or to care what they do mean," but to consider "that which led a man having an idea to express it in images."[15] The practice of allegorical poetry—Dante's visual imagination—was seen as a predecessor of the modernist poetry that Eliot himself practiced. Eliot found Dante's poem to be comprehensible on multiple levels even from the first reading, in which "we get a succession of phantasmagoric but clear images, of images which are coherent, in that each reinforces the last; of glimpses of individuals made memorable by a perfect phrase . . . and of particular longer episodes, which remain separately in the memory."[16] As examples of such memorable episodes, he cites Brunetto Latini in canto 15 and Ulysses in canto 26, among others. His interpretation of the Ulysses episode is particularly illustrative of his theory of Dante as an imagistic poet, whose poetry functions on multiple levels thanks to his use of allegory:

So Ulysses, unseen in the hornèd wave of flame . . . is a creature of pure poetic imagination, apprehensible apart from place and time and the scheme of the poem. The Ulysses episode may strike us first as a kind of excursion, an irrelevance, a self-indulgence on the part of Dante taking a holiday from his Christian scheme. But when we know the whole poem, we recognize how cunningly and convincingly Dante has made to fit in real men, his contemporaries, friends, and enemies, recent historical personages, legendary and Biblical figures, and figures of ancient fiction. He has been reproved or smiled at for satisfying personal grudges by putting in Hell men whom he knew and hated; but these, as well as Ulysses, are transformed in the whole; for the real and the unreal are all representative of types of sin, suffering, fault, and merit, and all become of the same reality and contemporary.[17]

Whether the image was historical or fictional, for Eliot meaning in Dante's poem consists in a narrative of experiences that grow richer the more one contextualizes them within the larger theological landscape of the poem.

If Eliot, the critic, saw in Dante's *Comedy* an example of universal poetry, as a poet Eliot found in Dante's poem the images with which he could represent the *Inferno* of his own times. His early poem "The Love Song of J. Alfred Prufrock" (1915) has as epigraph Guido da Montefeltro's words to the pilgrim (*Inf.* 27.61-66) and the more mature *The Waste Land* (1922) has references to the *Inferno* scattered across it.[18] The overall impression that one gets from Eliot's poetic employment of Dante's verse is that Eliot was using Dante and specifically the *Inferno* to paint the modern world as a drab kind of Hell populated with antiheroes such as Prufrock. Eliot wrote in passing in his 1929 essay that "Dante and Shakespeare divide the modern world between them; there is no third,"[19] but even more than the theater of Shakespeare, Dante's poetry was the compass according to which the direction of the modern world could be determined, both poetically and existentially. Eliot sought to be a Dante for the modern age, and Pound, for one, must have thought he had succeeded, since after Eliot's death he wrote of his fellow poet that "his was the true Dantescan voice."[20]

Although poets continued to read Dante and be influenced by his poetry throughout the twentieth century, the heroic engagement of early modernism with the *Inferno* never returned. In the meantime, however, the American academic engagement with Dante's poem developed into an institution on par with Italian Dante studies, but with its own distinctive voice. Twentieth- and twenty-first-century Dante criticism has for the most part focused on the same problems that arise in the epistle to Cangrande and in the early commentaries and on the same concerns for adapting those problems to the modern age that have provoked poets since the nineteenth century. The history of Dante criticism, in fact, might be described as a variation on the themes of history, poetry, and theology, and how to "Make it new!," to use Ezra Pound's modernist battle cry.

The question of poetry and theology took on a polemical tone in the criticism of Italian philosopher Benedetto Croce (1866-1952). In an effort to free the *Comedy* from the grips of overly zealous allegorizers and restore to it an artistic autonomy, Croce opposed all allegorical, and thus also theological, interpretation of the poem. He held that Dante's poetry, his art, must be separated from the doctrine behind the poem: in the *Comedy* there are "poetry" and "non-poetry," and only the former deserves the critic's attention. In an indicative passage from his *La poesia di Dante* (1921; *The Poetry of Dante*, 1922), Croce contends that each of the individual episodes of the *Inferno* "stands by itself and is a lyric by itself" outside of any structural technique and outside of Christian doctrine.[21] For Croce, the *Inferno* is the most artful of the three canticles, precisely because of the pathos of its many vignettes, which allows for an easier separation of the art from the theological superstructure of the poem itself.

The major critics both inside and outside Italy have spent the past century reestablishing these limits between poetry and theology in the *Comedy*. In the generation that followed Croce, Erich Auerbach (1892-1957) recuperated theology by making it into a rhetorical problem. Whereas Croce dismissed any universal meaning or consistent structure to the *Comedy*, in his 1938 essay "*Figura*" Auerbach argued that the *Comedy* is the ultimate fulfillment of the Christian "figural tradition," which describes the texts that mimic the temporal connection between the Old Testament (as promise of things to come) and the New Testament (as the fulfillment of the promise), a connection known as typology.[22] In the *sermo humilis*, or humble speech, of the Gospels and with a unique historical realism, the narrative of Dante's poem fulfills the promises of past history and fixes its characters in an "immutable existence" in the afterlife. In one of his most well-known interpretations from the later study *Mimesis* (first published in German in 1946; English translation, 1953), which concerns a fifty-odd-line passage from *Inferno* 10 (22-78), Auerbach presents the pilgrim's conversation with Farinata degli Uberti and Cavalcante de' Cavalcanti as an example of how Dante's poetry makes "man's Christian-figural being a reality," with the ultimate result that the "image of man eclipses the image of God" so that "even in Hell there are great souls."[23] Far from denying the theological strata of Dante's poem, however, in *Mimesis* Auerbach establishes Dante's poem as the apex of the Christian worldview and as the turning point in the history of literature from the ancient epic to the modern novel, from a literature with God at the center to one focused on humanity.

With Gianfranco Contini (1912-90) and his generation's cohort of Italian philologists, Italian criticism reacted to the problem of poetry and theology as it had been presented by Croce and gradually rehistoricized the *Comedy*. Although he was a convinced formalist (that is, he believed in the unity of form and content), Contini produced a historical analysis of Dante's language and style that paved the way for a new Italian philology and for historically contextualized readings of Dante's poetry. Two of his most important contributions are the separation of the subject-character of Dante's poem, the pilgrim, from the poet of the *Comedy* ("Dante as character-poet of the *Comedy*," 1958), so that the *Inferno* (and *Purgatorio*) become the theater of the sins and temptations that the poet has already overcome; and the historical analysis of Dante's language in the context of the poetic vernaculars of medieval Italy and in the development of Dante's own poetic lexicon across his career, or an "intertextual" and "intratextual" philological analysis as the basis for interpretation of the poem's meaning ("An interpretation of Dante," 1965).[24] Contini's legacy, combined with that of many other Italian philologists, has been the continued refinement of knowledge of the historical, linguistic, and semiotic layers of Dante's poem.

Contini's contemporary in the United States, Charles S. Singleton (1909-85), responded to Croce's legacy in an entirely different way, focusing almost entirely on the theological underpinnings of the poem.

Singleton's major insight into reading the *Comedy* was that it needs to be read in the context of the theological tradition of the Middle Ages. As did T. S. Eliot before him, Singleton found Dante's poem to be universal precisely because of its multilayered poetic allegories. Singleton suspended "both belief and disbelief," as Eliot had recommended in his 1929 essay,[25] and founded a school of Dante criticism that "believed" in the historical reality of Dante's journey, insofar as "the fiction of the *Comedy* is that it is not fiction," as his famous adage goes.[26]

In a famous reading of the first two lines of the *Inferno*, Singleton argued for an allegorical reading of the *persona* of the poem, a reading similar, though antecedent, to Contini's "Dante as character-poet."[27] Singleton believed that Dante intended his poem to be read as literally true, so that his individual experience ("I found myself") might become the "our life," the experience of any and every man. For Singleton, Dante's modus operandi in the poem was based on the Bible and on the long-standing tradition of interpreting the Bible alluded to in the epistle to Cangrande. In his two-volume *Dante Studies* Singleton expounds his allegorizing vision of Dante's poem, all but reducing it to a poetic rendition of the world according to the theology of Saint Thomas Aquinas.[28] For Singleton the *Comedy* is like a Gothic cathedral: each piece points beyond itself and is a part of a complex, hidden structure within the poem that imitates the majesty of God in the world.[29] Singleton's major insights do not lie in his opening up specific enigmas within the text of the poem but in his deriving a superstructure, both theological and artistic, according to which we can understand the poem.

Singleton's most faithful disciple, John Freccero, has responded to the monolithic readings of his teacher by pointing out that one of the major models beneath the narrative structure of the *Comedy* was Augustinian conversion. Thus, instead of reading the pilgrim's journey as a linear arc in which he becomes Dante the poet, Freccero reads the journey as a spiral that continually turns back in upon itself as it gradually moves forward. Defined as an example of "existential figuralism" by his own student Giuseppe Mazzotta,[30] Freccero's approach assigns central importance to the will in Dante's poem and to the nature of the narrative movement that begins when the poet dramatizes the crisis of the pilgrim's will in the first canto. For Freccero, the *Comedy* is a "novel of the self," a Christian autobiography, a story of reeducation and of conversion of the old self into the new. He shows how Dante rewrote classical ideas of education (Plato's *paideia*) and corrected them with Christian ideas of humility and grace. Armed with such a powerful paradigm, Freccero has proposed ingenious readings of small passages and episodes of the *Comedy*, many so strong that they can be seen to function across the whole breadth of the poem. From his interpretation of the *piè fermo*, or "firm foot," as the wounded will in *Inferno* 1.30 and that of the pilgrim's encounter with the three beasts as a dramatization of the failure of the will in the soul's ascent toward truth to his understanding of terza rima as the formal poetic representation of the spiral movement of conversion and his readings of Ulysses (example of a pilgrim who could not convert) and of the Geryon ("a self-conscious emblem" of the dangers of poetry), Freccero presents Dante's poem and the pilgrim's journey as a continuous reflection on Christian education and existential redemption through conversion.[31]

Twenty years ago the story of Dante criticism in the United States seemed to have come to a turning point with Freccero's virtuoso criticism in the wake of Singleton and Auerbach, with a plethora of responses—ranging from the orthodox to the fringe—to Singleton's strong approach, and a few of his contemporaries whose methods never took Singleton openly into account.[32] Today, however, new trends in Dante criticism have expanded on the legacy of Croce, Auerbach, Contini, Singleton, Freccero, and others to formulate new vistas on the artistic and philosophical landscape of the poem. Mazzotta has expanded and complicated Singleton's Thomistic and Freccero's Augustinian readings of Dante's theological underpinnings and, raising the question of the ambiguities of Dante's poetic language, has suggested that we read Dante's poem between exile and encyclopedia.

Only from the perspective of exile can the poet call into question the "falsifications and ambiguities that language harbors" and reformulate through the self-conscious language of poetry all fields of knowledge. To put it another way, Mazzotta understands the *Comedy* as a cry from exile that would encompass and reformulate all learning and all voices within it. For Mazzotta, the poetry and theology of Dante's poem are inseparable, since poetry was the instrument through which Dante tried to configure the universal knowledge that belongs to theology.[33]

Alternatively, but not entirely in contradiction with this reading, there is Teodolinda Barolini's formalist approach, which takes as its point of departure not Dante's theology but the formal demands— linguistic and stylistic—of the narrative of the *Comedy*, which the poet claims to be true. According to Barolini, only once the *Comedy* has been understood formally (not theologically) can its historical, cultural, and (therefore) theological contexts be reconstructed.[34] Other critics have sought to refine knowledge of Dante's political intentions and aspirations (Ferrante; Honess); of his relationship with classical antecedents (Hollander; Jacoff and Schnapp); of the novelty of his plurilinguism (Barański); of his use of mystic theology (Moevs), of Islamic philosophy (Stone), and of the Bible (Hawkins); and of his quest for authority (Ascoli)—not to mention increased interest in Dante's minor works (Ascoli; Barański; Harrison)—but this is not the place to review their approaches in detail.[35]

In the history of Western literature there has hardly been any other work of poetry that has sustained the amount of critical attention that Dante's *Comedy* has sustained over the years. It is a vast storehouse of poetic invention and knowledge that unveils as much as it conceals when probed. It is a profoundly generous poem in that it does not greedily withhold itself from the engaged attention of its readers. The more energy a reader puts into the *Comedy*, the more reward he or she reaps from it. Each time we return to the poem it renders new fruits, seemingly infinite. Not only critics have tried to come to terms with Dante and his poem, but poets also and especially have continually found in it a model for the capacity of poetry to represent and reform the world. Every critic, expert or novice, who sits down to read Dante's *Comedy* brings to it a different approach, a different reading, a different slant, but each and every critic must face the same questions that have intrigued readers since the earliest commentators: What does it mean to have written a poem about oneself and to have claimed that God had a hand in writing it? What are the relationships among poetry, history, and theology? How can we make this poem our own and how is it already a part of us? If the poem's fortune over the past seven hundred years holds for the future, then it will continue to speak to students, scholars, and poets the world over for a long time to come.

Notes

1. Peter Hawkins and Rachel Jacoff, eds., *The Poets' Dante: Twentieth-Century Responses* (New York: Farrar, Straus and Giroux, 2002).

2. Although there is still debate on whether or not Dante himself penned the letter, its importance as the founding document of Dante criticism goes unquestioned. For a brief outline of the history of the document and the debate on its authenticity, see Albert Ascoli, "Epistle to Cangrande," in *The Dante Encyclopedia*, ed. Richard Lansing (New York: Garland, 2000), 348-52. The interpretive sections of the letter are available in English translation with notes and an introduction in A. J. Minnis and A. B. Scott, *Medieval Literary Theory and Criticism, c. 1100-c.1375: The Commentary Tradition* (Oxford: Clarendon Press, 1988).

3. Psalm 113 in the Latin Vulgate Bible, which Dante knew, is Psalm 114 in other versions of the Bible.

4. Minnis and Scott, *Medieval Literary Theory*, 461.

5. Ibid.

6. His lectures have recently been translated into English by Michael Papio as *Boccaccio's Expositions on Dante's "Comedy"* (Toronto: University of Toronto Press, 2009).

7. Cristoforo Landino, *Comento sopra la "Comedia,"* 4 vols., ed. Paolo Procaccioli (Rome: Salerno, 2001), 1:285-86. Translations, unless otherwise noted, are my own.

8. See *Dante's Inferno*, adapted by Sandow Birk and Marcus Sanders, illustrated by Sandow Birk (San Francisco: Chronicle Books, 2004).

9. Vico's "Discoverta del vero Dante, ovvero nuovi principi di critica dantesca" (1728-29) has been translated by Cristina Mazzoni in *Critical Essays on Dante*, ed. Giuseppe Mazzotta (Boston: G. K. Hall, 1991), 58-60.

10. Mazzini (signed "Un italiano"), preface to *La Commedia di Dante Alighieri*, 4 vols., ed. Ugo Foscolo (London: P. Rolandi, 1842-43), 1:xii.

11. Francesco de Sanctis, "Francesca da Rimini," in *De Sanctis on Dante*, ed. and trans. Joseph Rossi and Alfred Galpin (Madison: University of Wisconsin Press, 1957), 38-39.

12. Ezra Pound, *The Spirit of Romance* (New York: New Directions, 1953), 127.

13. Ibid., 128.

14. See "Notes for Canto CXVII" in Ezra Pound, *The Cantos of Ezra Pound* (New York: New Directions, 1996), 822.

15. T. S. Eliot, *Selected Essays* (London: Faber and Faber, 1999), 242.

16. Ibid., 246-47.

17. Ibid., 247-48.

18. On the epigraph to "Prufrock," see Robert Pogue Harrison, "Comedy and Modernity: Dante's Hell," *Modern Language Notes* 102, no. 5 (Dec. 1987): 1043-61.

19. Eliot, *Selected Essays*, 265.

20. E. P. [Ezra Pound], "For T. S. E.," *Sewanee Review* 74, no. 1 (Winter 1966): 109.

21. Benedetto Croce, *The Poetry of Dante*, trans. Douglas Ainslie (New York: Henry Holt, 1922), 92.

22. Erich Auerbach, *Scenes from the Drama of European Literature: Six Essays*, trans. Ralph Manheim (1959; Minneapolis: University of Minnesota Press, 1984), 11-76.

23. Erich Auerbach, *Mimesis: The Representation of Reality in Western Literature*, trans. William R. Trask (1953; Princeton, NJ: Princeton University Press, 2003), 202.

24. These two essays were published in Italian as part of Contini's collected works on Dante, *Un'idea di Dante* (Turin: Einaudi, 1976).

25. Eliot, *Selected Essays*, 243. Charles Singleton's idea of Dante and his influences and heirs have become the subject of critical interest since his death in 1985. See, for example, Giuseppe Mazzotta, "The American Criticism of Charles Singleton," *Dante Studies* 104 (1986): 27-44, in which Singleton is related to American Transcendentalism, especially to Ralph Waldo Emerson; and Zygmunt G. Barański, "Reflecting on Dante in America, 1949-1990," *Annali d'Italianistica* 8 (1990): 58-87, where Singleton is related to the "St. Louis Hegelians," especially George Santayana.

26. Charles S. Singleton, "The Irreducible Dove," *Comparative Literature* 9 (1957): 129.

27. Singleton actually beat Contini to the idea of the separation of the pilgrim and the poet, but in regard to the *Vita Nuova*, in his *Essay on the "Vita Nuova"* (Cambridge, MA: Harvard University Press, 1949), 25.

28. See Singleton's *Dante Studies 1: Commedia. Elements of Structure* (Cambridge, MA: Harvard University Press, 1954) and *2: Journey to Beatrice* (Cambridge, MA: Harvard University Press, 1958).

29. For a famous example, see Singleton's "The Poet's Number at the Center," *Modern Language Notes* 80, no. 1 [Italian issue] (Jan. 1965): 1-10.

30. Giuseppe Mazzotta, "Reflections on Dante Studies in America," *Dante Studies* 118 (2000): 329.

31. I am referring to the subjects of the following essays, each available in the collected volume of Freccero's work, *Dante: The Poetics of Conversion*, ed. Rachel Jacoff (Cambridge, MA: Harvard University Press, 1988): "The Prologue Scene" (1-29), "The Firm Foot on a Journey Without a Guide" (29-54), "Pilgrim in a Gyre" (70-92), "Dante's Ulysses: From Epic to Novel" (136-51), and "The Significance of *Terza Rima*" (258-73).

32. See Dino S. Cervigni's introductory essay in the special issue of *Annali d'Italianistica* 8 (1990), "Dante and Modern American Criticism," the main aim of which is to find a new path for Dante criticism after Singleton. This is also the story that Rino Caputo tells in his *Per far segno: La critica dantesca americana da Singleton a oggi* (Rome: Il Calamo, 1993).

33. In addition to numerous essays, Mazzotta's two major contributions to Dante studies are *Dante, Poet of the Desert: History and Allegory in the "Divine Comedy"* (Princeton, NJ: Princeton University Press, 1979) and *Dante's Vision and the Circle of Knowledge* (Princeton, NJ: Princeton University Press, 1993).

34. Barolini's major essays on Dante, Petrarch, and Boccaccio have been collected in *Dante and the Origins of Italian Literary Culture* (New York: Fordham University Press, 2006), and Barolini has recently dedicated herself to the editing of Dante's early poetry, *Rime giovanili e della "Vita Nuova"* (Milan: Rizzoli, 2009). Her two major contributions to Dante studies are *Dante's Poets: Textuality and Truth in the "Comedy"* (Princeton, NJ: Princeton University Press, 1984) and *The Undivine Comedy: Detheologizing Dante* (Princeton, NJ: Princeton University Press, 1992). She explains her approach to Dante and medieval Italian literature in an interview with Simon Gilson, "Historicism, Philology, and the Text: An Interview with Teodolinda Barolini," *Italian Studies* 63, no. 1 (Spring 2008): 141-52.

35. I allude to the following studies: Albert Ascoli, *Dante and the Making of a Modern Author* (New York: Cambridge University Press, 2008); Zygmunt G. Barański, *Dante e i segni: Saggi per una storia intellettuale di Dante Alighieri* (Naples: Liguori, 2000); Joan M. Ferrante, *The Political Vision of the "Divine Comedy"* (Princeton, NJ: Princeton University Press, 1984); Robert Pogue Harrison, *The Body of Beatrice* (Baltimore: Johns Hopkins University Press, 1988); Peter Hawkins, *Dante's Testaments: Essays on Scriptural Imagination* (Stanford, CA: Stanford University Press, 2001); Robert Hollander, *Virgilio dantesco: Tragedia nella "Commedia"* (Florence: Olschki, 1983); Claire E. Honess, *From Florence to the Heavenly City: The Poetry of Citizenship in Dante* (London: Legenda, 2006); Rachel Jacoff and Jeffrey T. Schnapp, eds., *The Poetry of Allusion: Virgil and Ovid in Dante's "Commedia"* (Stanford, CA: Stanford University Press, 1991); Christian Moevs, *The Metaphysics of Dante's "Comedy"* (New York: Oxford University Press, 2005); and Gregory B. Stone, *Dante's Pluralism and the Islamic Philosophy of Religion* (New York: Palgrave Macmillan, 2006).

Bibliography

Ascoli, Albert Russell. *Dante and the Making of a Modern Author*. New York: Cambridge UP, 2008.

_____. "Epistle to Cangrande." *The Dante Encyclopedia*. Ed. Richard Lansing. New York: Garland, 2000. 348-52.

Auerbach, Erich. *Mimesis: The Representation of Reality in Western Literature*. Trans. William R. Trask. 1953. Princeton, NJ: Princeton UP, 2003.

_____. *Scenes from the Drama of European Literature: Six Essays*. Trans. Ralph Manheim. 1959. Minneapolis: U of Minnesota P, 1984.

Barański, Zygmunt G. *Dante e i segni: Saggi per una storia intellettuale di Dante Alighieri*. Naples: Liguori, 2000.

_____. "Reflecting on Dante in America, 1949-1990." *Annali d'Italianistica* 8 (1990): 58-87.

Barolini, Teodolinda. *Dante and the Origins of Italian Literary Culture*. New York: Fordham UP, 2006.

_____. *Dante's Poets: Textuality and Truth in the "Comedy."* Princeton, NJ: Princeton UP, 1984.

_____. *The Undivine Comedy: Detheologizing Dante*. Princeton, NJ: Princeton UP, 1992.

Boccaccio, Giovanni. *Boccaccio's Expositions on Dante's "Comedy."* Trans. Michael Papio. Toronto: U of Toronto P, 2009.

Caputo, Rino. *Per far segno: La critica dantesca americana da Singleton a oggi*. Rome: Il Calamo, 1993.

Cervigni, Dino S. "Dante and Modern American Criticism: An Introductory Essay." *Annali d'Italianistica* 8 (1990): 5-28.

Contini, Gianfranco. *Un'idea di Dante*. Turin: Einaudi, 1976.

Croce, Benedetto. *The Poetry of Dante*. Trans. Douglas Ainslie. New York: Henry Holt, 1922.

Dante. *Dante's Inferno*. Adapted by Sandow Birk and Marcus Sanders. Illustrated by Sandow Birk. San Francisco: Chronicle Books, 2004.

_____. *Rime giovanili e della "Vita Nuova."* Ed. Teodolinda Barolini. Milan: Rizzoli, 2009.

De Sanctis, Francesco. *De Sanctis on Dante*. Ed. and trans. Joseph Rossi and Alfred Galpin. Madison: U of Wisconsin P, 1957.

Eliot, T. S. *Selected Essays*. London: Faber & Faber, 1999.

Ferrante, Joan M. *The Political Vision of the "Divine Comedy."* Princeton, NJ: Princeton UP, 1984.

Freccero, John. *Dante: The Poetics of Conversion*. Ed. Rachel Jacoff. Cambridge, MA: Harvard UP, 1988.

Gilson, Simon. "Historicism, Philology and the Text. An Interview with Teodolinda Barolini." *Italian Studies* 63.1 (Spring 2008): 141-52.

Harrison, Robert Pogue. *The Body of Beatrice*. Baltimore: Johns Hopkins UP, 1988.

_____. "Comedy and Modernity: Dante's Hell." *Modern Language Notes* 102.5 (1987) 1043-61.

Hawkins, Peter S. *Dante's Testaments: Essays on Scriptural Imagination*. Stanford, CA: Stanford UP, 2001.

Hawkins, Peter S., and Rachel Jacoff, eds. *The Poets' Dante: Twentieth-Century Responses*. New York: Farrar, Straus and Giroux, 2002.

Hollander, Robert. *Virgilio dantesco: Tragedia nella "Commedia."* Florence: Olschki, 1983.

Honess, Claire E. *From Florence to the Heavenly City: The Poetry of Citizenship in Dante*. London: Legenda, 2006.

Jacoff, Rachel, and Jeffrey T. Schnapp, eds. *The Poetry of Allusion: Virgil and Ovid in Dante's "Commedia."* Stanford, Ca: Stanford UP, 1991.

Landino, Cristoforo. *Comento sopra la "Comedia."* 4 vols. Ed. Paolo Procaccioli. Rome: Salerno, 2001.

Mazzotta, Giuseppe. "The American Criticism of Charles Singleton." *Dante Studies* 104 (1986): 27-44.

_____. *Dante, Poet of the Desert: History and Allegory in the "Divine Comedy."* Princeton, NJ: Princeton UP, 1979.

_____. *Dante's Vision and the Circle of Knowledge*. Princeton, NJ: Princeton UP, 1993.

_____. "Reflections on Dante Studies in America." *Dante Studies* 118 (2000): 323-30.

_____, ed. *Critical Essays on Dante*. Boston: G. K. Hall, 1991.

Minnis, A. J., and A. B. Scott, eds. *Medieval Literary Theory and Criticism, c. 1100-c. 1375: The Commentary Tradition*. Oxford: Clarendon Press, 1988.

Moevs, Christian. *The Metaphysics of Dante's "Comedy."* New York: Oxford UP, 2005.

Pound, Ezra. *The Cantos of Ezra Pound*. New York: New Directions, 1996.

_____. [E. P]. "For T. S. E." *Sewanee Review* 74.1 (Winter, 1966): 109.

_____. *The Spirit of Romance*. New York: New Directions, 1953.

Singleton, Charles S. *Dante Studies 1: Commedia. Elements of Structure*. Cambridge, MA: Harvard UP, 1954.

_____. *Dante Studies 2: Journey to Beatrice*. Cambridge, MA: Harvard UP, 1958.

_____. *Essay on the "Vita Nuova."* Cambridge, MA: Harvard UP, 1949.

_____. "The Irreducible Dove." *Comparative Literature* 9 (1957): 129-35.

_____. "The Poet's Number at the Center." *Modern Language Notes* 80.1 [Italian issue] (Jan. 1965): 1-10.

Stone, Gregory B. *Dante's Pluralism and the Islamic Philosophy of Religion*. New York: Palgrave Macmillan, 2006.

Per lo 'nferno tuo nome si spande:
Politics in the Infernal City_____
Elizabeth Coggeshall

We live in an infernal society. As we read Dante's *Inferno*, we find
that much of the poet's fourteenth-century world still resonates with
ours. His insight into the human condition has maintained its complexity and subtlety in spite of the near seven centuries that separate us
from the poem's authorship. Certainly Dante's *Divine Comedy* continues to shape and inform our moral map. The twenty-first-century
reader can play video games of the *Inferno* or take online quizzes to
find his or her particular place in Hell (the lucky few end up in Purgatory, and I know no one who was admitted automatically into Paradise). Sandow Birk's 2004 illustrations of the *Inferno* update the pilgrim's speech and dress, and the 2008 toy-theater feature film that
animates Birk's illustrations includes a song-and-dance number about
corruption in the U.S. government during the pilgrim's visit to the circle of fraud. Modern and postmodern fascination with the poem has
waxed and waned, but the cultural relevance of the poem continuously
resurfaces. Hell is a franchise.

The *Comedy* can be read through a number of different lenses, as
centuries of criticism have attested. The real paradox of the poem,
however, is that it remains both familiar and foreign at the same time.
The richest reading of the text first explores the precise biographical,
cultural, and political landscape that produced the poem. Through this
reading we arrive at a comprehensive vision of the poem's implications both in its own time and in ours. It is nearly impossible for a
twenty-first-century reader to enter the text without some semblance
of notes, a Virgilian guidebook to explain what a Guelf is, or who the
Cavalcanti are, or what "barratry" means and why it matters so much to
our poet. The twenty-first-century reader can find the first passage
through a canto disorienting. It is the intention of this chapter to assist
the reader's orientation.[1]

The City

Unexpectedly, Dante's description of the otherworld remains tenaciously engaged with this world. Even as the pilgrim moves away from the earth in the *Paradiso*, the poet views his experience through the political realities that complicate the individual's ability to attain heaven. Civic responsibility is intrinsically bound to moral character. The poet never strays far from the struggles of the earthly cities, particularly of his own Florence: Florence remains a model for Dante of the *potential* of the earthly city to be either Heaven on Earth or the seat of tyranny, rebellion, and self-destruction. In both Heaven and Hell, "Florence remains a yardstick for the poet to measure corruption and its antithesis" (Scott 324). Heaven and Hell are, explicitly, cities: one a republic of communion and peace under a single ruler—God—and the other a space in which a complete breakdown of communication leads to isolation, disdain, self-pity, and disunity.

The city was not simply the location of social life and activity; it was the primary organizing principle of the medieval Italian community. One's identity, political and otherwise, was a symptom of one's native city. This concept is one that we now have difficulty understanding: in our age, one's native city is no longer necessarily the defining marker of one's character. We find one of the most bitter denunciations of Dante's native Florence in the full title he gives his poem in a letter: "Incipit Comoedia Dantis Alagherii, Florentini natione, non moribus" (Here begins the Comedy of Dante Alighieri, Florentine by birth, not by morals) (*Epistola* X.10; translation modified). This is a profoundly cynical statement about his civic identity, a bold distancing of himself from the sinful character of his Florentine compatriots.

Although he may desire to distance himself from Florence, Dante cannot simply erase the city's mark: the city is, for Dante as for all medieval Italians, one of the great determinants of self, as great as the positions of the stars at one's birth and as the branches of one's genealogical tree. Dante is a Florentine, and while he can choose to sculpt his morals after a mold different from that of his fellow citizens, he cannot erase Florence's stamp on his being. Nor would he want to.

The Italian city-state did not become the deepest marker of one's identity through a sense of civic pride trending through Italy in the period. Differences in the organization of space in medieval Europe determined this profound sense of connection to one's homeland. There were no nation-states in medieval Europe. Communities that incorporated cities into a larger unit were either empires, as in the case of the Holy Roman Empire, or greater confederations of cities tied together for political reasons. In either case, the city remained the heart of even these greater governmental units. The medieval city was walled for defense purposes, which often created a sense of isolation, enclosure, and exclusion. In Italy this isolation developed also linguistically: each city-state developed its own dialect of what would eventually be collectively called the Italian language. These dialects varied significantly from one city to the next, such that it could have been difficult for the citizens of one city to communicate well with those of a neighboring city.

Typically, no single peripheral authority, such as a king or bishop, governed city life and politics. Many medieval Italian cities were organized as communes, with democratically elected bodies of rulers that represented the interests of the people, at least theoretically. In practice many of the communes swore allegiance to one ruling body or another, and, in the case of Florence, these allegiances were often fickle and short-lived.

Florence established its independence as a free republic in 1115 and quickly became a European power. Giovanni Villani, a fourteenth-century chronicler of Florence, gives us some sense—albeit a biased sense—of the city's achievements. Thanks to innovations in banking and to the prosperity of its industries, particularly textiles, Florence was one of the largest and most successful cities in Europe. By 1300 the population exceeded some 100,000 citizens, second only to Paris. The strength of its industry gave rise to a merchant class, and soon class struggles broke out between the old regime, dominated by the nobility, and the new one, represented by the emergent middle class. As a result, the entire thirteenth century was marked by political instability. Rival factions sought to rout one another from the city so that they could seize control.

The two rival factions represented in Florence—the Guelfs and the Ghibellines—had a long history of strife. Originating in what is now Germany, the two names had represented noble families competing for the imperial throne. These two families eventually lent their names to conflicts that evolved and expanded as the Empire reached into neighboring states and regions. Factions in Tuscany adopted the two names during the thirteenth century to represent two groups vying for dominance of Tuscan lands: the Guelfs supported the papacy, which controlled large swaths of the southern Italian peninsula, and the Ghibellines defended the Empire, which controlled regions in the north of Italy.

Civil War

By the time the Guelf-Ghibelline conflict reached Tuscany, Florence was already experiencing its own struggle for dominance. The nobility of the city had begun to form loose familial alliances, and members of the burgeoning middle class were joining the political ranks, replacing the nobility who had dominated politics with the support of imperial power. By 1215 the two factions had already begun to emerge when the infamous murder of Buondelmonte de' Buondelmonti—killed by members of the Amidei and Uberti clans, whose relative he had spurned in favor of another bride—set off a chain of civil violence that continued for more than a century. Both Dante and his contemporaries, the chroniclers Giovanni Villani and Dino Compagni, attribute the factionalism that would tear Florence apart in the coming years to this moment. Dante places the perpetrator of the murder, Mosca dei Lamberti, in the *bolgia* of the sowers of discord and strife (*Inferno* 28.103-11).

On the murder and its aftermath, Compagni comments, "As a result of this death the citizens became divided, and relatives and allies were drawn in on both sides so that there was no end to this rift, from which many fights and murders and civil battles were born" (I.2). Villani claims that Buondelmonte's actions were "by the inspiration of the devil" and that the civil war that followed these events "will never have an end, if God do not cut it short" (V.39). Historian John M. Najemy nuances the medieval writers' black-and-white account of the event; in Najemy's view, the Buondelmonti murder was "more a symptom than a cause of this earlier division of the Florentine aristocracy" (83).

Whether or not the murder was in fact the true cause of the rift, after 1215 Florence became a battlefield. The Ghibellines, who endorsed imperial interests, represented the ancient noble families of Florence who primarily owned the Tuscan farming estates. The Guelf party, on the other hand, was composed largely of the wealthy merchant-class families who were politically aligned with the papacy and the Angevin court of France.

A long series of battles and mass expulsions between these two factions culminated at the Battle of Benevento in 1266, where Manfred, son of the late emperor Frederick II, was killed, the Ghibelline forces were defeated, and the families were collectively routed from the city, never to return to power. After years of civil strife and a number of battles, with defeats on both sides, the Guelf-Ghibelline conflict within the city walls had ended (which, sadly, did not mean a return to peace for the Florentines, as we will see below).

The vicissitudes of the conflict are narrated with considerable pathos in the pilgrim's encounter with Farinata degli Uberti in canto 10 of the *Inferno*. In the circle of the heretics we see the pilgrim engage in a political tête-à-tête with Farinata, one of the great Ghibelline leaders of Florence, head of one of its most powerful families. The pilgrim does not shy away from the gauntlet Farinata throws down with his question, "Chi fuor li maggior tui?" ("Who were your forebears?") (*Inferno* 10.42).[2] Virgil, aware of the tension between these two hot-blooded politicos, has already warned the pilgrim about watching his words. The pilgrim nonetheless jumps at the chance to claim his family's— and his party's—name, to which Farinata knowingly replies, "Fieramente furo avversi/ a me e a miei primi e a mia parte,/ sì che per due fiate li dispersi" ("Fiercely were they opposed to me and to my ancestors and to my party, so that twice I scattered them") (*Inferno* 10.46-48). Farinata's gibe here is a reference to the Ghibelline victories in the streets of Florence (1248) and at Montaperti (1260).

Dante, quick to defend his party's good name, notifies Farinata of the final defeat of the Ghibellines at Benevento in 1266. Farinata, who died in 1264, was unaware of his party's fate, and the pilgrim's final taunt falls hard on the Ghibelline's ears: if it is true, he says, "ciò mi tormenta più che questo letto" ("that torments me more than this bed") (*Inferno* 10.78). Farinata places the fortunes of his party even before his personal fate.

By the time Dante was born in 1265, the Guelf-Ghibelline conflict in Florence had all but ended. The Ghibellines posed little real threat to the Guelfs within the city proper, but Guelf allegiance was still palpable. As a young man Dante must have felt a strong party loyalty, perhaps even fighting on his party's behalf at the battle against the Ghibellines of Arezzo at Campaldino (1289). Dante was of course raised in a Guelf family and inculcated in Guelf values. As Najemy points out, it is Dante's "political education" in Hell that embitters his view of all nobles, Guelf and Ghibelline alike (85). In Hell it becomes apparent that it is the noble class that is at fault for the strife that Florence has seen. It is no longer a question of party affiliation.

Dante and his family were not of the noble class of *magnati* or *grandi*; rather, they were *popolani*, middle-class, and thus had always been prevented from holding office. Dante himself became a guildsman; guildsmen were middle-class members of associations based on various types of trade and labor. The guild members had long been excluded from politics, until changes in the governmental system in the late thirteenth century opened political doors to them. In the years intervening between victories of one party of *grandi* or the other, resolutions were sought to limit the amount of violence perpetrated between them, effectively excluding all nobles from politics. Between the Ghibelline victories in 1248 and 1260, for example, a regime known as the *primo popolo* formed. During that time it was decided that Guelfs and Ghibellines alike were to be barred from holding public office, and middle-class guildsmen rose to government positions. After the tenure of the *primo popolo*, battles at Montaperti (1260) and at Benevento (1266) placed Florence back in the hands of factionalist leaders.

The establishment of the priorate in 1282 was intended to end undemocratic rule. The priorate was a system of government in which six guild leaders would be elected for a two-month term, after which each was required to wait two years before reelection. Short terms allowed for a much greater number of formal participants in government. Even Dante held the office: he was elected in 1300, likely the first of his family to serve in government.

After the Guelf-Ghibelline conflict had been more or less resolved, the Florentine civic fabric began to tear again. Soon after their rise to firm control over the fortunes of the city, the Guelfs themselves divided into two factions, the Blacks and the Whites. Little is known about the reason for the split; Najemy refers to it as "one of the great mysteries of Florentine history" (81) and boils it down to a "feud" (91) between two families (à la Shakespeare's Capulets and Montagues). In this case, the feuding families were the Donati and the Cerchi, both *grandi*, both Guelf, bitterly divided over some unknown offense or incident.

The Papacy

Around the time that the Donati-Cerchi rivalry was heating, the papal see was also in disorder. After having held the high office for only five months and nine days, Pope Celestine V renounced the papacy in

1294, returning to his life as a hermit in Abruzzi (Villani VIII.5). His abdication represented, for Dante, the extreme act of cowardice, the "*gran rifiuto*" ("great refusal") as he calls it when he encounters the pope in *Inferno* 3 with the cowards, wretches, and neutrals. Despite the theological preference for the contemplative life over the active life in medieval Christian thought, it is imperative that "the man chosen to lead Christ's Church on earth must not retire from the world but must instead reform and guide the Church Militant on its path to salvation" (Scott 317).

What is worse than his display of cowardice, however, is that Celestine V's resignation made possible Benedetto Caetani's election to the papacy as Pope Boniface VIII. Boniface VIII was the converse of his predecessor: where Celestine V had been "simple and knew no letters," a hermit who wanted to "abandon the vanity of the world," Boniface VIII was "very learned in books, and in the things of this world much practiced and sagacious" (Villani VIII.5). While Dante abhors the feebleness of the *gran rifiuto*, Boniface's machinations that allowed his swift and corrupt rise to power are eminently more damnable. In fact, they are so damnable that Dante sees fit to damn the pope even before his death: a shade in the *bolgia* of simony mistakes the pilgrim for the pope who is to come and take the spirit's place. Assuming that he was misinformed about Boniface's death in 1303, the spirit cries out:

"Se' tu sì tosto di quell' aver sazio
per lo qual non temesti tòrre a 'nganno
la bella donna, e poi di farne strazio?"

"Are you so soon sated by the wealth for which you did not fear to marry the lovely lady fraudulently, and then to tear her apart?" (*Inferno* 19.55-57)

The reference is to Boniface's greed, the drive that sponsored his sudden and deceptive rise to the office of pope (the *bella donna* that he married is the Church), and which consumes him to the point that he allows the Church's devastation. Boniface VIII's reign was characterized by political intrigue, ambition, maneuvering, and fraud: embroiled in the various conflicts that afflicted all of Italy in the period, Pope Boniface continuously asserted the Church's authority over secular authorities and entangled the papacy even more deeply into temporal affairs.

Boniface VIII's politicized papacy coincided almost exactly with our poet's political life. Dante joined the Guild of Physicians and Apothecaries in 1295, and five years later, at the age of thirty-five, he was elected one of the six priors of the city of Florence. The year 1300 was a critical one for Dante's career: he claims to have made passage through the Underworld in spring of that year, and on June 18 he was elected one of the heads of state. The peak years of his political involvement were 1300 to 1302, the two-year period that marked "the sudden rise and equally precipitous fall of Dante Alighieri the politician" (Hollander 44).

Dante the Politician

As for the specifics of Dante's role in the Florentine political scene, we know that he was no minor figure, but the extent of his political recognition is unclear. Giovanni Boccaccio, a young man at the time of Dante's death, surely embellishes when he writes of Dante's political involvement:

> No legation was heard or answered, no law enacted or repealed, no peace established, nor a foreign war undertaken, and, in brief, never a deliberation of any responsibility made, until [Dante] first had given his opinion on the matter. All the public confidence, all trust, and, to sum up, all matters human and divine were sustained by his judgment. (18)

Dino Compagni writes considerably less of Dante in his chronicle of the city of Florence at the beginning of the fourteenth century.

Compagni mentions our poet only once in a list of the exiles banished from Florence in 1302 (II.25), although it should be noted that Compagni abandoned his chronicle in 1312, two years before the *Inferno* had been widely circulated. The true extent of Dante's political involvement obviously lies somewhere between the estimations of Compagni and those of Boccaccio.

We do know that the various government bodies in which Dante served in the period 1300-1302 faced certain decisions that were key to the future of Florentine politics, or at least to the vision of Florentine politics that Dante lays out in the *Comedy*. The decision that affected him most personally was the priors' vote to exile the leading members of both the Black and the White Guelfs in response to an attack on the government of the *popolo*. This resolution—which Dante supported—resulted in the banishment of Guido Cavalcanti, Dante's once best friend and poetic rival. Cavalcanti and his family, all White Guelfs, had been deeply entrenched in the conflict that had erupted: an attempt had been made on Guido's life while he was on pilgrimage in Spain, and he himself attempted to murder the leader of the Black Guelfs, Corso Donati, throwing a spear at Corso from a galloping horse (Compagni I.20). Guido contracted a fatal disease as a result of his exile and died in Florence shortly after his return. Dante must have struggled with his involvement in his friend's death, a dilemma that many critics find in *Inferno* 10, where we meet Guido's father and father-in-law (Farinata) sharing a tomb in the circle of heresy.

Dante too would experience the bitterness of exile. The Black and White Guelfs alike sought the aid of Boniface VIII, the pope to whose interests the entire Guelf party had sworn allegiance. The Blacks sent a mission explaining the treachery of the Whites, whom the Blacks claimed were supporting the Colonna family, bitter enemies of the pope. The Whites appealed with gifts and prayers, petitioning the pope as their lord. Boniface VIII, seeking to establish full and final control over the Tuscan state and to crush the supposed intentions of the

Colonna, called on Charles of Valois to assist his endeavors, employing him as "ambassador of peace" to Florence. But, as Compagni warns, "the pope sent enticing words with one hand and with the other set his lord over us" (II.11).

Nearly all of book II of Compagni's *Chronicle* is dedicated to Charles's assistance to papal schemes in Tuscany in 1301-2. Having been promised the crown of Sicily in exchange for Tuscan control, Charles entered Florence under the guise of peacemaker between the parties, with the secret objective of securing Black dominance. As he approached the city, a delegation—which likely included Dante himself—was sent to the pope in Rome to plead that Charles not take the city by force; Boniface reassured them. But, with another "long promise with a short keeping" (see *Inferno* 27.110 and notes), Boniface set Charles on the offensive before Dante returned to Florence. On March 10, 1302, the decree of exile on punishment of death was issued for all prominent White Guelfs; Dante was never to set foot inside the walls of his city again.

Exile

We have little understanding of the idea of "exile" in this century of mobility, connectivity, and networks. We assume that Shakespeare's Romeo overreacts when he cries "Ha! Banishment! Be merciful, say 'death;' for exile hath more terror in his look, much more than death: do not say 'banishment'" (*Romeo and Juliet* act 3, scene 3). The terror that exile instills in Romeo is created by real conditions in fourteenth-century Italy: for Dante and his contemporaries, the decree of exile was nearly tantamount to a death sentence. In medieval Italy, expulsion from one's city meant supreme dependence and supreme isolation. One was forced to turn to the generosity of courts in other cities for shelter, bread, and protection. Additionally, linguistic differences between one region and the next were drastic: the formal concept of an Italian language did not exist until Dante formulated it in his unfinished treatise *De vulgari eloquentia*, written in the early years of his exile. Dialects were strong and varied. Misunderstanding was inevitable.

Most of the politically active poets of the period experienced exile at one point or another, but none suffered it as Dante did. Dante's friends Guido Cavalcanti (whose exile is discussed above) and Cino da Pistoia both underwent exile for brief periods, and both exploited exile in their work as a metaphor for the psychological dissolution and seclusion inherent in the love experience. But Dante delved much more deeply into the experience of exile, both biographically and poetically. The Florentine Blacks tried to strike a deal with the exiles: if they confessed to charges of barratry—the buying and selling of political offices—they would be allowed to return to Florence, their lives spared in exchange for a brief prison term. Many accepted; Dante did not. As a result he spent twenty years depending on the kindness of courts.

Fortunately, the courts did not lack for kindness: Dante was hosted by some of the most powerful noblemen of northern Italy. With all their kindness, however, he never abandoned his love of home. Thus Florence is everywhere in the *Comedy*, most particularly in the *Inferno*. At the beginning of *Inferno* 26 he makes this explicit, just to be sure it does not escape any reader's notice:

> Godi, Fiorenza, poi che se' sì grande
> che per mare e per terra batti l'ali
> e per lo 'nferno tuo nome si spande!

Rejoice, Florence, since you are so great that on sea and land you beat your wings, and your name spreads through Hell! (*Inferno* 26.1-3)

Dante's relationship to his native city is caught between bitter scorn and tender memory. Historian John Najemy reads the relationship this way:

One possible interpretation of Dante's relationship to Florence would thus be that, belonging to the faction that lost the struggle for control of the city, finding himself exiled, and placing his hopes first in his fellow exiles and then in the grand dream of imperial peace, Dante rejected not only Florence and its politics, but the whole idea of the city as the proper and natural form of political association. (82)

Najemy makes a leap here: Dante's rejection of Florence is never so clear-cut as this. He denounced it fiercely, refused the city's offer of return at the cost of a confession to charges of corruption, and imprisoned many of its famed citizens in his Hell, yet to say that Dante rejected both Florence and the model of the city is to disregard the strength of his ties to the city and the pathos with which he wrote of his exile from it. He did not fully reject it; if he had, exile would not have been so bitter. He made vain attempts to soften the burden of distance from his homeland, but he felt that distance acutely, even—perhaps especially—at the furthest distance from it, in the city of God.

The poet, embittered and betrayed by the members of his party and by his fellow exiles, began to rethink his politics during his exile. It was the factionalism of city living that caused his banishment, that destroyed his city and dragged its citizens to Hell. How, then, could one combat such factionalism?

Empire

Dante's political leanings took a surprising turn late in his life and career. Initially fiercely opposed to the Empire's attempts to gain control over Tuscany, in exile he became an imperial sympathizer. This does not mean, however, that he would support the Empire in its current state. Rather, both in the *Comedy* and in the *Monarchia*, Dante's political treatise composed in the 1310s, he envisions a new system in which the entire human race is held under the authority of one man.

This single man is buttressed by philosophical teachings and is responsible for regulating moral order.

The dispute between papal and imperial authority that had been the nominal cause of the Guelf-Ghibelline split had been at issue since late antiquity. Medieval tradition held that the emperor Constantine had given imperial lands as a gift to the Church. This act, known as the Donation of Constantine, signaled the introduction of riches into the Church's purse, which made the Church, according to its critics, no longer poor, pristine, and above the fray of temporal concerns such as prosperity and greed. Dante rails against the Donation of Constantine in various places (see, for example, *Inferno* 19): he believes that the corruption of the Church can be traced to its entrance into worldly affairs. As Charles Till Davis points out, "In *Monarchia* he went so far as to claim that the emperor should escape cupidity by possessing everything, the pope and other clerics by possessing nothing" (72-73). Dante's hope was to restore both Church and Empire to their ideal states, as they were when Christ first came.

The Empire, for Dante, represents government rule over the entire human community. The authority of the emperor derives directly from God and is entirely unmediated. That is, no other authority stands between the emperor and divine authority, including (perhaps especially) the pope. The pope's authority surpasses that of the emperor, but the two do not conflict in any way: imperial rule governs the temporal realm and papal rule governs the spiritual realm, the latter being the greater of the two. The two even have distinct "advisers," so to speak: "The emperor relies on philosophical teachings to lead men to their human goal of temporal happiness; the pope relies on theological teachings to lead men to the divine goal of salvation" (Davis 68).

Dante's hope for the new imperial order was stirred by Henry of Luxembourg, who was declared emperor in November 1308. Emperor Henry VII had ambitions to bring peace to all of Italy, uniting it under one ruler; this is precisely Dante's dream for a theoretical king or emperor as he spells it out in *Monarchia*. Henry began to make his way to

Rome with Pope Clement V's endorsement and encouragement of Italian collaboration. Papal support meant that the ideal of an alliance between the two powers was possible. Dante eagerly wrote a letter to the people of Italy asking cooperation.

When Henry VII descended into Tuscany, however, Guelf Florence refused to admit him. He bypassed the city and went to Rome, where Clement V forced his early departure and warned him not to march against papal lands in southern Italy. Henry died shortly thereafter of malarial fever.

The rapid rise and anticlimactic fall of Henry VII took with it Dante's hopes for the restoration of peace in the commune of Florence, in the Italian peninsula at large, and in the community of Christians as a whole. The poet had even hoped that with peace would come his own reentry into Florence, where he would take on the mantle of poet laureate (*Paradiso* 25.7-9). But, he laments, Henry came before Italy was ready for him (*Paradiso* 30.137-38). Henry's place in Paradise is already reserved for him.

Conclusion: Dante Today

Why does all this political intrigue matter to a reading of a poem dubbed "divine"? Another way of phrasing the question is this: What do petty politics have to do with Dante's theology? It is easy to presume that the poem's significance resonates with modern readers more on the level of its moral blueprints than on that of its detailed political analysis of parties that have not existed since the time Dante wrote about them. But the political aspect of the poem is the root of its morality and theology; politics are crucial to Dante's theology. Dante's narrative is, first and foremost, his personal experience: it is the (purportedly) *true* autobiographical account of a struggling poet and politician in a midlife crisis visiting the otherworld. This is always taken as the crux of the *Comedy*'s fiction: in Charles Singleton's formulation, now standard to American Dante criticism, the greatest fiction of the poem

---

is that it is not a fiction. Dante has related his experience, dictated by his memory, of his conversion from sin to salvation. This conversion cannot take place without an examination of his political life.

The poem can be for its readers simultaneously familiar and foreign because it is specifically designed that way. This inferno is emphatically Dante's. In fact, we rarely lose his name when speaking of the *Inferno*: in popular culture it is always *Dante's Inferno*. But he constructs it as ours, too, and we can easily substitute our own characters in its circles: our own politicians and religious leaders, our own relatives and colleagues, our own friends and enemies. No matter what our political or religious circumstance, we can relate to his passionate appeal for love and justice in the face of ruthless adversity. To understand the political context of the poem is to meet it on its own terms, to engage Dante personally, as he is speaking to us through the text. Only once we have engaged the poem—and the poet—on this level can we then consider its modern analogues, taking from it the moral, philosophical, and theological lessons it expects of us.

Notes

1. The whole of this essay is indebted to the works listed below for dates and other pertinent historical information; however, each section relies more heavily on one text than the others. For "The City," see Scott (323-28), as well as the two chronicles. "The Civil War" follows Najemy's article in the *The Cambridge Companion to Dante*. For "The Papacy," see again Scott (317-21, 328-34). "Dante the Politician" looks to Boccaccio, Hollander (40-45), Najemy, and Scott (314-36). For the section titled "Exile" see Najemy. "Empire," obviously, leans much on Charles Till Davis's contribution to the *Cambridge Companion*, and on Scott (320-23).

2. All citations of and translations from the *Comedy* come from the Durling-Martinez edition, *The Divine Comedy of Dante Alighieri*.

Works Cited

Boccaccio, Giovanni. *The Life of Dante*. Trans. Vincenzo Zin Bollettino. New York: Garland, 1990.

Compagni, Dino. *Chronicle of Florence*. Trans. Daniel E. Bornstein. Philadelphia: U of Pennsylvania P, 1986.

Dante. *Dante's Inferno*. Adapted by Sandow Birk and Marcus Sanders. Illustrated by Sandow Birk. San Francisco: Chronicle Books, 2004.

_____. *Dantis Alagherii Epistolae: The Letters of Dante*. Ed. and trans. Paget Toynbee. 1920. New York: Oxford UP, 1966.

_____. *The Divine Comedy of Dante Alighieri*. Trans. Robert M. Durling. Intro. and notes by Ronald L. Martinez and Robert M. Durling. 3 vols. New York: Oxford UP, 1996, 2003, 2010.

Davis, Charles Till. "Dante and the Empire." *The Cambridge Companion to Dante*. Ed. Rachel Jacoff. New York: Cambridge UP, 1993. 67-79.

Hollander, Robert. *Dante: A Life in Works*. New Haven, CT: Yale UP, 2001.

Najemy, John M. "Dante and Florence." *The Cambridge Companion to Dante*. Ed. Rachel Jacoff. New York: Cambridge UP, 1993. 80-99.

Scott, John A. *Understanding Dante*. Notre Dame, IN: U of Notre Dame P, 2004.

Villani, Giovanni. *Villani's Chronicle: Being Selections from the First Nine Books of the "Chroniche Fiorentine" of Giovanni Villani*. Trans. Rose E. Selfe. Ed. Philip H. Wicksteed. London: Archibald Constable, 1906.

CRITICAL
READINGS

The Moral System of the *Commedia* and the Seven Capital Sins_____

Robert Hollander

Dante divides Hell into Aristotelian-Ciceronian compartments (as he himself tells us in *Inferno* XI), and Paradise into three Ptolemaic angelic triads (as he tells us in *Paradiso* XXVIII). Purgatory, on the other hand, is clearly and naturally ordered by the Seven Sins, corresponding to the seven terraces of the Mount. For various and good reasons, a few of Dante's commentators have wondered whether or not there is a common scheme of moral order which unites the three *cantiche*. The most recent (and partially successful) attempt to defy Dante's own statements about *Inferno* and *Paradiso* is that made by T. K. Swing in his often acute study, *The Fragile Leaves of the Sibyl: Dante's Master Plan*.[1] Swing's work, which refers to only six critics of Dante in its bibliography, does not take into account probably the most convincing of all attempts to make a unitary system for the moral plan of the three realms. This work is Luigi Valli's restatement and adumbration of his master's theories *L'allegoria di Dante secondo Giovanni Pascoli*.[2] Valli follows Pascoli in finding that Dante has organized the entire poem in accord with the Seven Sins in order to harmonize the Christian doctrine of Original Sin, the tripartite Aristotelian classification of evil, the Catholic doctrine of the Seven Sins, and the Ptolemaic system of nine spheres. Thus Pascoli, according to Valli, sees the opening of *Inferno* as a picture of "peccato originale non o invano redento (Selva Oscura)."[3] My own conclusion is that Dante did, albeit in small ways that are far from self-evident, pull the poem together in his use of the Seven Sins, but that he did so in a way that is of decorational importance rather than of primary structural significance. In this I oppose both Pascoli/Valli and Swing, all of whom argue for the revelation of a major secret in the poem's composition. Since Dante has told us clearly that he has organized *Inferno* in accord with Aristotle/Cicero and *Paradiso* in accord with the nine celestial spheres of Ptolemaic astronomy and the medieval hierarchy of angels, I see no way that we may look beyond his claims and find them intentionally misleading, which is the inevitable result of Swing's thesis; and I hesitate at the prospect of arid schematization which seems to me the result of Valli's approach.

Swing claims that he works backward from the plan of *Paradiso* to find the Seven Sins as the structural backbone of the entire poem. His work belies his claim. First of all, a quick glance will reveal that his treatments of the corresponding moments of *Purgatorio* and *Inferno* are quite long and detailed, while those of what he claims to be the corresponding parts of *Paradiso* are extremely brief and often forced. Had he consulted Valli he would probably have found that he had turned the Seven Sins, as they occur in *Paradiso*, precisely upside down. This is eventually rather damaging to his argument.

Since the Seven Sins are clearly enunciated only in *Purgatorio*, and since four of the seven give their names to four of the areas of *Inferno*, it is simplest to begin with the correlations between these two *cantiche*.

Inferno, once we get past the Neutrals and the Virtuous Pagans, starts out with the sins in the proper order. Canto V is Lust; VI, Gluttony; VII should then be Avarice, and it is. The fourth sin is Sloth, or *accidia*. Where is it? In the next canto, although it often goes unnoticed. As Virgil prepares Dante for the vision of the Wrathful, he tells his pupil that he is about to see those who were sad in the sweet air that is joyful in the sun, carrying within themselves an *accidioso* smoke, now saddened in the black slime of the Styx ("Tristi fummo/ ne l'aere dolce che dal sol s'allegra,/ portando dentro accidioso fummo:/ or ci attristiam nella belleta negra"—*Inf*. VII, 121-124). Together, the word *accidioso* and the posture, attitude, and behavior of those in Canto VIII spell not so much Wrath as Sloth. It is not clear to me whether Dante in Canto VIII wants us to think that all who practiced *ira* were essentially slothful, or that only some of them were. What does seem important is that he wanted to include the fourth sin at the appropriate juncture. For the fifth one is Wrath, and it is either described as the sin of Filippo

Argenti, thus intermingled with *accidia*, or it gets its turn in the next large division of the poem, which is that of Violence.

This area of the poem is subdivided into three categories: Violence is carried out against others, self, and God. As we approach the area we first see its guardian demon, the Minotaur, who is described as "ira bestial"—"bestial wrath" (*Inf.* XII, 33), and who guards the place where "ira folle"—"mad wrath" (line 49) is punished. That Dante thought of what he calls Wrath as at least to some degree including *accidia*, and of what he calls Violence as being principally the result of Wrath, is buttressed by a nice detail in *Purgatorio* XVII, among the Wrathful.[4] There the *exempla* of the sin which is to be purged on that terrace are three in number. Procne, Haman, and Amata are, respectively, if we think about it only a moment, *exempla* of each of the three categories of Violence we examined in Cantos XII through XVII of *Inferno*: Procne, of violence against others in that she slew her own son Itys in a frenzy of wrath (*Meta*. VI, 412f); Haman, of violence against God in that he, wrathful against Mordecai (Esther 3:5), wanted to slay all the Jews, God's chosen people; Amata, of violence against self in that she hanged herself when she thought Turnus was dead (*Aen*. XII, 595f).

The next great area of *Inferno* goes correctly by the name of Fraud. Did Dante think of it also as Envy, the sixth sin? If he did, he probably thought of Fraud as issuing from the passion of Envy, that is, thought of the Christian root of the pagan sin. This is far from certain, but the case is helped considerably because Dante twice uses the word for Envy, *invidia*, in its verb form, in the area (*Inf.* XXV, 99 and XXVI, 24).

This tentative argument is also bolstered when we consider that there is little doubt that the last area, Treachery, is seen in major respects to be the same sin as, or at least to issue from, Pride. For any Christian, Pride is Lucifer's other name; and it is the fallen angel who is the first *exemplum*, followed by the giants we also see at the bottom of Hell, and who is figured on the pavement of Pride in *Purgatorio* XII (25-36).

To review, we are certain that Dante uses the first three sins in their proper order in *Inferno*; we are almost positive that he refers to Sloth, Wrath, and Pride in the appropriate places; and then we can almost surely argue that he must have had Envy in mind for Fraud, thus supporting the relatively meager evidence we find within the poem at that point.

Although I disagree strongly with T. K. Swing about the moral order of *Paradiso*, my findings, though they are sometimes the result of a different way of thinking, are extremely close to his concerning *Inferno*. Again, however, I must emphasize a major distinction. I do not believe that Dante's careful ticking off of the Seven Sins in *Inferno* does away with the actual Classical division of sins which is put into Virgil's mouth in Canto XI, as Swing is wont to believe. Dante as usual has it both, indeed many, ways. Doctrinally, however, he must guarantee his vision with Christian doctrine, and so the Seven Sins should be somewhere, and in the right order, in *Inferno*. Secondly, as a poet, and as the kind of symmetry-loving and detail-conscious poet that he is, Dante enjoys small architectonic detail. The two instincts are not incompatible, as the whole work attests; speculation on which of them is stronger here is perhaps irrelevant and certainly beyond the possibilities of proof. A Christian reader today, like Professor Swing, may be most moved to celebrate the hidden doctrine. Another will be most pleased by the decorational detail, the compulsion to form *in parva*. They are both right.

If relatively little imagination is required to discover the way in which Dante hinges the broad and clear moral outline of *Purgatorio* to the complexities of the moral system of *Inferno*, what of the apparently antithetic moral structure of *Paradiso*? Since that part of the poem is to celebrate the virtues, where does it have room for the vices? One part of each celestial area is devoted not to the joy of blessedness but to the sinfulness of Earth. In each sphere someone makes a violent denunciation of sublunar behavior. These denunciations, then, are the logical places to look for traces of the Seven Sins. After the first two spheres,

Moon and Mercury,[5] four of the seven heavens (the first three and the last) contain denunciations of earthly behavior which connect with the Seven Sins, each in its proper place, all adhering to the proper order. The fourth, fifth, and sixth are less clearly identified or not referred to.[6] And yet even then, in the surrounding detail of each sphere, we find some supporting detail which might point to Dante's concern to include the Seven Sins even in *Paradiso*. The fact that the four spheres that almost certainly contain references to the Seven Sins also use subordinate detail to clarify the sins referred to in the denunciations helps to bolster the argument.

Why Dante chose to omit Moon and Mercury from the system is not particularly puzzling. He had nine spheres and seven sins, and he chose to omit the first two spheres. Venus, then, must be Lust. That is not surprising after all. This planet is believed by earthlings to ray forth "il folle amore" ("mad love"—*Par.* VIII, 2). Carlo Martello, Cunizza, and Folco all loved the world too much, and Cunizza even confesses to Lust, "because the light of this star overcame me" ("perché mi vinse il lume d'esta stella"—*Par.* IX, 33). These details certainly set the atmosphere for a correspondence between the Heavenly Venus and Earthly Lust. The inclusion of the reference to the presence in this sphere of Rahab the whore (IX, 115) adds to the overtone of the lust that typified life below for all present here. Then Folco concludes the canto and the sphere with his denunciation of Florence (127-142) for her coinage of the florin, which has turned the shepherd into the wolf. Thus it would seem to be only Avarice, and not Lust, which is the topic of his angry sermon—until we come to its final word, one that summarizes the sixteen lines that precede it, which is "l'adultero." To think of the coinage of, and the trading in of, money as fornication, as any reader of *Inferno* XVII will remember, was not strange to Dante or to his time. As usury was a form of fornication there, so cupidity seen from here is adultery. And thus, in this single word, which now attaches to the details of lust that were present in the souls we meet who recall their past lives, Dante ties together the sin of Lust and the continuing malefaction in the world below. Once again, as was frequently the case in *Inferno*, the detail is small, calling no great attention to itself.

Almost all of *Paradiso* XI is taken up by Thomas' thoroughly characteristic exposition of a phrase he has used previously, "u' ben s'impingua, se non si vaneggia" ("where there is good fattening if they do not stray"—*Par.* X, 96 and XI, 139). The image of sheep being properly fed and led follows from the previous similar shepherd-into-wolf image in *Paradiso* IX, 131-132, to which I have referred. Here the appropriate sin that should be referred to is gluttony. And, in Thomas' denunciation of the corruption of the Dominican order, bad shepherds now whereas their leader and founder had been a good one, the expression of their peculiar sinfulness is related to gluttony: Dominic's flock has grown so greedy for new foods that it can only stray through various wild pastures ("Ma 'l suo peculio di nova vivenda/ è fatto ghiotto, sì ch'esser non puote/ che per diversi salti non si spanda"—*Par.* XI, 124-126). The world has been understood to hunger (*gola*) for the news of Solomon's Song (*Par.* X, III), thus also setting the stage for the metaphoric equivalence of bad shepherding and gluttony in the denunciation. And so here, as in the sphere of Venus, the denunciation of bad conduct on earth is expressed with a striking metaphor which associates what would ordinarily be an unrelated sin to one of the Seven Sins. That this is the case is reinforced when we turn to the second denunciation in the Sun, that of degenerate Franciscans by Bonaventura. As the central action of this sphere has been the mutual and reciprocal praise of Franciscans by a Dominican and of Dominicans by a Franciscan, so each praiser once turns to blame those of his own order who have failed where the path was so clearly marked. Bonaventura's language of blame is parallel to that of Thomas' denunciation. The orbit of true faith and deed which circled about St. Francis is compared, in its degeneracy, to a loaf of bread turned to mold ("sì ch'è la muffa dov'era la gromma"—*Par.* XII, 114). The result of this turning from the true way is again compared to bad food: lines 119-120 refer to the parable in Matthew 13:24-30, 36-43, concerning the wheat and the tares. The degenerate Franciscans have given over the "verace manna" (line 84) for this rotten food, or accepted tares instead of wheat. Thus, throughout the three cantos in the Sun, the images of true food are contrasted with improper hunger; and Dante is able through metaphor to assert the less than immediately meaningful, although eventually telling, appropriateness of Gluttony.

In Mars, Cacciaguida denounces the current behavior of Florentines, invoking the woes of overzealous commercial life (*Par.* XVI, 52-84) and capping his description with the comparison of the ebb and flow of wealth to the instability of Moon-pulled tides; "così fa di Fiorenza la Fortuna" ("thus Fortune does with Florence"—line 84). We should remember the goddess Fortuna from *Inferno* VII, the canto of Avarice and Prodigality, where she is associated with the third of the Seven Sins, Avarice, which is the one we expect to find referred to here. The avarice of Florentines, treated as "adultery" when it is denounced in Venus (*Par.* IX, 142), is treated here as Avarice and Prodigality proper. To underline the point in the following canto, Dante has Cacciaguida say of Florence that there Christ Himself is bought and sold every day ("Cristo tutto di si merca"—*Par.* XVII, 51), behavior which surely betokens the height of Avarice and Prodigality.

In Jupiter Dante himself makes a denunciation for the only time in *Paradiso*. It concerns the Papal Court at Avignon. Against the bright star of Justice rises a smoke that vitiates its ray ("il fummo che 'l tuo raggio vizia"—*Par.* XVIII, 120). The passage continues by attacking the buying and selling in the temple that would seem to be connected with Avarice. However, the following *terzina* takes a second tack, scolding the Avignonian clergy for its withholding of communion and its sale of canceled excommunications in such a way that Sloth may be seen behind the words. Where the Crusaders fought with swords (line 127), these men merely withhold communion. Where Peter and Paul labored for Christ and wrote the Bible, these men write only to cancel excommunications for their own profit (130-131). In the final four lines of the canto Dante lets them speak for themselves, and we hear plainly the voices of self-absorbed, witty men, exemplars of *accidia*, condensed into this single imitation which would seem to be modeled from life. (The closest thing to it in the entire *Commedia* is probably the negligent, witty, self-absorbed speech of Belacqua, the very emblem of the slothful life.)

> . . . "I' ho fermo 'l disiro
> sì a colui che volle viver solo
> e che per salti fu tratto al martiro,
> ch'io non conosco il pescator né Polo."

> [. . . "I have so set my longing
> on him who wished to live solitary
> and was dragged to martyrdom by dancing feet
> that I do not know the Fisherman nor Paul."]
>   (*Par.* XVIII, 133-136)

The imaginary churchman who utters these words is, it seems to me, the picture of the physically comfortable and spiritually negligent creature who for Dante embodies Sloth. He cares only for the florin now being minted in Avignon that bears the picture of John the Baptist, who is represented, in the eyes of the lazy cleric of Avignon, merely as being a rather effete solitary who was sold for a dance of Salome. The jest, so distasteful and yet so perfectly realized, indicts the teller in such a way that the smoke we saw at the opening of Dante's denunciation may have now become associated in our minds with the first smoke we saw in the poem: that "accidioso fummo" of *Inferno* VII, 123, which there was the sign of *accidia*. The substance here certainly seems to fit Avarice better than Sloth. Yet I would argue for the tone of the entire passage, in conjunction with the possibly "loaded" word *fummo*, as indicating that it is Sloth which is on Dante's mind, embodied in his representation of the intellectually able but thoroughly lazy clergy he must have often encountered. In stark contrast to this scene of clerical misbehavior in *Paradiso* XVIII is the scene we found in the eighteenth canto of *Purgatorio*. There the zealous Abbot of San Zeno at Verona paid back his slothful days on earth by racing along the Terrace of Sloth. It is possible that Dante had *Purgatorio* XVIII in mind for *Paradiso* XVIII. And if the word for sloth is absent here, its manner does seem to be present.

As a place, as Valli points out, Saturn, "the mild" planet, is naturally opposed to anger. And in that place, denouncing the corrupt clergy, Peter Damian's contemplative patience gives way to righteous anger as he attacks "li moderni pastori" (*Par.* XXI, 130-135), who are, however, in no way associated with Wrath by Peter's words. The spirits who surround him end the canto with a shout of support for his denunciation which sound to Dante like thunder (142), the traditional sign of God's angry displeasure with man. And in the following canto Beatrice explains to Dante that what he has heard promises that God's vengeance ("la vendetta"—*Par.* XXII, 14) is soon to come. Similarly, at the conclusion of this canto Benedict, angry at clerical malfeasance, is joined by the spirits who surround him, and all go upward like a whirlwind ("come turbo"—*Par.* XXII, 99), that other natural sign of God's angry displeasure. These vestiges of anger—righteous anger—appear to be all we shall find here. For once there would seem to be no correlation whatsoever between the sin denounced and the appropriate one of the Seven Sins, unless in Dante's vision of Earth as the "threshing-floor which makes us so fierce" ("L'aiuola che ci fa tanto feroci"—*Par.* XXII, 151) human ferocity is to be understood as being synonymous with Wrath.[7]

In the sphere of the Fixed Stars, which Dante enters in the sign of Gemini (the Twins who themselves are a sign of concord) he encounters the cooperative spirit exemplified in the relationship revealed among Peter, James, and John, themselves representative of the communal accomplishments of the twelve Apostles. More impressive as proof that Dante is thinking of Envy here is the temporary blindness he undergoes (*Par.* XXV, 136-139), and which is figurally related to the blindness of Saul of Tarsus that was taken away by Ananias' hand (*Par.* XXVI, 12; Acts 9:10-18). For blindness has been the central image of Envy in *Purgatorio* XIII-XV, where Dante made use of the medieval etymology of the Latin *invidia* to see in Envy a form of blindness. His blindness here is fairly likely to be intended to remind us of that earlier version of the sin, which is countered there as here by images of fraternal love. Even in this high sphere of fraternal bliss we come upon a denunciation of earthly failings. Again it is directed against the corrupt clergy (as are all but two of the Paradisal outcries, the ones reserved for Florence). This time Peter holds forth against those who have usurped his place (*Par.* XXVII, 22), those ravening wolves in shepherds' clothing (55). Thus here the image which describes the procedures of covetousness is that of fraud. As we saw earlier, there seems to exist, for Dante, a correlation between fraudulence and Envy in *Inferno*, and my argument must rely on that thread to make the connection to Envy here. Again, as in the sphere of Saturn, the surrounding details must be primarily relied on in order to make the connection, although here there may be a little more justification in finding the trace of Envy in Peter's speech, the main purport of which is to assail the fraudulent practice of simony (XXVII, 40-60).

The *Primo Mobile*, where Dante is acquainted with the angels and their ranks, contains three denunciations, all made by Beatrice. The first, continuing that of Peter in the same canto (XXVII), attacks *cupidigia*, that radical sin which seems to be cognate with Pride ("Radix malorum est cupiditas") in the medieval imagination.[8] The second concerns the fallen angels (XXIX), and the third attacks puffed up preachers. This last (XXIX, 85-126) denounces false philosophy that is practised out of vanity, and thus bookish pride that cares only for applause and nothing for the truth. That Pride lies close beneath the surface of the first and third attacks is probably made certain by the middle one, in which Beatrice takes us back to *Inferno* XXXIV:

Principio del cader fu il maladetto

superbir di colui che tu vedesti

da tutti i pesi del mondo costretto.

[The beginning of the Fall was the cursed

pride of him whom thou didst see

constrained by every universal weight.]

(*Par.* XXIX, 55-57)

This reminiscence of Satan, with its specific reference to his pride against God, leaves little room for argument against the notion that in *Primo Mobile* Dante draws a clear line of opposition between proud Lucifer and the humble ("modesti"—line 58) angels he has just now seen.

Some of the evidence presented here is thin. Nevertheless, I believe there is enough that is solid to make it more than a likely possibility that Dante planned to reflect each of the Seven Sins, in programmatic fashion, in each of the three *cantiche* of the *Commedia*.

Notes

1. T. K. Swing, *The Fragile Leaves of the Sibyl: Dante's Master Plan*, Westminster, Md., 1962.

2. Luigi Valli, *L'allegoria di Dante secondo Giovanni Pascoli*, Bologna [1922], pp. 7-34.

3. In the diagram facing p. 32. Of *Inf.* I and II as corresponding to Eden after the Fall, see Chapter II of this study where I draw a similar conclusion for different reasons.

4. Lines 18-39.

5. Pascoli/Valli also exempt these two spheres. Their order, arrived at otherwise than mine, is in substance precisely the same. See Giovanni Pascoli's *La Mirabile Visione*, 3rd. ed. (Bologna, 1923), and his *Sotto il Velame* (Messina, 1900).

6. A pleasing parallel to the relative hiddenness of the corresponding sins of *In-*

ferno. In that *cantica* the first three are named, while in *Paradiso* the first three are more easily discovered than the fourth, fifth, and sixth. The seventh sin in each, Pride, is to be recognized emblematically in the references to Lucifer.

7. For this suggestion I am indebted to Peter Schäffer.

8. James E. Shaw's "'And the Evening and the Morning Were One Day' (*Paradiso*, XXVII, 136-138)," *Modern Philology*, XVIII (1921), 580-582, describes *cupidigia* as follows: ". . . that general sin which includes all others, which is the common disease of the whole world, which is the same as St. Augustine's 'amor privatus,' love of self. This is the sin that caused Lucifer to fall; the sin that, in his case, is often called pride."

Canto 1:
The Dark Wood_____

Wallace Fowlie

This first canto introduces the entire *Divine Comedy*. It defines each of the three realms that Dante the traveler has to visit in order to escape from the "dark wood" referred to in the opening tercet. *Una selva oscura* is the opening setting where the Florentine poet Dante Alighieri finds himself on the morning of Good Friday in the year 1300, in the thirty-fifth year of his life. He has lost his way and is frightened by the wildness of the wood.

The first tercet provides the motif and the motivation of the entire work. The motif is the journey of the poet who must find his way out of the dark wood. The motivation is the need to recover. Recover from what? What is the meaning of the dark wood and what has caused Dante's fear (the word *paura* is used twice in ten lines)? No precise answer is ever given to these questions. Today, some 680 years after the date of the poem's action, we would call the poet's condition that of alienation. And today we also know, or at least we believe, that the experience of alienation cannot be defined in any simple terms, that it is a complete situation formed by many causes.

Dante was indeed wise not to have attempted any strict analysis of his estrangement. If no specificity is possible in his case, we can be sure of the general cause which is always present, and often invisible, with every specific illness. Dante is estranged from the order of the world. This experience is a bitterness, comparable almost to death, in the sense that it has cut him off from the world. The real clue to this entire opening passage is Dante's confession that he cannot explain how he has come to this impasse: he was not conscious of losing his way. The reasons for his estrangement are as dark as the wood itself.

This bewildered man comes to the foot of a hill, and sees at its top the rays of the sun which he feels instinctively will guide him out of the darkness. But when he begins to climb, three animals, one after the other, impede his way, and again he loses hope, this time of reaching the summit:

io perdei la speranza de l'altezza.

[1:54]

[I lost hope of the height.]

By this line, and the reader has already followed an experience of help-lessness, frustration, and hopelessness. And already the reader's mind is perhaps moving beyond the literalness of this brief passage. The rays of light on the mountain top must be something more that the physical sun. The leopard, the lion, and the she-wolf, with their respective char-acteristics of litheness, fury, and leanness, must be more than the three beasts named in Jeremiah 5:6.

The wood, the hill, and the beasts appear to be outside of Dante, thanks to the poet's art, but we begin to realize that they are also within him, that they depict familiar fantasies we can easily recognize, fanta-sies created in the subconscious when one is "out of joint" with the world, when, like Dante and Hamlet, one is exiled, and relives, in some minor way which may yet be stupendous in a single life, the drama of man's fall from God's grace. Adam's dire experience is the archetype of innumerable kinds of experience that cause an individual to feel abandoned.

Until the sudden unexpected appearance of Virgil, the atmosphere of this opening canto is decidedly Hebraic. The lost way, the dark wood, the sense of bewilderment and estrangement are reminiscent of the fall of man in Genesis and the chosen people's intermittent separa-tions from God. The three beasts of Jeremiah were interpreted by Saint Jerome as representing sensuality (the leopard), pride (the lion), and greed (the she-wolf), and this moral interpretation seems as sound for Dante's passage as the political interpretations offered by some scholars.

When Virgil's figure emerges from the darkness, a new atmosphere develops. Virgil is a clearly delineated character from the classical world, explicit in his directions, the counterpart of Dante's muddled mind, which is half asleep, half terrorized. Virgil died nineteen years before the birth of Christ, and therefore stands at the end of the old world and at the beginning of the new. Appropriately, he will be the one to rescue Dante from the dark wood (he had already served as a guiding poet in Dante's development as a writer). *Poeta fui* (1:73), "I was a poet," he says, and Dante immediately acknowledges Virgil's rich inspiration for Italian verse (*quella fonte*, 1:79, "that fountain"). His recognition of Virgil is a moving moment in the action:

> Or se' tu quel Virgilio
> [1:79]
> [Are you then that Virgil?]

In total simplicity, Dante states Virgil's prevenience: the Latin poet was his master:

> Tu se' lo mio maestro
> [1:85]
> [you are my master]

In the form of a command, he asks for help: *aiutami* 1:89)—help me.

Before Virgil speaks of a way out from the predicament, we are reminded of the descent into Hades in the *Aeneid*, which was doubtless inspired by the same kind of descent narrated in Homer. We are reminded, too, of that passage in Virgil's fourth eclogue often interpreted as being a prophecy of the coming of Christ. Virgil is indeed the spiritual and historical and literary counterpart of Dante. From the very start, Dante accepts him as a doctor who prescribes.

Virgil's role as leader is clear in line 91:

A te convien tenere altro vïaggio

[you must take another way]

and with this statement we have a first insight into the entire scheme of the *Commedia*. The third beast, the *lupa*, has to be avoided at all costs because she will reign until a savior comes. She will finally be routed by a greyhound (*Veltro*, 1:101), but the time is not yet at hand. The history of political parties and political power does indeed count in the life history of the individual. Meanwhile, Virgil will serve as guide:

e io sarò tua guida

[1:113]

[and I will be guide]

Virgil then briefly describes the three realms that Dante must go through in order to escape not only the *lupa* impeding his way, but also the beast within him.

The first is an eternal place (*loco etterno*, 1:114) of suffering spirits (*spiriti dolenti*, 1:116) and cries. Such is the torment there that the spirits call out for a second death. The second realm is that place where there is suffering, but the sufferers are happy in the fire (*son contenti/ nel foco*, 1:118-19) because they know it is for a reason and that they will eventually move out of Purgatory into the third realm. Purgatory is a discipline for the higher life, for that place where the blessed live (*beate genti*, 1:120).

Dante gratefully consents to go wherever Virgil will take him. Virgil moves ahead, and Dante follows. It is the last line of the canto:

Allor si mosse, e io li tenni dietro.

[Then he moved on and I kept on behind him.]

The Latin poet Virgil, who had sung of Aeneas, founder of Rome, the eternal city where Christendom was to find its center, makes three promises to Dante before the beginning of the journey. These promises would seem to represent three kinds of salvation, and they embrace the entire poem. Virgil promises first a way of escape from the dark wood. This is the immediate, personal salvation of man who has reached an impasse in his thoughts and in his life. The man believes in God. He can see the rays of the sun on the distant hill and knows that God is the source of light and life, but he cannot, by himself, go to God. He is alienated in a mysterious psychic way and in such a state of confusion that he needs a slow, careful, documented picture of the ways in which transgressions against men and the cities of men result in blindness. All that Dante knows at this moment is that he is lost and impotent. This promise of a personal cure is made to him by a fellow poet of another age, his literary master, who, although not saved in the full Christian sense, lives eternally just outside of the realm inhabited by those spirits who, when they were on earth, willfully turned against the good and did not repent.

The second promise concerns Italy. Dante himself at this moment in his life is in exile from his beloved Florence. He has been forced by politics into the role of pilgrim and wayfarer. Virgil mysteriously names the one who is to save Italy *il Veltro* (the greyhound). Through the exercise of wisdom, love, and virile power (*sapienza, amore e virtute*, 1:104), he will restore Italy. In giving Virgil these words, Dante may have had in mind Can Grande della Scala, whose birthplace was Verona, a city that lies between Feltro in Venetia and Montefeltro in Romagna. Political hopes change more often than most, and Dante himself fixed his hopes on various leaders during the course of his life. The obscure line that names the birthplace as the nation of *il Veltro* (1:105) applies best to Can Grande:

> e sua nazion sarà tra feltro e feltro
> [and his nation will be between Feltro and Feltro.]

The third promise is more than one of immediate rescue from a serious predicament, and more than the political salvation of Italy. It is the promise of eternal life which is implied for Dante if he ascends the various heavens of Paradise. Virgil says that he will not be able to accompany the traveler there, but that he will leave him with a more worthy spirit. Beatrice is not named, but she is obviously referred to in line 123:

con lei ti lascerò
[with her I will leave you]

The three promises thus concern a man suffering from a mysterious but very real mental distress; a patriot exiled from a city ill-governed and without justice; and a soul which, like every other soul, is destined for eternal life.

Behind these promises there is at work a severe principle which penetrates the entire canto. Dante will not be saved without his own self-discipline. The descent into Hell will not be a sightseeing tour. And the spectacles will not only be exterior. Dante will also have to tame the various beasts that are within him. Help is promised him from a supernatural source, but that alone will not suffice. After all, the poem is called by the poet a *commedia*, which by definition implies the struggle of free will against forces that attempt to nullify it.

Thus, at the beginning of the *Commedia*, one finds the Hebraic image of man in need of God, and the classical image of man willing to help himself and exercise self-discipline. These two themes, the unseen God and the development of selfhood, will never be lost sight of.

In the first canto we witness a dramatic action—a man reaching the brink of despair where life is suddenly cast in the form of a dark wood. The confusion of Dante's spirit is here depicted in the tangled mesh of many growths: it is the sudden realization that he has gone too far in disorder. No one form of this disorder can be distinguished any longer: the multiple disorders have grown so closely together that their origins have been obscured.

Then, as Dante begins to climb the hill, three beasts arrest his progress as if they were the habits of disorder that keep him from emerging from his deep trouble. He can see the sun, and can thus hope that a cure may yet be effected. But in the action of the canto, the beasts appear and perform their function after Dante has seen the sun. Hope again has been blotted out, and the despair, the throttling sensation produced by dense, overgrown vegetation, is more marked than ever.

More than half of the canto, beginning with line 61, concerns the meeting with Virgil. Dante's bewilderment changes to awe. It is more than a meeting with a great poet of the past, because Virgil is Dante's poet. Dante has suddenly, unexpectedly found both his way and his predecessor:

> Tu se' lo mio maestro e 'l mio autore
> [1:85]
> [you are my master and my author]

The tone of awe and the acknowledgment of derivation are the same as those expressed by Eve to Adam in *Paradise Lost*:

> My author and disposer, what thou bidds't
> Unargued I obey.
> [4:635]

Eve, in her love for Adam, and Dante in his love for Virgil, both recognize their guide and their authority.

Thus, the first sixty lines of canto 1 reflect the Hebraic theme of man's estrangement from God, a theme never absent from the entire *Commedia*, because it emphasizes man's dependence on the Divine. But in the last seventy-six lines, the appearance of Virgil and his words of promise represent the classical strand in the poem by emphasizing the more purely human power of man to discover his true self.

Principal Signs and Symbols

1. *Dante*: the poet who is also the Christian sinner.
2. *Virgil*: the poet who is also human wisdom, the best that man can become without belief in Christ.
3. *The wood* (*la selva*): the error that hardens the heart or blinds the eye.
4. *The three beasts* (*le tre fiere*): the three types of sin that precipitate a soul into one of the three divisions of Hell (see canto 11):
    (a) the leopard (*la lonza*)—self-indulgence, carnality;
    (b) the lion (*il leone*)—violence or bestiality;
    (c) the wolf (*la lupa*)—malice involving fraud.
5. *Il Veltro* (the greyhound): the hoped-for leader the world continues to expect even today.

Selected Bibliography

Italian Editions of "The Divine Comedy"
Alighieri, Dante, *La divina commedia*. Testo critico della Società dantesca italiana; riveduto col commento scartazziniano; rifatto da Giuseppe Vandelli. Milan: 1957 (seventeenth edition).
Alighieri, Dante, *La divina commedia*. Edited and annotated by C. H. Grandgent. D. C. Heath: 1913.
Alighieri, Dante, *La divina commedia*. Edited and annotated by C. H. Grandgent. Revised by Charles S. Singleton. Harvard University Press: 1972.

Bilingual Editions with Commentary
Singleton, Charles S., *Inferno*. Vol. 1 text, vol. 2 commentary. Princeton: 1970.
The Inferno. Translated by J. A. Carlyle. Revised by H. Oelsner. The Temple Classics: 1970.
Dante's Inferno. Translated by John D. Sinclair. Oxford: 1974.

English Translations
The Comedy of Dante Alighieri. Cantica 1, *Hell*. Translated by Dorothy L. Sayers. Penguin Books: 1974.
Dante's Inferno. Translated by John Ciardi. Rutgers University Press: 1954.
Dante's Inferno. Translated by Mark Musa. Indiana University Press: 1971.

Commentary and Criticism in English

Auerbach, Erich, *Dante: Poet of the Secular World*. Translated by R. Manheim. University of Chicago Press: 1974.

Auerbach, Erich, *Mimesis*. Translated by W. Trask. Doubleday-Anchor: 1957. (See chapter 8, "Farinata and Cavalcante.")

Barbi, Michele, *Life of Dante*. Translated by P. Ruggiers. Cambridge University Press: 1955.

Bergin, Thomas G., *Dante*. Orion Press: 1965.

Brandeis, Irma, editor. *Discussions of The Divine Comedy*. D. C. Heath: 1961.

Brandeis, Irma, *The Ladder of Vision*. Chatto and Windus: 1960.

Charity, A. C., *Events and Their Afterlife: The Dialectics of Typology in the Bible and Dante*. Cambridge: 1966.

Eliot, T. S., "Dante" in *Selected Essays*. Harcourt, Brace: 1932.

Fergusson, Francis, *Dante*. Macmillan: 1966.

Freccero, John, editor. *Dante, A Collection of Critical Essays*. Prentice-Hall: 1965.

Musa, Mark, editor. *Essays on Dante*. Indiana University Press: 1964.

Snider, Denton J., *Dante's Inferno, A Commentary*. William H. Miner: 1892.

Strauss, Walter A., "Proust, Giotto, Dante." *Dante Studies* 96: 163-185.

Williams, Charles, *The Figure of Beatrice*. Noonday Press: 1961.

Aids to Reading the "Inferno"

Bodkin, Maud, *Archetypal Patterns in Poetry*. Vintage Books: 1958.

Dunbar, H. F., *Symbolism in Medieval Thought*. Oxford: 1929.

Vossler, Karl, *Medieval Culture: An Introduction to Dante and His Times*. Vols. 1 and 2. Harcourt, Brace: 1929.

Aeneas and Dante

David Thompson

In adapting the Ulysses story to depict his own spiritual autobiography, Dante plays Ulysses off against Aeneas. It might be well then, in conclusion, to inquire whether Aeneas also has a peculiar relevance to Dante's *itinerarium mentis*.

At first sight there appears to be more difference than similarity between the pagan hero and the Christian pilgrim. Asking the Sibyl for her help, Aeneas observes that others have descended to Avernus before him, and claims an equal right (*Aen.* 6. 119-23):

> si potuit manis accersere coniugis Orpheus
> Threicia fretus cithara fidibusque canoris,
> si fratrem Pollux alterna morte redemit
> itque reditque viam totiens. quid Thesea, magnum
> quid memorem Alciden? et mi genus ab Iove summo.

> [If Orpheus, relying on his Thracian lyre,
> was able to summon forth his wife's shade;
> if Pollux redeemed his brother, dying by turns,
> going back and forth so often—why mention Theseus,
> or mighty Hercules?—I too descend from Jove supreme.]

Dante also refers to his predecessors, but to make just the opposite point—he is not Prince Aeneas, nor was meant to be (*Inf.* 2. 13-15, 28-33):

> Tu dici che di Silvio lo parente
>   corruttibile ancora, ad immortale
>   secolo andò, e fu sensibilmente.
> . . . .
> Andovvi poi lo Vas d'elezione

per recarne conforto a quella fede

che è princípio alla via di salvazíone.

Ma io perchè venirvi? o chi'l concede?

Io non Enea, io non Paolo sono:

me degno a ciò nè io nè altri 'l crede.

[You say that the father of Silvius

still subject to corruption, went bodily

to the eternal world.

. . . .

Later the Chosen Vessel went there

to bring back comfort to that faith

which is the beginning of the way to salvation.

But I, why should I go there? Who grants it?

I am not Aeneas, I am not Paul:

neither I nor any one thinks me worthy of that.]

On the face of it, Dante's disclaimer seems obvious enough: confronted with the prospect of going to the other world while still in this life, he denies any similarity between himself and two heroes who had supposedly done just that. More specifically, Aeneas's *descensus ad inferos* would correspond to the first stage of the journey ahead of Dante, whereas Paul had told of a visit to Dante's celestial goal: "I knew a man in Christ above fourteen years ago (whether in the body, I cannot tell; or whether out of the body, I cannot tell: God knoweth;) such an one caught up to the third heaven. And I knew such a man . . . how that he was caught up into paradise, and heard unspeakable words, which it is not lawful for a man to utter" (II Corinthians 12: 2-4).

Paul's brief account (of what was generally taken to be his own experience) is certainly more suggestive than specific; but in Augustine and Aquinas's interpretations the *raptus Pauli* became the great exemplar of *visio intellectualis*, that is, the direct, unmediated, and indescribable knowledge of God which Dante himself attains at the end of his journey.[1]

As for Aeneas, Virgil's account of his descent was of course the major literary precedent for a physical journey to the other world by a man "in the body." But as we have seen, to a medieval reader the *Aeneid*, too, was more than just a history of physical events; and Bernard Silvestris's interpretation of Aeneas's *iter* may be directly relevant to the specific configuration of Dante's spiritual itinerary.

Glossing Aeneas's vision of Anchises near the end of book 5, Bernard says (27.25-28.1):

Monetur imagine patris ad inferos descendere visurus patrem ibi i. e. cogitatione quadam imaginaria quam de creatore habet. Non enim perfectam potest habere, cum deus incircumscriptus sit cogitatione. In qua ille monetur, ut ad mundana per cognitionem descendat, ibique videbit patrem quia quamvis in creatures non sit, cognitione tamen creaturarum cognoscitur. Ideoque iubetur apud inferos quaerere patrem licet celsa inhabitat.

[He is advised by an image of his father to descend to the infernal regions to see his father there; that is, by some imaginary thought which he has of the creator, for it cannot be perfect, since God is not circumscribed by thought. In it he is advised to descend for knowledge to worldly things, and there he will see his father; for although he is not in creatures, nevertheless he is known through a knowledge of creatures. And so he is ordered to seek his father among the infernal regions, although he dwells on high.]

Then in the introduction to his word-by-word commentary on book 6, Bernard discusses the descent of the soul in some detail. Initially, his explanations derive quite directly from Macrobius, who had observed that a *descensus ad inferos* could signify the soul's descent into the body:

antequam studium philosophiae circa naturae inquisitionem ad tantum vigoris adolesceret, qui per diversas gentes auctores constituendis sacris caerimoniarum fuerunt, aliud esse inferos negaverunt quam ipsa corpora, quibus inclusae animae carcerem foedum tenebris, horridum sordibus et cruore patiuntur.[2]

[Before the zeal of philosophers for the study of natural science grew to such vigorous proportions, those who were responsible for establishing religious rites among different races insisted that the lower regions were nothing more than the mortal bodies themselves, shut up in which souls suffered a horrible punishment in vile darkness and blood.]

Modifying Macrobius somewhat, Bernard begins as follows (28.15-18):

Antequam philosophia ad id vigoris adolesceret, theologiae professores aliud esse inferos quam corpora humana negaverunt, inferos autem corpora dixerunt eo quod in rebus nichil aliud inferius invenerunt.

[Before philosophy grew to its present vigorous proportions, the teachers of theology insisted that the lower regions were nothing more than human bodies, since among things they found nothing lower.]

Macrobius goes on in his next chapter to note that the Platonists gave *inferi* a more extensive meaning (or rather, several more extensive meanings, since three groups are discussed). Some called our perishable sublunary realm the infernal regions of the dead (9.6); and Bernard concludes with a reference to this "caducam et inferiorem regionem" (29.27).

However, the final and most interesting part of Bernard's introduction to book 6 seems to be his own invention.[3] There are, he explains, four kinds of *descensus ad inferos*. The first is every man's Fall (30.3-7):

Naturalis est nativitas hominis: ea enim naturaliter incipit anima esse in hac caduca regione atque ita inferis descendere atque ita a divinitate sua recedere et paulatim in vitium declinare et carnis voluptatibus assentire: sed iste omnium communis est.

[The natural descent is the birth of man; for by it the soul naturally begins to be in this perishable region and thus descend to the infernal world, departing thus from its divinity and gradually turning aside to vice and assenting to the pleasures of the flesh. But that is the common lot of all men.]

Most important in this context is the second sort of descent, made by Orpheus and Hercules (30.7-12):

Est autem alius virtutis qui fit dum sapiens aliquis ad mundana per considerationem descendit, non ut in eis intentionem ponat sed ut eorum cognita fragilitate eis abiectis ad invisibilia penitus se convertat et creaturarum cognitione creatorem evidentius agnoscat.

[There is, however, another descent, of virtue, which takes place when some wise man descends to worldly things for contemplation, not to concentrate on them, but so that having perceived their fragility he may cast them aside and turn himself completely to invisible things and through a knowledge of creatures may perceive the creator more clearly.]

Bernard later glosses *iter* as *ascensiones per creaturarum agnitiones*, explaining that the first step is from inanimate to insensible animate things, thence to irrational animals, rational animals ("i. e. ad homines," Bernard adds, with the optimism of an earlier age), the celestial orders, and finally to God: "Itaque per ordinem creaturarum itum est ad creatorem" (52.22: "And so through a succession of creatures one goes to the creator").[4]

Charles Singleton has glossed the three lights in the *Commedia* with the following statement by Aquinas: "There is a kind of vision for which the natural light of intellect suffices, such as the contemplation of invisible things according to the principles of reason; and the philosophers placed the highest happiness of man in this contemplation; there is yet another kind of contemplation to which man is raised by the light of faith . . . and there is that contemplation of the blessed in Heaven [*in patria*] to which the intellect is uplifted by the light of Glory"— which sometimes happens, as in Paul's case, to a man still in this life.[5] These three lights do not correspond to the tripartite division of the *Commedia*, for it is Beatrice who gives Dante wings for flight (*Par.* 10. 53-54), and his whole flight to God is a transhumanizing, a going beyond the human (*Par.* 1. 70: "trasumanar"), while his movement under Virgil's guidance was by the natural light of intellect.[6] *Inferno* and *Purgatorio* mark a first ontological stage, *Paradiso* a second.

In discussing man's threefold knowledge of divine things, Aquinas said: "prima est secundum quod homo naturali lumine rationis per creaturas in Dei cognitionem ascendit" (the first is when man, by the natural light of reason, rises through creatures to the knowledge of God)[7]— exactly the mediated, partial vision to which Bernard refers, vision that is not yet *facie ad faciem*. Thus, if Aquinas's whole formulation is a fair gloss upon the *Commedia*, Bernard's allegorized *Aeneid* assumes a striking resemblance to the Virgilian first stage of Dante's journey.

Virgil can lead Dante only so far: then Beatrice must take over. At this crucial point in the poem, as if to underline the parallelism between his own *iter* and that of Aeneas, Dante quotes from the climactic episode of *Aeneid* 6 (*Purg.* 30. 19-21):

> Tutti dicean: *Benedictus qui venis*,
> > e fior gittando di sopra e dintorno,
> > > *manibus o date lilia plenis*.

> [All were saying: *Benedictus qui venis*,
> > and, throwing flowers above and around,
> > > *manibus o date lilia plenis*.][8]

Christian and pagan: the one *iter* supersedes the other, but in so doing arises from and incorporates its predecessor.[9]

Before flying aloft to see God face to face, Dante undergoes a *descensus*, a *conversio* and an *ascensio*: he travels the same spiritual path along which the Sibyl had led Aeneas. Both journeys have the same pattern and the same basic epistemology. So despite his initial protestation, Dante becomes both an Enea and a Paolo, in quest of the heavenly *patria*, "quella Roma onde Cristo è romano" (*Purg.* 32. 102: "that Rome in which Christ is a Roman"). And it should be little cause for wonder if Bernard's mystic Virgil acts as his first guide, along that "cammino alto e silvestro" (*Inf.* 2. 142).

From *Dante's Epic Journeys* (1974) by David Thompson. Copyright © 1974 by The Johns Hopkins University Press. Reprinted with permission of The Johns Hopkins University Press.

Notes

All translations are by the author, unless otherwise indicated.

1. See Francis X. Newman, "St. Augustine's Three Visions and the Structure of the *Commedia*," *Modern Language Notes*, 82 (1967): 56-78.

2. *Commentarii in Somnium Scipionis*, ed. Iacobus Willis (Teubner: Leipzig, 1963), I, 10.9 (p. 43). The English version following is from *Commentary on the Dream of Scipio*, trans. William Harris Stahl (New York: Columbia University Press, 1952), p. 128.

3. Cf. Stanislaus Skimina, "De Bernardo Silvestri Vergilii Interprete," seorsum impressum ex *Commentationibus Vergilianis* (Cracow, 1930), 237-38: "Restat ut dicamus Bernardum, etiamsi aliorum libros exscriberet, quos quidem maxima libertate immutaret, multa addidisse quae eum ingeniosum atque inventionis vi praeditum fuisse ostendant." Skimina does observe, however, "Quorum nonnulla tam nova sunt adeoque praeter omnem opinionem accidunt, ut in incerto simus, utrum seriarum an iocosarum interpretationum loco numeranda sint."

4. Although Bernard's is not a Christianizing interpretation of the *Aeneid*, and there are obviously some elements in his commentary which would be difficult to square with Christian doctrine, he had good patristic sanction for the idea that pagans could know God through his creation. For example, in discussing the similarity between Platonism and Christianity, Augustine three times (*De civitate Dei* 8.6, 10, 12) cites Romans 1:19-20: "Quia quod notum est Dei, manifestum est in illis; Deus enim illis manifestavit. Invisibilia enim ipsius, a creatura mundi, per ea quae fatta sunt, intellecta, conspiciuntur; sempiterna quoque eius virtus, et divinitas."

5. Charles Singleton, *Dante Studies 2: Journey to Beatrice* (Baltimore: Johns Hopkins University Press, 1958), p. 15.

6. See Singleton, *Journey*, esp. pp. 26-31. A basically bipartite division of the poem is also suggested by Dante's use of classical mythology. See C. A. Robson, "Dante's Use in the *Divina Commedia* of the Medieval Allegories on Ovid," in *Centenary Essays on Dante*, by members of the Oxford Dante Society (Oxford: Clarendon Press, 1965), pp. 1-38.

7. Quoted by Singleton, *Journey*, 36, 23. The passage is also cited by Theodore Silverstein, "Dante and Vergil the Mystic," *Harvard Studies and Notes in Philology and Literature*, 14 (1932), p. 78.

8. Dante is adapting *Aen.* 6. 883: *manibus date lilia plenis* (give lilies with full hands).

9. Cf. Davis, *Dante and the Idea of Rome* (Oxford: Clarendon Press, 1957), p. 33: "Christ came, and Peter established the see of Rome, not to interrupt the tradition, but to fulfill it." Davis cites (p. 138) *Purg.* 30. 19-21 to illustrate Virgil's "dual role" as intermediary between the two Romes; but the historicity and historical importance of Virgil and Aeneas do not preclude allegorical significances, since in Dante's view a figure could be both historical and allegorical. The historical process is development, metamorphosis; and the same holds for a man's psychological progress. See *Purg.* 10. 124-26; *Par.* 1. 67-72; and Singleton, *Journey*, p. 28-29.

Dante's Knowledge of Florentine History[1]

John C. Barnes

For the purpose of this essay the term "history" includes pseudo-history, because without any doubt some of what passed for Florentine history in Dante's time was purely mythical. Dante briefly alludes to this in the fifteenth canto of *Paradiso*, where Cacciaguida is painting his idyllic picture of Florentine society in the late eleventh century and includes a glimpse of a Florentine matron in a domestic setting passing on a contemporary version of local history:

> l'altra, traendo a la rocca la chioma,
> favoleggiava con la sua famiglia
> d'i Troiani, di Fesule e di Roma.
> *(Paradiso*, XV. 124-6)

[Another, as she drew the threads from the distaff, would tell her household about the Trojans, and Fiesole, and Rome.]

In the interests of clarity, then, I shall begin by retelling the old tales that she would have been handing on.

I shall do so by summarizing a text known as *Chronica de Origine Civitatis* ["Chronicle about the City's Origin," the city being Florence], which was written in Latin in the first thirty years of the thirteenth century, or possibly at the end of the twelfth.[2] According to this text, the first ruler in Europe was Atlas, who, with the help of his astrologer Apollo, chose the best and healthiest site in Europe and there founded Europe's first city. This was Fiesole, which we know today as a small hill town five miles north of Florence, but was indeed an Etruscan and Roman city, much older than Florence. According to the legend Atlas and his wife Electra had three sons, of whom the eldest, Italus, succeeded his father and gave his name to Italy. Meanwhile the second son, Dardanus, the first soldier and the first man to train a horse to be ridden, went east in search of fresh territory, and founded a city on the Asiatic shore of the Hellespont which he named after himself (Dardania) but which was subsequently renamed Troy after Dardanus's grandson Troius.

According to Florentine legend, then, the city of Troy was a daughter of the city of Fiesole. Similarly, the city of Rome was a daughter of the city of Troy. This part of the legend is more familiar to us since it is the central story told in Virgil's *Aeneid*. As retold in *Chronica de Origine Civitatis*, it begins in the time of Troius's grandson Laumedon, whose daughter Hesiona was abducted by Talamon, a companion of Hercules, while Troy was destroyed by Hercules himself. Laumedon's son Priam rebuilt Troy and married Hecuba, who gave him many offspring of both sexes including Hector and Paris. Paris it was who avenged the events of his grandfather's generation by going to Greece and abducting Helen, the wife of King Menelaus, and destroying Menelaus's city (Sparta). But this led to further retaliatory action, the final destruction of Troy (by Menelaus's brother Agamemnon), and the long, eventful voyage of twenty shiploads of survivors led by Aeneas, eventually disembarking on the west coast of Italy. Aeneas married Lavinia, daughter of one of the Italian kings, and after many generations their descendants founded Rome. This is how Rome was a daughter of Troy. The story told in *Chronica de Origine Civitatis* continues with the beginnings of Christianity, the coming of St Peter to Rome and the foundation there of St Peter's basilica. At the time of that foundation Rome was protected from devils by large quantities of incense; the smell of the incense drifted northwards, and since the Latin word for "incense" is *thus* the area to the north of Rome was named Tuscany.

Not only was Rome the daughter of Troy and ultimately Fiesole's granddaughter: Florence was a daughter of Rome and thus a great-granddaughter of Fiesole. The starting-point for this part of the legend is the (historic) conspiracy of Catiline, who planned a revolution in 65 BC but was compelled to flee from Rome two years later during

Cicero's consulship. According to *Chronica de Origine Civitatis*, Catiline settled in Fiesole, making Fiesole an anti-Roman city, a characteristic it retained permanently thereafter. Although Catiline was killed in the Battle of Pistoia (in 62 BC: that much is established fact), the Roman authorities were determined to destroy Fiesole for its resistance to Rome, and sent an army to besiege the Tuscan city, an army which encamped on the site where Florence was later to be founded. During the siege the Fiesolans killed the Roman commander, Florinus, at night by stealth. When Fiesole eventually capitulated, Florence was founded in order to ensure that Fiesole would never be rebuilt. It was called Florence for a number of reasons, one of which was that it marked the spot where Florinus had been slain, another being that it was colonized by the flower (*flos, floris*) of the Roman nobility. It was also topographically modelled on Rome, with fine walls "ad similitudinem urbis Romae" ["in the likeness of the city of Rome"] and a Capitol and various other buildings "sicut erat in urbe romana" ["as it was in the city of Rome"].[3]

Thus Florence was quintessentially a Roman city where Fiesole had been quintessentially an anti-Roman city. Of course such a statement is still cast in legendary terms, and the legend would have originated much closer to the twelfth century than to the first century BC. In fact Nicolai Rubinstein has shown that it would have originated in the twelfth century itself as an expression of what he calls "the beginnings of political thought in Florence," at the time when Florence began to emerge as an autonomous city-state from the feudal structure inherited from the Roman Empire.[4] It was not uncommon for medieval nations and cities to trace their origins to Roman or Trojan ancestors, but Charles Davis has observed that no other Italian town made so much out of its Roman connections as "the aggressive Tuscan metropolis of Florence."[5] So, a few generations after *Chronica de Origine Civitatis* was written, it is not surprising to find Dante, in his *Convivio* (I. 3. 4), referring to the city of his birth as "la bellissima e famosissima figlia di Roma" ["Rome's most beautiful and famous daughter"]; nor is it surprising to read in his seventh epistle (VII. 25) of Rome as the city "que ad ymaginem suam atque similitudinem fecit illam [Florence]" ["which made her (Florence) in her own image and after her own likeness"]. This pseudo-historical background also casts light on a couple of lines in the sixth canto of *Paradiso*, where the soul of Justinian says that the Roman eagle treated Fiesole harshly:

> a quel colle
> sotto 'l qual tu nascesti parve amaro.
> (*Paradiso*, VI. 53-4)

[to that hill beneath which you were born it showed itself bitter.]

This is a reference to Rome's legendary destruction of Fiesole in the aftermath of Catiline's conspiracy.

Chronica de Origine Civitatis is anonymous, and it is unclear whether the version that has come down to us was compiled all at once from various remote sources, or whether it is partly based on earlier compilations which have been lost. As the evidence stands, however, the text is quite a considerable compilation, taking material from at least half-a-dozen sources, some of them ancient and some less so. The earliest legendary material appears to derive from the *Fabulae* attributed to the first-century Spanish writer Hyginus, who was a friend of Ovid's. Virgil's *Aeneid* was a source, and so was Servius's commentary on the *Aeneid*. So too, perhaps, were the accounts of the Trojan War attributed to Dares of Phrygia and Dictys of Crete. The *Naturalis Historia* of Pliny the Elder may also be a source (directly or indirectly), as may the work of Livy. Less ancient sources certainly include the *Historia Romana* of Paul the Deacon (from which whole sentences are lifted) and the work of Paulus Orosius, probably the *Etymologies* of Isidore of Seville, and possibly St Augustine's *De Civitate Dei*.[6]

Chronica de Origine Civitatis remained a well-known work throughout the thirteenth century and beyond. Its contents were known to Dante and to other cultured Florentines, such as Brunetto Latini, and in the early part of the next century Giovanni Villani used it as one of the many sources of his great work, the *Nuova cronica*.[7] Another index of its popularity lies in the fact that numerous early manuscripts survive in which it—or a version of it—is contained. But it was a characteristic of the more popular medieval chronicles that they tended to be taken over as public property and revised with new emphases. *Chronica de Origine Civitatis* is a case in point: at least five redactions of it survive, two in Latin (the second evidently written in 1264) and three in Tuscan.[8] One of the Tuscan versions, written between 1284 and 1330 and known as the *Libro fiesolano* ["The Book of Fiesole"], adapts and enlarges the original quite drastically.[9] One small but significant alteration is seen in the fact that whereas in what we have to take as the original version Italus and Dardanus consult their unnamed oracle before Dardanus departs to found Troy, in the *Libro fiesolano* they consult Mars, thus implicating the influence of the god of war in Troy's foundation:[10] we shall see the significance of this shortly. More dramatically, the *Libro fiesolano* has Catiline survive the Battle of Pistoia and become the ancestor of the Florentine Uberti family (of which Farinata was a member), via his son Uberto Cesare, who—the *Libro fiesolano* tells us—was readmitted to Rome with great honour after Catiline's death and subsequently ruled Florence in Rome's name, after which his son, Uberto Catellina, and other descendants ruled the area around Florence evidently with some degree of permanence.[11] Thus the *Libro fiesolano* seems to have been concocted to provide an ancient genealogy for the Uberti family, who even after their exile from Florence in 1267 still exercised great influence on Tuscan affairs.

According to *Chronica de Origine Civitatis* and its various revised versions, since Florence's foundation coincided with the destruction of Fiesole, the new city was populated partly by colonists from Rome and partly by the former inhabitants of Fiesole, who had been left homeless.[12] This is the background to a famous passage in the fifteenth canto of Dante's *Inferno*, where Brunetto Latini three times makes a highly "racist" distinction between the two components of Florence's demographic make-up, but not without first implying that the Roman element has actually been obliterated, or almost obliterated, by the Fiesolan. He appears to refer to the *whole* of Florence's population—or at least the whole of it except Dante—as

> quello ingrato popolo maligno
> che discese da Fiesole, ab antico,
> e tène ancor del monte e del macigno.
> (Inferno, XV. 61-3)

[that thankless, malignant people, who of old came down from Fiesole, and still smack of the mountain and the rock].

He then (lines 65-6) contrasts the "lazzi sorbi" ["bitter sorb-trees"] (the population of Florence) with the "dolce fico" ["sweet fig"] (Dante, in his solitary splendour); and replicates that contrast in the images of (lines 73-4) the "bestie fesulane" ["Fiesolan beasts"] and the "pianta" ["plant"], and again (lines 75-8) in the images of "letame" ["dung"] and

> la semente santa
> di quei Roman' che vi rimaser quando
> fu fatto il nido di malizia tanta.
> (Inferno, XV. 76-8)

[the holy seed of those Romans who remained there when the nest of so much wickedness was built (that is, when Florence was founded).]

The implication seems to be that the exiled Dante is the only—or virtually the only—surviving representative of the Roman element of the original settlement.

The remainder of the narrative of *Chronica de Origine Civitatis* consists essentially of three events. The first is the city's (fictitious) destruction by Totila, the king of the Ostrogoths who did in fact besiege (though not destroy) Florence in 542, and who in medieval sources was commonly confused with Attila the Hun, "the Scourge of God" ("quel' Atila che fu flagello in terra": *Inferno*, XII. 134). In all versions of the *Chronica* Totila succeeded in destroying Florence only by extreme treachery. This event was predictably accompanied by the rebuilding of Fiesole. The second of the remaining events was the (equally fictitious) rebuilding of Florence by the Romans, smaller than the original city ("muris giraverunt modico circuitu") according to the *Chronica* though larger ("maggiore e piú forte che prima") according to the *Libro fiesolano*,[13] but in either case stronger than before and again modelled on the topographical lay-out of Rome, this time Christian Rome. According to the *Libro fiesolano* Florence was freshly colonized by noble Roman citizens on this occasion. The third and final event arose from the fact that Fiesole was not destroyed when Florence was allegedly rebuilt, so that an "inimicitia maxima" ["great hostility"] grew up between the two cities,[14] which were too close to each other for them both to prosper. This led to the final destruction of Fiesole by the Florentines (a historical event which we can situate in 1125) and a fresh wave of Fiesolan refugees moving into Florence. This is the point at which the *Chronica* ends: its author's intention seems to have been to account for everything that preceded the "modern" history of Florence. And his deeper objective was to formulate what today would be called nationalist propaganda, the function of the legends he assembled being to dignify a petty local rivalry between Florence and Fiesole which in point of historical fact could not have been very old when Fiesole was destroyed in 1125. Since, as Rubinstein demonstrates, such political propaganda could only have come into existence after the death of Countess Matilda of Tuscany in 1115,[15] we may note in passing that it seems anachronistic for Dante to picture his Florentine matron telling the stories of "the

Trojans, and Fiesole, and Rome" in 1091, the year of Cacciaguida's birth.

Dante makes occasional references to the later events narrated by the *Chronica*. In *Inferno* XIII (lines 148-9), where the topic is Florence, he mentions "quei cittadin' che poi la rifondarno/ sopra 'l cener che d'Atila rimase" ["those citizens who afterwards rebuilt it on the ashes left by Attila"]. In Book II of *De Vulgari Eloquentia* (II. 6. 4) he wishes to convey the extreme treachery by which Charles de Valois brought about the Florentine crisis of 1301-2; and he does so by calling Charles de Valois a second Totila ("Totila secundus"). In his sixth epistle, where he warns the Florentines of the dire consequences of resisting Emperor Henry VII, he threatens them with a second destruction of their city (VI. 24): "O miserrima Fesulanorum propago, et iterum iam punita barbaries!" ["O most wretched offshoot of Fiesole! O barbarians punished now a second time!"].

If we bundle all the versions of *Chronica de Origine Civitatis* together as a single chronicle, we may now move on to the second surviving Florentine chronicle, which is the first of two texts entitled *Gesta Florentinorum* ["The Deeds of the Florentines"].[16] This work is not anonymous, though almost the only information we have about its author is the paradoxical fact that his name was Sanzanome (which translates as "without a name"); his chronicle also tells us that he took part in Florence's war for the conquest of Semifonte in 1202 and the destruction of Castel Montalto in 1207.[17] He appears to have written his *Gesta Florentinorum* in the 1230s. By then it was over a hundred years since the destruction of Fiesole, an event which had proved a turning-point in Florentine history as the first significant expansionist conquest by Florence in a long sequence of such victories that had transformed the city into a major player on the Tuscan stage. It was because the destruction of Fiesole had come to be perceived as a crucial turning-point that *Chronica de Origine Civitatis* had ended with that event: its author's purpose had been to recount the *pre*-history of contemporary Florence—hence the title, "Chronicle about the City's *Ori*-

gin." From this point of view Sanzanome's work complements its predecessor perfectly, in that, after a very brief preamble summarizing the story from the death of Catiline to the rebuilding of Fiesole by Totila (which it derives from the *Chronica*), it begins with the second and last destruction of Fiesole in 1125 and brings the narration down to 1231. It is in fact explicit in viewing 1125 as the beginning of modern Florence: "A destructione [. . .] Fesularum modernis temporibus facta victoriarum sumatur initium" ["The beginning of (Florence's) victories should be taken as dating from the destruction of Fiesole achieved in modern times"].[18] But that is about as far as any connection between the two works goes: although they are both written in Latin and both products of the same militant patriotic outlook, they are very different in nature. Sanzanome's *Gesta Florentinorum* proceeds strictly year by year, and records only Florence's military campaigns against feudal castles in the *contado* and the overcoming of other obstacles to Florentine expansion (together with some reverses in the city's fortunes). In an amateur sort of way, it is also a text with greater literary pretensions than its predecessor, taking more care over its sentence structure and frequently providing its protagonists with eloquent disquisitions in direct speech, which among other things emphasize again Florence's Roman origins.

We do not know of any sources from which Sanzanome drew his post-1125 material. It seems obvious that his own experience would have been his most important source; otherwise, he may have had access to records, official or otherwise, that are now lost.

We have seen that Dante knew the content of *Chronica de Origine Civitatis*, but it is not clear that he derived it directly from any of the versions of that work that have come down to us. In the case of Sanzanome, though, it has been claimed that verbal parallels prove direct derivation. It has been suggested, for example, that the reference to Florence that we have already quoted from Book I of the *Convivio* (I. 3. 4), as "la bellissima e famosissima figlia di Roma" ["Rome's most beautiful and famous daughter"] elaborates Sanzanome's statement,

"Nobilissima civitas florentina [. . .] patrum est huc usque secuta vestigia" ["The most noble city of Florence has so far followed in the footsteps of its fathers"]. It has also been suggested that Dantesque expressions derive directly from a sentence about the Fiesolans at the beginning of *Gesta Florentinorum*. Sanzanome writes, of Fiesole: "Erat [. . .] super asperum montem sita et undique circumdata muris et saxis ultra modum appositis in eisdem" ["It sat on a harsh mountain and was surrounded on all sides by walls and an enormous number of rocks placed against them"]. This, it has been claimed, could possibly be the inspiration behind the lines in *Inferno* XV which are also quoted above:

> quello ingrato popolo maligno
> che discese da Fiesole, ab antico,
> e tène ancor del monte e del macigno.
> *(Inferno*, XV. 61-3)

[that thankless, malignant people, who of old came down from Fiesole, and still smack of the mountain and the rock].[19]

But this evidence seems far from conclusive, in which case it perhaps remains wiser not to insist on a verbal debt to Sanzanome's chronicle on Dante's part.

On the other hand, however he acquired the information, Dante's knowledge of Florentine history does coincide with the content of Sanzanome's chronicle. Since Sanzanome is so exclusively concerned with Florentine expansion into the *contado*, the point at which that coincidence shows itself is the middle of *Paradiso* XVI, where Cacciaguida talks about the same thing, though from the point of view of the city as the recipient of immigrants from the vanquished towns and castles. In lines 49-66 Cacciaguida mentions seven places which were outside the Florentine state in the early twelfth century but within it in Dante's day, and thus sources of immigration into the city in the twelfth and thirteenth centuries. Four of these, and their respective subjugations, are covered by Sanzanome's *Gesta Florentinorum*: Montebuono Castle, the seat of the Buondelmonti family in the Greve Valley to the south of the city, destroyed in 1135; Acone, a village about twelve miles east-north-east of Florence in the Sieve Valley, which had been sustained by the neighbouring Monte di Croce Castle, destroyed by the Florentines in 1154; Figline, a town in the upper Arno Valley, south-east of Florence, which was totally destroyed in 1168 (though Sanzanome says 1170); and Semifonte, a strong fortress in the Elsa Valley, south-west of Florence, captured and destroyed in 1202 after a four-year siege.[20] Furthermore, it is almost certain that a fifth of these locations was originally covered by Sanzanome's *Gesta*. To the best of my knowledge only one early manuscript of the work survives,[21] but it appears that there must have been at least one other because the scribe of the surviving manuscript leaves gaps which seem to correspond to missing pages in the parent manuscript or some other obstruction to reproducing its content. One of these gaps eliminates the years between 1208 and 1219, and that period was believed to have included, in 1209, Florence's acquisition of Montemurlo Castle, northwest of Florence between Pistoia and Prato. (In fact Montemurlo was not sold to Florence until 1254, but the fourteenth-century chronicler Giovanni Villani, who used Sanzanome's *Gesta* as one of his many sources, still thought the event had taken place in 1209.[22])

Of the seven places mentioned by Cacciaguida, then, only two remain to be accounted for by some source other than Sanzanome's *Gesta:* Campi, a village in the Bisenzio Valley, about nine miles north-west of Florence, and Certaldo, twenty-nine miles south-west of Florence in the Elsa Valley. Since Dante knew the extent of the Florentine state in his own day, and since he knew the pattern of Florentine expansion in the previous couple of centuries narrated by Sanzanome, he could have worked out for himself that Campi and Certaldo were two other places that had been absorbed into the state between Cacciaguida's day and his own.

In our chronological itinerary we are close to another turning-point in Florentine history, the split of the citizenry into the Guelf and Ghibelline factions, supposedly caused by the murder of Buondelmonte de' Buondelmonti in 1216. But I defer any further mention of that, because the lacuna in *Gesta Florentinorum* between 1208 and 1219 makes it impossible to say whether or not Sanzanome, with his apparently exclusive interest in expansionist conquests, permitted himself to deal with even such an important internal matter as the Buondelmonte murder.

If—once again—all the versions of *Chronica de Origine Civitatis* are reckoned as one chronicle, we have now summarily covered two of the surviving chronicles of Florence which were written before Dante left his home town for the last time in 1301. Two others remain to be considered, making a total of four such chronicles altogether. But before we proceed to the third it will be advantageous to look briefly at a text which is not a chronicle but looms large in the literary tradition that Dante looked back on, *Li Livres dou tresor* by Brunetto Latini, which Brunetto wrote in France, and in French, while he was in exile from Florence between 1260 and 1266.[23]

Although we are proceeding chronologically as far as the writers are concerned, the point of mentioning Brunetto's *Tresor* takes us back to the legendary foundation of Florence by the Romans in the first century BC. It will be recalled that the *Libro fiesolano* implicates the influence of Mars in the foundation of Troy by having Italus and Dardanus consult the god of war before Dardanus ventured forth to Phrygia. Medieval writers were also aware that Mars was the presiding deity of ancient Rome, Troy's daughter; indeed the Romans themselves had made Mars the father of their city's founders, Romulus and Remus.[24] In both cases the underlying idea was presumably to stress the warlike nature of the city in question and of its people, the implication being that they were also destined to be victorious in warfare and thus to dominate other cities and nations. In due course Mars was similarly associated with the foundation of Florence, and the point of mentioning

Brunetto Latini is that he is the first writer in whom that association is evident.

Chronica de Origine Civitatis had said that Florence was founded on the site of a village called Camartia ("villa Camartiae"), without further comment.[25] Brunetto, in his survey of world history (*Tresor*, I. 37. 2), interprets this toponym as deriving from the name of Mars: "Sachés que la place de tiere ou Florence est fu jadis apelee chiés Mars, c'est a dire maisons de batailles; car Mars, ki est une des vii. planetes, est apelés deus de batailles, ensi fu il aourés anciennement" ["You should know that the piece of land where Florence now is was formerly called Head of Mars, that is, the house of battles, for Mars, which is one of the seven planets, is called God of Battles, and thus was he called and revered in olden times"]. Brunetto continues (§3): "Por ce n'est il mie merveille se li Florentin sont tozjors en guerre et en descort, car celui planete regne sor aus" ["For this reason it is not surprising if the Florentines are always at war and in discord, for that planet rules over them"].[26] In other words, the warlike influence of Mars has had not only the positive effect of making Florence a successful military power, but also the baleful, negative effect of internal warfare, between the Guelf and Ghibelline factions. Dante is very much of the same opinion as Brunetto on this point. In *Inferno* XIII (143-4) he has a character refer to Florence as "la città che nel Batista/ mutò il primo patrone" ["the city that changed her first patron for the Baptist"—the first patron having been Mars]. And the speaker continues (lines 144-5): "ond' ei per questo/ sempre con l'arte sua la farà trista" ["on which account he (Mars) with his art (war) will ever make her (Florence) sorrowful"].

Rather than getting sidetracked into Dante's interpretation of history, I move on to the third of our four chronicles, though it has the distinction of being a chronicle that does not exist. The fourteenth-century Lucchese chronicler Tolomeo of Lucca says that one of his sources was a work called *Gesta Florentinorum*.[27] Modern scholarship has been unable to unearth this work, which remains anonymous; but the fact that various other fourteenth-century compilers also used it has made it possible for the lost *Gesta Florentinorum* to be reconstructed, by Bernhard Schmeidler.[28] It seems that it was in Tuscan, though that does not prevent it having been a translation of a still earlier version in Latin. The identity of titles may suggest that this *Gesta Florentinorum* has something to do with the work of Sanzanome; but it does not. The two texts are radically different. Whereas Sanzanome's chronicle focuses almost exclusively on Florence's Tuscan conquests and gives quite detailed accounts of some of the campaigns with a tendency towards rhetorical elevation, the anonymous *Gesta* is a far leaner and plainer record of a much more varied selection of events, beginning in the year 1080 and (in Schmeidler's reconstruction) continuing the record to 1278:[29] indeed this work might be seen as the kind of seed out of which Giovanni Villani's great chronicle was to grow in the following century.

It is the anonymous *Gesta Florentinorum*, then, that contained the earliest known account of the Buondelmonte murder in 1216 and its supposed consequence, the division of the citizenry into the Guelf and Ghibelline factions. The lost work also chronicled quite carefully the fluctuating fortunes of the two factions in subsequent decades, with the periodic expulsion from the city and readmission to the city of each of them in turn. The democratic interlude (the *primo popolo*) between 1250 and 1260 was highlighted in the anonymous *Gesta*, together with its resounding military successes, ending, however, with the dramatic defeat by Ghibelline Siena in the Battle of Montaperti in 1260. Florence's revenge on the Sienese, at Colle di Val d'Elsa in 1269, was also recorded. The narrative included several references to Count Guido Guerra VI and an adequate account of the constitutional novelty in 1266 when two Jovial Friars from Bologna, Catalano dei Malavolti and Loderingo degli Andalò, had jointly occupied the post of *podestà* in Florence and created the short-lived council of thirty-six *buoni uomini*. And, earlier than any of that, this chronicle put the story of twelfth-century Florence's territorial expansion into some sort of perspective by telling how in 1185 Emperor Frederick Barbarossa had stripped Florence of all the territory it had acquired outside the city walls, and how three years later by imperial decree the territory within a ten-mile radius of the city had been restored to Florentine jurisdiction, so that expansion beyond that limit had had to be started all over again. The anonymous *Gesta* also recorded two campaigns against Figline in 1223 and 1252 that had not been mentioned by Sanzanome.

The connections between Dante and the events I have picked out from the anonymous *Gesta Florentinorum* are not difficult to discern. The Buondelmonte murder and its consequences are mentioned more than once in the *Comedia*, most notably by Cacciaguida in *Paradiso* XVI:

> La casa di che nacque il vostro fleto,
> per lo giusto disdegno che v'à morti,
> e pose fine al vostro viver lieto,
>
> era onorata, essa e i suoi consorti:
> o Bondelmonte, quanto mal fuggisti
> le nozze sue per gli altrui conforti!
>
> Molti serebber lieti, che son tristi,
> se Dio t'avesse conceduto ad Ema
> la prima volta ch'a città venisti.
>
> *(Paradiso*, XVI. 136-44)

[The house of which was born your weeping (the house of Amidei, which was offended by Buondelmonte's termination of his engagement to his Amidei fiancée; and the "you" here is plural—you modern Florentines), by reason of its just resentment which has slain you (thirteenth-century Florentines) and put an end to your glad living, was honoured (in the early twelfth century), both itself and its consorts. O Buondelmonte, how ill for you that you did fly from its nuptials at the promptings of another. Many would be happy who now are sad (because of eighty-four years of factional strife) if God had committed you to the Ema the first time you came to the city! (that is, if God had *drowned* you in the Ema, a river that the Buondelmonti had to cross when they immigrated to Florence from their castle at Montebuono).]

The fluctuating fortunes of the Guelfs and Ghibellines in Florence are memorably alluded to in *Inferno* X, where Farinata degli Uberti, the leader of the Ghibellines until his death in 1264, taunts the Guelf Dante with the fact that he (Farinata) was twice responsible for the expulsion of the Guelfs; to which Dante retorts that the Guelfs always managed to return from their exile, which is more than the Ghibellines did (lines 46-51). The Battle of Montaperti is another event that crops up several times in Dante's poem, including Canto XI of *Purgatorio*, where Dante the character is told that Provenzan Salvani was lord of Siena

> quando fu distrutta
> la rabbia fiorentina, che soperba
> fu a quel punto.
> *(Purgatorio*, XI. 112-14)

[when the rage of Florence was destroyed, which was proud then.]

The return match at Colle di Val d'Elsa in 1269 is mentioned—again from the Sienese point of view—by Sapia of Siena only two cantos later:

> Eran li cittadin' miei presso a Colle
> in campo giunti con loro aversari [. . .].
> Rotti fuòr quivi e vòlti nelli amari
> passi di fuga.
> *(Purgatorio*, XIII.115-19)

[My townsmen had joined battle near Colle with their adversaries (. . .): there were they routed and turned back in the bitter steps of flight.]

Guido Guerra VI is one of the violent against nature named in Canto XVI of *Inferno* (lines 34-9)—Dante expresses great respect for him (lines 58-60). And the *bolgia* of the hypocrites (*Inferno*, XXIII. 103-8) is where we find Catalano and Loderingo, who had shared the office of *podestà* in Florence when Dante was one year old.

The fourth and last chronicle to be considered, and the earliest extant Florentine chronicle which was originally drafted in the vernacular, is anonymous but known as the chronicle of Pseudo-Brunetto Latini, because it was once erroneously attributed to Brunetto.[30] It spans the years between 1002, when Henry II was elected Emperor, and 1300.[31] The autograph manuscript, however, has a final paragraph in a different hand which continues the narrative down to 1303; and there are earlier passages that must have been written in 1303 or later, which makes it questionable whether this chronicle could have been available before Dante left Florence in 1301—though in an earlier version perhaps it could have been. The narrative contained in this chronicle is interrupted by a large gap between the years 1249 and 1285; and since Dante was twenty in 1285 and would not by that time need chronicles to inform himself about current events, it is the part before the gap that concerns us here. This early part of the Pseudo-Brunetto chronicle proceeds by elaborating a non-Florentine work, Martin of Troppau's *Chronicon Pontificum et Imperatorum* ["Chronicle of the Popes and the Emperors"],[32] with a Florentine slant, interpolating material that is fundamentally parallel to the anonymous *Gesta Florentinorum*, but at times much more detailed.

The Pseudo-Brunetto chronicle may cast some light on a point in *Paradiso* XVI that we have already visited. It will be recalled that two places mentioned by Cacciaguida as regrettably having become part of the Florentine state since his lifetime are Campi and Certaldo (line 50). And Pseudo-Brunetto, in his coverage of the destruction of Semifonte Castle (which is near Certaldo) in 1202, is the first to state that this castle belonged to the Counts of Certaldo (to which it may be added that the Counts of Certaldo were a branch of one of the biggest feudal families in Tuscany, the Conti Alberti).[33] This may be sufficient to explain why Dante singles out Certaldo as a place that Florence has cause to regret incorporating into its *contado*.

Otherwise, the Pseudo-Brunetto chronicle does not have a great deal to add to what earlier texts could have taught Dante about Florentine history—with one outstanding exception: it does give an extraordinarily full account of the Buondelmonte murder in 1216 and its consequences.[34] It begins the story at an earlier point than other sources; and it begins it in Campi, which, as in the case of Certaldo, may explain why Dante singles out Campi as a place that Florence has cause to regret incorporating into its *contado*. According to Pseudo-Brunetto, in 1215 (*calculus florentinus*) Messer Mazzingo Tegrimi de' Mazzinghi invited other Florentine aristocrats, including Buondelmonte, to his residence at Campi (about nine miles north-west of Florence), but at dinner a brawl broke out between them, during which Buondelmonte stabbed Oddo Arrighi in the arm. After their return to Florence Oddo Arrighi and his kinsmen, who were to become the leading Ghibellines, decided to make peace with Buondelmonte, and that this peace should be sealed by a marriage between Buondelmonte and a girl of the Amidei family whose mother was Oddo Arrighi's sister. This, we read, was the background to Buondelmonte's first engagement. But, the narrative continues, Madonna Gualdrada, the wife of Messer Forese de' Donati (not the one in *Purgatorio* XXIII, who lived about three generations later), taunted Buondelmonte with cowardice in being manipulated by the powerful proto-Ghibelline families and persuaded him to marry her daughter instead . . . and the rest is pseudo-history. It may well be, then, specifically to Madonna Gualdrada that Dante refers in *Paradiso*, XVI. 141, where Cacciaguida says Buondelmonte broke his first engagement "per gli altrui conforti" ["at the promptings of another"].

The proto-Ghibellines' reaction to the broken engagement, Pseudo-Brunetto continues, was to discuss the situation at a meeting held in the church of S. Maria sopra Porta: various suggestions were made, such as beating Buondelmonte with a stick or disfiguring his face; but the decisive contribution came from Mosca de' Lamberti with his famous phrase "Capo à cosa fatta," as Dante puts it in *Inferno*, XXVIII.107— or, in the words of Pseudo-Brunetto's autograph, "Cosa fatta cappa à,"[35] the sense being in either case "No half-measures, which will only lead to retaliation: a completed job is required." In his account of the actual murder, on Easter morning (10 April 1316), Pseudo-Brunetto is the first writer to locate it by the statue of Mars at the end of the Ponte Vecchio, thus—possibly—completing the background to Dante's view of the half-ruined statue as blighting Florentine life with a continuing influence of Mars, engendering belligerence among the citizens. Dante mentions the statue in *Inferno* XIII:

> e se non fosse che 'n sul passo d'Arno
> rimane ancor di lui alcuna vista,
>   quei cittadin' che poi la rifondarno
> sopra 'l cener che d'Atila rimase,
> avrebber fatto lavorar indarno.
>   (*Inferno*, XIII. 146-50)

[and were it not that at the passage of the Arno some semblance of him (Mars) still remains, those citizens who afterwards rebuilt it (Florence) on the ashes left by Attila would have laboured in vain.]

Here the presence of the statue is, superstitiously, a condition of Florence's survival. But in *Paradiso* XVI its significance becomes positively pagan:

> Ma conveniasi, a quella petra scema
> che guarda 'l ponte, che Firenza fesse
> vittima nella sua pace postrema.
>   (*Paradiso*, XVI. 145-7)

[But it was fitting that Florence, in her last peace, should offer a victim to that mutilated stone which guards the bridge.]

Pseudo-Brunetto has a very similar view to Dante of the significance of Buondelmonte's murder: "In quello giorno si cominciò la struzione di Firenze" ["That day Florence's destruction began"].[36] And in recounting the division of the citizenry into Guelfs and Ghibellines, he makes the interesting comment that the Ghibellines called themselves the imperial party, even though they were well-known as Paterine or Cathar heretics ("e' Ghibellini s'apellarono Parte d'Inperio, avegnadio che' Ghibellini fossero publici paterini"). He also says a little later, "Il'una parte è Guelfa traditori e l'altra sono Ghibellini paterini" ["one faction consists of Guelf traitors and the other of Ghibelline Paterines"].[37] This may not be unconnected with the fact that three of the four heretics identified in *Inferno* X are Ghibellines.[38]

A last point of interest in Pseudo-Brunetto's passage about the beginnings of Florentine factionalism is that Campi again appears as a place that Florentines might think of with heavy hearts. After Buondelmonte's murder the proto-Ghibelline families gathered at Campi but were treacherously attacked and defeated there by the Buondelmonti and other proto-Guelf families. And it was from Campi that the leading families brought their conflict into the city itself.

My examination of Dante's literary and not-so-literary precursors in the specific area of Florentine historiography is now complete, but we still need to ask ourselves—briefly—the very important question of whether the surviving written sources account fully for Dante's knowledge of Florentine history. And we quickly realize that they do not. A number of awkward questions remain. How, for instance, did Dante know that the della Bella family had been elevated to the aristocracy by Margrave Ugo (*Paradiso*, XVI. 127-30)? How did he know that the Caponsacchi family had originally immigrated from Fiesole (*Paradiso*, XVI. 121-6)? How did he know about Bellincione Berti de' Ravignani (*Paradiso*, XV. 112-14; XVI. 94-9), who, to the displeasure of his son-in-law Ubertino Donati, married one of his daughters to a member of the Adimari family (*Paradiso*, XVI. 115-20), and another of whose daughters, "la buona Gualdrada" ["the good Gualdrada"—not the bad Gualdrada who pressed Buondelmonte to marry *her* daughter], was to become a grandmother of Guido Guerra VI (*Inferno*, XVI. 37)? How did Dante know that in the first half of the twelfth century the Florentine knighthood had been only a fifth of the size that it had reached by 1300 (*Paradiso*, XVI. 46-8) or that the forty families he identifies in the second half of *Paradiso* XVI (lines 82-147) had been prominent in the early twelfth century? Turning to the thirteenth century, how did Dante know about Iacopo Rusticucci and Tegghiaio Aldobrandi degli Adimari, mentioned together in *Inferno* VI (lines 79-80) and encountered together in *Inferno* XVI (lines 40-5)? How did he know that Tesauro de' Beccheria had been executed by the Florentines (*Inferno*, XXXII. 119-20; the event took place in 1258), or that Bocca degli Abati had betrayed the Florentine army in the Battle of Montaperti (*Inferno*, XXXII. 79-81)? How did he know about the political prominence of Farinata degli Uberti, and specifically about his role in saving Florence from destruction at the Council of Empoli later in 1260 (*Inferno*, X. 91-3)? How did he know about the treachery of Gianni de' Soldanieri (*Inferno*, XXXII. 121), who in 1266 betrayed the Ghibelline faction, to which he belonged, siding with the *popolo*, by whom the Ghibellines were exiled?

To all these questions there would appear to be two possible answers: either the information reached him by word of mouth or he read it in sources that have been lost. It does not seem implausible that the information about the thirteenth century reached him by oral tradition: it would be analogous to our knowledge of the sinking of SS *Titanic*, or of Lindbergh's first solo flight across the Atlantic, or of the conquest of Everest. Admittedly, Dante lived before the age of school history lessons as we know them and before the age of mass media, and even before the age of the printed word; but on the other hand we are here referring to his knowledge of Florentine affairs, not world affairs; and if he can picture a Florentine matron telling the story of the Trojans and Fiesole and Rome, *we* can surely picture *him* being told the story of Montaperti in far greater detail than surfaces in his poem. But since Dante also lived several centuries before the invention of the tape-recorder, we shall never have any direct evidence of oral tradition during his lifetime.

It might be tempting to imagine that Dante had access to all sorts of written sources that we can no longer locate;[39] but I am tentatively suggesting that this is not necessarily the most economical assumption, at least as far as the thirteenth century is concerned. If we now look back at our unanswered questions about the twelfth century, we notice that all of them are concerned in one way or another with population, family prestige and genealogy. Dante's material on Florentine families, especially the long passage in the second half of *Paradiso* XVI, may be compared to similar material in two fourteenth-century Florentine chronicles, the *Nuova cronica* of Giovanni Villani, and the *Storia fiorentina* ascribed to Ricordano and Giacotto Malispini; the Malispini chronicle was formerly thought to be another thirteenth-century text but has been shown to be a late fourteenth-century forgery copied from the *Libro fiesolano* and from an abridgement of Villani's *Nuova cronica*, with insertions designed to glorify certain Florentine families (another case of chronicles becoming quasi-public property).[40] All three of these texts—Dante, Villani and Malispini—contain the same sort of information about Florentine families;[41] and indeed Kenneth Hyde demonstrated, on the basis of a wider field of investigation than just Florence, that what he called the "social chronicle," giving such information as the various families' antiquity, current social standing, place of residence within the city, coat of arms, and so on, was quite an established genre in medieval literature.[42] Crucially, though, Dante, Villani and Malispini, while to a large extent overlapping, all give different accounts of Florence's major families;[43] and, even though the Malispini chronicle is now regarded as an imposture, it seems very likely that whoever put it together, around 1380 or even later, had a source other than Dante and Villani for what he wrote about Florentine society—that the short passages of social chronicle embedded in the Malispini text, unlike the rest of the Malispini chronicle, *do* represent genuine thirteenth-century material.[44] This genuine thirteenth-century material could also have been used, separately, by Dante and by Villani (though presumably Villani consulted Dante as well).

My conclusion is, then, that the surviving thirteenth-century sources account for Dante's knowledge of Florentine history rather more satisfactorily than might be imagined, but that one of his sources is missing: some account, whether official or otherwise, of the composition of the more prominent classes in Florentine society, continues to elude us.

From *Dante and His Literary Precursors: Twelve Essays* (2007) edited by John C. Barnes and Jennifer Petrie. Copyright © 2007 by the University College Dublin Foundation for Italian Studies. Reprinted with permission of the University College Dublin Foundation for Italian Studies.

Notes

1. I thank Antonio Corsaro for checking a detail in a Florentine manuscript for me.

2. *Chronica de Origine Civitatis*, in *Quellen und Forschungen zur ältesten Geschichte der Stadt Florenz*, edited by O. Hartwig, 2 vols, I (Marburg, Elwert, 1875), 35-69. For the date of composition see *Quellen und Forschungen*, I, xix; N. Rubinstein, "The Beginnings of Political Thought in Florence" (see n. 4 below), p. 199; G. Aquilecchia, "Dante and the Florentine Chroniclers," *Bulletin of the John Rylands Library*, 48 (1965), 30-55 (p. 32). T. Maissen, "Attila, Totila e Carlo Magno fra Dante, Villani, Boccaccio e Malispini: per la genesi di due leggende erudite," *Archivio storico italiano*, 152 (1994), 561-639, suggests that this chronicle was composed early in 1228 (p. 572). The year 1264 is unconvincingly put forward as the date of composition in the unpersuasive critical edition of Anna Maria Cesari: "Chronica de Origine Civitatis Florentie," edited by A. M. Cesari, *Atti e memorie dell'Accademia toscana di scienze e lettere La Colombaria*, 58 [new series 44] (1993), 185-253. In these notes reference will be made to both editions, though only Hartwig's will be quoted; in any case, except at the end, where Cesari admits as part of the original text a few lines which presumably constitute a later addition, the two editors' texts are almost identical.

3. *Chronica de Origine Civitatis*, p. 55 col. 1 (Hartwig), p. 248 (Cesari).

4. N. Rubinstein, "The Beginnings of Political Thought in Florence: A Study in

Medieval Historiography," *Journal of the Warburg and Courtauld Institutes*, 5 (1942), 198-227.

5. C. T. Davis, "Topographical and Historical Propaganda in Early Florentine Chronicles and in Villani," *Medioevo e Rinascimento*, 2 (1988), 33-51 (p. 33).

6. *Quellen und Forschungen*, I, XX-XXIV; N. Rubinstein, "The Beginnings of Political Thought in Florence," pp. 199-201.

7. G. Villani, *Nuova cronica*, edited by G. Porta, 3 vols (Parma, Fondazione Bembo/Guanda, 1990-1); G. Aquilecchia, "Dante and the Florentine Chroniclers," p. 32; N. Rubinstein, "The Beginnings of Political Thought in Florence," pp. 200-1; F. Ragone, *Giovanni Villani e i suoi continuatori: la scrittura delle cronache a Firenze nel Trecento* (Rome, Istituto Storico Italiano per il Medio Evo, 1998), pp. 47-8.

8. Broadly speaking, there are three main versions, one—evidently the earliest— in Latin and two in the vernacular. Of the Latin text four manuscripts are known, and three have been edited: MS II. II. 67 of the Biblioteca Nazionale Centrale in Florence by O. Hartwig in column 1 of his *Quellen und Forschungen*, I, 35-69; MS XXIX. VIII of Florence's Biblioteca Medicea Laurenziana, dated 1264, by E. Alvisi in his *Il libro delle origini di Fiesole e di Firenze* (Parma, Ferrari and Pellegrini, 1895), pp. 49-73 (unnumbered); and Latin MS 5381 of the Bibliotheca Apostolica Vaticana, Rome (dated 1334) by A. Del Monte in his "La storiografia fllorentina dei secoli XII e XIII," *Bullettino dell'Istituto Storico Italiano e Archivio Muratoriano*, 62 (1950), 175-282 (pp. 265-82). Cesari's edition is based on the first two of these manuscripts. (The fourth, MS II. IV. 109 of Florence's Biblioteca Nazionale, is described by P. Santini, *Quesiti e ricerche di storiografia fiorentina* [Florence, Seeber, 1903], p. 19.) A vernacular translation is represented by Gaddi *reliqui* MS 18 in the Biblioteca Laurenziana and by MS 40 of the G. B. Orsucci collection in the Lucca State Archive, the second of which is edited in the second column of Hartwig's *Quellen und Forschungen*, I, 35-69. Another, expanded, vernacular version, entitled *Libro fiesolano*, presumably because the additions concern Fiesole rather than Florence as well as establishing a spurious descent of the Uberti family from Catiline, is represented by MS C. 300 of Florence's Biblioteca Marucelliana, which Hartwig edits in column 3 of his *Quellen und Forschungen*, I, 35-69. See O. Hartwig, *Quellen und Forschungen*, I, xxix-xliii; P. Santini, *Quesiti e ricerche*, pp. 17-26, 51-3; N. Rubinstein, "The Beginnings of Political Thought in Florence," pp. 198-9 n. 1. The Gaddian manuscript has recently been edited (confusingly under the title *Il libro fiesolano*) by Colette Gros, who baldly states (p. 17) that "il contient la plus ancienne version de la légende": "La Plus Ancienne Version de Il *Libro fiesolano* (la *Légende des origines*)," edited by C. Gros, *Letteratura italiana antica*, 4 (2003), 11-28.

9. G. T. Gargani edited the *Libro fiesolano* among the "Opuscoli scelti inediti e rari" published as an appendix to his *Letture di famiglia* (Florence, Galileiana, 1854). It is to the *Libro fiesolano* that Giovanni Villani refers in his *Nuova cronica* (II. 4) when, scornfully dismissing the account in "alcuno scritto" of the alleged descent of the Uberti from Catiline, he says: "Questo non troviamo per autentica cronica che per noi si pruovi."

10. *Chronica de Origine Civitatis*, p. 40 cols 1, 3 (Hartwig), p. 241 (Cesari).

11. *Chronica de Origine Civitatis*, pp. 64-5.

12. *Chronica de Origine Civitatis*, pp. 54-5 (Hartwig), p. 248 (Cesari), p. 25 (Gros).

13. *Chronica de Origine Civitatis*, p. 59 cols 1, 3 (Hartwig), p. 250 (Cesari).

14. *Chronica de Origine Civitatis*, p. 60 col. 1 (Hartwig), p. 251 (Cesari).

15. N. Rubinstein, "The Beginnings of Political Thought in Florence," pp. 204-5. For a different perspective on the Florentine legends see M. Dozon, *Les Légendes de fondation de Fiesole et de Florence au temps de Dante* [Centre de Recherches de Langue et Littérature Italiennes: Documents de travail et prépublications, no. 31] (Paris, Université Paris x-Nanterre, 1983). See, too, A. Benvenuti, "'Secondo che raccontano le storie': il mito delle origini cittadine nella Firenze comunale," in *Il senso della storia nella cultura medievale italiana (1100-1350)*, by various authors (Pistoia, Centro Italiano di Studi di Storia e d'Arte, 1995), pp. 205-52.

16. *Sanzanomis Gesta Florentinorum*, in Hartwig's *Quellen und Forschungen*, I, 1-34; also in *Cronache dei secoli XIII e XIV* (Florence, Cellini, 1876), pp. 125-54. References hereafter are to Hartwig's edition.

17. *Sanzanomis Gesta Florentinorum*, pp. 12, 16.

18. *Sanzanomis Gesta Florentinorum*, p. 2.

19. See *Sanzanomis Gesta Florentinorum*, pp. 30, 2; G. Aquilecchia, "Sanzanome," in *Enc. dant.*, V, 17.

20. *Sanzanomis Geste Florentinorum*, pp. 5, 7, 10, 12. For the date 1168 see G. W. Dameron, *Episcopal Power and Florentine Society, 1000-1320* (Cambridge, Mass.-London, Harvard University Press, 1991), p. 75.

21. *Quellen und Forschungen*, I, XIV-XV.

22. See the anonymous *Gesta Florentinorum* (n. 28 below), p. 251; *Cronica fiorentina compilata nel secolo XIII* (n. 30 below), p. 115 (Schiaffini), p. 230 (Villari), p. 223 (Hartwig); G. Villani, *Nuova cronica*, VI. 31 (1, 258); R. Davidsohn, *Storia di Firenze* [1896-1927], translated by G. B. Klein and R. Palmarocchi, 8 vols (Florence, Sansoni, 1956-65), II, 599.

23. B. Latini, *Li Livres dou tresor*, edited by F. J. Carmody (Berkeley-Los Angeles, University of California Press, 1948).

24. See "Romulus and Remus," in *The Oxford Classical Dictionary*, edited by N. G. L. Hammond and H. H. Scullard, second edition (Oxford, Clarendon Press, 1970), p. 936.

25. *Chronica de Origine Civitatis*, p. 54 col. 1 (Hartwig), p. 247 (Cesari).

26. B. Latini, *The Book of the Treasure*, translated by P. Barrette and S. Baldwin (New York-London, Garland, 1993), p. 26. For a fascinating study of the Martian element in Florentine culture see L. Gatti, "Il mito di Marte a Firenze e la 'pietra scema': memorie, riti e ascendenze," *Rinascimento*, 35 (1995), 201-30.

27. *Die Annalen des Tholomeus von Lucca in doppelter Fassung*, edited by B. Schmeidler [*Monumenta Germaniae Historica: Scriptores Rerum Germanicarum, Nova Series*, 8] (Berlin, Weidmann, 1930), p. 3.

28. *Die Gesta Florentinorum von 1080-1278*, appendix to *Die Annalen des Tholomeus von Lucca*, pp. 243-77.

29. A. Del Monte, "La storiografia fiorentina dei secoli XII e XIII," infers that the anonymous *Gesta Florentinorum* ended around 1270 from the fact that although Tolomeo of Lucca's last reference to it concerns 1260, some of his material

relating to the next decade is similar in form to what he has derived from the *Gesta* (p. 185).

30. *Cronica fiorentina compilata nel secolo XIII* ["erroneamente attribuita a Brunetto Latini"], in *Testi fiorentini del Dugento e dei primi del Trecento*, edited by A. Schiaffini (Florence, Sansoni, 1926), pp. 82-150; previously published by P. Villari as an appendix to his *I primi due secoli della storia di Firenze*, 2 vols (Florence, Sansoni, 1893), II, 193-269. Earlier still, extracts containing all the Florentine material had been published as *Die sogennante Chronik des Brunetto Latini*, in *Quellen und Forschungen zur ältesten Geschichte der Stadt Florenz*, edited by O. Hartwig, 2 vols, II (Halle, Niemeyer, 1880), 209-37. None of these editions includes the long initial section covering the years before 1002, which merely summarizes Martin of Troppau (see n. 32 below) with almost no mention of Florence. The five brief passages where Florence or Fiesole is mentioned (including one which purports to record the building of the Florentine Baptistery as a pagan temple in 102 AD) are printed by Villari in his *I primi due secoli della storia di Firenze*, II, 187 n. 1.

31. P. Villari, *I primi due secoli della storia di Firenze*, II, 186, 190, and others (e.g. P. Santini, *Quesiti e ricerche*, pp. 54, 56) state that the autograph part of Pseudo-Brunetto's chronicle ends in 1297, which is certainly the last date given there. The last event narrated, however, is a visit to Florence, as papal peacemaker, by Cardinal Matteo d'Acquasparta, which took place in May 1300 (and was followed by a second such visit in 1301). It is true that the Cardinal had also visited Florence at the end of 1297, but on that occasion his purpose had been to enlist support for the papal "crusade" against the Colonna family (see A. Frugoni, "Matteo di Acquasparta," in *Enc. dant.*, III, 868-9). In my view Pseudo-Brunette's emphasis on the Cardinal's peace-making role indicates that his final paragraph cannot have been written before 1300. The *Cronichetta inedita della prima metà del sec. XIV* ("contenuta nel cod. magliabechiano XXV. 505"), published by P. Santini in his *Quesiti e ricerche*, pp. 89-144, records the two visits as follows: "MCCLXXXVII venne in Firenze messer Matteo d'Aquasparta [*sic*], cardinale e legato del papa, e bandí la Croce sopra e' Colonnesi e perdono, chome chi andasse sopra a' saraceni: molta gente v'andò di Firenze. [. . .] MCCC [. . .] Nel detto anno venne in Firenze messer Matteo d'Acquasparta, e giunse a dí x di giugno, per pacificare e' fiorentini Neri e Bianchi" (pp. 122-3).

32. *Martini Oppaviensis Chronicon Pontificum et Imperatorum*, edited by L. Weiland, in *Monumenta Germaniae Historica: Scriptores*, 32 vols in 34 (Hanover, Hahn; Leipzig, Hiersemann, 1826-1934), XXII, 377-482.

33. *Cronica fiorentina*, p. 112 (Schiaffini), p. 227 (Villari), p. 222 (Hartwig). On the Counts of Certaldo see G. W. Dameron, *Episcopal Power and Florentine Society*, pp. 107-8.

34. *Cronica fiorentina*, pp. 117-20 (Schiaffini), pp. 233-6 (Villari), pp. 223-6 (Hartwig). For an assessment of the significance of the Buondelmonte murder in the poet's view of Florentine history see R. J. Quinones, "Foundation Sacrifice and Florentine History," *Lectura Dantis*, 4 (Spring 1989), 10-19, subsequently developed in his *Foundation Sacrifice in Dante's "Commedia"* (Pennsylvania, Penn State University Press, 1994), Ch. 1 (pp. 9-29).

35. *Cronica fiorentina*, p. 119 (Schiaffini), p. 234 (Villari), p. 225 (Hartwig).

36. *Cronica fiorentina*, p. 119 (Schiaffini), p. 235 (Villari), p. 225 (Hartwig).

37. *Cronica fiorentina*, pp. 119, 120 (Schiaffini), pp. 235, 236 (Villari), pp. 225, 226 (Hartwig).

38. See also P. Armour, "Dante's Brunetto: The Paternal Paterine," *Italian Studies*, 38 (1983), 1-38, especially pp. 19-23.

39. L. Green, *Chronicle into History: An Essay on the Interpretation of History in Florentine Fourteenth-century Chronicles* (Cambridge, Cambridge University Press, 1972), pp. 155-64, considering the sources of Giovanni Villani's *Nuova cronica*, written in the decades immediately after Dante's death, finds ample evidence of lost texts, demonstrating, for example, that as regards the years 1080-1278 (the period covered by the anonymous *Gesta Florentinorum*), in addition to the known texts, "other sources unknown to us must [. . .] be presumed to have provided [Villani] with further factual material that enabled him to elaborate and expand his narrative" (p. 157).

40. R. Malispini, *Storia fiorentina, col seguito di Giacotto Malispini, dalla edificazione di Firenze sino all'anno 1286*, edited by V. Follini (Florence, Ricci, 1816); C. T. Davis, "The Malispini Question," in *A Giuseppe Ermini = Studi medievali*, third series, 10 (1970), 215-54, reprinted in his *Dante's Italy and Other Essays* (Philadelphia, University of Pennsylvania Press, 1984), pp. 94-136; J. C. Barnes, "Un problema in via di chiusura: la Cronica malispiniana," *Studi e problemi di critica testuale*, 27 (October 1983), 15-32; C. T. Davis; "Recent Work on the Malispini Question," in his *Dante's Italy and Other Essays*, pp. 290-9; G. Porta, "Le varianti redazionali come strumento di verifica dell'autenticità dei testi: Villani e Malispini," in *La filologia romanza e i codici*, edited by S. Guida and F. Latella, 2 vols (Messina, Sicania, 1993), II, 481-529; L. Mastroddi, "Contributo al testo critico della *Storia fiorentina* di Ricordano Malispini," *Bullettino dell'Istituto Storico Italiano e Archivio Muratoriano*, 103 (2000-1), 239-93.

41. See G. Villani, *Nuova cronica*, V. 10-13 (I, 179-82); R. Malispini, *Storia fiorentina*, Chh. 52, 103 (pp. 46-50, 83-6).

42. J. K. Hyde, "Italian Social Chronicles in the Middle Ages," *Bulletin of the John Rylands Library*, 49 (1966), 107-32.

43. C. T. Davis, "The Malispini Question" (1984), pp. 116-24.

44. V. Lami, "Di un compendio inedito della *Cronica* di Giovanni Villani nelle sue relazioni con la *Storia fiorentina* malispiniana," *Archivio storico italiano*, fifth series, 5 (1890), 369-416. C. T. Davis, "The Malispini Question" (1984), p. 123 n. 66, however, is inclined to doubt this.

Nature's Revenge

Francesca Guerra D'Antoni

Flakes of fire rain down on a smoking desert plain garlanded by charcoal stumps of trees that encircle the wood of suicides. Observing the phenomenon, Dante as Pilgrim of the infernal journey recalls a similar scene he had once witnessed from an Alpine mountaintop, when snow fell in a perfectly vertical pattern into the valley on a windless day. But falling snow at any angle is natural, even a blessing at times. Falling fire instead manifests a reversal of natural laws, a curse upon the earth, the Creator's garden of all beauty and bounty. Therefore, in his vision of burning sands the poet prepares us to expect a reversal of everything we consider natural, orderly or logical in the landscape and its inhabitants.

We enter with Vergil and the Pilgrim into the third ring of the circle of "matta bestialitade" and brute violence, where the burning sands resembling Sodom and Gomorrah begin. At sight of this gloomy "rena arida e spessa" deforested of all vegetation, the Pilgrim heightens the drama for us by recalling Cato's account of the Lybian sands in Lucan's *Pharsalia*, and again by comparing his vision with Medieval accounts describing the fiery plains of India trodden by Alexander's troops. So familiar is this poetic landscape to us that its banality blinds our perceptions to the finer, more momentous details which it introduces.[1] Yet the next phenomenon, generally neglected by interpreters, offers a surprising new perspective on both literal and deeper, allegorical levels of meaning, ultimately affecting our understanding of the entire *Commedia*. The Pilgrim, confronted by a human tragedy unfolding ahead under the raining fire, marvels:[2]

> d'anime nude vidi molte gregge
> che piangean tutte assai miseramente
> e parea posta lor diversa legge.

(I saw many herds of naked souls, who were all lamenting very miserably; and different laws seemed to be imposed upon them.)

Upon witnessing this grim spectacle the Pilgrim contemplates the fearful vengeance of God upon a disordered universe. Nature had wreaked her revenge on the inhabitants as well as the land. The different law by which these naked shades expose their sin alludes to their dehumanization. They resemble herds of animals. Having reverted from a human nature to brutishness, some of the "gregge" lie supine, others crouch in clusters, still more run in an eternal chase to overtake one another. Nature has stripped these sinners of a quality that differentiates beasts from humans: intelligence. The bizarre pastoral scene recalls Circe's island and its bestialized men, with smoke encircling the palace of their sorceress.[3]

This interpretation, therefore, considerably qualifies the meaning of Dante's burning sands. A Circean quality in both landscape and inhabitants reveals itself with increased intensity as the wayfarers descend gradually into deeper darkness. Of immediate concern as we contemplate Dante's imagery of these souls despoiled of their humanity is the poet's suggested inspiration on the ancient platonic theory of metempsychosis. As briefly mentioned in the introduction, this means that souls of the wicked shrink to beastly form. Yet, strangely, their bodies retain their human shapes.[4]

Most likely, the poet's source of inspiration for this idea was Boethius, for whom Dante had reason to nourish a sense of fellowship when composing the *Commedia*.[5] It should not surprise us to discover a meeting of minds in these two exiles; for each in his own time experienced fears that his city, which he served and cherished, faced imminent destruction in a fiery conflagration at the hands of invaders. Representing the Early and Late Middle Ages respectively, Boethius and Dante shared another bond. In their literary masterpieces both philosophized about nature, fortune and the wages of greed, themes which dominate both the *Consolation of Philosophy* and Dante's vision of Sodom in the *Commedia*.

The poet's literary debt to Boethius for his metempsychosis theory appears clearly in *Convivio* II vii 4, where he comments:

E però chi da la ragione si parte, e usa pur la parte sensitiva, non vive uomo, ma vive bestia, sí come dice quello eccellentissimo Boezio: "Asino vive." Direttamente dico, però che lo pensiero è proprio atto de la ragione, perchè le bestie non pensano, che no l'hanno; e non dico pur de le minori bestie, ma di quelle che hanno apparenza umana e spirito di pecora, o d'altra bestia abominevole.

(So anyone who sets reason aside and uses only his sensitive part lives not as a man but as a beast, a point made by the most excellent Boethius when he says: "He lives as an ass." I quite agree, for thought is the act proper to reason; animals do not think, because they lack that faculty—a description that fits not only the lower animals but those who have a human appearance but the spirit of a sheep or of some other vile beast.)

Dante transfers this reasoning from his own "banquet of wisdom" to his scenario of burning sands, dramatizing bestiality of the human spirit as perversion of nature's laws.

Ignoring the significant literal meaning of Dante's imagery alluding to dehumanized men as herds of miserable disease-ridden brutes, traditional critics assumed that "gregge" for the poet metaphorically implied merely crowds of people. Consequently, the poem's real meaning of sins against nature has remained obscure. One can object that the poet later calls the souls running along the bank of the arena a "schiera" (*Inf.* XV 16). Yet here too an ironic ambiguity results from a term that could signify a troupe of men, usually military, or a swarm of insects. The same can be said of Dante's terms, "traccia" (*Inf.* XV 33), "masnada" (*Inf.* XV 41) and "torma" (*Inf.* XVI 5), all ambiguously charged with double meanings associated with herding patterns of animals. The leader of the second troupe of runners apologizes for their mangy look, the most prestigious among them appearing "nudo e dipelato" (*Inf.* XVI 35). These repeated allusions to bestiality, far from exhaustive, expose the misery of the grim scenario. Brunetto senses no guilt over his perdition, blaming "fortuna o destino" (*Inf.*

XV 46) for the Pilgrim's presumed damnation and implicitly for his own.

Bruno Migliorini notes the negative connotation of "gregge" as a term likening herds of animals to people who blindly follow indiscriminately after any leader or new trend.[6] And new trends threatening imperial and ecclesiastical authority in Dante's Italy were nationalism and commercialization of society, which the nobility espoused eagerly, blindly serving foreign local interests as they sought power and fortune for themselves.[7] Dante saw these trends as underlying causes of partisan rivalries for pre-eminence. For ordinary citizens these social changes meant oppressive labor, with loss of peace and prosperity; for they became burdened with heavy taxes and overproduction of fields in order to support internecine wars.

Meanwhile, the aristocrats obligated to protect the citizens shirked their duties as defenders and peacemakers. Those whom Dante confines to his burning sands were all Christians, implicitly surrogates of the Good Shepherd, who knows his sheep as they know him, and who sacrifices his life for them (John 10:14-5). Projected against this Christological ideal, harmonizing for Dante with the equally sacred Roman ideal embodied in the pious Aeneas, failure of magistrates to protect the people from injustice perverted the spirit of Roman world government. Therefore, we can easily understand how the poet would perceive his fellow Italian aristocrats as blasphemers against Christ's law fulfilled in the Roman ideal.[8]

Capaneus was their prototype. According to Statius this foolish warlord defied Jove's will to save Thebes from destruction by attempting to steal his thunder, snatching the lightning bolt out of the sky.[9] As the law of nature would have it, he was fulminated. Bestial rage dehumanized him, for it impaired his power of discretion. This typology of dehumanization depends on a rich and universal tradition in literary history. Biblically, Esau, described as hairy, suggesting bestiality, typifies bellicose men of violent habits that impair reasoning; unwittingly he trades his patrimony for a bowl of soup (Gen. 25:24-8). In secular tradition his counterpart appears in Ovid, who describes the same typological hairiness of an Arcadian king to enrich his story of Circe's power over men ruled by violent passions. The king's garments undergo transformation, along with his body, so that his clothes become shaggy hair, his arms turning into legs. He is transmuted into a wolf, retaining only traces of his human shape, with the same gray hair and fierce face. His eyes gleam in beastly savagery.[10]

Something akin to this reversal of natural laws governs Dante's vision of perversity in the burning sands. Sinners who wielded greater earthly power retain the least degree of freedom. Capaneus was a king; he suffers total deprivation of powers he once wielded abusively. As he ignored nature's limits placed on human force, so nature now ignores his impotent, defiant rage. Next on the infernal scene come several groups of runners fleeing from each other eternally, suggesting their violent competition for fast profits, which they pursued on earth with the same arrogance and rash action as the prefigural Capaneus whom they resemble as figures of power and fame. As noted men of wisdom resembling those in Dante's Noble Castle, they should move with a slow, grave pace suitable to their reputation. Instead the Pilgrim now sees in this desert resembling Sodom only dehumanized fugitives running with mercurial speed.[11] Brunetto identifies only three and advises silence about the rest, for time would not permit naming so many. Could Dante have known such a horde of homosexuals in his time, or in history? While sodomites condemned by historians and Medieval moralists were generally idle monks caught in the snares of the noonday devil, idleness and boredom were not characteristic of Dante's fellow nobles. These were ambitious and intelligent. Italy's faustians. All were "cherci e litterati grandi e di gran fama . . . d'un peccato medesmo al mondo lerci" (*Inf.* XV 106-8). Those whose approach Brunetto fears were Dante's boyhood heroes and only horror of the fire keeps the Pilgrim from joining them, with Vergil's approval (*Inf.* XVI 46-8). In the face of these contradictions in the poet's vision of Sodom, can it be that homosexuality was far from the only "sin against nature" known to

Dante and his tradition? The momentous question upon which the validity of this study hinges will answer itself as this study progresses.[12]

Meanwhile, the group of usurers crouched at the edge of the burning sands with moneybags suspended from their necks stare in apparent ecstasy at the gaudy crests of noble families finely tooled on the flaps. Ironically, these heraldic symbols feature diverse animals: a lion; a goose; a sow (*Inf.* XVII 60-4). In the gestures of these sinners brutishness more strongly suggests itself than in the previous categories. The undignified poses of the usurers recall the way donkeys even today are restrained, with feedbags hanging from their muzzles while they remain harnessed to their load. Sheer irony informs their imagery, which, as noted briefly in the introductory chapter, shares some of the typology of classical literatures. Like the asinine Midas yoked to his cart loaded with indigestible gold, the usurers cannot hope for sustenance from the contents of their pouches.

Dante's most forceful appeal to our perception of dehumanization in this imagery comes from his description of a usurer who distorts his mouth, his tongue extended to lick his nostrils. Imagination invites us to hear him braying as he hails the advent of a "cavalier sovrano" carrying his pouches crested with figures of three billy goats (*Inf.* XVII 72-3). Other brutish gestures of this group mimic animal behavior. All the usurers swat themselves like dogs fending off flies "ora col ceffo, ora col piè, quando son morsi" (*Inf.* XVII 50). Charles Grandgent reminded us long ago that "doglike, bovine, disgusting as these creatures are, they came of noble stock."[13] This whole macabre pastoral scene becomes a parody of the locus amoenus, which for Dante was Italy. His burning sands suggest a complete negation of an edenic garden, now virtually a wasted land where nature shows no mercy upon a depraved, brutish, destitute humanity.

We can now bring Dante's figures of dehumanization forward and prepare this herd of miserable shades weeping over their loss for stern judgment at the bar of Boethian ethics. Anticipating Dante by some seven hundred years, Boethius had linked man's bestialization with inordinate ambition for power and craving for material possessions. Philosophically, he asked:[14]

Sic rerum versa condicio est ut divinum merito rationis animal non aliter sibi splendere nisi inanimatae supellectilis possessione videatur?

(Is the state of nature so upside down that man, a living and rational—and therefore a godlike—animal, can only appear splendid to himself by the possession of lifeless stuff?)

To paraphrase Boethius' lengthy reply to his own question, only when a man learns to know himself does he rise above the need for material things in nature to enhance his stature. If he does not know himself he remains lower than brutes. Man strays from his true nature when he seeks to improve upon the way God created him, when he measures his earthly importance with things external to himself. Power gained by earthly possessions harms the possessor, threatening both his physical and moral safety. For power debases the human spirit. When greed makes a human being crave possessions, he thinks himself worthier than others to possess power and wealth. In such thirst for worldly things lies the perverted seed of pride.[15]

And in self-righteousness, Dante's illustrious men now lying, running or helplessly bound to earthly things in his burning sands enact their perverse pride, sterile seed of life that makes vain all works of nature. For Boethius, pride and inordinate ambition work together to disrupt the order of nature. The idea was hardly new. Cicero had observed that superior minds often cause men of great genius to become overly ambitious for military authority, power and renown, and that such men often fail to prevent injustices when self-interest leads them to neglect those whom they are obligated to protect.[16] Cicero was also probably as instrumental as Boethius in defining Dante's ideas on natural law. Nature for the Stoic measures the proper course of action for both animals and humans, both endowed with instincts of self-preservation, which drive them to provide such necessities as food, shelter, defense and procreation. But beasts are moved by the senses, with no perception of past or future, cause or consequence; humans are moved by reason to comprehend these in a universal scope. Therefore, humans can perceive a need for order and moderation that govern the world of spirit.[17]

The world of spirit is inhabited by men who recognize laws of human fellowship that bind them to live, not for themselves, but to serve their country. When humans fail in this regard, avarice is the controlling motive. Inherent in our nature there is a law that recognizes certain duties of public service, which are violated when bravery and intelligence are motivated by self-aggrandizement.[18] Conversely, true philosophic greatness of spirit consonant with moral goodness, to which Nature aspires, requires a man to remain indifferent to worldly fortunes and to stake everything in defense of the common good. Civic virtue exercised for selfish ends instead of the common good becomes a vice; courage becomes effrontery. The exalted spirit reveals only a barbarous nature when it tolerates injustice.[19]

This barbarous nature which Cicero perceives in great men who succumb to unmanly ambitions characterizes Dante's aristocrats in the burning sands, whose forms appear bestialized. The "diversa legge" or strange law alluding to their dehumanization is the common contrapasso of all the sinners, whether they lie supine, run with mercurial speed, or bend over burdens of useless money. In subjecting them all to one identical contrapasso the poet follows the rigid categorical scheme he imposes in all his vision of Hell. This arena is not, as critics have supposed, a poetic exception to structural rules; for such a case would make the ring of blasphemers anomalous. If Dante had intended to expose a miscellany of unrelated sins in his burning sands, he most logically would have selected a plural phrase, "diverse leggi," to denote plural punishments. Further, the raining fire makes no distinction between sinners; it scorches all bodies whether they lie, run or crouch.

Analogous instances from two other categories in the *Inferno* will clarify the confusion of critics by showing how all sinners in each category suffer a common general contrapasso, with specific variations only in mode. Poetically, the only function of such modulations within a scene is enhancement of dramatic impact. In the canto of adulterers all sinners are buffeted by the "bufera infernal" (*Inf.* V 31). Yet Paolo and Francesca suffer this hellish hurricane in an eternally inseparable embrace symbolizing their sinful love; for this poetic modulation dramatizes their own unique life story, stretching the moment of their fatal sin into an eternity. The whole effect emphasizes the sublime irony of their love which can never be consummated. Likewise, among the false counsellors in the division of fraud all sinners are punished by the same contrapasso, tongues set aflame. But the specific poetic modulation of inseparably twinned tongues in the case of Diomedes and Ulysses symbolizes and eternalizes their cooperation in the ruse of the wooden horse (*Inf.* XXVI 56-60).[20]

Dramatic modulations similarly enhance the scene in the burning sands. There is no authorial intent to differentiate between the sin of Capaneus and those of the runners or usurers. One example serves to clarify the issue. When the Pilgrim attempts to solace his beloved teacher Brunetto by offering to sit a while with him, the miserable shade counters:[21]

> O figliuol . . . qual di questa greggia
> s'arresta punto, giace poi cent'anni
> sanz'arrostarsi quando 'l foco il feggia.

(O son . . . whoever of this flock stops even for an instant must then lie a hundred years without brushing off the fire when it strikes him.)

This lament clarifies the common fate of all sinners in the fiery arena. If Brunetto would risk the same punishment dealt to Capaneus by stopping, could his contrapasso change, or his sin be substituted for another? Such speculations make nonsense of Dante's structural system of the *Inferno*.[22] Brunetto's lament reveals, instead, that Capaneus and the runners committed basically the same sin of blasphemy.[23]

By inclusion in the same ring of blasphemers who exerted human force against God or his things, Dante then equates the sin of the usurers with those of Capaneus and the runners who occupy the same circular space under the rain of fire. This claim will surely raise objections from critics who insist that emphatic allusions to the contrary inhere in the poet's specific mention of "Soddoma e Caorsa" as symbolic of quite separate transgressions. How could Dante logically combine these as identical types of sin, further equating both with the defiance of Capaneus against Jove? Can poetic integrity ignore such glaring illogic? Is Dante himself committing an unreasoning error by presuming to compare the incomparable?

These objections vanish once we submit Dante's poetic logic to the test of Boethian and Ciceronian opinion of what is required by the laws of Nature, as summarized here. If Nature, as Cicero held, requires men to value the common good above personal fortunes, all of Dante's sinners in the burning sands perverted such a natural law, which ultimately comes from God. In Dante's moral vision they committed blasphemy. The outrages against humanity committed by Capaneus at Thebes, by the Sodomites against the wayfarers and by the moneylenders of Cahors in Dante's time differ only in the means employed by the aggressors.

In the introduction to this study we already observed how the quality of mercy underlies the surface, literal meaning of each of the crimes punished in the burning sands. Given the fact that Dante here condemns men of power, privilege and authority, we might logically conclude that their common failing concerned lust for domination. In each case powerful men reciprocated God's goodness bestowed upon them with perverse, merciless, violent acts. Capaneus outright defied Jove's decision to save Thebes, reaching for the thunderbolt with which to light his torch, a large uprooted tree. He had planned to hurl this weapon into the battlefield, while he stood advantageously safe on the city's wall.[24] Defiance of divine mercy also figures in the story of Sodom; for Yahweh promised Abraham to save the city if any just men be found there. And in his *Monarchia* Dante also addresses the issue of God's mercy in determining Rome's manifest right to universal rule, as Vergil had previously claimed.[25] Therefore, Dante deplored the self-serving, factious quests of Italy's aristocrats for pre-eminence among themselves; for in his mind these sowed the seeds of Rome's destruction. In their lust for domination they blindly aided the rise of nationalism that accompanied the commercialization of Europe. The poet believed these were abusing the civilizing arts which they should have practiced in a spirit of service as taught by Cicero. In each of the three cases of blasphemy to which Dante alludes in his burning sands we can perceive a refusal of divine mercy, defiance of natural laws and abuse of the civilizing arts, be these civic, military, clerical, economic or even domestic.

Besides the amplified interpretation of blasphemy implicit in this argument, we need also give closer scrutiny to Dante's wider definition of usury. In the poem we find no proof that he employed the terms "usura" and "usuriere" (*Inf.* XI 95, 109) technically, referring only to moneylending. In its broader meaning, the Italian term "usura" means "abuse" generally, or harmful actions. Dante's contemporary, Bono Giamboni, in his popular treatise on virtues and vices, defined usury as "uno studioso desiderio d'avere alcuna cosa oltre la sorte."[26] This definition as it affects the sinners in Dante's vision of Sodom becomes strikingly significant, for it reduces them all to mindless dupes of the goddess Fortuna. Implicitly, therefore, the poem's pecuniary themes condemning "subiti guadagni" as destructive of "cortesia e valor" in Italy (*Inf.* XVI 67, 73) accuse Capaneus as well as all the other sinners. The charge is most appropriate, for he was a mercenary warlord commissioned along with six other kings of surrounding cities to destroy Thebes.

Another textual element supports this broader interpretation of usury. The term "art" as Vergil defines it in the context of his reply to the Pilgrim's question concerning usurious practices embraces all the human arts, not merely banking (*Inf.* XI 97-111). And appropriately, all Dante's figures in the burning sands, from Capaneus to the usurers, embody the highest human arts, requiring superior intelligence in the conduct of military, civic, clerical and financial affairs.[27] To abuse any of the human arts, therefore, offends nature. And to offend nature incurs a charge of blasphemy, for nature is God's child. This is substantially the lesson which Vergil gives to his protégé.

Giamboni's broad definition of usury as ambition to possess things "oltre la sorte" imposes a greater task on us of reassessing Dante's fortune themes in his burning sands. In her analysis of the language of commerce characterizing the figure of Brunetto, Joan Ferrante notes this magistrate's preoccupation with fortune in his familiarity with terminology of the marketplace. Yet, Ferrante remains puzzled over the poet's combination of commerce and sodomy as coherent themes in his burning sands.[28] Ferrante's quandary is understandable, since she rejected both André Pézard's and Richard Kay's interpretations of sodomy as having other than sexual significance in the poem.[29] Ironically, Ferrante's detailed account of the rank materialism of Dante's century, revealed in his language of the commercial world, pleads a better case for the position taken by Pézard and his followers than their own arguments.

Brunetto's inability to detach himself from the material world with its distortion of language, first discernible from his expressed belief that "fortuna o destino" (*Inf.* XV 46) had undone his former protégé and himself as well, remains an integral aspect of his eternal suffering. His anger over his damnation, which he cannot understand, shares some affinity with the rage of Capaneus. Neither seems capable of recognizing his condemnation as nature's vengeance upon him for his self-righteous presumption to disregard her laws, and to merit a greater share of her bounties because of his power to coerce.

Such is the beastly world of commercial competition as Dante most probably expected to lay it bare in all its wastefulness that blesses nei-

ther rich nor poor. Deeper implications of all the literary transmuta-
tions associated with instincts overruling reason, introduced so far,
will receive lengthy discussion in the following chapters. From textual
observations aired here it seems clear that the poet intended no enigmatic artifices to puzzle readers, but that our difficulties are merely
linguistic.

Notes

1. Singleton, *Inferno 2: Commentary*, pp. 230-31; cf. Lucan *Pharsalia* 9. 431-37;
cf. Albertus Magnus, *De meteoris, Opera omnia*, Vol. IV, eds. Auguste and Emile
Borgnet (Paris, 1890-99), 1. 4.9.

2. *Inferno* XIV 19-21.

3. Homer *Odyssey* 10. 135-44. Though Ulysses' men turn into swine, he sees
prowling about the palace of Circe wolves and lions subdued by and fawning over
their mistress. In Italy, the Orvieto Museum preserves a fourth century B.C. urn with
sculptured relief depicting Ulysses forcing Circe to restore his men to human form.
The sculpture shows these men with animal heads and human bodies, suggesting metempsychosis, or partial transmutation, rather than a complete metamorphosis. Curi-
ously, also, the heads of the figures resemble lions and rams, not swine. An illustration
of this sculpture appears in *New Larousse Encyclopedia of Mythology* (London:
Prometheus Press, 1973), p. 137.

4. Unlike the blasphemers in the circle of violence, the fraudulent blasphemers
undergo complete metamorphosis later in a snake pit where Vanni Fucci and others
writhe as they are transmuted into serpentine forms (*Inf.* XXIV 82-151, XXV all). See
the commentary of Attilio Momigliano, *Dante Alighieri, La Divina Commedia*, Vol. I:
Inferno (Florence: Sansoni, 1964), pp. 181-95. In English consult Singleton, *Inferno
2: Commentary*, pp. 414-6.

5. Boethius *Consolation* 4. 1-5, prose passage.

6. Giulio Cappuccini and Bruno Migliorini, *Vocabolario della lingua italiana*
(Turin: G. B. Paravia & Co., 1945), s.v. "gregge," "masnada," "schiera," "torma,"
"traccia." Though critics generally assume that Dante used these terms metaphorically, assuring readers the poet intended no negative connotations, such an interpretation contradicts *Convivio* II vii (viii) 4, just quoted.

7. Lester K. Little, *Religious Poverty and the Profit Economy in Medieval Europe*,
Chapter 2: "Adapting to the Profit Economy" (Ithaca: Cornell University Press, 1978),

pp. 19-41. For an idea of the impact which the commercialization of Europe had on the Italian nobility, see Aldo Vallone, *Studi su Dante medievale*, "Il Canto XVI dell'*Inferno*" (Florence: Leo S. Olschki Editore, 1965), pp. 179-98.

8. *Monarchia* II xi 8. Dante affirms the general Christian belief that Christ chose to be born under Roman rule during the monarchy of Augustus in order to signify the validity of Imperial Rome.

9. Statius *Thebaid* 10. 741-939. Statius excels in describing unrighteous battles which neither side wins. After the blameless young hero Menoeceus sacrifices his life as willed by Jove, the Argives lose despite attempts of their strongest warrior Capaneus to besiege the city. Statius achieves dramatic heights describing the failed attempt of the gigantic but foolhardy Capaneus to light his torch with Jove's invincible sword, the thunderbolt.

10. Ovid *Metamorphoses* 1. 236-40.

11. Boethius *Consolation* 4. 47-69, prose passage. The author may be Dante's source for Circean imagery originating with Homer but probably learned from Vergil. Lady Philosophy entertains her disconsolate listener with demonstrations of the power of evil to change men into bestial forms, while their human nature remains only an appearance. Plunderers become wolves; careless talkers asses; deceivers foxes; angry men lions; fearful men deer; sluggards asses; fickle men birds; incontinent men sows. Boethius then imagines a Ulyssean ship of fools (4. 3.1-39, lyric passage), wherein Circe serves an herbal drink that reshapes men into boars, lions, wolves, tigers and swine.

12. Identified figures in Dante's burning sands are: Capaneus, king and military strategist; Brunetto Latini, rhetorician and civic magistrate; Priscian, rhetorician and professor; Francesco d'Accorso, jurist and professor; Andrea de'Mozzi, jurist and prelate; Guido Guerra, military commander; Tegghiaio Aldobrandi and Iacopo Rusticucci, civic magistrates; Guglielmo Borsiere, courtier. The usurers remain anonymous, identifiable only by heraldic symbols on their moneybags.

13. *La Divina Commedia di Dante Alighieri*, ed. Charles H. Grandgent (Boston: D. C. Heath and Company, 1933), p. 151.

14. Boethius *Consolation* 2. 5.72-5, prose passage.

15. Boethius, *Consolation* 2. 5.85-100, prose, and 2. 5.1-14, lyric passages.

16. Cicero, *De officiis* 1. 8.26; 1. 9.28. Similarly, concerning Buondelmonte's murder for his injustice against the Amidei, Dante's Cacciaguida suggests the moral principle that it is a serious crime to offend a noble but even more serious for persons privileged by nature or events to fail in their obligations (*Par.* XVI 136-44).

17. Cicero, *De officiis* 1. 4.11-4.

18. Cicero, *De officiis* 1. 7.23-4; 1. 8.27.9; 1.9.28.

19. Cicero, *De officiis* 1. 19.62-5; 1. 20.67-70; 1. 21.70-3; 1. 22.74-8.

20. Aldo Vallone, *Studi su Dante medievale*, "Il peccato e la pena," Vol. 80, Ser. I, Biblioteca dell' *Anchivum Romanicum* (Florence: Leo S. Olschki Editore, 1965), pp. 111-23. Vallone stresses Dante's gradation of transgressions as related to degree of abuse of reason. Incontinence involves darkened reason; violence absence of reason; fraud conscious subordination of reason.

21. *Inferno* XV 37-9.

22. Pézard, *Dante sous la pluie de feu*, p. 77, fn. (1).

23. Ibid., pp. 73-8.

24. Statius Thebaid 10. 741-939.

25. *Monarchia* II viii 1-17. Dante claims that Aeneas possessed both inherited nobility, being of godly lineage, and proven nobility for his labors in founding Rome. As Colin Hardie notes, Dante considered Vergil's *Aeneid* a prophetic book and the poet a prophet of the stature of biblical prophets. See *Monarchy*, p. 35, fn. 1.

26. Giamboni, *Libro de' vizi e vertudi*, p. 52.

27. Pézard, *Dante sous la pluie de feu*, pp. 279-82, favors a general conclusion that Dante's men of letters blasphemed against the Holy Ghost in their presumption of impunity for abusing the human arts.

28. Joan M. Ferrante, *The Political Vision of the Divine Comedy* (Princeton University Press, 1984), pp. 311-79.

29. Ibid., p. 161, fn. 40.

Canto 4:
Limbo (First Circle)_____

Wallace Fowlie

There is no way of knowing how long Dante sleeps. According to the rigorous chronological plan of the poem, the descent through Hell occupies about twenty-four hours, but we are really outside of time during this period.

The sleep, perhaps equivalent to a spiritual death or a moment of grace, is long enough for the poet to be rested when he opens his eyes. The words *occhio riposato*, in the fourth line, remind us that "eye" (*occhio*) is the most often used noun in *The Divine Comedy.* All of Hell is dimly lit—no sunlight penetrates to any of its parts. Dante has to strain his eyes to see, and here in limbo one has a sense of Dante trying to penetrate the dark to see the noble figures he is anxious to meet, and striving also to comprehend and perhaps accept the harsh theology represented in this first division of the underworld.

The theological reasons for assigning unbaptized infants and the noble human figures who lived before Christ to Hell are so hard to follow that the mind clings to the word *sospesi* (4:45) which fills the canto. These spirits are "suspended" between the states of condemnation and salvation. Dante the theologian and Dante the man are in conflict here, and the conflict does not stimulate his greatest poetical powers. He is content to draw pictures as best he can of a dignified scene, of honorable men, using the word "honor" five times within twenty-five lines, while listening to a more than garrulous Virgil point out his own circle and his companion poets who dwell in this strangely neutral and lifeless scene.

The word *limbo* comes from *lembo* meaning "hem" or "margin." We are on the outskirts of Hell. We have not yet met Minos, who judges the damned. Here on the brink of the abyss of Hell, Dante pauses and hears the accumulated wailings of all the spirits resounding in his ears like continual thunder. He sees Virgil grow pale, *tutto smorto* (4:14), and wonders how he can follow so fearful a guide. Then when he hears the explanation, given briefly and in abstract terms (these spirits in the first circle lived before Christ and thus could not worship God in the right way) he feels overcome with sadness. He knows he will meet among the "suspended" spirits many of great worth.

Here, more than in any other section of Hell, damnation has a sense of beauty about it, a degree of greatness and goodness. Virgil is its hero. He talks about his eternal abode where there are no cries and no torture, and presents it to Dante in the aspect of a school (*la bella scola*, 4:94) or a company (*con molti compagni*, 4:121; *la sesta compagnia*, 4:148). This motif of the group is accompanied by the motif of two singular figures who stand somewhat apart from the group and represent it: Homer, the first of the poets of antiquity (4:86), and Aristotle, "the master of those who know" (*il maestro di color che sanno*, 4:131).

Dante's sleep, broken at the beginning of the canto, may be recalled by the reader when Homer, "the sovereign poet," appears, because of the sleep of Odysseus in book 13 of the *Odyssey*, when his sailors took him back to Ithaca. The theme of sleep initiates the canto and would seem to bear some relation to the sin or lack of sin that explains limbo. These spirits are not damned, but "suspended" in exile from Heaven and from God for having failed to acknowledge and worship him. *Non adorar debitamente a Dio* is the key line of explanation (4:38), "They did not worship God as they should have." Theologically, there is vagueness and hesitation in the canto, and we can almost surmise that limbo is another break in the walls of Hell, that there is hope behind the obdurate laws.

Dante's sadness,

> Gran duol mi prese al cor
>
> [4:43]
>
> [great sadness took me at the heart]

---

urges him to ask the question: "Did anyone leave limbo?" Virgil's answer is affirmative. Christ, at his death, came to this part of Hell and released his Jewish ancestors. This is called the "harrowing of Hell" and is related in the apocryphal book, the Gospel of Nicodemus. The name of Christ is never spoken in Hell. Virgil refers to him as *un possente* (4:53), "a mighty one" who came to liberate Adam, Abel, Noah, Moses, Abraham, David, Jacob, Isaac, and many others not named specifically.

In referring to this act of Christ, Dante reapplies the doctrine of the chosen people. He thus adheres to a theological belief of the Middle Ages, but shows such admiration for the heathen of antiquity that his heart seems to oppose his mind. Is he protesting against a theological law, or is he indicating some future possible mitigation of the rigorous law? A faint motif of protest moves through *The Divine Comedy* as an undercurrent. "Protest" is perhaps too strong a word—it might be best described as the vain struggle of a finite mind to come to terms with the infinite.

Limbo was as overpowering a problem for a mind of the fourteenth century as it is for a mind of the twentieth. In light of Christian theology, what can be said concerning such eternal figures as Socrates, Plato, and Aristotle, the three among all those named who would have the most meaning for us today? Dante does the best he can to rescue such men from ignominy, by casting limbo in the shape of Elysium. His picture is a Greek elysian field where the good live after death as in classical mythology. Virgil summarizes the fate of the good heathen in the words, "without hope we live in desire":

> sanza speme vivemo in disio.
> [4:42]

"Living in desire" would be salvation, but "living in desire without hope" is limbo.

We are now at the scene of Dante's recognition of those Greeks and Romans, his literary masters, representing his preferences, who are joined with Virgil and whom he finds joined in Hell. The canto is more than half over before any spirit speaks to Dante and Virgil. Then in line 80, one of the spirits—it is not clear who—greets Virgil:

> Onorate l'altissimo poeta
> [honor the great poet]

Virgil, who had left the group, is now welcomed back into it.

The first group, composed of poets, is led by Homer, appropriately enough since Homer's myth of the apocalypse is the basis of *The Divine Comedy*. Although Dante did not read Greek and probably did not read Homer even in translation, the Roman poets whom he studied had ascribed first place to Homer. "Sovereign poet" Dante calls him in line 88:

> quelli è Omero poeta sovrano
> [that is Homer, the sovereign poet]

The four Latin poets represent the major poets of Dante's literary culture: Virgil first; then Lucan who sang of Caesar and the Empire in his *Pharsalia*; Ovid, whose *Metamorphoses* are used by Dante; and Horace, both satirist and lyricist. They give to Dante the sixth place and thus honor him. Is this pride on the part of Dante? Possibly. But it can easily be argued that the literary world today would place Dante, not sixth in such a group, but beside Homer, as the second poet.

The poets then move toward a light which seems to come from a castle and a green meadow. There are seven walls and seven gates in this noble castle, which is surrounded by a small river. The poets come to a fresh green meadow.

The second group of spirits in the meadow is composed of Romans and Trojans, active spirits who once engaged in war. There is also one Arab. Thirteen are mentioned, eight of whom are women. There are no Greeks here.

The third group is made up of scientists and philosophers. Nearly all of these are Greek. Here the central figure is Aristotle. They have a light of their own in this dark region, and converse with one another, thus maintaining in limbo their speculative attitudes and interests. The problem of what to do with men like Socrates and Plato must have been puzzling for Dante. Saint Thomas had put them in Hell. Dante does better by putting them in a limbo of their own. These spirits have not been formally condemned.

Dante seems to feel more sympathy for the Greek and Roman second half of limbo than he had shown for the Jewish-Christian first half. The scholastic philosophers spoke of a limbo for unbaptized babies, and another limbo for the heathen fathers. Dante fuses these into one. The vestibule of the neutrals in canto 3 was his own invention, and there is a significant relationship between Dante's vestibule and his limbo. The vestibule exists for those spirits who made no choice in their lives; limbo is reserved for those spirits who were given no choice.

The picture is a symposium. Its hero is Virgil and he is very much at home. It is also a fantasy scene in which there is almost no talk, a circle of suspense. The words in line 45 pervade the canto: *eran sospesi*— they were suspended. And Dante also appears "suspended," hesitant in his description, uncertain of the meaning of this scene, which for us today is too close to allegory.

The figure of Aristotle is memorable. In his *Nicomachean Ethics*, which Dante knew in translation, the underworld has two divisions: upper and lower Hell. In upper Hell, the sins punished are those of incontinence. In Dante's Hell, the vestibule and the six upper circles are also the places where incontinence is punished. It is difficult to understand how incontinence applies to the neutrals of the vestibule and to the worthy heathen of limbo. Were they deficient in the exercise of their will? Were they faulty in willing the highest good? It is hard to reach a satisfactory answer to this basic question, and a modern reader has to rely on the fact that these noble figures have not been judged as the truly incontinent have been judged.

Principal Signs and Symbols:

1. *Limbo* (4:45) or the first circle of Hell: dwelling of the unbaptized and the virtuous pagans. Baptism is the first sacrament, and has been called the "gateway to faith," although this definition is not accurate. Faith is a gift from God. Baptism, as the first sacrament, opens the way to the other sacraments.

2. *The suspended* (*sospesi* 4:45): these spirits know no torment. They are excluded from Heaven and from the other parts of Hell. They live in desire, but without hope.

3. *The harrowing of Hell* (4:52-53): this is mentioned by Virgil and refers to Christ's descent into limbo to liberate the souls of the Jewish patriarchs.

4. *The noble castle* and *the green meadow* (*un nobile castello e il prato di fresca verdura* 4:106-11): this seems to be Dante's version of the elysian fields.

5. *Homer, the sovereign poet* (*Omero, poeta sovrano* 4:88): he carries a sword because his name is so closely associated with the Trojan War.

6. *Aristotle*: "the master of those who know" (*il maestro di color che sanno* 4:131).

Selected Bibliography

Italian Editions of "The Divine Comedy"
Alighieri, Dante, *La divina commedia*. Testo critico della Società dantesca italiana; riveduto col commento scartazziniano; rifatto da Giuseppe Vandelli. Milan: 1957 (seventeenth edition).
Alighieri, Dante, *La divina commedia*. Edited and annotated by C. H. Grandgent. D. C. Heath: 1913.
Alighieri, Dante, *La divina commedia*. Edited and annotated by C. H. Grandgent. Revised by Charles S. Singleton. Harvard University Press: 1972.

Bilingual Editions with Commentary

Singleton, Charles S., *Inferno*. Vol. 1 text, vol. 2 commentary. Princeton: 1970.

The Inferno. Translated by J. A. Carlyle. Revised by H. Oelsner. The Temple Classics: 1970.

Dante's Inferno. Translated by John D. Sinclair. Oxford: 1974.

English Translations

The Comedy of Dante Alighieri. Cantica 1, *Hell*. Translated by Dorothy L. Sayers. Penguin Books: 1974.

Dante's Inferno. Translated by John Ciardi. Rutgers University Press: 1954.

Dante's Inferno. Translated by Mark Musa. Indiana University Press: 1971.

Commentary and Criticism in English

Auerbach, Erich, *Dante: Poet of the Secular World*. Translated by R. Manheim. University of Chicago Press: 1974.

Auerbach, Erich, *Mimesis*. Translated by W. Trask. Doubleday-Anchor: 1957. (See chapter 8, "Farinata and Cavalcante.")

Barbi, Michele, *Life of Dante*. Translated by P. Ruggiers. Cambridge University Press: 1955.

Bergin, Thomas G., *Dante*. Orion Press: 1965.

Brandeis, Irma, editor. *Discussions of The Divine Comedy*. D. C. Heath: 1961.

Brandeis, Irma, *The Ladder of Vision*. Chatto and Windus: 1960.

Charity, A. C., *Events and Their Afterlife: The Dialectics of Typology in the Bible and Dante*. Cambridge: 1966.

Eliot, T. S., "Dante" in *Selected Essays*. Harcourt, Brace: 1932.

Fergusson, Francis, *Dante*. Macmillan: 1966.

Freccero, John, editor. *Dante, A Collection of Critical Essays*. Prentice-Hall: 1965.

Musa, Mark, editor. *Essays on Dante*. Indiana University Press: 1964.

Snider, Denton J., *Dante's Inferno, A Commentary*. William H. Miner: 1892.

Strauss, Walter A., "Proust, Giotto, Dante." *Dante Studies* 96: 163-185.

Williams, Charles, *The Figure of Beatrice*. Noonday Press: 1961.

Aids to Reading the "Inferno"

Bodkin, Maud, *Archetypal Patterns in Poetry*. Vintage Books: 1958.

Dunbar, H. F., *Symbolism in Medieval Thought*. Oxford: 1929.

Vossler, Karl, *Medieval Culture: An Introduction to Dante and His Times*. Vols. 1 and 2. Harcourt, Brace: 1929.

The Portrait of Francesca:
Inferno V _____

As far as we know, there is no record of the love story of Francesca da Rimini before Dante's account in Canto V of the *Inferno*. His portrait of her emerges in astonishingly few verses and, in its passion and pathos, emulates and rivals Virgil's portrayal of Dido. Francesca tells us nothing of her life in the first part of her monologue, apart from her place of birth, which she identifies with elegant periphrasis. Instead, she sums up in retrospect the genesis, consummation and fatal consequences of the love she shared with her inseparable companion in Hell, whom she does not name. Her celebrated apostrophe to love, the unforgettable anaphora on "Amore," is at once succinct and profound, a rhetorical representation in miniature of consciousness and interiority without precedent in the Middle Ages. We shall see that part of it is ultimately derived from Plato's *Phaedrus*, yet it anticipates the "subjectivity" we associate with the modern novel.

In three anaphoric *terzine*, Francesca describes love and its effects, not abstractly, as had other poets and especially Guido Cavalcanti in his abstruse *canzone*, *Donna me prega*, but existentially, relating how she and her lover fell prey to that passion and so were led to their death. This first half of her meditation ends with a prophetic imprecation consigning their killer to the circle of Cain. The name of the original fratricide identifies the killer as her lover's brother. When the opening lines of the next canto refer to the couple as in-laws ("i due cognati [VI, 2]"), we have all we need to know about Francesca's marriage, adultery and death.

After a pause and the pilgrim's compassionate plea that she explain how she succumbed to her dubious desires, she resumes her monologue in a different key, narrative rather than analytic, to describe the "first root" of their love. They were reading together of Lancelot, seized by love. Here too, she provides no external detail, describing

---

The Portrait of Francesca: *Inferno* V   **179**

only their solitude, their glances and their embarrassment. She relates only one event: the notorious "kiss."[1] This second half of her monologue is of the same length as the first, but contradicts it in one important respect. In the first, love was described as spontaneous combustion, "kindled quickly in a gentle heart," which would mitigate the lovers' culpability. In the second part, she describes the occasion of their sin and the mediation of the book by which they were seduced. Like the first half, this part too ends with a curse: "Galeotto fu il libro e chi lo scrisse" ["A Galeotto (was) that book and so was he who wrote it"; Pinsky] (v. 137). She first cursed the fratricide for their death and now the book for their damnation. The two parts of Francesca's monologue are like what came to be called *engaño* and *desengaño* in Spanish drama of the Golden Age, the juxtaposition of the illusion of love with the stark reality of its consequences.

Francesca was an historical personage, the aunt of Guido Novello, Dante's host in Ravenna. The details of her life were probably well known to the poet and his sympathetic portrait of her has often been taken as his tribute to the generosity of his friend. Nevertheless, he gives us few of those details. He does not say that she was duped into her marriage, nor does he suggest that her sin was a singular tragic encounter, rather than the habitual conduct that would merit damnation. When Francesca says that she and her lover were led by love to a single death, it is unlikely that this means the simultaneous death at the hands of love's assassin. The text alludes to her murder only obliquely—"'l modo ancor m'offende" ["in a fierce manner that still torments my soul, (my fair body) was torn untimely away from me"; Pinsky] (v. 102)—and to its perpetrator never by name. We are familiar with what are supposed to be the exterior circumstances of her story, some of them wildly improbable, from glosses on the text written by Boccaccio, who forged them into a coherent plot in what might be called the medieval "romance" of Francesca.

We owe to the commentary of that master story-teller the exculpatory *mise-en-scène* of the affair: a fraudulent marriage, true lovers caught *in flagrante* by a predictably ugly and deformed husband, Paolo's attempted escape, the swashbuckling climax in which the lovers are killed by a sword-thrust meant for Paolo, but skewering the interposed Francesca instead. A second thrust then reaches its mark, killing her hapless lover. The next day they were buried together in the same tomb.

The account of a botched attack by Francesca's husband probably reflects Boccaccio's desperate attempt to translate Dante's verse literally: "Amor condusse noi ad *una* morte [love led us to a single death]" (v. 106), which the commentator construes to mean that her husband first killed her by accident, since he truly loved her, and then his original target. With that, Boccaccio turns Dante's tremendous figure into lurid literality. We shall see, however, that all such fearsome loves, in pursuit of the absolute, result in a single death.

With Boccaccio's pop version of the tale, Francesca and Paolo attained their legendary status.[2] As Virgil transformed Dido, the founder and sober Queen of Carthage, into a tragic and lovesick heroine, so Dante gave to an historical personage the consciousness and voice of love's secular martyr. It remained for Boccaccio, however, to turn her into the heroine of medieval romance and, eventually, of nineteenth century melodrama. Boccaccio's story became something of a "penny-dreadful," the Victorian version of pulp fiction, having little to do with Dante's text. In illustrations of the critical moment, the jealousy-crazed husband was depicted as interrupting their first embrace, the open book lying face-down at Francesca's feet, like a grotesque parody of the Annunciation.[3] The sword drawn as the couple embrace hints at double vendetta: to kill them before they have time to repent, so as to send them directly to Hell. The scene is pruriently fascinating, but theologically absurd. In Dante's system, first-time offenders are sentenced to Purgatory. Hell is reserved for obdurate sinners, whose sin is grievous, habitual and premeditated. Even then, as we learn from Buonconte da Montefeltro in Purgatory (V, 88ff.), pierced in the throat and uttering the name of "Maria," forgiveness is only a gasp away.

Robert Browning was more faithful than his Victorian contemporaries to Dante's style. His "dramatic monologue,"[4] *My Last Duchess*, is reminiscent of Francesca's story, but told from the perspective of the Duke, the lady's husband. Showing a visitor a portrait of his late wife, he is terse, enigmatic, and a touch defensive. His description of her is ominously understated: "[she had] a heart—how shall I say?—too soon made glad." The circumstances under which the Duchess died are suspicious, but never revealed, and remain the subject of conjecture.

Dante's text, in its stunning originality, is no hackneyed romance. It represents Francesca's meditation, a pithy anatomy of love's progress. It lacks the exculpatory detail, social context and sentimental clichés of Boccaccio's narrative and relates only one action. Paradoxically, it is in fact a proleptic critique of the genre into which Boccaccio tried to transform it. When the pilgrim asks the question perennially posed to the guilty by the presumptively innocent—"how could you?"—she turns away from the illusions of romance and acknowledges that, like actors, they were reading themselves into an all too familiar script. What she imagined to be a unique and spontaneous passion turns out to have begun as the mimicry of someone else's story. Reading about Lancelot and Guinevere was the first root of their love and their kiss was its first incarnation.

The phenomenon of mimetic desire is at the center of the work of René Girard, one of the most powerful theorists of culture of our time. Perhaps because his early work on the novel has been overshadowed by his profound influence in anthropology, social studies and comparative religion, few students of Dante seem to know his essay of fifty years ago, dedicated to the canto of Francesca. In the briefest of terms, his point was that the desiring subject imagines, as does Francesca, that desire springs spontaneously from within, while the truth that is revealed by Dante and the greatest of novelists, is that desire is always triangular, "mediated" by the desires of the other—in this case, as in the case of Don Quixote, by a book. In a few mordant pages, Girard debunked the romantic reading of Francesca's story, showing that it was simply a repetition of her own initial mystification. When Girard wrote, the best-selling love story of the time was entitled *By Love Possessed*; Girard's title was polemic, summing up the delusion propagated by all such "romance" stories: "By Literature Possessed." His point was that desire is essentially imitative, searching for a model, and that literature provides it with an imaginary map. Dante's text was not complicit in "romantic" deception. On the contrary, Francesca's last words exposed the *roman* as a panderer and seducer, leading the lovers to their destruction. Her story anticipated those of Chaucer, Shakespeare and Cervantes in the genre of the *"anti-roman."*[5]

Nevertheless, Boccaccio's "romance" of Francesca had its effect on learned as well as popular speculation about her character. So real did she appear to Dante's readers that even serious critics debated her moral qualities, her relative guilt or innocence, as though she were a "personality," rather than simply a character in the infernal drama. The debates have been so vigorous that a distinguished scholar, in his survey of the bibliography, classified the critics as "hawks" or "doves," according to whether they disputed her human weakness or the justice of her condemnation.[6] Yet, her guilt is undeniable; it is axiomatic in Dante's moral system. To dispute that would be to call all of Hell into question.

Leaving aside the naïveté of some of the commentaries, however, the situational irony of Hell fosters the illusion of what György Lukács called "real personality" in Dante's poem, distinguishing it from earlier literature and foreshadowing the rise of the modern novel.[7] Only in Hell do we find a clash between the worldly outlook of the characters and the mute otherworldly reality to which they are unwillingly subject. For Lukács, such discord is absent in the epic, where heroes may fight mightily against monsters and gods, but nevertheless inhabit the same homogenous reality, observing the same rules of the game. In contrast, the novel, Lukács' principal concern, recounts an interior adventure, in which the protagonist is alienated from a fragmented world, separated from all others by an unbridgeable gap. The novel is the "epic of a world from which God has departed." In Dante's poem, which might be thought of as an epic of transcendence, the *Inferno* is an autonomous realm, a "doloroso regno" totally separate from God. It corresponds exactly to Lukács' definition of "novelistic reality." For this reason, he thought of it as the transition from ancient epic to the modern novel.

In Hell, the sinners are alone, even when they are together, individual and separated from the Church and the communion of saints. They are banished from the kingdom of heaven, where God is King ("il re dell'universo" [*Inf.* V, 91]). The illusory "personality" of Francesca and of all of the dramatic figures in Hell who have occasioned debates between "hawks" and "doves" is a function of their respective "singularity." They are surd elements in a hegemonic otherworld. There is no such singularity in the happy family of the blessed and therefore no possible debate among critics about their moral character. No one has ever questioned the heroism of Manfred or the virtue of Piccarda.

The stories recounted by the sinners are inevitably self-serving. Like the testimony of convicts, the truth of their stories can often be impugned. If they have been "framed" in this blind prison (*Inf.* X, 58-59), it is not by false accusation, as in crime stories, but literally, in a thematic sense, by the author, who frames his characters within the larger context of his fiction. Hell is the *cornice* for their stories, an infernal decameron, in which the surroundings cast doubt over the inmates' tales. The contrast between their defensiveness and the self-evident judgment against them casts shadows of doubt in the open mind of a reader who is neither "hawk" nor "dove" and further enhances the illusion of "real personality."

The stories within Dante's story invite ironic interpretation and critical debate, as do the tales told by prisoners protesting their conviction. But in Dante's autobiographical story, he is at once the prosecution and the defense. There are two Dantes, just as there are two Augustines in the *Confessions*. Italian editors of the latter work take pains to distinguish "Agostino narrato" from "Agostino narratore" in their commentaries. In Dante studies, the distinction between the pilgrim and the poet serves the same purpose. In a conversion narrative, the distinction creates the temporal illusion of an experience retrospectively recounted. The relevance of this for the portrait of Francesca is that its moral ambiguity arises from the clash between the secular and human perspective of the damned, once shared by the pilgrim and now by most readers, and implacable Justice, which is the perspective assumed by the poet. The compassionate pilgrim "narrato" is en route to becoming the stern "narratore," who, paradoxically, has been with us from the beginning.

When the accretions of oral history and romance have been removed, Dante's text reveals itself to be at once the origin and the refutation of its own midrashic tradition. Like the barnacles and shells scraped away from the body of Glaucus to restore the sea-god's form (*Republic* X, 611), the sentimental "romance" of Francesca has often served to obscure Dante's pristine conciseness, nuance and intellectual rigor. When it is cleared away, there emerges the simulacrum of a "real personality," the more poignant for having been condemned by its creator.

In the following pages we survey the dominant themes of the canto: the analysis of desire, reciprocity in love, the adumbration of subjectivity and the mediation of the book. We shall see that Dante owes many of these themes to Augustine, who has been called the discoverer of the "inner self."

I. The Wings of Desire

Dante's Hell is an autonomous region, totally separate from deity, where the sinners are sorted according to the coils of a monster's tail. Minos, the judge of Virgil's underworld, is transformed into a Kafkaesque bureaucrat, impersonally and implacably meting out punishment as though the sinners' guilt were a weight seeking its appropriate place in the abyss, according to its specific gravity. The "weight of love" (*pondus amoris*) is a structural principle in the *Commedia*, derived from the Augustinian formula, "pondus meum, amor meus" (*Conf.* XIII, 9, 10). It determines the placement of the sinners, the massiveness of Satan and the spontaneous ascent of the pilgrim through the heavenly spheres. It suggests that one *is* metaphorically what one loves and that sin is therefore its own punishment. Justice is immanent in the sinners; among them, the carnal sinners are the least culpable. They are the best of the worst.

The Kingdom of Heaven, according to the *Gospel of Matthew* (13.31), is like a flourishing tree, where the birds of the air come to rest in its branches. In the kingdom of Hell, the avian imagery is chaotic. The subterranean sky is filled with sinners swept up in a maelstrom, like dense flocks of starlings in winter, impelled by shifting winds and driven in every direction. The paratactic verse "di qua, di là, di giù, di sù li mena" (V, 43) mimics the staccato blasts and intermittent lulls in the infernal hurricane.

Out of the shifting swarm, there emerges in contrast a formation of souls, flying like cranes in single file, as though passing in review. The verse which introduces them is not only syntactically flowing, but rhythmic as well: "E come i gru van cantando lor lai,/ faccendo in aere di sé lunga riga." The ending of the verse, "lunga riga," is spondaic, as though to extend the "line," in the image as well as the meter. Virgil, guiding Dante, then calls the roll of more than a thousand "donne antiche e' cavalieri," the ladies and knights of old, as they peel off from the nameless and innumerable horde.[8]

The avian similes are juxtaposed, but sharply contrasted. The flight of starlings is random, while cranes fly in linear order, "cantando lor lai." The word "lai" is usually understood as "lamentations," but one can scarcely avoid the association with its literal sense: the "lais" sung by the troubadors, or the Breton "lais" of Marie de France, in which the theme is love. Given that nuance, the literary overtones of the verse are reinforced by the ancient belief that the patterns traced by cranes flying in consort were signs, portents, or even letters of the alphabet. Such formations were the closest thing to sky-writing the world had ever seen before the invention of the airplane.[9] If cranes may be said to "chant their lays," then starlings merely make noise. The thematic importance of these emblems of disorder and order at the beginning of the infernal descent is clear: to distinguish the notorious and aristocratic lovers catalogued by Virgil from the swarms of common and anonymous carnal sinners. So, nothing is further said of the generically lustful crowd. The ancient ladies and their knights, however, constitute a pantheon of the literature of love.

Avian imagery permeates the work of the poet who claimed to have flown from the highest perch of Tuscan poetry (*Purg.* XI, 99) to the nest of Leda in the starry heaven (*Par.* XXVII, 98) and whose surname suggests "a bearer of wings" (Latin *aliger*). In a masterful essay on the ancient theme of the wings of love, Leo Spitzer traced its variations, including the dantesque, from Plato to the *Vol de nuit* of Saint-Exupéry.[10] Here in Canto V, the imagery serves a narrative purpose. Starlings connote the chaos of lust, while the flight of cranes suggest the channeling of passion into the formulae of the literature (or even the courtly religion) of love. They are apt emblems of popular literature, flying unswervingly in an aerial "follow-the-leader," corresponding to the tradition of what Girard calls the "mensonge romantique": "imitators imitating imitators in the name of spontaneity."[11]

From the flock of Dido, "la schiera ov'è Dido," there emerge a pair of doves, marking at the same time the emergence of Dante from his literary forebears and his contemporaries. In a lull in the blasts of the infernal wind, Francesca and Paolo respond to the pilgrim's affectionate cry:

> Quali colombe dal disio chiamate
> con l'ali alzate e ferme al dolce nido
> vegnon per l'aere, dal voler portate;
>> cotali uscir da la schiera ov'è Dido
> a noi venendo per l'aere maligno,
> sì forte fu l'affettüoso grido.
>> (*Inf.* V, 82-88)[12]

The simile is a reminiscence from the fifth book of the *Aeneid:* "As a wild dove when startled into flight/ Beats her affrighted way over the fields/ . . . But soon in quiet air goes floating on/ with wings extended motionless . . ." (V, 274).[13] Dante's verses are close enough to Virgil's to make the difference between them all the more salient. Virgil's comparison describes the gliding of a boat after furious strokes of its oars. Dante's doves are impelled by thoroughly human emotions: the doves are called forth by desire and moved by will. The metaphorical wings of Paolo and Francesca, who yearn for peace, echo Virgil's words, but are more reminiscent in sentiment to the poignant verses of *Psalm* 54: "Who will give me the wings of the dove [*pennas colombae*] so that I might fly away and be at rest?" (54.7). In his commentary on this Psalm, St. Augustine suggests that the psalmist in these words longs in vain for the peace of death (*Enarrationes in Psalmos, ad loc. Ps. 54v*). That longing is Francesca's *leit-motif.*

Like cranes, the doves too are emblems of love, but they bear Dante's inimitable theological mark. As they descend from their flock, so Dante parts company from his literary predecessors. Doves appear elsewhere in the poem: in the *Purgatorio* (II, 120) in a penitential setting, as Casella "sings" a *canzone* from the *Convivio*. In the *Paradiso*, Sts James and Peter lavish their affection on each other, murmuring like doves, but this time, the literary allusion is to the Gospels.

The wings of the dove in the *Inferno* are called by desire and moved by will. The words "desire" and "will" may at first seem redundant, but Dante is, as always, precise: they are called from without by [the object of] desire and impelled from within by the will. They seek the sweet nest, as all do, the peace and quiet that doves may reach, but that human lovers will never find. At best, they hover, during a pause in the infernal storm.

The insatiability of human desire is a major theme in the *Inferno*. Its specific emblem is the insuperable she-wolf of the prologue scene, "la bestia sanza pace" (I, 57), but its sway goes beyond the sensitive appetite and infects the mind and heart as well. Francesca yearns for "pace," deliverance from desire, but even death provided no escape for her. As Virgil says of souls in Limbo, "sanza speme vivemo in disio" (IV, 42). The peace for which Christians pray, as the lovers would, were they God's friend (v. 90-91), is the peace of the Lord, the *quies* that "passes understanding" (*Philippians* 4.7). From this, as from death, the souls of the damned are eternally excluded. Francesca is the exemplary victim in Hell of an "unquiet heart."

St. Augustine's *Confessions* begins and ends with this theme. In the first paragraph of what has been called his "pilgrimage of the soul" he says, "you made us for yourself and our heart is unquiet until it rests in you [fecisti nos ad te et inquietum est cor nostrum donec requiescat in te]" (Augustine 1992, I, 38). He returns to the theme in the final paragraph of his work: "we hope that we shall have found rest when you admit us to the great holiness of your presence [nos requieturos in tua grandi sanctificatione speramus]." In our day, Jacques Lacan was perhaps thinking of this passage when he said that the tense of desire is always in the future perfect (cf Bowie 185).

This desire is a metaphysical hunger that cannot be satisfied except by the beatific vision. Appetites, human or animal, are readily, if only temporarily sated, but yearning always exceeds its putative object, seeking the absolute. The first books of the *Confessions* trace metonymically the trajectory of desire throughout Augustine's stages of development: the breast in his infancy, human love in his youth, fame and glory as an adult, but none of these can bring *quies* to the soul. Even what he takes to be the truth of the faith, after his conversion, cannot diminish the heart's yearning.

The wings of human desire, unlike those of doves, will never find rest. Hannah Arendt, who wrote a remarkable thesis on St. Augustine under the tutelage of Karl Jaspers, does not mention Dante, but virtually paraphrases the meaning of his simile: ". . . the very act of desiring presupposes the distinction of an "inner" act ["volere"] and its "external" object ["disio"], so that desiring, by definition, can never attain its object, unless the object, too, is within man, and so within his power" (Arendt 21).

Twenty years after writing his simile of the doves, Dante returned to the distinction between desire and will at the ending of the *Paradiso* and resolved the paradox of desire in a supernatural dimension, exactly as Arendt said was its only possible resolution. The last lines of the poem describe the experience of beatific vision: "già volgeva il mio disio e 'l *velle,*/ sì come rota ch'igualmente è mossa,/ l'amor che move il sole e l'altre stelle [my desire and will were moved, as a wheel is evenly moved, by the love that moves the sun and the other stars]" (*Par.* XXXIII, 143-45). The otherwise perpetually exterior object of desire is internalized in the beatific vision and the descent of desire is arrested and transformed into what the theologians call fruition, the love of God within the soul. What Arendt does not say, but Dante must, is that this interiorization is not in man's power, but is a gift of grace.

All wheels on earth move in two directions at the same time, since they rotate around their own center, and, at the same time, move forward, thanks to their tangency with the ground. So the *motus rotabundus* of beatitude is a simultaneous movement in two directions: an *inner* rotation of the soul around God, now at its center, but also a forward revolution thanks to its integration with the universe, around God, center of the cosmos. In the last sentence of the poem, Love moves desire and will together, along with the sun and the other stars.

The downward course of desire is implicit in its etymology. Etymologists generally agree that the word "desiderare" shares its root with the word "considerare": the noun *sidus, sideris,* meaning "star." However, there seems to be no agreement about the significance of that common origin. In an essay written many years ago, discussing the circular dance of the theologians in the heaven of the sun, I suggested that the word "considerare" was an evocation of the platonic analogy between the circular movement of the heavens and the circular movement of mind, eternally thinking the same thoughts (see Freccero

1986, 226). This would account for both the etymology and the meaning of the word "consideration." The theory usually advanced, that the etymon might have to do with augury or astrology, seems to be excluded by the prefix "con," meaning "with," and by a suffix derived from a verb of action. The etymology I proposed, "to move with the stars," seemed more probable. Essentially, "consideration" is like "contemplation," except that its locus is the heavens rather than a temple. The same hypothetical root, *siderare*, with the prefix of "de" instead of "con," yields an equally ancient significance for "desiderare": "to fall from the stars."

The myth of such a fall was widespread in neoplatonic spiritualism and in the religion of the Gnostics. A passage in the commentary of Macrobius on the "Dream of Scipio" serves to illustrate the mythic theme in a widely diffused text that echoes Plotinus and that Dante probably knew: "the blessed souls, free from all bodily contamination, possess the heavens; but the soul that from its lofty pinnacle of perpetual radiance disdains to grasp after a body . . . yet allows a secret yearning for it to creep into its thoughts [*desiderio latenti cogitaverit*] and gradually slips down to the lower realms because of the very weight of its earthy thoughts" (Macrobius 132-33). This yearning for the body was said to be the cause of the fall from the stars of several mythic angels and souls in the religion of the Gnostics. In some versions, an angel named Sophia gazed lovingly at the earth, like Narcissus at the pool, and fell from the stars to become Helen, the companion of Simon Magus, whom Dante apostrophizes at the opening of Canto XIX. Etymologically, as well as mythically, the circularity of "consideranza" and the linear plunge of "disio" are as far apart as Heaven and Hell.

Francesca's lament is a death wish, to still her "unquiet heart." Human desire is insatiable because it is a thirst for the absolute. If God is excluded in the search, the only other absolute within reach would seem to be annihilation. The descent of the doves in Canto V are reminiscent of the doves of Venus, but they do not alight. Their descent is a "desiderare," an eternal dying fall in search of peace.

II. The Po Descends to the Sea

Courtly love is sometimes referred to as the religion of love; often it has little to do with sexual appetite. It demands the total devotion of the lover, with no claim to reward except for the gracious condescension of his lady. In Augustinian terms, it is quintessentially idolatrous, indifferent or hostile toward marriage and social values. Andreas Capellanus is famous for having written an etiquette book called "The Art of Courtly Love," setting forth the rules of conduct for courtly ladies and their faithful knights. Before Dante's time, the legends of Tristan and Iseult and of Lancelot and Guinevere were adapted into Lais and Romances embodying the courtly code. With some difficulty, the literature struggled to find some contrivance to reconcile courtly love with the code of knightly chivalry. When all else failed, there was always the love potion to mask the incompatibility.

Tristan was a dedicated knight of King Mark, yet he loved Iseult, who was betrothed to the King. Lancelot was a knight of the round-table, who nevertheless slept with Guinevere, King Arthur's Queen. The lovers are portrayed as not being responsible for falling in love, since in both cases there were extenuating circumstances: Tristan and Iseult unwittingly drank a love potion, and Lancelot and Guinevere were seduced by the blandishments of Gallehaut. Nevertheless, their respective cases ended in death or dishonor, not to mention the end of Camelot. Death was the choice for lovers like Tristan and Isolde, the eponymous lovers of Wagner's revival of the story, which ended in a "liebestod." Although Francesca and Paolo were murdered by her husband, their love too bore within it the seeds of its own destruction.

Francesca speaks as a lady in a romance, to mitigate her culpability. She refers to God, from whose sight she is banished, with courtly circumlocution, "il Re dell'universo" ["the King of the universe"] and, of course, to her seduction by Gallehaut. The lines she uses to tell about her birthplace, Ravenna, contain a hint of a courtly motif: "Siede la terra ove nata fui/ su la marina dove 'l Po discende/ per aver pace co' seguaci sui." Singleton translates "The place where I was born lies on the shore where the river Po descends to be at peace with its followers" (see I, 1, 53), but the English misses an exquisite nuance, without which it would be difficult to account for the memorability of the topographic detail. If the Po descends to seek peace (like the dove of *Psalm* 54), a dispersion into the sea, it must be that it is *pursued*, rather than merely followed, by its tributaries—we might say "hounded," until its dissolution. The striking assonance, "seguaci sui," invites an association with the phonetically and semantically related word, "segugi," meaning "hounds," hinting that the tributaries are like hunting dogs, yapping at the heels of a delicate prey. The faint allusion is to the motif of the erotic hunt, the "caccia amorosa."

In antiquity, the most famous example of such a hunt is the death of Acteon, in book III of Ovid's *Metamorphoses*, who was punished by Diana for gazing at her as she was bathing naked in the forest. In indignation, she splashed him, transforming him into a stag, to be pursued and then killed by his own hounds. The Ovidian tale was widely read, elaborated and embellished in the Middle Ages, but perhaps the most famous variation was the lai of Marie de France entitled *Guigemar.* There is no evidence that Dante knew it, but several of its motifs re-emerge in Francesca's story: a knight, who seemed immune to love, hunts and wounds a white hind, strangely transgendered with the antlers of a hart. He is himself wounded by the ricochet of one of his arrows and is swept away down a river in a magic boat, which eventually carries him out to sea. He comes to a castle, where he falls madly in love with the Queen (who has been burning a copy of Ovid's *Remedia amoris*!) and has a passionate and adulterous relationship with her. Her husband discovers them, they escape separately, but after many vicissitudes, are ultimately reunited.

The dream-like fantasy of Marie in the 12th century, with the ricochet arrows of Cupid and the irresistible flow of the river in a magic boat, is brutally de-mystified two centuries later with Boccaccio's nightmare version of the "caccia amorosa." In the fifth book of the

Decameron, Nastagio degli Onesti has an infernal vision of a naked woman hunted by her spurned knight and ripped apart by his dogs, only to be resurrected the following week, when the chase is resumed. The moral of this recurrent nightmare is the lover's wish-fulfillment: a lady should not spurn the advances of her suitor. The cautionary tale from the dark side of courtly love was made socially acceptable, barely, when it was portrayed in four exquisite panels by Botticelli, the last of which was a happy wedding banquet.

The amorous hunt and its history from antiquity through Petrarch to the Renaissance were exhaustively studied by D. C. Allen in an essay on Marvell's "Nymph's Complaint on the Death of her Fawn."[14] He missed one author, however, who provides us with a gloss on Dante's text. In 1502, Antonio Fregoso, a mediocre poet from Genova, wrote an allegorical poem about the pursuit of virtue called the *Cerva Bianca*. Dante may or may not have known *Guigemar*, but Fregoso certainly did. His "white hind" is also transgendered, since it has the antlers of a hart. The hermaphroditism is the emblem of heterosexual love, as it is in Guido Guinizelli's words in *Purgatorio* XXVI, 82: "il nostro peccato fu ermafrodito [our sin was hermaphrodite]." The mythical animal is clearly neither male nor female, but a *surrogatus amoris*, Love itself.

There is little of romance in Fregoso's earnest allegory, except for the landscape. What is most interesting for us are the hunter along the banks of a river and the names of his hounds: they are called "desio" and "pensier," and are so labeled in the frontispiece. These are the words used by the pilgrim in Canto V when he breaks into Francesca's monologue to express his compassion: "Oh lasso,/ quanti dolci *pensier*, quanto *disio*/ menò costoro al doloroso passo! [Alas, How many sweet thoughts, what great desire, drove them to the woeful pass!]" (*Inf*. V, 112-14). With the echo of these verses, the hounds pursuing the "cerva bianca" are interiorized as the inner struggle of love, the *erotomachia*, implicit in the story of Acteon and allusive in the descent of the Po, sweeping away Francesca to her doom.

Critical Insights

III. Eros and Anteros

The verses that follow have become familiar throughout the centuries to virtually every literate Italian. They confirm the role of Francesca as at once the heroine and the victim of love, from its inception to its death. It is a rhetorical tour de force:

> Amor, ch'al cor gentil ratto s'apprende,
> prese costui della bella persona
> che mi fu tolta; e 'l modo ancor m'offende.
> Amor, ch'a nullo amato amar perdona,
> mi prese del costui piacer sì forte,
> che, come vedi, ancor non m'abbandona.
> Amor condusse noi ad una morte.
>
> (*Inf.* V, 100-06)[15]

In a famous essay, Renato Poggioli doubted that Dante intended with the first verse of this anaphora to allude to his own famous sonnet in the *Vita nuova, Amor e cor gentil son una cosa* [love and the gentle heart are one], and to the "school" of like-minded poets.[16] The easy rejoinder to Poggioli's doubt is that, if he is correct, then Dante was running the risk of being badly misunderstood. It is true that his early sonnet specifically credits Guido Guinizelli with that definition of love, but it is equally true that it came to be universally associated with Dante, if not from the little book, certainly from the *Inferno*. In the *Knight's Tale*, Geoffrey Chaucer writes, "pitee renneth soone in gentil herte" (890), which unmistakably echoes Francesca's "pietà" and suggests that by Chaucer's time, Dante owned the allusion, even if he was not its sole proprietor. When Dante invokes the spirits to descend to the travelers (*Inf.* V, 80), it is not in the voice of the poet, but in the voice of the pilgrim, who is very much a character in this canto. We are not told what his affectionate cry ("affettuoso grido") is, but it is in a language that Francesca understands and to which she responds. He calls her in the name of the love that still drives the lovers ("per quello amor che i mena" [v. 78]), which can only be desire. Early in his career, in the "dolce stil novo," Dante spoke the same language.

The point is critical, because it involves the dialectic of pilgrim and poet. If the allusion to the "gentle heart" is in whole or in part attributed to the young Dante, then it is clearly palinodic on the part of the mature poet, who would be rejecting his own theory as he rejects Francesca's. If this is the case, it would explain the celebrated fainting of the pilgrim at the end of the canto as a crisis of remorse for his naive acceptance of a then current poetic cliché. If, on the other hand, the allusion to the "gentle heart" is Dante's Olympian rejection of the theory of his erstwhile school, then the fainting spell at the end of the canto is merely an awkward transition to the next canto. That may be true, but it would certainly be uninteresting.

The second iteration of "Amor" is more complex: "Amor, ch'a nullo amato amar perdona." The observation that love should be requited is banal enough for critics to have adduced many potential sources for Dante's verse, from Scripture to Andreas Capellanus, without being particularly persuasive. What is distinctive about the verse is not the sentiment, but the wordplay. The proposition conveys the idea of reciprocity of love by repetition of its verbal root, just as Pier delle Vigne conveys the contagiousness of envy with variations on the word "infiammare": *infiammò—infiammati—infiammar* (*Inf.* XIII, 67-68). This sort of diction suggests the style of a rhetorician, rather than the biblical or medieval sources usually cited.

The early books of Augustine's *Confessions* are replete with virtuoso plays on the word "Amor," with the Silver Age rhetoric for which he is famous. He tells us that he loved most of all to love and to be loved (*amare et amari*), even when he had not yet loved (*nondum amabam, et amare amabam*). These were the loves which "Agostino narratore" deeply regrets. The closest analogue in his text to Dante's verses is one that stresses a moral imperative to reciprocate friendship, rather than physical love. In the fourth book of the *Confessions*, he explains what it is that is loved in friends: "Hoc est quod diligitur in amicis, et sic diligitur ut rea sibi sit humana conscientia si non amaverit redamantem aut si amantem non redamaverit [this is what we love in friends. We love to the point that the human conscience feels guilty if we do not love the person who is loving us, and if that love is not returned]" (Augustine 1998, 61).

In his extraordinary book, *The Politics of Friendship*, Jacques Derrida gives Augustine's discussion great prominence in the ancient tradition of the literature of friendship from Plato, Aristotle and Cicero, subjecting it to an exhaustive and brilliant philosophical analysis. Of this passage in particular, he observes that its intricacies could be the object of "interminable meditation" (Derrida 186). The similarity of the play on words to Francesca's suggests that it was so for Dante as well. Love in the physical sense ("two souls in one flesh") would appear to be antithetical to friendship ("one soul in bodies twain"); Francesca's play on the word "amare" elides the sharp distinction.

The question is whether body or soul constitutes the "oneness" of love. Francesca loved her lover with her body, so there is no hint in her words of the caveat that Augustine adds to his: "nihil quaerens ex eius corpore praeter indicia benevolentiae [without demanding any physical response other than the marks of affectionate good will]" (Augustine 1998, 61). In the context of Augustine's remarks, a paean to the memory of his beloved friend, so fervent as to strike us as homoerotic, the admonition is critical. At stake is the clear line separating *caritas* from *cupiditas*, of love from lust. Proof that Dante knew Augustine's text is his version of the same caveat in the *Purgatorio*, where he offers a restriction on the obligation to reciprocate a proffered love. When the poets meet Statius, Virgil explains why he responds to Statius' love: "Amore, *acceso di virtù*, sempre altro accese" (XXII, 9-10). A love "kindled" by virtue is perforce chaste. Before Augustine's absolutism, the line between friendship and physical love was sometimes blurred.

Augustine's wordplay in turn precisely reveals his classical source. When he tells us that "the human conscience feels guilty if we do not love the person who is loving us, and if that love is not returned," not only does he invoke a moral imperative to which Francesca seems also to allude ("nullo amato amar *perdona*"), but he also indulges in "echolalia" more intricate than the poet's: "si non amaverit redamantem aut si amantem non redamaverit." The rare word "redamare" was coined by Cicero in *De Amicitia*. Wishing to indicate the reciprocity necessary in friendship, the orator apologizes for the neologism he uses to describe a friend, who "vel amare, ut ita dicam, *redamare* possit [is able to love or—if I may use the word—"re-love"]."[17] As the saying goes, "the Greeks had a word for it," even if Cicero did not. He knew Plato's work well enough to have translated some of the *Timaeus*, the only Platonic dialogue known in the Latin Middle Ages. It seems reasonable to assume that he invented the word "redamare" to render the word "anteros" from Plato's *Phaedrus* (255D), the *locus classicus* for the theme of erotic reciprocity.

The passage in Plato contains many of the themes we have been discussing. We shall have to quote it at length:

. . . as a breeze or an echo rebounds from the smooth rocks and returns whence it came, so does the stream of beauty, passing through the eyes which are the windows of the soul, come back to the beautiful one . . . filling the soul of the beloved also with love. And thus he loves, but he knows not what; he does not understand and cannot explain his own state; he appears to have caught the infection of blindness from another; the lover is his mirror in whom he is beholding himself, but he is not aware of this. When he is with the lover, both cease from their pain, but when he is away then he longs as he is longed for, and has love's image, love for love lodging in his breast [*idolon erotos anterota echon*], which he calls and believes to be not love but friendship only, and his desire is as the desire of the other, but weaker; he wants to see him, touch him, kiss him, embrace him, and probably not long afterwards his desire is accomplished. (Plato 50)

The objective of the older lover in this difficult passage is to mask his seduction of the beloved by convincing him that whatever responses the boy may have are a product of his own god-like beauty rather than to the lover's importunate advances. A. W. Price paraphrases the sense of the passage: "desire overflows the eyes of the lover, and, like a sound echoing back to its source, re-enters the eyes of the boy . . . who in turn falls in love, but with what or whom he cannot tell. In a way, he is a Narcissus in love with his own reflection. . . . Like Ganymede loving Zeus, who is a god, he loves the other as a god whom his own god-like beauty has attracted . . . his return of love (*anteros*) is a reflection of love (*eros*)."[18] The boy mistakes this love for friendship, but, inevitably, with day-to-day contact, in the gymnasium and elsewhere, and although his love is weaker than the fervor of the lover, the beloved succumbs to physical love.

According to Erwin Panofsky, "Plato's [metaphysical] theory of love has left no trace in Greek and Roman poetry" (99). The word "anteros" was sufficiently obscure, he tells us, that when it was revived in the Renaissance it was sometimes misinterpreted to refer to the rival brother of the profane and blindfolded Cupid; that is, "anti-eros," ultimately a symbol of sacred love. Yet this passage of the *Phaedrus* seems to have left some traces, not only in Latin prose, with Cicero and Augustine, but also, however faintly, in the poetry of Ovid.[19] Plato's paragraph reads as if it were the meditation of a still-mystified Narcissus, at once losing and finding himself in his image, an erotic *cogito*: "Iste ego sum!" (*Metamorphoses* III, 463). It begins with the streams of beauty reverberating like an echo. The exchange of glances, the lover as a mirror in which the beloved unknowingly beholds himself, create desire and the response to it, with desire, face to face. Only the endings of the two accounts are different. Plato seems tolerant of the slippage from friendship to physical love, but the myth ends in disaster, commemorated by the flower, marking the place where Narcissus died.

We should observe in retrospect that in Augustine's account of the death of his friend there is as well an erotic *cogito*, a wisp of potential narcissism in his love for his friend, a reminiscence of Ovid's "iste ego sum," but posthumous: "ille alter etiam." We assume that the premature conversion and death of his boyhood friend saved Augustine from experiencing any of the ulterior temptations of intense friendship such as those described in the *Phaedrus*. The echo of Ovid may very well be fortuitous, but the textual similarity of the two declarations underscores the potential narcissism of friendship when it is expressed as the identification, the *immedesimarsi*, of one with the other.

Plotinus was more severe than either Plato or Ovid, condemning any fall from the realm of ideal beauty to physical consummation. He used the myth of Narcissus as a caution to the lover to turn away from the physical embodiment of beauty to pursue instead the ideal. The descent of Narcissus in the following passage may have been the inspiration for Macrobius' cosmological version of the descent of desire, which we have discussed:

> ... when a man sees "the beauty in bodies, he must not pursue them ... they are images, traces and shadows. . . . If a man runs to the image and wants to seize it as if it was [sic] a reality—like a beautiful reflection playing on the water, which some myth recounts that a man wanted to catch, only *to sink down into the stream and disappear* [cf. Macrobius: "paulatim in inferiora delabitur"]—then this man who clings to beautiful bodies and will not let them go, will be precipitated, not in body but in soul, like the man in the story, down into the dark depths of Hades." (*Enn.* I.6.8.10 ff.)[20]

The narcissism described by Plotinus is not the vanity of self-sufficient autonomy, but the mistake of seeking a spiritual absolute in the corporeal beauty of the other. Plotinus' use of the plural ("beautiful bodies") suggests that the stunning allusion to the error of Narcissus in the *Paradiso*, "l'error . . . ch'accese amor tra l'omo e 'l fonte [the error . . . that kindled love between the man and the fountain]" (III, 17) evokes Plotinus more than Ovid. I have written elsewhere about that extraordinary simile; here I wish simply to point out that the pilgrim sees "più facce [many faces]" in the heaven of the Moon, rather than just his own.[21] This would seem to be a neoplatonic, rather than an Ovidian reading of the myth. In any case, on any reading, the love of Narcissus is clearly suicidal.

Given these fatal overtones, the last apostrophe to love, "Amor condusse noi ad una morte," seems impoverished by the literal interpretation it has usually been given, as though it were a stage direction for Ingres or other illustrators of the final scene. But the rhetorical efficacy of repetition, such as the anaphora of "Amore," depends upon its being a linear progression, without which it is merely boring, as Spitzer, in a different context, has observed.[22] Love's anaphora is precisely that: a causal linearity, moving from love's genesis, in a dependent clause, to the "entanglement" of reciprocity in a second dependent clause, to a direct dénouement in its definitive ending. The portentous finality of Francesca's words describes a personified Love so fearsome in its pursuit of the absolute that it annihilates its acolytes.

Thematically, the indefinite singular article, "una," reinforces the motif of the physical unity of the lovers, but it serves a rhetorical purpose as well, ensuring an echo of "amore" in the words "una morte [unA-MORte]." In the folk-etymology of Dante's poetic contemporaries, the lethal ending of such a passion was implicit in its name. The verse echoes the etymon "amor" with which it, like the passion, began. It suggests that the death wish of Love, the *Liebestod*, was merely assisted by a contemptible assassin, who is identified by Francesca only with a pronoun and dismissed with a curse.

The pseudo-etymological pun was used by Guittone d'Arezzo and was a commonplace, according to Gianfranco Contini, in the poetry of the time (Contini 87). He cites Federigo dall'Ambra: "Amor, che tutte cose signoreggia,/ Non fu chiamato amor senza cagione:/ Amor dai savi quasi A MOR S'espone;/ Guarda s'AMOR A MORte s'apareggia [Love, which is Lord of all things, was not by chance called 'Amor': by the learned it was defined as 'A-MORte'; behold how 'Amor' equals 'A-MORte']." The verse is doggerel, but the sentiment is tremendous. It is this deadly power of love that led Guido Cavalcanti in his definition of love to describe it as "fero e sì altero [fierce and haughty]," which is itself a play on words.

There are logical, as well as thematic grounds for arguing that such a love was doomed to end in impasse. In her monologue, there are two Francescas: her consciousness and, in loving memory, her beautiful body ("la bella persona che mi fu tolta"). Of Paolo we can say nothing (as he says nothing), except that he weeps and he is *there*. Dante is at pains to portray in parallel verses the crossed symmetry of their erotic transaction: "prese costui/ mi prese del costui," but all we know of Paolo is that his gaze, directed at her beautiful body, kindled his passion for her and in turn awakened in her a mirrored passion for her own body, valorized by his glance. Now that they are severed from their bodies, the grounds for their love is gone, and they are left as disembodied souls, alone together.

There is a touch of condescension in Francesca's "Amor, ch'a nullo amato amar perdona," distinguishing her love from his. He loved her first and, so, presumably, more. Like the beloved in the *Phaedrus*, her desire is weaker, as if it were in part a moral obligation, as in friendship. But her loving memory of her own beauty and her enduring resentment for its loss ("'l modo ancor m'offende") suggest that her murder was a narcissistic wound that still festers. As she mourns her beauty in retrospect, she gives the impression of a consciousness whose physical charms, like those in a flirtation or a seduction, were instruments of foreign policy, serving as foils for her detached self-love. In abandoning her body to Paolo, she was paying homage to a virtual image of herself, projected into the eyes of the other and reflected in his ardor. Francesca's desire was *to be desired* and only then to reward her suitor.

This consideration sheds light on an ambiguous phrase in her words: "Amor, [. . .] mi prese del costui piacer sì forte che, come vedi, ancor non m'abbandona" (vv. 103-04). It has been argued that, to complete the symmetry of the transaction, Paolo's "piacere" should be translated as the counterpart of Francesca's "persona": as he loved her body, so she loved his "piacere," a word that Dante uses in the *Purgatorio* to indicate the physical manifestation of beauty, derived from Provençal "plazer," meaning charm. It is difficult, however, to understand how Paolo's body could continue to be so attractive to Francesca, now (in the present—*ancora*) that it is gone. It seems more likely that the word "piacere" is to be construed to mean "his *pleasure*," indicating her (narcissistic) satisfaction in the pleasure he took in the beauty of *her* body, now lost to both of them.

This construction would be consonant with the topos of the *Phaedrus*, *anteros* as a reflection of the *eros* emitted by the lover. Otherwise, her love would be a spontaneous and coincident replication of his *eros*, unmotivated by anything other than physical desire for his body. The compulsion that she felt (*a nullo amato amar perdona*) would then be inexplicable. Their coming together would be simply the physical transaction of beautiful and consenting adults, having nothing to do with the tremendous mystery of love.

An interior distance separates Francesca's consciousness from her "bella persona."[23] The transient physical contiguity of the lovers' bodies has had no effect on her inner self. The lovers persist as mutually isolated subjects, who objectified each other, and now, without bodies, are alone together. We have no idea of Paolo's consciousness. Because he is mute, he is simply a pawn in Francesca's analysis of her own love. For all we know, his love was a physical response to Francesca's beauty. Physical beauty can kindle lust as well as love, in hearts gentle or otherwise. In contrast to the law of reciprocity, the hallmark of friendship, consensual physical love tolerates dominance and acquiescence.

The fiction of Hell dramatizes in concrete terms the doubling of the self we experience when we withdraw within ourselves, conscious of an interior distance separating us from the reality in which we live, with our bodies as the front line between that inner self and the world. In the *Inferno*, where the sinners are removed from both the body and the world, Hell is the front line; there is no return from that inner state, which is their sole mode of existence. The great figures in Hell look back with resentment, delusion or bitter regret, fixed and isolated in their respective memories. This permanently "subjective" state, their singularity in conflict with the established order, endows them with that novelistic "personality" that was, in its time, uniquely dantesque.

Although Dante seems to have had no antecedents in western literature for the portrayal of self-reflexive consciousness, such a doubling of the self was of course implicit, in antiquity as well as Christianity, in what came to be called the "examination of conscience," the moral evaluation one makes of one's own actions in the world. It should be mentioned that Latin and the major European languages do not have separate words for "conscience" and "consciousness": both meanings are assigned to the word *conscientia* and its modern derivatives. We have already seen an example of the reduplication of consciousness, or conscience, in Augustine's meditation on friendship, quoted above. He explained that, "the human conscience feels guilty if it does not love in return" (Augustinus 1998, 61). The reflexive construction of the verb expresses the guilt of an inner self: "rea sibi sit humana conscientia."

This interior distance is the forerunner of modern phenomenological analyses of consciousness from Hegel to Heidegger and Sartre; its ancient roots are to be found in Augustinian meditations. According to Phillip Cary, it was the spatialization of memory in Augustine's theory of time that led to what Cary calls "the invention" of the inner self, living in a "memory palace," with a ceiling open to heaven.[24] To know oneself, for Augustine, it was necessary to close the doors (*extra nos*), enter within (*intra nos*), and rise above ourselves (*supra nos*). The metaphor of the "house of the soul" survived, in a radically different version, until the Enlightenment. John Locke described the self as an empty room, a "camera obscura," through which reality entered only through a pinhole in the wall.

In the prison house of the damned there is access neither to the world nor to the stars. The inmates are pure subjectivities, with only memories of a "tempo felice." We might note in passing that the durative "tempo felice" which contributes to Francesca's "dolore" gives the lie to the idea that the lovers' love was consummated in one brief moment, before they were killed. If, as Jacques Lacan maintains, desire is always in the future perfect, it is also true that mortal sin is always in the imperfect: that is, premeditated and obdurate. "Tempo felice" undoubtedly refers to a protracted liaison.

IV. Love by the Book

Having shaken with her words one key myth of courtly love, the myth of reciprocity, Francesca now smashes one most sacred, not only to courtly lovers, but to poets of the "sweet new style" as well, including Dante himself. She refutes the theory of the spontaneous nature of love, in spite of its importance for disproving premeditation in their sin, by confessing that their love took root first of all in their reading. The lover of Plato saw his reflection in the mirror of the beloved, while Ovid's Narcissus saw his reflection in a drowning pool. Francesca saw herself in the equally fallacious mirror of the book: the *roman* of Lancelot:

> Noi leggiavamo un giorno per diletto
> di Lancialotto come Amor lo strinse;
> soli eravamo e sanza alcun sospetto.
> Per più fiate li occhi ci sospinse
> quella lettura, e scolorocci il viso;
> ma solo un punto fu quel che ci vinse.
> Quando leggemmo il disiato riso
> essere basciato da cotanto amante,
> questi, che mai da me non fia diviso,
> la bocca mi basciò tutto tremante.
> Galeotto fu 'l libro e chi lo scrisse:
> quel giorno più non vi leggemmo avante.
> (*Inf.* V, 127-38)[25]

In the *Phaedrus*, the lover is the mirror of the beloved, who then condescends to love in return, with a love that is somewhat weaker. In the context of platonic dualism, the slippage from friendship to physical love compromises the aspiration to ideal beauty in an effort to achieve total identity, body and soul, between the lovers. The *homology* of friends in the texts we have examined determines that the physicality to which they sometimes "descend" must be correspondingly homologous, which is to say *homoerotic*, so that their bodies, as well as their souls, mirror each other. On the other hand, heterosexuality means *difference*, a complement, rather than a replication, of one's body, with no *necessary* claim to spiritual unity beyond compatibility and mutual consent. The illusion of "Amor," in Francesca's "romantic" definition, is that one can find a soul mate and model in one who is simultaneously a heterosexual partner.

If there is a mirror in heterosexuality, a reflection of the self, it cannot be in the opposite gender; it can only be in one's own. The pool of Narcissus is located in inner space. Francesca's mirror is the book, in which, if she can persuade herself that her poor lover is a Lancelot, she can be the "virtual" Queen of Camelot, the fairest of them all, with no "Snow White" to challenge her. The first root of their love was not a mysterious, irresistible passion, but a casting call for one more performance of *Lancelot du Lac*, in which she assigned herself the role of Guinevere, with Paolo as a colorless stand-in for the greatest lover of the realm.

The scene of reading as a scene of seduction had an historical precedent in the century before Dante. In Peter Abelard's *History of My Calamities*, the renowned philosopher seduced the brilliant and beautiful Heloise, entrusted to him as a pupil by her uncle, the Canon Fulbert. As punishment for their scandalous elopement, Fulbert sent his henchmen to capture Abelard, whom they surprised in his sleep and castrated, after which Heloise was forcibly cloistered. The lovers achieved canonical status in François Villon's *Ballade des dames du temps jadis*. In the popular imagination of the 19th century, they were historical counterparts of Francesca and Paolo. In exactly the same year of Ingres' famous painting of the murder of Francesca and Paolo, 1819, Jean Vignaud depicted the discovery of Heloise and Abelard in a scene almost identical to Ingres' painting, except that it is the canon Fulbert, in clerical garb, instead of Gianciotto, who looks in on the lovers from the doorway of their room.

Peter Dronke called attention to the parallel between the distraction from the text of Abelard's lovers and that of Dante's, as well as verbal similarities in the description of their exchange of glances and their respective embarrassment (see Dronke). The critical difference in the scenes is that the book is irrelevant for Abelard: "Our speech was more of love than of the books which lay open before us; our kisses far outnumbered our reasoned words. Our hands sought less the book than each other's bosoms—love drew our eyes together far more than the lesson drew them to the pages of our text. . . . What followed? No degree in love's progress was left untried by our passion . . ." (Abelard 14). Abelard's passion, as he portrays it, was pure lust. Of Heloise's love, faithful to death, we know little except for her letters, authentic or not. One suspects that her story would have resembled the "romance of Francesca," even to the detail of the single tomb, now in the cemetery of Père Lachaise.[26]

In contrast, Francesca's reading of the book is critical in her story. The verses that set the stage for her performance ought to be (and in fact have often been!) read *crescendo* to help us understand the role she intended to assume: "quando leggemmo il disïato riso esser basciato da cotanto amante . . . [when we read of the longed-for smile kissed by such a lover . . .]." The culmination of her romantic illusion, the delicate circumlocution of "disïato riso" to indicate Guinevere's lips and the description of Francesca's now silent but weeping partner as a substitute for the greatest of lovers, bring us to the cusp separating romance and reality. The very next word shatters the illusion. The bare demonstrative pronoun "questi," indicating, perhaps with a perfunctory gesture, her companion in misery, is said, indelicately, to have kissed her mouth, rather than her lips, all trembling.

The gap separating the erotic fantasies of literature from their sometimes awkward re-enactment in real life was exploited for comic effect in antiquity by Terence (*Eunuchus* III, 5), but for St. Augustine, it was no laughing matter. In the first book of the *Confessions*, the most "logocentric" Father of the Church rails against the seduction of the young by literature and uses the play by Terence as an example. He inveighs against the mythological fables of Homer, whose stories of the adulteries of Jupiter, the "thunderer," encourage his followers to commit adultery, while claiming the authority to do so by mimicking false "thundering." Augustine quotes the words of the young man in the play, gazing at the picture of Jupiter, impregnating Danae in a shower of gold: "what a god he is! His mighty thunder rocks the sky from end to end. You may say that I am only a man and thundering is beyond my power. But I played the rest of the part well enough and willingly, too!" (Augustine 1961, 37).

The imitation of a book is a moral precept in Christianity, the basis for the *imitatio Christi* and, in popular religion, for moral guidance in the *sortes biblicae*, the random consultation of the Bible for a sign. In the eighth book of the *Confessions*, the scene of conversion, Augustine is commanded, through the voices of children, to take up the book and read: "tolle! lege!" He obeys because he remembers Ponticianus' story of the conversion of two young men when they read the life of St. Antony, who was in turn converted by the words he heard in a sermon. I have written elsewhere that conversion is a textual as much as a spiritual event, effected by the Word of God *in bono*, or, *in malo*, by the words of books.[27] Girard has observed that Don Quixote, infected by his reading, follows the precepts of chivalric romance and imitates Amadis of Gaul with the fervor of a Christian imitating the life of Christ (see Girard 1966). Instead of a god, he worships an idol. The efficacy of both the Word of God and the words of man, the permeability of the heart to words of antithetical provenance, helps to understand why the cult of romantic love should have reached its apogee precisely in the age of faith.

For Augustine, language is born in desire, even in the infant's paralanguage of gesticulation. The infant "breaks in its mouth" to the sounds of language in order to express desire, which is insatiable, always exceeding the infant's needs.[28] Nevertheless, the "heart" seeks to channel overflowing desire with various "objects" of desire, chosen from a world that adults have named. It will never find its rest, unless and until [*donec*] it rests in God. Meanwhile, the literature that Augustine bitterly condemns offers myriad surrogate and illusory objects of desire, culled from a world meant to be used (*uti*), rather than enjoyed (*frui*), as only God should be. To enjoy what should be used is to counterfeit love and substitute for it idolatry. Diverting the heart away from its goal requires a powerful enchanter.

The words "galeotto fu il libro e chi lo scrisse" compare the writer's craft to the mediation (to use the polite word) of Prince Gallehaut, between Lancelot and Guinevere. The analogy became a topos almost immediately. In the context of Francesca's damnation it has the ring of a curse, but Boccaccio's *Decameron* proudly bears the subtitle of "Prencipe Galeotto," as if to announce boldly the seductive intent of the book: to bring solace to idle ladies, disappointed in love. In Chaucer's *Troilus and Criseyde*, the lady's uncle, Pandarus, fulfills the role of Gallehaut and bequeaths his name to the English language in a less polite word for erotic mediation: "pandering." Chaucer's masterpiece is a deft denunciation of cheap romance. After dozens of verses in which Pandarus extols the beauty and virtues of Troilus to cajole his niece, she finally sees Troilus from her window and asks herself "who gave me drink?" meaning, of course, a love potion (*T.C.* III, 1555). When Pandarus finally succeeds in getting the lovers into bed, he tucks them in and retires to the fire to read his "old romance."

Francesca's last words, "quel giorno più non vi leggemmo avante [in its pages that day we read no more]," use what rhetoricians call "reticentia," a figure to express by pointed suppression a meaning that is obscene, horrible, or otherwise unspeakable. Francesca's words allude to meaning, which is clearly, almost vulgarly, obscene. Yet Dante's *reticentia* is never quite that obvious. In the Canto of Ugolino, for example, an equally famous instance of reticence are Ugolino's last words: "poscia, più che 'l dolor poté il digiuno" (*Inf.* XXXIII, 75), the meaning of which was debated by critics as famous as Byron and Shelley, who respectively affirmed and denied the allusion to cannibalism in the verse.

At opposite poles of the *Inferno*, what these two instances of reticence have in common is that they are both spoken in the dramatic monologues of characters in Dante's fiction. Those characters perforce disappear at the borderline, where literature meets the voiceless reality of flesh and blood. In Dante's parlance, flesh and blood is the realm of the sensitive soul, the pre-human animality of sex, in the case of the lovers, or the post-human noise of a dog, with a bone in his maw. The clinical insistence on the mouth in both episodes marks the transition from words to the flesh.

We have seen that Francesca is what Lukács called a "novelistic" personality, whom we might think of as a medieval *Madame Bovary*. Whatever Flaubert meant by his enigmatic identification with his heroine, "Madame Bovary, c'est moi," it would apply at face value to the character "Dante" in this canto. The words placed in Francesca's mouth sound very much like words used by the poet as a young man, the religion of the "gentle heart," the spontaneity of love, the dark eros of the *Rime Petrose*. Her retraction in the second part of her monologue is at the same time his palinode. The character "Dante" disappears with her, falling as a dead man falls, silenced, leaving behind the stern narrator to revive him for the next stage of his pilgrimage.

From *MLN* 124.5 Supplement (December 2009): S7-S38. Copyright © 2010 by The Johns Hopkins University Press. Reprinted with permission of The Johns Hopkins University Press.

Notes

I wish to acknowledge with gratitude the invaluable help of Melissa Swain of NYU for choosing and assembling the illustrations for this article [not included in this re-printing]. I owe to the tireless efforts of Igor Candido and Francesco Caruso my sincere thanks for their help in preparing this article for publication. I am indebted to them and to my friend and colleague Walter Stephens, The Charles S. Singleton Professor of Italian at Johns Hopkins, for the invitation to revisit the university.

[*Editor's Note:* All translations citing Pinsky are from *The Inferno of Dante*, translated by Robert Pinsky (New York: Farrar, Straus and Giroux, 1994).]

1. For the kiss, see Perella.

2. For a reading of Dante's construction and Boccaccio's "elaboration" of the figure of Francesca, see Barolini.

3. The popular theme of the Annunciation in medieval and renaissance visual art is taken from *Luke* 1.26-38, in which the Angel Gabriel appears to the Virgin Mary to announce the forthcoming incarnation of Christ. In the later medieval visual tradition following St. Bernard's textual gloss as well as other popular theological writings of the time, the Virgin is often depicted as having been interrupted in the act of reading. In some instances, the text of Isaiah is reproduced in the image (*Isaiah* 7.14, "behold, a virgin shall conceive and bring forth a son, and his name shall be called Emmanuel").

4. See Parker.

5. See Girard 1978.

6. See Dronke.

7. See Lukács.

8. Cranes in the poem are associated with writing and its inspiration. In the *Purgatorio*, after Dante's definition of his poetry, Bonagiunta says: "io veggio ben come le vostre penne/ di retro al dittator sen vanno strette/ che de le nostre certo non avvenne" (XXIV, 58-60). There follows a simile of cranes, suggested by the word "penne" ("quills") and the words "sen vanno strette." The allusion is possibly to a poem by Guido Guinizelli, addressed to Bonagiunta, in which different poets are said to be as varied as species of birds. Two cantos later, a particularly contrived "hypothetical" simile of migrating cranes represent the penitent lover-poets, homosexual and heterosexual: "Poi, come grue ch'a le montagne Rife/ volasser parte, e parte inver' l'arene,/ queste del gel, quelle del sole schife . . ." (*Purg.* XXVI, 43-45).

9. Sky-writing is described in the heaven of Justice (*Paradiso* XVIII-XX), where Dante executes spectacular variations on a theme from Lucan: the successive tracing and undoing of letters formed by cranes.

10. See Spitzer.

11. See Girard 1978.

12. "As doves called by desire, with wings raised and steady, come through the air, borne by their will to their sweet nest, so did these issue from the troop where Dido is, coming to us through the malignant air, such force had my compassionate cry" (Singleton I, 1, 53).

13. Fitzgerald's translation 132.

14. See also Thiebaux and Barberi Squarotti.

---

15. "Love, which is quickly kindled in a gentle heart, seized this one for the beautiful body that was taken from me in a way that still offends me. Love, which absolves no one loved from loving, seized me so strongly with his pleasure that, as you see, it still has not left me. Love led us to one death" (Singleton I, 1, 53).

16. See Poggioli.

17. Cicero, *De Amicitia*, 14.49. Quoted by O'Donnell in Augustine 1992, II, 232, along with other citations.

18. See the commentary *ad. loc.* by A. W. Price 87, who notes the resemblance to Narcissus.

19. See Goldin.

20. Quoted from Plotinus 53.

21. See Freccero 1998.

22. See Spitzer.

23. I take the phrase from Georges Poulet's *Études sur le temps humain, II: La distance intérieure*.

24. See Cary, Chapter 10, "The Origin of Inner Space," 125 ff. The reference to John Locke is Cary's.

25. "One day for pastime, we read about Lancelot, how love seized him; we were alone, suspecting nothing. Several times that reading urged our eyes to meet and took the color from our faces, but one moment alone it was that overcame us. When we read how the longed for smile was kissed by so great a lover, this one, who never shall be parted from me, kissed my mouth all trembling. A Gallehaut was the book and he who wrote it; in its pages that day we read no more" (Singleton I, 1, 55).

26. One can imagine what a "Romance of Paolo" might have been, before his damnation. Brothers, thinking that they love each other, gradually become consumed with mimetic envy, vying for the hand of the fair Francesca, who is simply a pawn. Gianciotto wins, but is ultimately defeated by the adulterous love of his wife for the dashing Paolo. Together, the lovers kill Gianciotto. Such a plot would correspond to Cervantes' novella contained within the *Quixote*, "El curioso impertinente," as read by René Girard in Girard 1961. Girard's first chapter deals with "external mediation" in *Don Quixote*.

27. Cf. Freccero 1986.

28. These remarks are a synopsis of the theme as represented in Book I of the *Confessions*. Quotations are from *Confessions* 1998, 18-19.

Works Cited

Allen, Don Cameron. "Marlowe's *Dido* and the Tradition." *Essays on Shakespeare and Elizabethan Drama in Honor of Hardin Craig.* Ed. R. Hosley (London: Routledge, 1963), 55-68.

Arendt, Hannah. *Love and Saint Augustine* (Chicago: The University of Chicago Press, 1996).

Augustine, St. *Confessions.* Trans. R. S. Pine-Coffin (London; New York, N.Y., U.S.A.: Penguin Books, 1961).

_____. *Confessions*. Commentary by J. O'Donnell. 3 vols. (Oxford: Clarendon Press; Oxford; New York: Oxford University Press, 1992).

_____. *Confessions*. Trans. with an introduction and notes by H. Chadwick (Oxford: Oxford University Press, 1998).

Bàrberi Squarotti, Giorgio. *Selvaggia Dilettanza: La caccia nella letteratura italiana dalle origini a Marino* (Venezia: Marsilio, 2000).

Barolini, Teodolinda. "Dante and Francesca da Rimini: Realpolitik, Romance, Gender." *Speculum* 75.1 (January 2000): 1-28.

Bowie, Malcolm. *Lacan* (Cambridge, MA: Harvard University Press, 1991).

Cary, Philip. *Augustine's Invention of the Inner Self: The Legacy of a Christian Platonist* (Oxford: Oxford University Press, 2000).

Contini, Gianfranco, ed. *Poeti del dolce stil novo* (Milan: Mondadori, 1991).

Derrida, Jacques. *The Politics of Friendship*. Trans. G. Collins (London: Verso, 2005).

Dronke, Peter. "Francesca and Héloïse." *Comparative Literature* 27.2 (Spring 1975): 113-35.

Freccero, John. *Dante: The Poetics of Conversion*. Ed. R. Jacoff (Cambridge, MA: Harvard University Press, 1986).

_____. "Moon Shadows: *Paradiso* III." *Studies for Dante: Essays in Honor of Dante Della Terza*. Ed. F. Fido et al. (Fiesole: Cadmo, 1998), 89-101.

Fregoso, Antonio and Bartholomeus Simonetta. *Opera nova del magnifico cavaliero messer Antonio Philaremo Fregoso intitvlata Cerva biancha: corretta novamente* (Venice: Printed by Nicolo Zopino, 1525).

Girard, René. *Deceit, Desire, and the Novel: Self and Other in Literary Structure* (Baltimore: The Johns Hopkins University Press, 1966).

_____. *Mensonge romantique et vèrité romanesque* (Paris: Grasset, 1961).

_____. *To Double Business Bound: Essays on Literature, Mimesis, and Anthropology* (Baltimore: The Johns Hopkins University Press, 1978).

Goldin, Frederick. *The Mirror of Narcissus in the Courtly Love Lyric* (Ithaca, NY: Cornell University Press, 1967).

Lukács, György. *The Theory of the Novel*. Trans. A. Bostock (Cambridge, MA: MIT, 1971).

Macrobius. *Commentary on the Dream of Scipio*. Ed. and trans. W. Stahl (New York: Columbia University Press, 1952).

Panofsky, Erwin. *Studies in Iconology: Humanistic Themes in the Art of the Renaissance* (New York: Oxford University Press, 1967).

Parker, Patricia. "Dante and the Dramatic Monologue." *Stanford Literature Review* 2.2 (Fall 1985): 165-83.

Perella, Nicholas J. *The Kiss, Sacred and Profane: An Interpretive History of Kiss Symbolism and Related Religio-erotic Themes* (Berkeley and Los Angeles: University of California Press, 1969).

Peter Abelard. *Historia calamitatum. The story of my misfortunes: An autobiography*. Trans. H. A. Bellows (Saint Paul, MN: T. A. Boyd, 1922).

Plato. *Phaedrus*. Ed. B. Jowett (Teddington: The Echo Library, 2006).

Plotinus I. Porphyry on the life of Plotinus and the order of his books. Enneads I. Trans. A. H. Armstrong (Cambridge: Harvard University Press, 1967).

Poggioli, Renato. "Tragedy or Romance? A Reading of the Paolo and Francesca Episode in Dante's Inferno." *PMLA* 72.3 (1957): 313-58.

Poulet, Georges. *Études sur le temps humain, II: La distance intérieure* (Paris: Plon, 1965).

Price, A. W. *Love and Friendship in Plato and Aristotle* (Oxford: Clarendon Press, 1990).

Singleton, Charles S. *The Divine Comedy*. Trans. with a commentary by C. S. Singleton. 3 vols. in 6 tomes (Princeton, N.J.: Princeton University Press, 1970-1975).

Spitzer, Leo. "The Poetic Treatment of a Platonic-Christian Theme." *Comparative Literature* 6.3 (Summer 1954): 193-217.

Thiebaux, Marcelle. *The Stag of Love: The Chase in Medieval Literature* (Ithaca, NY: Cornell University Press, 1974).

Virgil. *The Aeneid*. Trans. R. Fitzgerald (New York: Random House, 1983).

Echoes of Andromache in *Inferno* X_____

Joseph Luzzi

The critical literature on *Inferno* X, one of the most studied cantos in the *Commedia*, tends to focus either on the psychological complexities of the Pilgrim's encounter with the ghost of his *primo amico*'s father, Cavalcante de' Cavalcanti, or on the linguistic misunderstanding that transpires during this dialogue—a *malinteso* with, of course, profound theological implications.[1] Stimulated by the biographical and contextual criticism of the Romantics, pioneering interpretations by Francesco de Sanctis and Erich Auerbach helped initiate a parallel line of readings that focuses on the canto's historical and political aspects, especially in the prophecy of Dante's exile by the unforgettable Farinata degli Uberti, a character emblematic of Dante's surging "realism" and genius for dramatic effect.[2] The prominence of the canto in the criticism is understandable, given its privileged access to such defining elements of Dante's writing as palinode and autobiographical reflection, the tension between secular and spiritual concerns, and the abiding question of Florence. Notwithstanding the attention devoted to the Virgilian subtext of *Inferno* X (especially in the commentary tradition),[3] the scholarship has not to my knowledge produced a sustained treatment of the canto's allusion to Andromache's dialogue with Aeneas at Buthrotum in *Aeneid* III (cited below), an exchange that permeates Cavalcante's tortured inquiries about his son Guido's whereabouts and impacts the Pilgrim's entire journey through the *al di là*.

> piangendo disse: "Se per questo cieco
> carcere vai per altezza d'ingegno,
> mio figlio ov'è? e perché non è teco?"
>
> (*Inf.* X, 58-60)

"[. . .] vivisne? aut, si lux alma recessit,
Hector ubi est?" dixit, lacrimasque effudit et ominem
implevit clamore locum. [. . .]"

(Aen. III, 311-13)

("Are you [Aeneas] alive? If the light of life has left you, [. . .] [w]here is
Hector?" As she [Andromache] spoke she burst into tears and her cries
filled the grove.)[4]

I will argue that Dante's *translatio* of Andromache's voice via
Cavalcante triggers an elaborate thematic construction in which the
Pilgrim—like Aeneas confronted with the task of founding a new Rome
and leaving behind the false "little Troy" (*parva Troia*) of *Aeneid* III—
overcomes the personal, philosophical, and literary-historical nostalgia elicited by his meeting with the Florentine patriarchs.[5] By situat-
ing Guido Cavalcanti's notorious "disdegno" (63) in the subtext of
Andromache's effusive tears, "lacrimasque effudit" (312), Dante connects the Pilgrim's spiritual ascent with the formal exigencies of the
epic genre, the historical considerations of Roman imperial ideology,
and the theological dimensions of his impending exile as prophesied
by Farinata. In a manner that anticipates Andromache's subsequent
haunting of Western literary history, the *Inferno*'s lyric inscription of
the *parva Troia* episode shows how the private or hidden affective
qualities of a literary allusion can challenge and even reverse the more
public, explicit, and superficially referential elements of the source
text, however prestigious and paradigmatic.

The critical lacuna on the legacy of Andromache in *Inferno* X
comes as no surprise, for her voice resurfaces in an extremely mediated
fashion: as an approximate auditory fragment or echo, as John Hollander describes the term in his study of the figure.

[Echo is] a way of alluding that is inherently poetic, rather than expository,
and that makes new metaphor rather than learned gestures. [. . .] Poets [. . .]

seem to echo earlier voices with full or suppressed consciousness that, and of how, they are so doing, by accident or by plan, but with the same shaping spirit that gives form to tropes of thought and feeling. Whether these figurative echoes constitute a kind of underground cipher-message for the attentive poetic ear, or perhaps a private melody or undersong hummed during composition by the poet as a spell or charm, matters less [. . .] than that the revisionary power of poetic allusive echo generates new figuration.[6]

This notion of echo, as an allusive practice that aurally gestures in the direction of a source yet simultaneously establishes its freedom from origin by generating new formal and thematic structures, epitomizes the revisionary process at work in Dante's recapitulation of the Virgilian subtext in *Inferno* X.[7] The voicing of Andromache's lament by Cavalcante depends on a figurative and linguistic repetition, whereby "the repeated sound is not only contingent upon the [source], but in some way a qualified version of it (a metaphor of the decaying dynamics of successive echoes, perhaps)."[8] In *Inferno* X, the transition from Virgil's Latin to Dante's Tuscan further mediates the sonic distancing inherent in poetic echo. The verbal refraction of Andromache's voice represents but one of many instances in which Dante employs an aural reference meant both to evoke a predecessor text and obscure or manipulate that source's presence and meaning. In *Inferno* V, for example, when Francesca repeats to Dante the celebrated Guinizzellian figure of the *cor gentil* overcome by passion ("Amor, ch'al cor gentil ratto s'apprende"; "Amor, ch'a nullo amato amar perdona"; and "Amor condusse noi ad una morte"),[9] the sentiments expressed in the anaphoric construction and their accompanying images actually undermine Francesca's would-be defense of her adultery, for her words represent a sinful notion of love from the poem's Christian perspective. Francesca is not "citing" Guinizzelli, but rather loosely recapitulating any number of lyrical representations of *amor* by the Stilnovisti (especially Cavalcanti), a move that allows Dante to engage in literary-historical reflection of a most intimate and, given the unyielding moral economy of the *Commedia*, stringent kind.[10] The unstable echoing lines in Francesca's discourse on love, with their implication of a lack of agency and incantatory evocation of overwhelming emotion, recall the figurative body of that same Lord of Love who haunted and daunted the Dante of the earlier *Vita Nuova*. The confluence of metaphor, precept, and theme in Francesca's ersatz allusion to Guinizzelli's *cor gentil* thus operates on a range of sensorial, cognitive, and affective planes, for it is aural (spoken by Francesca and heard by the Pilgrim), textual (written and cited by the Poet), and indeed *felt* by the Pilgrim (he swoons after Francesca's speech, arguably because of his own guilty hand in composing the kind of poetry reflected in her misplaced passion). However one wishes to gloss Francesca's Guinizzellian misprision, it is plausible to argue that the scene's dramatic possibilities derive in great part from the resonance of a purposefully ambivalent echo in which Dante's vaunted powers of synthesis assume a decidedly acoustic dimension.

Whereas composition generally entailed an overt display of allusive skill for such later writers as Petrarch and his fellow literary humanists, Dante faced less or at least a different kind of pressure in this regard. From his earliest compositions in the Stil Novo to the *Commedia* of his poetic maturity, Dante does of course weave a rich intertextual tapestry of ancient and medieval authors—an intertextuality laced, moreover, with tireless allusions to his own work. Yet, to a greater degree than Petrarch, Dante's rewriting of other texts quite often seeks, for moral or religious reasons, to eclipse the source or reduce it to an ethereal and shadowy presence, fittingly enough in the case of the supremely ectoplastic Andromache. The ambiguities of the spectral Andromache are intensified in *Inferno* X by another ghostly presence with whom Dante also grapples in this canto of settling accounts (albeit provisionally): Guido Cavalcanti.[11] By locating the Andromachean lament for Hector in Cavalcante's plea for his son, Dante suggests the Oedipal and epic-like pitch of his own unresolved tension vis-à-vis his initial *maître à penser*, Guido. One is tempted to posit that Dante's tortuous allusion to Andromache represents a defensive invocation of his first poetic mentor (Guido) through a version of the anxious, antithetical model of influence described by Bloom: i.e., that mode of referring to a predecessor poet by avoiding explicit reference and masking the textual ligature or debt in a web of evasions, false leads, even silence.[12] At the risk of acquiescing to a critical anachronism, I believe there is something to be gained by this Freudian line of interpretation; yet one does not need modern theory to diagnose the canto's psychological pressures, since Dante renders these symptoms fully manifest through an extended intertextual dialogue with Virgilian and Stilnovistic sources.

The subtext of Dante's allusive anxiety in *Inferno* X is one of the more poignant episodes in the *Aeneid*. With the flames of his lost city left behind, Aeneas lands in Carthage and recounts to Dido how he left Troy in tears ("lacrimans," *Aen*. III, 10) and as an exile ("exsul," 11). He narrates his false starts and failed attempts to resurrect his city, first at the eponymous Aeneadae, where the specter of the slain Polydorus emerges to warn away the Trojans; later in Crete, where a dream vision of the Penates once again disperses the castaways with a prophecy of their true destination: "est locus, Hesperiam Grai cognomine dicunt,/ terra antiqua, potens armis atque ubere glaebae;/ [. . .] hae nobis propriae sedes" (163-64, 166-67): "There is a place—Greeks call it Hesperia—an ancient land, strong in arms and in the richness of her soil. [. . .] This is our true home." Fortified with this promise, the Trojans set sail in search of a second Troy in what is now the Italian Peninsula. Blown off course, the ships eventually deter into the coast of Epirus and the city of Buthrotum. "Here," Aeneas recounts to Dido, "there came to our ears a story almost beyond belief" ("Hic incredibilis rerum fama occupat auris," 294)—a tale whose emphatic doubling and mix of the familiar and spectral bring to mind elements of the Freudian uncanny. Buthrotum, it turns out, is a city under the rule of Priam's son Helenus, who has taken Andromache, former wife of the great Hector, as his queen and assumed control of the kingdom (and the bride) previously under the dominion of the Greek king Pyrrhus after the Trojan War. So Aeneas discovers Andromache returned to that same family that housed her before the calamities of war with Greece, but her restoration, he learns, is anything but felicitous.[13] The land he has stumbled upon is a copy of his lost home, peopled by old friends and with a citadel modeled on the Trojan Pergamum. Initially, the reproduced homeland fills Aeneas with joy. He embraces the threshold of the Scaean Gate, and his fellow Trojans enjoy their twin city ("simil urbe," 352) and attend a welcoming feast. Yet a funereal atmosphere pervades the city, to which Aeneas refers with the pejorative tag of "parva Troia" ("little Troy"). In her unstinting grief and obsession with the past, Andromache seems more dead than alive, and Buthrotum's Xanthus River itself is "dry" ("arentem," 350). Virgil refashions the Trojan *polis* into a kind of necropolis, a city consecrated to the past and memories of the dead. Eventually, Aeneas will have to acknowledge the pact between Juno and Jupiter that there can be no *Troia rediviva*, and that he will perforce continue to seek not a second Troy but a new Rome, which for all its glory and regenerative force will always remind him of a former life lost. Aeneas will recreate the old Troy in the new Rome in part by a *translatio imperii* of a literal kind, by carrying the Penates into Alba Longa. Following Maurizio Bettini's suggestive rhetorical reading of the episode ("Ghosts of Exile," 29-30), one could describe Aeneas's political translation in terms of metonymy: the Penates are representative parts that serve the subsequent reconstitution of a larger whole, the Trojan *Italia*. Andromache, on the other hand, will resort to a less successful, more metaphorical act of translation. Her *parva Troia* merely approximates the original city by reproducing it through an impoverished analogy. Employing the painful grammar of immigration, Virgil portrays an Andromache unable to release herself from the claims of the past and the material world that houses it, and so she spends her days marking time backward and futilely rebuilding a domestic sphere history has undone.

This Virgilian scene and its themes have proved resurgent in writers ranging from Dante and Yeats to the French authors Racine, Baudelaire, Mallarmé, and Roubaud.[14] Thomas Greene even suggests that Virgil's creation of the *parva Troia* episode and its stubborn resonance in the *Aeneid* embodies a quintessential "tragic anachronism" of Western literary history.

> The *Aeneid* displays an awareness of tragic anachronism that Virgil's culture did not formulate discursively, and as the central classic of Western civilization it inscribed this awareness, this ambivalent sympathy, upon our whole tradition. It authorized the regret that stems from turning one's back, as the poem as a whole turns its back. Andromache and Helenus are signs for the dominance of that Homeric past from which Roman epic struggles to free itself, but not without misgivings, and these misgivings have remained to define our intercourse with our past.[15]

Particularly instructive is Greene's observation that the political and cultural burdens either narrated or anticipated by the Homeric *Ur*-text— in the above case, the dominion of the conquering Greeks over Andromache and the Trojans—mirror the formal challenges faced by Homer's heirs, especially Virgil. Homeric epic provided Virgil with a master narrative about heroism, homecoming, and the waxing and waning of great civilizations; from Homer Virgil was also able to wrest a poetic protocol whereby a physical space is consecrated in the name of the transcendental ideals that sanction its ideological underpinnings. The voice of Andromache, however, surfaces above the din of the epic's historical struggles to remind each successive generation of readers that, in this literary genre as in life, there are winners and there are losers.[16] In order to advance the claims of the *Aeneid*, Virgil circumscribes the voice of Andromache—and, by extension, the architectural echoes binding Buthrotum to the razed city of Troy—in a remote outpost whose gravitational melancholy the agent of historical progress, Aeneas, hastens to exit. The resilient voice of Andromache and her failed replication of Troy appear in the *Aeneid* as a ghostly trace

that the Virgilian master narrative suppresses yet never wholly eliminates nor comfortably absorbs.[17]

Several centuries later, Virgil's disciple Dante would face a similar
challenge from the phantoms of epic inheritance, imperial ideology,
and nostalgic exile in *Inferno* X, a canto that scholars (however divided over issues related to Dante's exchange with Cavalcante) generally acknowledge to be one of the more figuratively dense in Dante's
poetry.[18] Andromache's image of the sweet light in her aforementioned
lines from *Aen*. III ("aut, si *lux alma* recessit,/ Hector ubi est?" 311-12)
resurfaces as the photographic negative of Cavalcante's description of
Dis as a blind prison ("Se per questo *cieco*/ *carcere* vai per altezza
d'ingegno,/ mio figlio ov'è?").[19] Cavalcante's further questioning of
the Pilgrim—"non fiere li occhi suoi [Guido's] lo dolce lume?" 69—
also echoes both Andromache's "lux alma recessit" and her later query
"quid puer Ascanius? superatne et vescitur aura?" (III, 339: "What
about your [Aeneas's] boy Ascanius? Is he alive and breathing the
air?"). The city of Dis in which Dante encounters the Epicureans is,
like Buthrotum, an urban conglomeration of painful recollection and
incurable nostalgia. Here, where the Epicureans ("che l'anima col corpo
morta fanno," *Inf.* X, 15) have their burial place, Dante encounters open
graves, similar to Aeneas's discovery of Andromache by an empty
grave for Hector in the *parva Troia*. In *Inferno* X, the emphasis on the
physicality of the sinners' spiritual poverty recalls the comparable fate
of Andromache, who cannot transcend her warrior-husband's corporeal
death and, in Epicurean-like fashion, views the world *sub specie mortis*.
However macabre the respective scenes, Aeneas and the Pilgrim desire
the same thing: to speak to people from their city. Dante's wish to see
Florentines, which he initially hides from Virgil, is not frustrated. In
keeping with the canto's aural focus, the magnanimous Farinata hears
the Pilgrim's accent and greets him as a fellow citizen ("O Tosco"),
then immediately inquires about his ancestors.[20] Farinata's genealogical rhetoric finds a melancholic echo in the miserable figure of his in-
law Cavalcante, a mirror image of Andromache. Like her, Cavalcante

is weeping ("piangendo," 58) and looking for another ("Dintorno mi guardò," 55). Just as Andromache sees Hector everywhere, especially in Aeneas, so too does Cavalcante discern his son Guido in all parts, particularly in Dante ("mio figlio ov'è? e perché non è teco?" 60).

As is well known, it has not been definitively established just whom ("cui") Guido disdained ("ebbe a disdegno"), for Dante has—perhaps purposefully—left the referent of the pronoun in line 63 unclear.[21] Beyond the vagueness of the "cui," the Pilgrim's choice of the past tense in "ebbe a disdegno" troubles Cavalcante, who interprets these words to mean that his son Guido no longer lives. By putting the word "dolce" in the mouth of Guido's father Cavalcante and simultaneously echoing Virgil's Andromachean lament (especially her mention of the "lux alma" in line 311), Dante thereby associates the Dolce Stil Novo of Cavalcanti et al. with a categorical materialism that reduces existence to an Epicurean worldview engulfed in *Inferno* X by the funereal atmosphere of the *parva Troia* subtext.[22] Of equal importance, the passage feminizes Cavalcante in order to emphasize the unmanly impotence of his grief, a gesture in the direction of the uncontrollable passions of the same Stilnovistic lyric that the *Commedia* associates with, among other things, the sinful carnality and excessive ardor of Francesca in *Inferno* V. At the same time as Cavalcante's words evoke the issue of gender, they also signal the disappearance or occlusion of such matters of identity, for the blanketing ambiguity of his Andromachean lament dematerializes his physical presence in the name of an absent—and, as far as he is concerned, dead—son, just as the Stilnovistic lexicon he cites buckles under the pressure exerted upon it by Dante's Christian allegory. The overall effect is to spread the reader's interpretive energies over the range of the four-fold model of exegesis outlined in the Letter to Can Grande, which authorizes references to the literal level (in *Inferno* X, the pathos of the suffering father Cavalcante) to coexist alongside competing and often conflicting moral and theological discourses.[23] If readers of the *Commedia* have learned to read Dante's poetic construction of *contrapasso* as a system of reified metaphors turned against the sinners themselves, Dante's contrapuntal echoing of Andromache's mournful words suggests that the reification reaches inside the verbal tissue of these metaphors and infuses their sonic articulation. Viewed from this rhetorical perspective, the Cavalcante that emerges from *Inferno* X is a literary pastiche comprised of Virgilian and Stilnovistic citations, fragments, and textual allusions, whose operatic pathos Dante exploits in tandem with his manipulation of the vertiginous temporality of the biography of Cavalcante's son Guido.[24] By implicating Guido in the judgment of his father, Dante, in Aeneas-like fashion, challenges the nostalgia binding him to Florence as he attempts to come to terms with the exile that Farinata later prophesies in the canto. As a whole, *Inferno* X obsessively tropes on the imagery, themes, and words of the dismal Virgilian *parva Troia* in order to debunk any false promise of return by the Pilgrim to Florence, which in *Inferno* X assumes the form of a moral and historical *parva Florentia*.[25]

Though the various literary séances inspired by the primal scene of Andromache mourning the ghost of Hector in *Aeneid* III may differ from Dante's in nature and theme (see note 12), his rendition of the episode establishes a transhistorical point of reference for later authors as a major post-Virgilian refashioning of Andromache that implicates issues of historical progress, cultural tradition, and literary authority. Virgil's own treatment of Andromache and the *parva Troia* was more an invention than an allusion, and thus an act of literary autonomy with regard to Homeric epic. Neither the razing of Troy nor the failed Trojan replication of the destroyed *patria* appears in Homer, whose poetry moreover does not seem to manifest the preoccupation with authority and cultural belatedness that informs Virgil. Like Virgil, the Dante who invokes Andromache has an explicit epic inheritance that he negotiates partly through his manipulation of the *parva Troia*, a consummate literary symbol of belatedness and distance from origin. Writers in Dante's wake dealt with similar burdens of literary genealogy. For example, Jean Racine observed in the second preface to *Andromaque* that his eponymous protagonist was known primarily as Hector's widow and Astyanax's mother, and that her tears move the audience principally because they are shed for the child of so great a hero.[26] Thus, her abundant weeping—a figurative debt to the Virgilian *lacrimae* in the *parva Troia* episode—attains its full affective impact as the nostalgic invocation of a lost golden age that Andromache herself passively remembers but never actively re-experiences. Yet, for all its pretense of promoting a heroic ethos and the classical unities, Racine's play exhibits qualities that diminish the selfsame atmosphere of antiquity that the author sought to promote in the *Querelle des Anciens et Modernes* surrounding the text's composition. Andromache's forlorn suitor and eventual husband Pyrrhus appears more as a dallying and indecisive lover from what Dryden called the eminently "modern" sentimental stage of Shakespeare than from any warrior-king in, say, Sophocles.[27] Moreover, Hermione's arbitrary cruelty toward Orestes at play's end fails to evoke the workings of fate and codes of justice-retribution that were central to the ancient Greek stage. The brilliance of Racine's *Andromaque*, perhaps against his presumed intentions, seems to lie in an unresolved tension between ancient Greco-Roman and contemporary neoclassical elements that Racine generates through a compelling use of anachronism.

Perhaps the sharpest reworking of themes similar to Dante's reinscription of Andromache in *Inferno* X appears in an author far removed from the moral absolutes and spiritual certainties of the *Commedia*, Charles Baudelaire. He begins his poem "Le cygne"—the first edition of which carried the epigraph "Falsi Simoentis ad undam" ("[O]n the banks of a [false Trojan] river Simois") from *Aen*. III, 302—with the apostrophe "Andromaque, je pense à vous!" (1).[28] The urgency of the address is felt immediately in the exclamatory opening: we two are one, the voice seems to say, and the narrative presence, in its identification with a bereaved ancient widow, appears deeply out-of-joint with the historical moment. Unlike Aeneas or Dante the Pilgrim, however, the narrator in Baudelaire's poem is in no hurry to depart from the nostalgic funereal rites of his *parva* Paris, the lost medieval section of his beloved city razed by Haussman's modernizing boulevards. In "Le cygne," Andromache's tears have sanctified the stream of the Xanthus, and her "majesté" (3) makes "fertile" (5) the poet's memory, which blossoms forth with a series of reflections on the nature of temporality. Andromache's Troy functions in the narrator's mind as the coveted, unattainable allegory of a beloved "old Paris," now "no more," for "a city, alas, changes more quickly than does a man's heart" ("Le vieux Paris n'est plus [la forme d'une ville/ Change plus vite, hélas! que le coeur d'un mortel]," 7-8). In his somber urban elegy, the poet privileges the memory of a symbol, the swan, whose combination of majesty and misery, like the figure of Andromache, extends its associative powers to the poet's imagination.[29] A *signe* as *déplacé* and *déraciné* as the poem's narrator himself, the magnificent white-plumed "cygne" now finds itself bathed in dust and reduced to parched wandering ("Sur le sol raboteux traînait son blanc plumage./ Près d'un ruisseau sans eau la bête ouvrant le bec/ Baignait nerveusement ses ailes dans la poudre" [19-21]). Filled with memories of its lost native lake, the exiled beast emits the elegaic cry: "Eau, quand donc pleuvras-tu? quand tonneras-tu, foudre?" (23). The creature's dried, dusty environs, Baudelaire's version of the Virgilian *Xanthus arens*, serves as a "sad mirror" ("triste miroir" [2]) of the poet's alienated consciousness, which fails to move in sync with history and adapt itself to change: "Paris change! mais rien dans ma mélancolie/ N'a bougé!" (29-30). Dante, of course, could never accept the inertia and marginality of Baudelaire's *flâneur*. The Pilgrim moves away from any figurative *Arnus arens* of the false "second Florence" in *Inferno* X and toward the heavenly city of *Paradiso*, a fusion of the secular and sacred Rome and the urban correlative to his shadow selves, the Aeneas and St. Paul of *Inferno* II, 32 ("Io non Enea, io non Paulo sono"). He also moves forward from the death of Guido Cavalcanti—and the self-fragmenting "Epicurean" Stilnovistic lyrics that shadow the invocation of his former *primo amico* in *Inferno* X—to the theologically inflected encyclopedic poetry that makes the *Commedia* possible. Thus, in his treatment of the Andromachean source, Dante stands closer to Virgilian epic and is more "ancient" than the more paralyzed, self-conscious, and self-referential lyrical representation of the *parva Troia* by Baudelaire. Yet there are elements in Dante that suggest the proximity of the literary subtext of *Inferno* X to the issues raised in "Le cygne." When Virgil's Aeneas bids farewell to Andromache and Helenus at Buthrotum, the official language of his valediction (cited below) compels the reader to guess at his emotions, for, as we have been told countless times by authorities ranging from Voltaire to Lukács, the epic hero's private thoughts tend to cede pride of place to his public actions.

> vivite felices, quibus est fortuna peracta
> iam sua: nos alia ex aliis in fata vocamur.
> vobis parta quies:
>
> (*Aen.* III, 493-95)

("Live on and enjoy the blessing of heaven. Your destiny has been accomplished. But we are called from fate to fate. Your rest is won.")

Like the above, *Inferno* X obliges the reader to decode the raw emotions of nostalgia, likely shaded by guilt and grief, in both the Pilgrim and Poet; but, as in Baudelaire's "Le cygne," the locus of the canto's affective pressure derives as much from its foregrounding of a choice literary subtext in *Aeneid* III as from the narration of the events at hand. Though the melancholy in *Inferno* X seems more mobile and protean than the fixed *tristesse* in "Le cygne" ("rien dans ma mélancolie/ N'a bougé!"), Dante follows Baudelaire in using Andromache's voice to express a crisis of conscience and historical dislocation devoid of the imperial certainties (however costly) that sustain the *Aeneid*.

As a whole, Dante's virtuoso refashioning of the Virgilian source reveals how a pressing cultural, intellectual, and spiritual question—in

---

Dante's case, his inheritance as a Christian poet of the Virgilian epic genre and its pagan, imperial associations—can be subjected to the revisionary power of poetic echo, a practice that Dante employs to subvert many of the governing principles of the same source he aurally invokes. The referencing of Andromache's Latin in Cavalcante's Tuscan speech testifies to the capacity of figurative discourse to transcend the limitations and restrictions of the historical framework that surrounds it. For, by giving his ear to the mournful words of a defeated Trojan queen, Dante collapses the temporal distance separating the *parva Troia* from its Florentine urban counterpart in Dis and, as a consequence, sets their oceanic cultural and historical differences into a dialogue that informs both the overall design of the *Commedia* and the nature of the Christian faith that subtends it. In so doing, he echoes a voice of regret that, for some two thousand years now, has been a touchstone in Western literature's ongoing dialectic with the wages of historical progress.

Readers of the *Commedia* have long been accustomed to the strategies by which the poem's elaborate and unshakable Christian allegorical framework eventually explicates and assigns meaning or value to what at first appear to be the inscrutable details, questions, and issues of the Pilgrim's journey. This essay has endeavored to establish that the compass of the *Commedia*'s typological structure extends to the aural dimension, through a process in which the seemingly inchoate verbal refractions and permutations of one of the *Commedia*'s many subtexts ultimately resonate with meanings never voiced within their initial context. It is a testament to the restless sweep of Dante's imagination—and to the tuning of his poetic ear—that the often radical otherness of his disparate sources can be transfigured in such a way as to enhance their aesthetic effect, even when their forms and themes are shaped by what is in some cases (and certainly for Virgil) an alien typology. The interplay between citation and "riscrittura" that defines Dante's treatment of the *parva Troia* episode in *Inferno* X calls to mind the words of T. S. Eliot on the praxis of allusion.

You cannot effectively "borrow" an image, unless you borrow also, or have spontaneously, something like the feeling which prompted the original image. An "image," in itself, is like dream symbolism, is only vigorous in relation to the feelings out of which it issues, in the relation of word to the flesh. You are entitled to take it for your own purposes in so far as your fundamental purposes are akin to those of the one who is, for you, the author of the phrase, the inventor of the image; or if you take it for other purposes then your purposes must be consciously and *pointedly* diverse from those of the author, and the contrast is very much to the point; you may not take it merely because it is a good phrase or a lovely image.[30]

In keeping with Eliot's prescriptions, Cavalcante's voicing of the Virgilian subtext to express his paternal anguish meshes with Andromache's pained queries about the ghost of her late husband—hence Dante's capture of the visceral sentiment of the original as it links "word to flesh." Moreover, whereas the *parva Troia* episode in the *Aeneid* makes Andromache and her artificial Troy a sacrificial altar upon which personal memory must give way to the public recollection of imperial destiny, the *Commedia* can know no such collective certainties (thus Dante's "pointed" difference from source). When Dante exits the circle of the Epicureans, he bids farewell to a *parva Florentia* and is left to envision an alternate version of that same Roman Empire that Aeneas steadfastly and successfully pursued after abandoning his second Troy. The Pilgrim, one could say, gains the self and loses the world as his journey through the afterlife increases the momentum of its celestial ascent. Aeneas, avatar par excellence of historical *gravitas*, moved in an opposite and more immanent direction, and so the *Aeneid* ends—with a selfless hero's loss of identity through the brutal murder of Turnus—where Dante's journey, in the dark wood, begins.

From *Dante Studies* 122 (2004): 27-43. Copyright © 2004 by the Dante Society of America. Reprinted with permission of the Dante Society of America.

Notes

1. Readings of the canto consulted in preparation for this essay include Michele Barbi, "Il canto di Farinata," *Studi Danteschi* 8 (1924), 87-109; Bruno Nardi, "L'averroismo del 'primo amico' di Dante," *Studi Danteschi* 25 (1940), 43-79; Guido Mazzoni, "Il disdegno di Guido (*Inf.* X, 62-63)," in *Almae luces, malae cruces: Studii danteschi* (Bologna: Zanichelli, 1941), 213-19; Antonino Pagliaro, "Il disdegno di Guido," in *Saggi di critica semantica* (Messina-Florence: D'Anna, 1953), 355-79; Mario Casella, "Il canto X dell'*Inferno*," *Studi Danteschi* 33 (1955), 35-42; Charles S. Singleton, "*Inferno* X: Guido's Disdain," *MLN* 77 (1962), 49-65; Arsenio Frugoni, "Il canto X dell'*Inferno*," in *Nuove letture dantesche* (Florence: Le Monnier, 1968), 261-83; Anthony K. Cassell, "Dante's Farinata and the Image of the *Arca*," *Yale Italian Studies* 1 (1977), 335-70; John Freccero, "Ironia e mimesi: Il disdegno di Guido," in *Dante e la Bibbia*, ed. G. Barblan (Florence: Olschki, 1988), 41-54; and Robert M. Durling, "Canto X: Farinata and Cavalcante," in *Lectura Dantis: Inferno*, ed. A. Mandelbaum, A. Oldcorn, and C. Ross (Berkeley: University of California Press, 1998), 136-49.

2. For a representative expression of this critical perspective, see Auerbach: "We cannot but admire Farinata and weep with Cavalcanti. What actually moves us is not that God has damned them, but that the one is unbroken and the other mourns so heartrendingly for his son and the sweetness of the light. [. . .] The image of man eclipses the image of god. Dante's work made man's Christian-figural being a reality, and destroyed it in the very process of realizing it" ("Farinata and Cavalcante," *Mimesis: The Representation of Reality in Western Literature*, trans. W. Trask [Princeton: Princeton University Press, 1953], 200, 202). In a related vein, De Sanctis observes that the "grandi figure poetiche" and "personaggi eroici" in Hell, including Farinata and Cavalcante, lead the reader out of "astrattezze mistiche e scholastiche" and to the "possesso della realtà" (*Storia della letteratura italiana*, ed. G. Contini [Turin: UTET, 1989], 234). De Sanctis's influential essay "Il Farinata di Dante" first appeared in *Nuova antologia* (May, 1869); see "Farinata," in *De Sanctis on Dante*, ed. and trans. J. Rossi and A. Galpin (Madison: University of Wisconsin Press, 1957), 53-86. For discussion of *Inferno* X in its political and historical contexts, see Benedetto Croce, *La poesia di Dante*, 7th ed. (Bari: Laterza, 1952). 76-77. See also John Scott, *Dante's Political Purgatory* (Philadelphia: University of Pennsylvania Press, 1996): "[Dante's] six years of active involvement in Florentine politics only served to drive home the lesson of the mutability of human affairs as exemplified in his native city. It is therefore not surprising that the poet of the *Comedy* chose two thirteenth-century Florentines—Farinata degli Uberti (d. 1264) and Cavalcante de' Cavalcanti (d. before 1280)—to illustrate the truth of Christ's warning that 'every city or household divided against itself shall fall' (Matthew 12:5)" (8).

3. In his sixteenth-century commentary on *Inf.* X, 52-63, Daniello describes Guido Cavalcanti as a "dottissimo & eccellente Filosofo," observing that "di Costui [Guido] dimanda il padre à Dante, lodando il figliuolo, dicendo che se gli era conceduto l'andar per l'Inferno da grandissimo ingegno, doveva esser seco ancora il suo Guido: come Virg. in persona d'Andromaca ad Enea di suo marito, nel 3.

dell'Eeneid. Nate Dea? vivisne, aut, si lux alma recessit: Hector ubi est?"
(*L'espositione di Bernardino Daniello da Lucca sopra la Comedia di Dante*, ed. R.
Hollander and J. Schnapp with K. Brownlee and N. Vickers [Hanover, New Jersey:
University Press of New England, 1989], 56). See also the commentaries by N.
Tommaseo, ed., *La Comedia di Dante Allighieri col comento di N. Tommaseo* (Naples:
Cioffi, 1839), 125; G. Fallani, ed., *La Divina Commedia: Inferno* (Messina-Florence:
D'Anna, 1965), 111, and C. Singleton, ed., *The Divine Comedy*, 6 vols. (1970-75;
Princeton: Princeton University Press, 1989-91), II, 153.

4. References are taken from, respectively, Dante, *La Commedia secondo l'antica
vulgata*, ed. G. Petrocchi, 4 vols. (Milan: Mondadori, 1966-67); and *The Aeneid of Virgil: Books 1-6*, ed. R. D. Williams (1972; London: St. Martin's Press, 1992); trans. D.
West, *The Aeneid: A New Prose Translation* (New York: Penguin, 1991).

5. For a biographical discussion of Dante's overcoming of nostalgia and his abandonment of the idea of returning to Florence through a military conspiracy with his fellow exiles, see Giuseppe Mazzotta, "Life of Dante," *The Cambridge Companion to
Dante* (Cambridge: Cambridge University Press, 1993), 9.

6. John Hollander, *The Figure of Echo: A Mode of Allusion in Milton and After*
(1981; Berkeley: University of California Press, 1984), ix. For general studies of allusion, see William Irwin, "What Is an Allusion?" *The Journal of Aesthetics and Art
Criticism* 59 (2001), 287-97; and Christopher Ricks, *Allusion to the Poets* (Oxford:
Oxford University Press, 2002).

7. Dante's persistent echoing of Virgil's *Aeneid*, at once the *Commedia*'s privileged literary source as well as its textual foil, recalls Thomas Greene's notion of
"heuristic imitation," i.e., an author's thematizing of the relationship of his own
work to that same source that serves as literary model or touchstone (*The Light in
Troy: Imitation and Discovery in Renaissance Literature* [New Haven: Yale University Press, 1982], 40). See the discussion of Dante's allusive strategy vis-à-vis
Virgil in R. Jacoff and J. Schnapp, eds., "Introduction," in *The Poetry of Allusion: Virgil and Ovid in Dante's "Commedia"* (Stanford: Stanford University Press,
1991), 2-5.

8. Hollander, *Echo* 3.

9. *Inf.* V, 100, 103, 106.

10. See Teodolinda Barolini, "Dante and Cavalcanti (On Making Distinctions in
Matters of Love): *Inferno* V in Its Lyric Context," *Dante Studies* 116 (1998), 31-63.

11. For studies of Dante's relationship to Cavalcanti, see Mario Marti, "Cavalcanti,
Guido," *Enciclopedia dantesca*, ed. U. Bosco, 6 vols. (Rome: Istituto della
Enciclopedia Italiana, 1970-78), I, 891-96, esp. his mention of "talune note
cavalcantiane" in Dante's poetry (892); Robert Pogue Harrison, *The Body of Beatrice*
(Baltimore: The Johns Hopkins University Press, 1988), 69-90, esp. the discussion of
Cavalcanti's "phantasmology of the self" (70), which makes him the perfect analogue
for the Andromache who haunts *Inferno* X; and Gianfranco Contini, "Cavalcanti in
Dante," *Un'idea di Dante: Saggi danteschi*, 3rd ed. (Turin: Einaudi: 2001), 143-57.
For an analysis of the philosophical underpinnings of Cavalcanti's presence in *Inferno*
X, see Maria Corti, *Dante a un nuovo crocevia* (Florence: Sansoni, 1981), 77-85. A
study of the legacy of both Cavalcanti and Guinizzelli in Dante's poetry is in

Teodolinda Barolini, *Dante's Poets: Textuality and Truth in the "Comedy"* (Princeton: Princeton University Press, 1984), 123-153.

12. See Harold Bloom, *The Anxiety of Influence: A Theory of Poetry* (New York: Oxford University Press, 1973), *passim*.

13. Maurizio Bettini describes the marriage of Andromache and Helenus as a "levirate," the inheritance by a younger brother of his dead sibling's wife, and thus more a transfer of ownership than an actual marriage. See "Ghosts of Exile: Doubles and Nostalgia in Vergil's *parva Troia* (*Aeneid* 3.294ff.)," trans. L. Gibbs-Wichrowska, *Classical Antiquity* 16 (1997), 8-33. Emphasizing the spectral nature of Andromache's marital status, Bettini notes that through her levirate she "has in some sense reproduced her own past," and that this second marriage is an emblem for the diminished *parva Troia* she inhabits (11).

14. Literary debts to the scene with Andromache in *Aeneid* III appear in Jean Racine, *Andromaque* (1667); Charles Baudelaire, "Le cygne" (1860); Stéphane Mallarmé, "Le vierge, le vivace et le bel aujourd'hui" (1885); W. B. Yeats, "No Second Troy" (1910); and Jacques Roubaud, *La forme d'une ville change plus vite, hélas, que le coeur des humains* (1999). Though Mallarmé's poem does not allude directly to Andromache, it recalls the displaced figure of Baudelaire's swan and the erasure of the past in the modernizing city, and also draws on the rhetoric of temporal exile and dislocation typical of the Virgilian, Dantesque, and Baudelairean versions of Andromache. Yeats's unattainable "second Troy" evokes the breakdown of the "mythical method" associated with the high Modernism of such authors as T. S. Eliot and manifests a nostalgic effect similar to the one at work in Dante's and Baudelaire's refashioning of Virgil. Roubaud draws the title of his collection of poems nearly verbatim from a line in "Le cygne" and, like Mallarmé (and in a manner akin to the Virgilian *Ur*-text), exploits the theme of a modern city's erasure of its own past.

15. Thomas Greene, "History and Anachronism," in *Literature and History: Theoretical Problems and Russian Case Studies*, ed. G. S. Morson (Stanford: Stanford University Press, 1986), 205-220, p. 211.

16. For a study of the epic genre as a dialectic between, on the one hand, the Virgilian tradition of conquest and empire and, on the other, narratives of the defeated and republican liberty (e.g., Lucan's *Pharsalia*), see David Quint, *Epic and Empire: Politics and Generic Form from Virgil to Milton* (Princeton: Princeton University Press, 1993). Quint notes that Aeneas's abandonment of Andromache's city and the historical memories it embodies contributes to a transition in genre in which the first half of the *Aeneid*, reminiscent of Odysseus's wanderings, eventually passes into its more properly "epic" second half, modeled on the *Iliad* but with the critical difference that the heirs of Troy emerge victorious (58-59, 64-66).

17. Freud employs an urban metaphor similar to the *parva Troia* to exemplify his theory of the "memory-trace," by comparing mental life—in which "nothing which has once been formed can perish," and whose repressed memories can ultimately resurface independent of conscious intent—to the ruins of civilization's great cities. According to Freud, if Rome were not a physical but a "psychical entity," the palaces of the Caesars would rise alongside those of the Renaissance and the Fascists (*Civilization and Its Discontents*, ed. and trans. J. Strachey [1961; New York: W. W. Norton,

1989], 16, 18). The concepts and metaphors of the Freudian memory-trace recall the resurgence of the *parva Troia* in both *Aeneid* III and *Inferno* X, for the episode of memory represented by Andromache and her diminished "second Troy" reappears as an unexpected challenge that a putatively preemptive ideal (Rome's imperial mission for Virgil and a Christian, anti-Stilnovistic poetics for Dante) represses yet never completely erases.

18. In addition to the canto's literary substrata, scholars have actively identified its many biblical allusions: see, for example, Durling ("Canto X" 143) for discussion of Cavalcante's question about his son ("mio figlio ov' è?" 60) as a parallel to God's query to Cain about Abel in Genesis 4:9 ("Ubi est Abel frater tuus?"); and Freccero's claim that the subtext of Augustine's *Confessions* VII (esp. in the phrase *dedignantur ab eo discere* ["they disdain to learn from him [Christ]"]) permeates the "ebbe a disdegno" of *Inf.* X, 63 ("Ironia e mimesi," 48).

19. *Inf.* X, 58-60 (my italics). For discussion of the term "cieco carcere" in the context of Dante's relationship to the *Aeneid*, see Michael C. J. Putnam, "Virgil's *Inferno*," in *Poetry of Allusion*, 94-112.

20. *Inf.* X, 22. Auerbach underscores the canto's aurality by discussing the vocative "O" from Farinata's greeting to the Pilgrim as an example of Dante's use of the "O thou who" construction from ancient epic ("Farinata and Cavalcante" 179). Auerbach also notes the sonic contrast between "the regularly constructed clauses which come to the listener [from Farinata] while he is still conscious of the irregular and plaintively thronging questions of the other [Cavalcante]," and raises the possibility that Dante may have modeled Cavalcante's words on Andromache's mournful encounter with Aeneas in *Aeneid* III (181). See also Barbi, "Farinata" 95 for a discussion of the affective impact on Farinata of the Pilgrim's voice (which represents to Farinata "la voce della sua Firenze").

21. From the earliest commentaries on the *Commedia* to well into the nineteenth century, the widespread belief was that the referent of "cui" in line 63 was Virgil. Recent criticism, however, has tended to argue on behalf of Beatrice as the target of Guido's disdain (see Pagliaro, "Disdegno di Guido," for an influential exposition of this view). For a comprehensive inventory of this famous crux, see Pier Luigi Cerisola, "Il 'disdegno' di Guido Cavalcanti (*Inf.* X, 61-63)," in *Aevum* 52 (1978), 195-217, who proposes Virgil as the referent of "cui," as the emblem of Dante's turn to a politically motivated poetics disdained by Guido; see also his summary of the scholarship that propose God as the referent in question (201-202). I share the view that the "cui" refers to Beatrice.

22. For discussion of the metaphor of blindness and the theological implications of Cavalcante's line "non fiere li occhi suoi lo dolce lume," especially as it relates to the conflicting conceptions of love in Dante and Guido Cavalcanti, see Giuseppe Mazzotta, Dante, *Poet of the Desert: History and Allegory in the "Divine Comedy"* (Princeton: Princeton University Press, 1979), 289-94.

23. For Singleton, Cavalcante is the first "anti-allegorist" of Dante's interpreters on record, for he remains blocked at the literal level of meaning and fails to recognize the transcendental implications of the Pilgrim's reply that he is being led by one whom Guido "ebbe a disdegno" ("Guido's Disdain," 62-63).

---

24. Dante was one of the Florentine priors who agreed to exile Guido, along with other leading members of the White and Black Guelph factions, for political extremism in June 1300. Though he was soon recalled to Florence, Guido contracted malaria in exile and died later that same year on August 29, 1300. Thus, within the fictional timeframe of Dante's meeting with Cavalcante in *Inferno* X (April 1300), a pre-exilic Guido still lives—though, of course, he had already died well before Dante commenced the composition of the *Inferno* (in 1304, according to Petrocchi).

25. Underscoring the subtext of Augustine's divisions between the Heavenly and Earthly Cities in *Inferno* X, Cassell notes that the Pilgrim's arrival in Dis parallels his descent into the "bickerings and internecine strife of the earthly *polis*—in this case those of the Guelphs and Ghibellines of his own city, Florence, transported to Hell and used as an exemplum" ("Image of *Arca*" 336).

26. See Jean Racine, *Oeuvres complètes* (Paris: Gallimard, 1950), I, 243; and discussion in Bettini, "Ghosts of Exile," 22-23.

27. See John Dryden, *An Essay on Dramatic Poesy* (1684), in *Literary Criticism: Plato to Dryden*, ed. A. Gilbert (New York: American Book, 1940), 637-39.

28. Charles Baudelaire, *Oeuvres complètes*, ed. C. Pichois (Paris: Gallimard, 1961), 81-83. For an interpretation of the poem in relation to the Virgilian subtext, see Lowry Nelson, Jr., "Baudelaire and Virgil: A Reading of 'Le Cygne,'" *Comparative Literature* 13 (1961), 332-45; and Bettini, "Ghosts of Exile" 12-13. Like *Inferno* X, "Le cygne" contains issues of paternity and poetic apprenticeship, for it was dedicated to Victor Hugo—bard of that same razed medieval Paris lamented in Baudelaire's poem—with a letter from December 7, 1859: "Voici des vers faits pour vous et en pensant à vous. Il ne faut pas les juger avec vos yeux sévères, mais avec vos yeux paternels . . ." ("Here are some verses written with you in mind. You should not regard them with severe eyes but rather with paternal ones . . ." [cit. Pichois, *Oeuvres complètes*, 1537-38]).

29. Like Dante's Cavalcante *lacrimans*, Baudelaire's distressed swan compresses in a single image the affective energies emanating from the *parva Troia* subtext. See Baudelaire's aforementioned letter to Hugo: "Ce qui était important pour moi, c'était de dire vite tout ce qu'un accident, une image, peut contenir de suggestions, et comment la vue d'un animal souffrant pousse l'esprit vers tous les êtres que nous aimons, qui sont absents et qui souffrent . . ." ("What was important to me was to say quickly all that an accident, an image can contain by way of associations, and how the prospect of a suffering animal pushes the spirit toward all those beings whom we love, who are absent and who suffer . . ." [cit. Pichois, *Oeuvres complètes*, 1538]).

30. T. S. Eliot, *The Bible as Scripture and as Literature*, Address, Boston, December 1932, Houghton Library; b.MS.Am.1691 (26), 11-12. Cited by Ricks, *Allusion*, 4.

Beginning to Think about *Salò*[1]

Gabrielle Lesperance

> Four manner of things appear: good and evil, life and death: but the tongue
> ruleth over them continually.
>
> —Sirach 37:18:1[2]

When analysing films based on written narratives (other than screen-plays, naturally), one always runs the risk of oversimplifying the cine-matic critique, basing it on points of intersection and divergence between the original and filmic texts (Marcus 1-25). Delineating Dantesque allusions in Pier Paolo Pasolini's films is a relatively easy exercise, as Pasolini borrows repeatedly from the *Divine Comedy*, in spirit and in kind, from his first film, *Accattone* (1961), to his last, *Salò o le 120 giornate di Sodoma* (1975). This paper is less an attempt to enumerate these *accenni* to Dante than a means of returning to an anal-ysis of Pasolini's cinematic texts, in this case through the filter of the *Divine Comedy*, with the goal of offering a new perspective on a film which all too frequently in the past has been maligned as some psy-chotic, homosexual, sadomasochistic fantasy. While a thorough analy-sis of Pasolini's final film would require more space than is available in this volume, this essay will focus on *Salò*'s more subtle connections with Dante's influential poem.

The main issue to be considered in this inquiry is Pasolini's treatment of justice, crime, and punishment, much of which depends, as it does in the *Commedia*, on spatial structure, symmetry, and how identity is de-veloped in *Salò*. In Dante's world, punishment is perfectly suited to the sins committed and is, in fact, the mirror image of sins. Because retri-bution is divine, punishment is viewed as both fixed and logical: fixed (and preordained) because Hell is created simultaneously with the rest of the world, and therefore created together with original sin; logical because it is made in the image of God. In this sense, justice can exist only because a perfect system of punishment is in place.

In Pasolini's world, punishment is enforced because of the existence of dysfunction and bureaucracy. Here, the rules are stated and even scripted in the form of a code of conduct, but then are subject to change at the will of the libertines. For example, in the *Antinferno* the Eccellenza establishes the villa's laws in a speech from the balcony. One of these rules is that no heterosexual intercourse among the prisoners will be allowed. The punishment for any male prisoner in violation of this law is said to be the loss of a limb. Yet when Enzo, one of the recruited soldiers, is caught *in flagrante* with his servant girlfriend, both are fatally wounded. Not only does this action gravely exceed the penalty set forth by the 'law,' but it also arbitrarily punishes another party where no discipline had been prescribed. Also, while the Libertines try to project the image of a preordained system of punishment to the extent that the laws are written in book form, much is legislated on a case-by-case basis. When one of the female victims reveals Enzo's secret affair in order to save herself, she asks, 'What will become of me?' The Monsignore responds, 'I don't know . . . it will be decided tomorrow . . . many things will be decided tomorrow.' Because of the fluid nature of punishment (and the imaginary status of 'sin') in *Salò*, there is no justice here.

According to David Schwartz, Pasolini 'had wanted for some time to do a work built on the principle of Dante's "theological verticalism": levels of blessing, layers of Hell' (Schwartz 640-1). Naomi Greene appears to agree that this is what Pasolini actually accomplishes in his film when she states that '*Salò* echoes the "theological verticalism" of the *Inferno* as, like a descending spiral, it takes us from one circle of horrors to the next' (Greene 197). I would contend that *Salò* does not follow Dante's principle of 'theological verticalism' because the punishment is not just, and there are no blessings. However, the film's moral relativism, a result of such an 'imperfect' Inferno, serves only to underscore the perfection and ideological symmetry in the *Divine Comedy*. Any viewer of *Salò* who recognizes Pasolini's Dantesque references will almost certainly also have expectations of theological verticalism in the film in recalling Dante's system of grace and retribution. Instead, when the viewer is confronted with the contrary system in *Salò*, the effect is much more powerful than had Pasolini utilized 'theological verticalism' in its purest form.

At the same time that there exists an uneven bureaucracy in *Salò*, the film's physical symmetry could be considered overwhelming. This degree of glacial perfection has both political and semiotic implications. While *Salò*'s symmetry gives the impression of complete dominance by man over his surroundings, it, in fact, reveals the limits of human control. 'The obsession with precise formulas and bureaucratic regulations that characterizes his libertines represented, [Pasolini] declared, the strategies embraced by *all* power in its pure arbitrariness, that is, its own anarchy' (Greene 204). Though power is arbitrary in *Salò*, it is manifested in an extremely organized fashion.

Concerning the physical symmetry found in *Salò*, Naomi Greene notes: '[T]he world of *Salò* is one where everything is mathematically composed, geometrically balanced, endowed with a precise function and meaning' (Greene 198). Greene does not go on, however, to explain precisely how this world is composed, balanced, and endowed. I would like to offer the following explications as they resonate with the structure of the *Divine Comedy*.

While Dante's threes are a constant reminder of the divine structure of the afterlife, where there is perfection through forgiveness, Pasolini's fours (4 libertines, 4 narrators, 16 [4 × 4] victims, 4 guards, 4 conspirators, 4 companions, 4 wives/daughters) suggest symmetry. However, this symmetry is not divine, but apocalyptic, if we consider the biblical significance of the number four.[3] Furthermore, the repetition of the number four suggests, in spatial terms, a cubic construction or box. A closer look at the artwork decorating the villa reveals Cubist paintings, which serve to emphasize this pattern of thought. The majority of the film consists of interior shots, which repeatedly present viewers with almost identical boxes.[4]

I would go so far as to suggest that Pasolini is, in fact, consciously toying with the interplay of Dante's divine threes and *Salò*'s apocalyptic fours, with the theme of fours appearing in the narrative structure of the film. For example, while it might seem that there are three acts or circles (the *gironi delle manie, della merda, e del sangue*), there are really four when we include the *Antinferno*. Additionally, the male and female victims begin as nine each (3 × 3), but they number sixteen in total (four squared) after one male and one female victim are killed. It should be noted that Pasolini underlines the numeric aspect of the killings, when after the murder of each of the first two victims the President offers a joke based on the change in numbers. Even the narrators appear to be three, but are actually four since the accompanist is classified as a narrator.[5] In the *girone del sangue*, Pasolini seems to attempt a reversal, insinuating a divine finale with a destruction of the symmetry he had so carefully constructed earlier in the film. Enzo's death signals a reduction from four to three soldiers, which is soon followed by a similar reduction in the number of narrators when the accompanist commits suicide. Both deaths seem sacrificial and somewhat Christ-like. In the sequence directly following the suicide, the four libertines separate for the torture with the three torturers and the one spectator, rotating roles so that each man is both spectator and participant. In other words, even though there is a physical division between the spectator and the three participants, the manner in which the libertines exchange these roles so effortlessly suggests that there is very little practical difference between the functions of the two roles. Therefore, the 'trinity' of torturers is actually a foursome.

Besides the numerological aspect of the symmetry found in *Salò*, there is also the important question of symmetry as it relates to physical perfection and to identity. Unlike *Inferno*, where shades are grotesque, here physical imperfection (i.e., a missing tooth) results in the rejection and/or immediate death of the victims. As opposed to the disfigurements of the libertines in Sade, Pasolini's libertines are perfectly typical, making their behaviour seem simultaneously more heinous and thoroughly conceivable (Schwartz 644). In other words, the grotesque appearance of Sade's characters renders them fantastical in semblance to the reader, thereby making their actions sublime but innocuous, as the characters are unabashedly fictitious. Instead, the lack of hyperbole in Pasolini's depiction of the libertines is odious in that monstrous behaviour is perpetrated, not by aberrant, unbelievable characters, but by those of 'normal' superficies.

The film's symmetry skews identity and, through the use of mirrors and the employment of certain lighting techniques, camera shots, and angles, makes all things equal. The first identity crisis occurs with the introduction of the libertines in a darkened room where it is nearly impossible to distinguish one from another. Not only are their identities obscured by the low lighting of the shot, but the libertines prolong the confusion by addressing each other by titles which are similar (Monsignore, Presidente, Eccellenza, Duca) and which reveal little about their personalities or backgrounds other than the bureaucratic nature of their roles.[6] In all, there is little effort made to differentiate them. As a consequence, the act of the libertines marrying each other's daughters becomes incestuous and further obfuscates their relationships and identities.

Contrary to Dante's *Inferno*, where the names of the shades take on a great deal of importance, here, after the initial listing of victims' names, they nearly cease to denominate the characters. The one exception to this tendency is the crimes list, where the President writes down names and offences. In his capacity as record keeper, the President becomes a modern Minos but does not allow the 'sinners' to distinguish themselves by listing their own sins; instead, this becomes another mundane, bureaucratic duty. In the *Comedy*, the punished find solace and remembrance in their speech acts; in *Salò*, utterances by the victims usually result in obliteration. Besides the lack of identity attributable to the victims' 'namelessness' and relative speechlessness, the children also are deemed interchangeable because of their nudity (Greene 203) or, in the case of the guardsmen, because of their sumptuary uniformity.

In the transition from the *Antinferno* to each of the *gironi*, Pasolini adds complexity to the identities of the narrators more so than he does with any other group of characters within the film. The title shot of the first circle, the *girone delle manie*, dissolves into a shot of the image of the first narrator, Sra. Vaccari, in a mirror as she prepares for her 'performance.' The problem? The shot presents an image with no referent. Sra. Vaccari then visits another mirror on a closet door, where we see two images of her and the image of another vanity with a mirror. Furthermore, the act of opening and closing the closet door catapults her reflected image across the room and across the screen. When she exits the room, we see yet another mirror. Clearly, this is a hall of mirrors. Cinematically, such a multiplicity of disparately positioned reflections already signals an identity crisis. The reproduction of images confuses the audience; which is the image we should watch? As Sra. Vaccari walks down the marble steps to the storytelling room, her image is reflected in the table, making her appear to rise as she descends. Her descent into the first 'circle,' unlike Dante's descent, is easy. The children, guards, wives, other narrators, and libertines are placed in groups around the room, against the wall, not in a circular formation, as would be the expected arrangement of an audience about to hear a story or an oral history, but in the shape of a square. At this point, Sra. Vaccari initiates her narrative by recounting her childhood.

The second circle, the *girone della merda*, is nearly identical to the first, involving a different but remarkably familiar room with a storyteller in front of a mirror. This narrator is seen on both the left and right sides of the frame as both referent and mirror image. In her grooming, screen position, and reflections, Sra. Maggi is identical to Sra. Vaccari, reducing the viewer's ability to demarcate the two women. Given the Dantesque reference to the *gironi*, one would expect to find the characters in a distinct location, as this is a new circle. Instead, Sra. Maggi descends the same stairs in the same way to the same room where the audience is in the same configuration as in the previous *girone*. Sra. Maggi says she will not tell the audience of her childhood as Sra.

Vaccari has done. Of course, given the continuum of the characters, there is no need for her to do so, as the two narrators experienced what must be considered, for all intents and purposes, the same childhood. Rather, she begins her narration where the first storyteller left off. In other words, Sra. Maggi is being 'plugged' into the role formerly inhabited by Sra. Vaccari, with no discernible differences between the two. In this way, the film suggests that what passes for identity is very slippery, indeed, and here degenerates into what could be better deemed prefabricated standardizations than true identity.

Because, cinematically speaking, Sra. Vaccari, Sra. Maggi, and Sra. Castelli are being constructed as one character divided or fractured, we expect to see the image of Sra. Castelli in a bedroom mirror in a transition from the *girone della merda* to the *girone del sangue*. Instead we are met with three cross-dressed libertines, each looking in a different mirror as he finishes his preparations, and each reflected in the others' mirrors. This transvestism presents the crisis of a third sex, which 'puts in question identities previously conceived as stable, unchallengeable, grounded, and "known"' (Garber 12-13). Instead of being introduced to one woman (or rather, our three women in one), in this episode Pasolini positions the three men where they are neither expected nor, in some ways, welcome. In Western cinema, women are generally assigned to the centre of the frame to emphasize their 'to-be-looked-at-ness' or to the left side of the screen because this is the weaker, less active position. Here, instead, the three libertines inhabit a traditionally female, spectacular space. Additionally, the topos of the dressing room could be considered almost exclusively feminine or feminized, and certainly has been a feminine locus within the film until this moment.

It should be noted that this act of transvestism should not be seen merely as a case of sexual or gender role *jouissance*, but as a serious challenge to power and gender construction. These men are not trying to 'pass,' as neither the Eccellenza nor the Duca depilates for his performance, but the three are co-opting female functions while maintaining their masculinity. The libertines' interruption of the narration implies their incontrovertible mastery over categories. They are allowed to slide in and out of roles, but with deadly results. In other words, the libertines may seem to be only burlesquing in this sequence, but because of the real effects of the torture and because the others are not permitted the same kind of spatial and gender freedom, it really must be viewed as something graver. Aside from the identity crisis resulting from the cross-dressing episode, the highly fragmented and multiple images arising from the numerous mirrors utilized here serve to emphasize the libertines' physical dominance of the room and the screen, while suggesting something akin to a reproduction or cloning of their power. Pasolini is making us question the nature of power, gender, and position through his constant interplay of the same. It should be noted that the narrative tension created by the sequence of transvestment is eventually relieved when the temporarily displaced Sra. Castelli later makes the descent to the storytelling room in the same manner as the first two storytellers had, thus resuming the female ritual.

The presentation of the third circle purposely interjects the libertines into the 'space' of the narrators in order to show that the females are every bit as culpable in the torture as the libertines, because they are responsible for producing the stimuli which result in torture. In other words, the libertine bureaucrats are barren of ideas and must rely on the narrators for 'original' ideas. Without the narrators, the libertines would be impotent. Ironically, because the libertines have managed to infiltrate and colonize the narrators' space, the women are ultimately and literally eliminated from the screen. After attempts to surfeit the men's appetites have been made, the galvanizing presence of female creativity is no longer deemed necessary as a stimulus for the libertines.

Finally, ascension in Dante signals the transition from Inferno to Purgatory. Since the pilgrim's climb toward Purgatory begins in Inferno, the two regions are described as being physically connected as well as created concurrently, so that the one could not exist without the other. Ascension here is classified as hopeful since sinners can be redeemed. Pasolini instead creates ascensions which are every bit as diabolical as the descents. The rituals that occur on the top floor of the villa seem promising at first glance, with wedding ceremonies associated with both societal approbation and eventual procreation, but they prove fruitless when the libertines once again subvert these events. Instead, these rituals serve to reinforce another kind of sterility demonstrated by the libertines' dependence on the narrators for stimulation. In the film's final ascension following the three wedding ceremonies, the accompanist, who has tried to intervene on behalf of the victims, manifests her inability to influence the destiny of the children when she plunges to her death. She is no Beatrice, Mary, or Lucia. Perhaps the key to Pasolini's rendering of 'theological verticalism' is to be found in the convoluted role of the four narrators, who, rather than mediating divine intervention leading toward salvation, inspire only torturous death.

Notes

1. This title is a play on words on the title of a painting by artist-translator Tom Phillips. That work, entitled *Beginning to Think about Dante* (1978), served as an important springboard to Phillips' illustrated translation of Dante's *Inferno* (1983), which led to his collaborative television series on the *Inferno*, *A TV Dante* (1988). Both *Beginning to Think about Dante* and *A TV Dante* are examined in this collection.

2. This biblical (KJV) reference to the number four seems particularly apt in light of the importance of the speech act in *Salò*. The role of the number four and symmetry in the film is discussed later in this paper.

3. Frequently, the number four appears in the Bible in describing winds (Job 1:19 and Dan. 7:3); punishment or destruction arising from God's anger (Ezek. 7:2 and Amos 1:3-2:7); beasts (Dan. 7:3-8); and the number of enemy troops, companies, or deceased (Gen. 32:6, 33:1, Judg. 9:34, and 1 Sam. 4:2). The apocalyptic usage of the number four is most sensational, of course, in the Book of Revelation.

4. A viewer familiar with the Italian retro films of the 1970s cannot avoid associating the cubism of *Salò* with a striking flashback in Liliana Cavani's *Night Porter* (1973). In this flashback, the Nazi protagonist presents his victim-lover with a box containing the decapitated head of a man believed to be a threat to their relationship.

5. This is done cinematically in the balcony sequence. While the Eccellenza discusses the daily orgies, the camera holds on each of the storytellers, with the accompanist presented as the second of the four narrators in the series of shots.

6. As Greene suggests, Sade's aristocrats are replaced by bureaucrats (203).

Bibliography

Adair, Gilbert. '*Salò o le 120 giornate di Sodoma.*' *Monthly Film Bulletin* 46.548 (Sept. 1979): 200-1.

Bachmann, Gideon. 'Pasolini and the Marquis de Sade.' *Sight and Sound* 45.1 (Winter 1975-6): 50-4.

_____. 'Pasolini on de Sade.' *Film Quarterly* 29.2 (Winter 1975-6): 39-45.

Barthes, Roland. *Sade, Fourier, Loyola.* Trans. Richard Miller. New York: Hill and Wand, 1976.

Boarini, Vittorio, Pietro Bonfiglioli, and Giorgio Cremonini, presentati da. *Da Accattone a Salò: 120 scritti sul cinema di Pier Paolo Pasolini.* Bologna: Tip. Compositori, 1982.

Cavani, Liliana, dir. *Portiere di notte.* 1973.

Dumont, P. '*Salò* ou l'impossible représentation du fantasme.' *Cinéma* 302 (Feb. 1984): 8-10.

Finetti, U. 'Nella struttura di *Salò*: La dialettica erotismo-potere' and 'La condanna di *Salò* nella sentenza del tribunale.' *Cinema Nuovo* 25.244 (Nov.-Dec. 1976): 428-43.

Garber, Marjorie. *Vested Interests: Cross-Dressing and Cultural Anxiety.* New York: Routledge, 1992.

Greene, Naomi. *Pier Paolo Pasolini: Cinema As Heresy.* Princeton: Princeton University Press, 1990.

Klossowski, Pierre. *Sade My Neighbor.* Trans. Alphonso Lingis. Evanston, IL: Northwestern University Press, 1991.

Marcus, Millicent. *Filmmaking by the Book.* Baltimore: Johns Hopkins University Press, 1993.

Pasolini, Pier Paolo, dir. *Salò o le 120 giornate di Sodoma.* 1975.

Rumble, Patrick. *Allegories of Contamination: Pier Paolo Pasolini's Trilogy of Life.* Toronto: University of Toronto Press, 1996.

Rumble, Patrick, and Bart Testa, eds. *Pier Paolo Pasolini: Contemporary Perspectives.* Toronto: University of Toronto Press, 1994.

Sade, Marquis de. *The Marquis de Sade: The 120 Days of Sodom and Other Writings.* Ed. and trans. Austin Wainhouse and Richard Seaver. New York: Grove Press, 1966.

Schwartz, Barth David. *Pasolini Requiem.* New York: Pantheon Books, 1992.

Waller, Marguerite. 'Signifying the Holocaust: Liliana Cavani's *Portiere di Notte.*' *Italian Women Writers from the Renaissance to the Present: Revising the Canon.* Ed. and introd. Maria Ornella Marotti. University Park, PA: Pennsylvania State University Press, 1996. 259-72.

Dante's Monsters in the *Inferno*:
Reimagining Classical to Christian Judgment _____

Patrick Hunt

Introduction

Dante deliberately amalgamated relict Classicism and his own Christian vision. He did not revive Classicism to the letter or even to the spirit thereof as followed in the Renaissance through Petrarch onward, but instead created a unique medieval epic looking both deeply backward and forward in time. This diachronicity is expanded by imbibing Classical material in one direction and moving toward the Last Judgment in the other direction. By altering aspects of antiquity in his own long view of eternity, he fictionalizes myth truths that may at times wear the complicated garb of "falsehoods" (*mezogna*)[1] or reimagined truths. This is especially fitting in his use of Classical monsters like Geryon, Cerberus, Medusa and others, where he transforms them into allegories of both spiritual and political significance.[2] While others in the medieval world, mostly clerics, invented fictional otherworldly journeys for moral or didactic religious intent,[3] Dante made of his *Commedia* a cosmic topos of genius where myth and history meet, where he summons real rather than imaginary personages who curse their chosen hells alongside imaginary beasts and creatures of poetic lore. Given the many studies of Dante's monsters,[4] here only a few selective monsters are discussed.

Dante's repeated use of Classical authors is well known, for example, as Brownlee shows in echoes of Virgil, Statius, Lucan and Ovid, also especially in Canto 20 where his ancient diviners appear as metonymy of their ancient authors.[5] In many places in the *Inferno*, Dante even minimizes biblical references, as Barolini and others have noted, whereas Classical references abound. While many scholars trace Virgilian allusions in Dante, a great debt to Ovid can be overlooked, where Dante not only imbibes figurative language and narrative but also stylistic features.[6] Where understanding Classical Rome

Dante's Monsters in the *Inferno* **245**

meant looking only backward in Dante's time, even after a more than a millennium, Christian Rome was mostly forward looking in terms of both individual accountability and the Last Judgment, as "Christianity gave Rome its future orientation."[7] If Western Civilization became this inevitable fusion of Classical and Christian worlds, when Roman Christianity triumphed over Roman paganism even while syncretizing some of its elements, Dante is one of its original architects not so much by choice as by the force of his creative *nous* ("mind"). His monsters trebly serve as vehicles of Classical *imitatio*, medieval Christian symbolism and rhetoric as well as Mediterranean and especially Italian history. Jewell asserts:

> The reasons for the centrality of Italian literature to the topic of the monstrous are many. They run much deeper than Italy's ties to Classical Greece and Rome where mortals and demigods were recurrently dogged by monsters of mythic and epic memory . . . the medieval period was characterized by a Christian renegotiation of classical, especially Neoplatonic, thought, and the idea of the monstrous played an important role in this phenomenon.[8]

Dante's imitations alone of Virgil run into the hundreds of passages, either stylistic or thematic.[9] His use of monsters found earlier especially in the *Aeneid*, however, has the added function of Christological trope, among other meanings. For example, Hercules conquered both Geryon on earth and Cerberus at the gates of the Underworld, like Christ who broke down the gates of Hell in his visit after Calvary, winnowing Pre-Christian souls from Purgatory. Thus, Dante's monsters not only "show" connections to the supernatural in their polyform nature, graphically expressing their hybridity as harbingers of unseen divine power but also, like their Classical prototypes, are outworkings of divine justice.

While in Classical myth monsters (from *monstrare*, "to show") arise out of disrupted nature to punish human hubris on earth—note their likely etymological derivation from the Greek declension of *hubris* to *hubridis*[10]—Dante's monsters are divine instruments of punishment in the *Inferno*, "ministers of divine justice."[11] In addition to major passages about Cerberus (Canto VI) and Geryon (Canto XVII), Dante also mentions Medusa (Canto IX), the Minotaur (Canto XII) and centaurs like Nessus (Canto XII) and Cacus (Canto XXV), but this discussion will concentrate mostly on the first two major monsters. As mentioned and elaborated in prior literature,[12] Cerberus, Geryon and Nessus and Cacus were all overwhelmed, tamed or killed by Hercules, a Pre-Christian salvific type invested with probable Neoplatonic symbolism, and other salvific heroes who were sons of Jupiter and Neptune in myth, Perseus and Theseus, likewise conquered Medusa and the Minotaur respectively. Such myth congruences of heroes and monsters integrating Classical and Christian traditions are necessary for Dante and are purposefully woven together to make a whole new literary fabric out of separate threads. Tensions that may thus occur therein are harmonized by the historicity of his denizens of hell, many from among his own contemporaries.

Dante's monsters are both predictable in the sense that they somewhat mirror Virgilian episodes and somewhat unpredictable in the Christian ethos that the poet creates specifically for each. As Jewiss noted:

> The most obvious place to look for monsters in the medieval world is hell, the dark margins of God's creation, a space retrieved from Classical antiquity and transformed into the Christian repository for evil. Within a Christian framework, sin must be coupled metaphorically with the monstrous, for transgression is that which deforms and makes ugly.[13]

In this way, monsters fit Dante's worldview and his theological intents to make Christian allegories of antiquity.

Erinyes (Furies) and Harpies

The Erinyes or Furies (Canto IX) and Harpies (Canto XIII) also serve Dante's rhetorical purposes as monstrous, but are not necessarily perceived as monsters themselves even in classical antiquity. In the *Inferno*, instead the Furies add horrific purpose, bloodstained, girdled in bright green hydras about their waist and crowned with vipers at their brows, screaming, howling and baying as they wound themselves. In Canto IX.38-48 Dante imitates the Underworld of *Aeneid* VI.545 & ff. with its triple steel walled Tartarus and moated red-hot Phlegethon where the Fury, Tisiphone in her "blood-wet" dress guards its towered gate, but in typical triplicity Dante adds her sisters Megaera and Alecto.

The mournful thicket of the Harpies opening Canto XIII is a puzzling place, one Dante describes in repetitive negative "nons" (not yet reached other side, unmarked by paths, not green leaves, unsmooth bark, no fruit, no beast infests so rough and dense a wood), all reserved for suicides in their ultimate negation of self. Dante's Harpies (*Arpie* from Latin *Harpeia*) nesting in this poisonous wood are described as *odio*, loathsome, winged and with bird talons for feet, feathered bodies with distended stomachs, yet with human heads, but even these cannot fully articulate human speech in their screeching *lamenti*. Dante's pilgrim is horrified to learn the harpies feed on the thorny foliage, causing pain because inhabiting the stumps were disembodied humans whose voices cry out, and he also discovers to his horror this is the wood of suicides.

Harpies (from Greek ʼαρπυια) in mythology were greatly feared, harpy literally meaning "snatcher" (in Greek *harpazein* means "to snatch"). At times Harpies may also have been thought to be sudden gusts of wind with mournful sounds, and in superstition they were blamed for sudden disappearances. Hesiod was one of the first Greek poets to mention Harpies in *Theogony* 265 onward, connected to both winds and birds.

Generally female—Virgil says that they had the faces of maidens but were obscene in their habits—as filthy and ravenous bird monsters with human heads, in legend they befouled and stole food from wanderers like the Trojans of Aeneas who stopped on the island of Strophades in *Aeneid* III.216-58 and were imagined thus in Italy in *Aeneid* VII.107-20. In some myths and, for example, on sculpted Classical Greek friezes from the so-called Harpy Tomb of Xanthos, c. 470 BCE, they appear to carry off human souls of the dead.[14] In some myths Harpies may have also stolen souls of sleeping babies as some have interpreted, and in other variants they abducted and tortured souls en route to Tartarus, but since they were insatiably hungry, it was usually food they pilfered after befouling everything else with excrement as they robbed stranded seafarers. Dante has the Harpies stripping what little withered foliage exists in the mostly barren, thorny wood of the suicides, which pains the human souls occupying the twisted, bleeding trees, and Dante's Harpy monsters are the "embodiment of fear" in this wood of despair.[15]

Medusa

While some have seen Medusa as out of place in the *Inferno*, like its sinners her curse was self-inflicted, her original human beauty became a monstrous curse because of how she misapprehended it, an omen of her hubris. Even Christine de Pizan said it was originally Medusa's beauty that was arresting,[16] and its transformation from beauty to horrification is suggested by Dante's description of the Furies even though they are only harbingers of Medusa. After her disfiguring transformation Medusa was always deemed a monster, as the Furies invoke in almost reverse apotropaic intent that Medusa is worse than their own effect because like a basilisk she can silently turn to stone with one fractional gaze of being seen, whereas they can be seen in all their ugliness. Hollander not only calls her a "watchdog of Dis" but also sees her as an allegory personifying "that which turns hard the will of man in sin" in Dante's use of her.[17] Freccero's reasoned essay on Dante's Medusa also makes much of the baffling use of allegory in sightedness and antitheses of "covering" and "uncovering" with the poet's veil (*velami*) and antitheses of *dottrina* and Medusa as Dante commands readers to see (*mirate*) and understand what lesson is beneath the veil of strange verses (*sotto 'l velami de li versi strani*): "it is because the pilgrim averted his eyes from the Medusa that there is a truth to be seen beneath the veil," both an interpretive and moral threat of doom of petrification, which will happen if the pilgrim does not "turn" (conversion) because then he will never "return" above.[18]

Apotropaic devices possessed much of the similar force in their ability to ward off evil, as eyes painted on ships' prows, and often warding off evil by evil, as in the myth of Athena/Minerva's wearing of the Gorgoneion (severed Medusa head) on her aegis, or sculpted eyes that could still see while being seen on profile relief in antiquity, or to protect against the *fascinum*, "evil eye" in ancient Roman superstition,[19] which practice Virgil mentions through the mouth of Menalcas about bewitching herd animals in *Eclogue* III.103: "*Nescio quis teneros oculos mihi fascinat agnum.*" But here in Dante's *Inferno*, however, the threat of seeing Medusa to the "living" pilgrim is still very much "alive" and powerful in the realm of the dead.

Charybdis and Cacus

While ancient monsters often included Charybdis as the maelstrom in the Straits of Messina where two contrary seas meet, in the *Inferno* (Canto VII) she is reduced to figurative language alluding to monstrous destructive waves that crash together and separate again as describing the hordes of the damned rushing about in their half-circle collisions where chaos rules. Charybdis was an oceanographic phenomenon, the worse of two evils relative to Scylla in the idiom "between a rock and a hard place," a way for myth to explain nature and the dangers of the sea.

Cacus, on the other hand, was treated by Virgil in *Aeneid* VIII.195-230 & ff. with considerable detail in a narration by King Evander of Latium, some of which Dante echoes. In myth, thieving Cacus was the son of Vulcan and Medusa—having a few characteristics of both in his fire-breathing, horrific evil character—who lived awhile on the Aventine Hill, where in myth he had "often turned the stones under the Aventine mount into a lake of blood," *sotto 'l sasso di monte Aventino, di sangue fece spesse volte laco*, much like Nero of old if Suetonius is credible.[20] Having stolen some of Hercules's cattle, Cacus thought he could hide his crime by forcing the cattle to walk backward into his cave, thus trying to fool anyone who might track them. Hearing a pilfered heifer lowing from within the mountain as he drove his herd past, Hercules discovered the theft and clubbed the half-human monster in his destroyed cave with a hundred blows, only the first ten of which he lived through. In a sense this heroic overkill may spill over into Dante's hell where sinners are punished beyond physical death.

Dante's Cacus is thus apropos in Canto XXV's Circle of Thieves, Bolgia 7, although here in centaur form. While not necessarily always thieves, centaurs were prone to trying to steal women like Deianira the wife of Hercules and Hippodameia the bride princess of the Lapith king Pirithous in the most famous Centauromachy in myth. Cacus the violent centaur is covered with snakes, also bearing a dragon fire-breathing like the original Cacus of myth, and the following transformation of Florentine shades and serpents has likely allegorical power as well, possibly about degradation of the *Imago Dei* or bestial antithesis to the divine in *nostra effige*.[21] Early commentators assumed Dante's centaurs were *condottieri*, mercenaries hired out by tyrants, often violent but nonetheless instruments of rule however harsh,[22] and this centaur's full rage (*centauro pien di rabbia*) deserves Dante's *contrapasso* equivocating the sin in life with the punishment in hell.[23]

Early in Canto XXV, the pursuit of the Florentine Fucci by Cacus, where a centaur form is emblematic of violence, with "the load of serpents for his many thefts" and "the fiery dragon for his sacrilege and blasphemy—for he [Fucci] had stolen from the Church"[24]—predispose the passage to an allegory of fugitive justice; the myth endorses in Hercules' destruction Cacus, as in *Aeneid* VIII where the kingdom of

Latium is also thereby freed. In myth, dual-natured centaurs are instruments of chaos whose bestiality usually undermines their humanity.[25]

In Canto XXV Dante often either uses synonymic or derived words of transmutation (e.g., *mutare, mutato, converte* and *trasmutare*) alongside slightly negativized words of amalgamation (e.g., *confusi, mischiar*), his poetic text—mentioning other Roman poets and works like Ovid's *Metamorphoses* and Lucan's *Pharsalia* both of whom he slightly demeans, possibly relative to Virgil—might appear to be steeped in hermetic alchemy in descriptive colors of brown, black and white as well as "livid" earlier, all newly changed by the agency of fire partly seen through smoke: *Mentre che 'l fummo l'uno e l'altro vela di colore novo* ("while the smoke veils the one and then the other with new color"), and with allegorical details somehow evoking what one would see in a metalworker's forge where metal flows serpent-like when molten,[26] evocative considering the father of Cacus was Vulcan in myth. The Latin name Cacus may derive from the Greek *kakos*, "evil," which would be consonant with his place in the *Inferno* as a creature given over to wickedness and without redeeming qualities, although Augustine would have evil only as an absence of goodness, where "no creature is evil, in spite of the fact that some creatures are worse than others,"[27] and even Dante's demi-monsters like Cacus are creatures that bear traces of the *Imago Dei*, however marred.

Minotaur

The Minotaur is a more obvious classical monster with hybrid nature conjoining man and bull, regardless which part wears head or body. At the broken edge of the chasm, here rages the *l'Infamia di Creti*, the "Infamy of Crete." Long ago in myth, instead of sacrificing the bull from the sea to Poseidon as a votive, King Minos of Crete wanted the magnificent bull to stud his cows and the sea god gave him more than he wanted, seeding his wife whose bent mind desired the bull. The captive inventor Daedalus, at the bidding of Queen Pasiphae whose lust for the white bull knew no natural bounds, created a fake cow for her to climb inside for the bull to mount, and the Minotaur was conceived inside the cow, *concetta ne la falsa vacca*, perhaps also an allusion to the birth shell of Venus, Goddess of Love since *concetta* can ambiguously suggest both "shell" (Latin *concha*) as well as the normal "conceived." Theseus, as Duca d'Atene, slew the Minotaur but also descended into the Underworld to steal Persephone, and never returned, so when Virgil wonders, "Perhaps you think you see the Duke of Athens," it is partly because Dante reminds that in *Aeneid* VI.618 "wretched Theseus sits forever" trapped in Virgil's Tartarus for his thwarted hubristic crime of abduction.

Seeing the poets, the violent Minotaur rages, his mind crazed as he "gnawed himself in rage" (*sé stesso morse, si come quei cui l'ira dentro fiacca*), the Italian repetitive with alliteratively rich velar consonants (*come, quei, cui*), and he can only rage not the least because he has a beast-human duality of mind that will never be resolvable. The structure of Canto XII, itself about dualities, "conceals" an image about the human body: "neither the Minotaur nor the centaurs can produce more than half a human body each";[28] even Chiron, the noblest of centaurs, is still half a beast. The threatening way in which the Minotaur plunges back and forth on the rocks, *guardata da quell'ira bestial*, makes the monster's direction as unpredictable as his mind and body, neither of which can move in unison. Even the Minotaur's rageful gnawing himself is a form of self-punishment, the accursed pain one nature violently inflicts on the other. Mindless or not, however, typical of the *Inferno*'s quasi-biblical denizens, rage and gnashing of teeth are eternal (*Gospel of Matthew* 13:42, 50).[29]

Cerberus

Cerberus was the monstrous triple-headed Hell Dog guarding the Gates of Hell in Canto VI of the *Inferno*, appropriated by Dante after having guarded the mythical gate of the Classical Underworld from

Greek through Roman myth, his task also used by Virgil, allowing the dead to enter but none to escape, as Hesiod first said in *Theogony* 767-74:

> There, in front, stand the echoing halls of the god of the lower-world, strong Hades, and of awful Persephone. A fearful hound guards the house in front, pitiless, and he has a cruel trick. On those who go in he fawns with his tail and both his ears, but suffers them not to go out back again, but keeps watch and devours whomever he catches going out of the gates of strong Hades and awful Persephone.[30]

As one of his last punitive labors Juno (Hera) sent Hercules (Heracles) to the Underworld to bring back Cerberus, hoping he would be trapped and never return, but as protectress of heroes Minerva (Athena) came to his aid, showing him how to tame the monster with brains instead of muscling the monster with brawn. In several passages, Virgil locates Cerberus in the Underworld (*Aeneid* VI.395-6) for the successful passage of Hercules, where Hercules contravened the normal function of Cerberus by dragging him away from the gate and then has Aeneas face him in following lines (417-18).[31] For Dante, Cerberus was also used as an allegory of uncontrolled gluttony or incontinence of appetite. For the tormented sinners who yielded to gluttony in the Third Circle, implying they were moved more by their stomachs than any beauty, Cerberus rakes them and rips at the embodied spirits with his monstrous claws:

> [Cerberus] is the prototype of the gluttons. . . . He has become Appetite and as such he flays and mangles the spirits who reduced their lives to a satisfaction of appetite. With his three heads, he appears to be a manifestation of Lucifer and thus another distortion of the Trinity.[32]

In Luciferian allegory, Dante directly refers to Cerberus as *il gran vermo*, "the Great Worm" alluding to many biblical possibilities from

Genesis 3 with the serpent in Eden to the great warring dragon of *Apocalypse* (*Revelation*) 12:3-4 whose demonic tail drew down a third of the stars in the sky, although in the biblical passage the dragon has seven heads, not three, but the reptilian nature is derogated by Dante, reduced in scorn to being a worm.[33] As in almost every Dante reference, triplicity and Trinitarian allusions abound even in logical but antithetical ways; if God has three persons so must the Devil. The ternary correlation with angels fits that after Lucifer's expulsion from Heaven, the third of the stars are fallen angels swept down with his prideful fall.

Dante's Cerberus makes direct imitative reference to Virgil's description of the Underworld passage of Aeneas, where Dante has Virgil throwing dirt clods into the monster's gaping, fanged mouths to distract it when it sees the two poets approaching:

> With this action, Virgil imitates the action of the Sibyl who, leading Aeneas through the Underworld, placates Cerberus by casting honeyed cakes into his three throats (*Aeneid* VI.417-423). By substituting "dirt" for the Virgilian cakes, Dante emphasizes Cerberus' irrational gluttony.[34]

Where the Sibyl throws drugged honeycakes in order to subdue it, Dante scornfully reduces the "food" to dirt, not only which the monster finds indistinguishable from other sustenance but also reductively apropos of its underworld locus. Dante describes Cerberus as behaving just like a food-distracted dog, quieting only to bolt its food down, "a hungry cur fighting with only its food," thus leaving the two poets alone to pass by more safely.

Dante's description of Cerberus echoes Virgil in other ways in *Aeneid* VI.417-18: "Huge Cerberus sets these regions echoing with his triple-throated howling, crouching monstrously in a cave opposite" as both Virgil and Dante describe Cerberus as monstrous, triple-throated, noisily howling and Hell's guardian, Dante's description of Cerberus, however, is also much more ample than Virgil's standard version: the *Inferno*'s Cerberus has red eyes (*occhi . . . vermigli*), a greasy black beard (*barba untra . . . atra*) and a great belly (*ventre largo*), signifying its unbridled motivation to eat. For Virgil, Cerberus howls, where for Dante the monster deafeningly barks and thunders. In Canto IX.98-99 the ugly throat of Cerberus is also described as scraped clean due to Hercules having temporarily dragged him away while he resisted his destiny. Most of all for Dante, Cerberus is a monster dispensing divine justice; the cruel claws rake, scar and flay the sinners (*graffia li spiriti, scuoia e disquatra*), something the classical monster could never do, as it could only devour anyone trying to escape back. Even as an incorporeal shade, the disjunction in devouring a shade is nonetheless still a potent threat.

Cerberus is similar to the animation of soul-devouring in the vignette in Egypt's Hall of Two Truths, Chapter-Spell 125 A-D of the *Egyptian Book of Going Forth by Day* (*Book of the Dead*), where the fearful triple hybrid Ammit (combining a wigged crocodile head with either a hyena or maned lion torso and a hippopotamus rear as a monster) forever gobbles the souls of those whose sins made their "hearts" weigh more than the proverbial feather of justice of Ma'at. Thereafter the souls have no future.[35] This relict ancient classical function of triple-headed Cerberus—devouring any who might try to leave Hell—bears great resemblance to triple-hybrid Ammit, which was most likely a distant source for some of the Greek Kerberos (Cerberus) myth tradition. In this case triplicity is not only a Danteesque device but also a potent myth function of the *hubris-hubridis* formula already mentioned.

Geryon

The most complicated of Dante's monsters may be Geryon, ". . . one of the most fantastic of Dante's monsters, Geryon the emblem of fraud,"[36] whose place here has long been debated because his nature is so enigmatic and Dante's description and use are not in keeping with the classical three-headed Iberian giant slain by Hercules.[37] In myth

Geryon lived on the "red" island of Erytheia in the far west, always tinted by sunset, and Hercules appropriated and drove away his herd of red cattle after killing him. According to Hesiod, *Theogony* 287-290, Geryon's mother was Kallirhoe, daughter of Ocean, and he was at first only triple-headed. Many have pointed out how often Greek monsters are connected to Poseidon and Ocean, as Hesiod lists, including those in the *Inferno* like Geryon, including Medusa and her Gorgon sisters (*Theogony* 273-5), Harpies (*Theogony* 264-69) and Cerberus (*Theogony* 311). The Erinyes were born from the drops of blood of castrated Uranus falling on earth (*Theogony* 176-77), and the Minotaur was born of the bull Poseidon sent from the sea (Apollodorus, *Bibliotheke* III.1.3-4). The connection of Geryon and the other monsters to Poseidon and Ocean can account for them as instruments of chaos, like the uncontrollable sea. Other than as manifestations of chaos, these classical text monsters have less in common with Dante's highly symbolic schemata of punishment.

But Dante has other uses for Geryon that do not need to mirror every classical myth, however much his conquest by the salvific Hercules foreshadows a heroic figure of Christ who himself descended in his harrowing of Hell after his death. By changing Geryon from a triple-bodied giant with three similar bodies or merely a giant with three heads—forms of the classical image as seen on black-figured Greek vase paintings and Roman mosaics[38]—to a giant hybridizing different creatures in one person, Dante offers a bolder allegory:

> Geryon . . . combines the wise man with the scorpion's tail. As this passage makes clear, he combines the three natures of man, beast, and serpent delineated in the *Liber monstrorum di diversis generibus*. . . . The most enigmatic of Dante's monsters escapes definition as he metamorphoses under the poet's pen . . . described as one who swims and flies . . . Geryon is the ever-changing monster who ushers Dante into the realm of fraud, the sin of deception and false appearances.[39]

In Canto XVII.10 & ff., Geryon is described as having a just man's face, outwardly kind, but that is his only human part. His wingless torso is serpentine, with hairy fur from his paws to his armpits, and his back and breast are marked with intricate designs Dante does not divulge; in 27-28 his tail is armed with a venomous stinger like a dreadful scorpion's. This hybrid form also echoes his Classical triple form, with a benign human head at one end with a scorpion's toxic poisonous tail on the other end, a dangerous mixture for Dante's persona to read: which part best expresses of the beast's truer nature? Because the only way down into the Abyss is on the monster's back, Dante has to overcome his greatest fears. The fact that face and body do not match is part of the fraud; if fooled by the huge kindly face one might never see the arcing scorpion stinger coming overhead to pierce behind, which is part of what Dante feared so greatly and why Virgil sat behind him for protection in the descent.

Since Dante's guide is Virgil, perhaps the most appropriate Geryon sources for Dante are *Aeneid* VI.289 and VIII.202, where as has been pointed out in VI.289 in Aeneas' underworld descent that Geryon is periphrastically alluded in the words *forma tricorporis umbrae*[40] as a "triple-bodied shade." But in using Geryon to different ends than Classical myth, Dante manipulates many different images to create a holistic monster, mostly lacking Classic monstrousness in terms of malevolence and instead rendering a composite being who acts as a vehicle for transporting Dante and Virgil to the abyss. Here Dante "collapse[s] a wildly incompatible range of literal senses into a single level of narrative. . . . Geryon conflates classical myth, Christian doctrine, literary criticism and exegetical terminology as literal meanings of creatures."[41]

Geryon is also ambiguous in exact medium through which he moves in the Abyss, because Dante describes his locomotion in various figurative ways: "Geryon remains in a disquietingly indeterminate position as he travels through a medium described as air and water."[42] One of the most interesting recent studies about Dante's description of Geryon and his flight down into the Abyss comes not from a literary analysis but from a physicist. Dante's prescience about an aspect of science is not entirely surprising given his powers of description. When Dante carefully describes the gradual downward motion of Geryon spiraling into the Abyss (100-108) while swimming though air, he remarks in the absence of seeing anything that while he knows they must be descending in wheeling round, he has no perception of motion and can only perceive motion by the wind against his face.[43] The physicist Ricci believes the perceptive poet intuitively grasped what Galileo established centuries later as the Galilean invariance principle regarding the imperceptibility of motion without a visual frame of reference and the physicist was not surprised given Dante's incredible sensory detail and immense powers of description.

Synthesizing Christian apocalyptic lore, Dante's Geryon is also a figure of the *Antichristus mysticus* derivable for Dante from the biblical *Apocalypse* (*Revelation*) 9:7 about the deep Abyss, where, after the fifth angel sounds his trumpet, a star falls to the earth with a key to unlock the Abyss. Then smoke rose from the Abyss "as from a giant furnace" and where locust-like creatures with thundering wings and human faces came out of the smoke with tails of scorpions and the power of scorpions to sting.[44] Since Dante describes Geryon as a composite creature out of the Abyss, a beast bearing a human face but having a scorpion's tail, the comparison is apt. Dante's Geryon thus sums up past, present and future judgment in a fusion of Classical and Christian tradition, taking the long view of time and eternity as might be expected from such a great poet.

Conclusion

Dante's monsters may be derived from classical sources but are transformed into very different, allegorical creatures, each one at a symbolic junction of the story and with a specific association with both sinners and divinely-assigned tasks to fulfill, a liminal function as boundary markers of infernal sub-territories, each on a different turf.

Each circle below Limbo is inhabited or guarded by a monster. More precisely, monsters dwell at the edges, at notable thresholds on the pilgrim's journey. Thus in addition to marking the transition from one level to another, they help to define the entrance to the Gates of Hell and to Hell proper, the gates of the city of Dis and the exit from the eternally dark realm. Most significantly, monsters appear at difficult junctures on the journey, places where the terrain is impossible to traverse without their intervention.[45]

While Dante's monsters derived from Classical myth—Cerberus, Erinyes, Harpies, Medusa, Cacus, Geryon and others—are not creatures of obvious order, nonetheless they order the *Inferno* in a different way. They mete out punishment appropriate to each circle of hell where, often similar to their sinners in appropriate locations, they too mostly suffer and rage as they painfully maim sinners who are also their bait because Dante has crafted them as the direst personification of fear. Dante's sinners might have wished that only earthly foreshadowings of accountability and judgment in this life were as effective as their horrific encounters after the fact. In the face of his monsters who link Classical and Christian worlds through the past, present and future, Dante warns, *Caveat lector*: "Reader beware." As he claims he did, Dante the Poet wishes to make us tremble.

Notes

1. Lansing, 107.
2. Gurevich, 144: "Dante's Other World is allegorized. Though allegory for medieval man was not equivalent to fiction, and it is unlikely that for Dante hell, purgatory and paradise were mere poetic metaphors, nevertheless this impressive picture of otherwordly reality was created precisely by Dante."
3. Frayling, 159: "well-known literary genre of 'otherworldly visits' . . . [in

Dante] the condemned in hell are not plagued by reptiles and fanged beasts of sculpture . . . they are plagued forever by their worldly sins . . . Other world . . . which Dante transformed from the world of folklore to the world of art. . . ."

4. Gérard Luciani. *Les Monstres dans "La Divine Comédie."* Paris: Lettres Modernes, 1975 (according to Jewiss "the most thorough treatment of the topic"); many others have written extensively on Dante's monsters, e.g., Christopher Kleinhenz. "Notes on Dante's Use of Classical Myths and the Mythological Tradition." *Romance Quarterly* 33 (1986) 477-484. I do not yet have text for what looks to be a promising study: Christopher Livanos. "Dante's Monsters: Nature and Evil in the Comedy," in C. Kleinhenz, ed. Symposium on Dante Alighieri and the Medieval Cultural Traditions. *Dante Studies*, forthcoming.

5. Kevin Brownlee. "Dante and the Classical Poets," in Rachel Jacoff, ed., *The Cambridge Companion to Dante*, 2007 ed, 141-60, esp. 141, 148, 150, 152 & ff.

6. Madison Sowell, ed. *Dante and Ovid: Essays in Intertextuality.* Medieval & Renaissance Texts & Studies, vol 82. Center for International Scholarly Exchange, Columbia University, vol. 2. Binghamton, NY, 1991, 11. Also see Teodolinda Barolini, "Re-Presenting What God Presented: The Arachnean Art of Dante's Terrace of Pride." *Dante Studies* 105 (1987) 43-62, and elsewhere.

7. O'Grady, 1.

8. Jewell, 12.

9. Curtius, 359, "Dante's hundreds of imitations of the *Aeneid* . . . ."

10. Regarding *hubris-hubridis*, I tried this idea out on John Boardman in early 2007, and he encouraged my reading.

11. Sinclair, 164.

12. Lansing, 274n43.

13. Jewiss, 181.

14. Archaic style Lykian tomb monument, British Museum. GR 1848-10-20.1 (Sculpture B287). Not all agree they are Harpy representations, but rather sirens. One of the figures shown seated on the Lykian tomb relief may have been the dynastic Lykian king Harpagus, hence the possible homophonic association with the mythical harpy (᾿αρπυια).

15. Sinclair, 176.

16. Garber and Vickers, writing about Pizan's *Book of the City of Ladies* in *The Medusa Reader*, 57.

17. Robert Hollander. *Allegory in Dante's Commedia*. Princeton: Princeton University Press, 1969, 240, 253.

18. John Freccero, ch. in Garber and Vickers, 110-112 & ff.

19. Matthew W. Dickie. "Heliodorus and Plutarch on the Evil Eye." *Classical Philology* 86 (1991) 17-29.

20. Suetonius, *De Vitae Caesarum: Vita Neronis* 28-29, 37; Tacitus, *Annales* XV 39-40, 44, where Nero's uncontrollable lusts and violent thievery bathed Rome in blood, robbed Romans of all classes and persecuted Christians to death, including burning them as torches at his orgies by his Domus Aurea lake.

21. Priest, 21 & ff.

22. Sinclair, 164.

23. Note of Nicole Pinsky in Robert Pinsky's *Inferno* translation, 340.

24. Sinclair, 317.

25. Patrick Hunt. "Kentauros: Near Eastern and Not-So-Greek-Hybrid." Yale University Graduate Classics Colloquium paper, April, 1999.

26. Classical Hebrew makes this clear where *nahash* (נחש) is serpent and *nehoshet* (נחשת) is bronze serpent in the fiery serpent biblical passage of *Numbers* 21:5-9, although for Dante to have known this is not attestable.

27. Derivable from Augustine, *De Natura boni contra Mani* 14 in Eleonore Stump and Norman Kretzmann. *The Cambridge Companion to Augustine*, Cambridge University Press, 2001, 44.

28. Tambling, 881.

29. *Matthew* 13:42, 50: "And [God] shall cast them into a furnace of fire: there shall be wailing and gnashing of teeth."

30. Hesiod *Theogony* 767-74, tr. Hugh G. Evelyn-White. *Hesiod's Theogony*. Cambridge, MA: Harvard University Press; London, William Heinemann Ltd. 1914.

31. Raymond J. Clark. "The Cerberus-Like Function of the Gorgons in Virgil's Underworld (*Aen.* 6.273-94)." *The Classical Quarterly*, 53.1 (2003) 308-309. Virgil's placement of Cerberus corresponds with the location of other monsters and snakes in a lost Heracles catabasis, 309n6.

32. Musa, 59.

33. Christopher Kleinhenz. "Infernal Guardians Revisited: 'Cerbero, il gran vermo.'" (*Inferno* VI.22) *Dante Studies* 93 (1975) 185-99.

34. Musa, 59.

35. Raymond Faulkner, Carol Andrews, eds. *The Egyptian Book of the Dead: The Book of Going Forth by Day*. San Francisco: Chronicle Books, 2000, 115-18. From the *Papyrus of Ani*, see the British Museum sheet EA 10470/3 or from the *Papyrus of Hunefer*, see the British Museum sheet EA 9901/3, both 19th Dynasty, around 1275 BCE.

36. Becker, 179.

37. Friedman, 109, esp. in "Dante's figure of fraud hardly resembles the classical Geryon, a three-headed Spanish king slain by Hercules."

38. E.g., Archaic c. 540 BCE. Black-Figure Vase, Musée du Louvre, Paris F3, Beazley 310309; and the magnificent late Roman mosaics in the late 3rd century CE Triclinium at Villa Romana del Casale near Piazza Armerina, Sicily, depicting The Labors of Hercules show a bleeding triple-bodied armored giant felled by the hero.

39. Jewiss, 183.

40. Friedman, 109.

41. Lansing, 107.

42. Jewiss, 183.

43. Ricci, 717: "The poet's vividly imagined flight unwittingly captures a physical law of motion. In 1632 Galileo described his experience of motion aboard a large ship and exposed in detail the invariance principle. . . . I suggest that more than three centuries earlier, in the *Divine Comedy*, his fellow countryman Dante Alighieri intuitively grasped what Galileo was later to establish."

44. Friedman, 112.

45. Jewiss, 184.

Bibliography

Barolini, Teodolinda. "Re-Presenting What God Presented: The Arachnean Art of Dante's Terrace of Pride." *Dante Studies* 105 (1987) 43-62.

Becker, Christopher Bennett. "Dante's Motley Cord: Art and Apocalypse in *Inferno* XVI." *Modern Language Notes* 106.1 Italian issue (1991) 179-83.

Brownlee, Kevin. "Dante and the Classical Poets," in Rachel Jacoff, ed., *The Cambridge Companion to Dante*, 2007 ed, 141-60, esp. 141, 148, 150, 152 & ff.

Clark, Raymond J. "The Cerberus-Like Function of the Gorgons in Virgil's Underworld (*Aen.* 6.273-94)." *The Classical Quarterly* 53.1 (2003) 308-309.

Curtius, Ernst Robert. *European Literature and the Latin Middle Ages.* "Dante" (Chapter 17). W.R. Trask, tr. Bollingen Series XXXVI. Princeton: Princeton University Press, 1990 [1953] 7th pr., 348-79.

Dickie, Matthew W. "Heliodorus and Plutarch on the Evil Eye." *Classical Philology* 86 (1991) 17-29.

Faulkner, Raymond, and Carol Andrews, eds. *The Egyptian Book of the Dead: The Book of Going Forth by Day.* San Francisco: Chronicle Books, 2000.

Frayling, Christopher. *Strange Landscape: A Journey Through the Middle Ages.* London: Penguin Books, 1995, 159.

Freccero, John. Foreword, in Robert Pinsky, tr. *The Inferno of Dante.* New York: Farrar, Straus and Giroux, 2000. 11th pr.

Freccero, John. "On Dante's Medusa," in Marjorie Garber and Nancy Vickers, eds. *The Medusa Reader.* New York: Routledge, 2003, Chapter 45, 109-121 [reprinted from Freccero, *Medusa: The Letter and the Spirit*, 1972].

Friedman, John Block. "Antichrist and the Iconography of Dante's Geryon." *Journal of the Warburg and Courtauld Institutes* XXXV (1972) 108-122.

Garber, Marjorie, and Nancy Vickers, eds. *The Medusa Reader.* New York: Routledge, 2003, 57.

Gurevich, Aron. *Medieval Popular Culture: Problems of Belief and Perception.* J. M. Bak and P. A. Hollingsworth, trs. Cambridge: Cambridge University Press, 1997 repr., 144.

Hollander, Robert. *Allegory in Dante's Commedia.* Princeton: Princeton University Press, 1969, 240, 253.

Hunt, Patrick. "Kentauros: Near Eastern and Not-So-Greek-Hybrid." *Yale University Graduate Classics Colloquium* paper, April, 1999.

Jewell, Keala, ed. *Monsters in the Italian Literary Imagination.* Wayne State University Press, 2001, 12.

Jewiss, Virginia. "Monstrous Movements and Metaphors in Dante's *Divine Comedy*," in Keala Jewell, ed. *Monsters in the Italian Literary Imagination.* Wayne State University Press, 2001, 179-184 & ff.

Kleinhenz, Christopher. "Infernal Guardians Revisited: '*Cerbero, il gran vermo.*'" (*Inferno* VI.22) *Dante Studies* 93 (1975) 185-99.

Kleinhenz, Christopher. "Notes on Dante's Use of Classical Myths and the Mythological Tradition." *Romance Quarterly* 33 (1986) 477-484.

Lansing, Richard. *Dante and Classical Antiquity: The Epic Tradition*. [Dante: The Critical Complex, vol. 2.] London and New York: Routledge, 2002, 107.

Luciani, Gérard. *Les Monstres dans "La Divine Comédie."* Paris: Lettres Modernes, 1975.

Musa, Mark, ed. *Dante's Inferno*. Indiana Critical Edition. Bloomington: Indiana University Press, 1995, 59.

O'Grady, Desmond. *Rome Reshaped: Jubilees 1300-2000*. New York: Continuum Books, 1-5, 63-5 on Dante.

Pinsky, Robert, ed. *The Inferno of Dante*, foreword by John Freccero. New York: Farrar, Straus and Giroux, 2000. 11th pr.

Priest, Paul. "Looking Back from the Vision: Trinitarian Structure and Poetry in the *Commedia*." *Dante Studies* 91 (1973) 113-30.

Ricci, Leonardo. "History of Science: Dante's insight into Galilean invariance (*Inferno* VI.103-08)." *Nature* 434 (2005) 717.

Sinclair, John D. *Dante: The Divine Comedy: 1. Inferno*. New York: Oxford University Press, 1961.

Sowell, Madison, ed. *Dante and Ovid: Essays in Intertextuality*. Medieval & Renaissance Texts & Studies, vol 82. Center for International Scholarly Exchange, Columbia University, vol. 2. Binghamton, NY, 1991, 11.

Stump, Eleonore, and Norman Kretzmann. *The Cambridge Companion to Augustine*. Cambridge University Press, 2001.

Tambling, Jeremy. "Monstrous Tyranny, Men of Blood: Dante and *Inferno* XII." *The Modern Language Review* 98.4 (2003) 881-97.

Canto 11:
The Plan of Hell _____

Wallace Fowlie

Dante chooses this point in his poem, at the conclusion of the brilliant meeting with Farinata and Guido Cavalcanti's father, to give an interlude, an exposition of the system of punishments in his *Inferno*. The gravity of the tone of the sixth circle is enhanced by Dante's use of *voi*, the polite pronoun, in speaking to Farinata and Cavalcante Cavalcanti, the pronoun he will use on only one other meeting, that with Brunetto Latini, in canto 15. With all the other shades he uses *tu*, the familiar form of address.

Thus canto 11 is a necessary pause before the real descent into the city of Dis begins, and it serves many purposes. For the action of the poem, it reveals the knowledge of Virgil, who expounds a system of classification based on scholastic philosophy, that of Saint Thomas Aquinas, who leaned heavily on Aristotle and Cicero for matters related to ethics. And consequently it reveals at the same time a fuller insight on the part of Dante concerning the region of the dead he is crossing, thus enabling us to see more clearly the structure of the work, the highly rational ordering of sins.

Dante's mind is full of memories of the battle career of Farinata, of his proud strong nature still manifest in Hell. In a way, the great Ghibelline illustrates the hardness of the Medusa head with which Dante himself had just been threatened when he and Virgil had tried to enter the gate of Dis. The change that deeper Hell will bring is prepared in this opening image of the archheretic. The sixth circle separates the upper Hell of the incontinent from the lower Hell formed by the three circles of violence, fraud, and treachery. The sins of violence, in the seventh circle, have a deeper place in Hell than those of incontinence because they accentuate the bestial side of man's nature. They are the sins of the lion (*leone*), the second beast encountered by Dante in canto 1. The sins of fraud or malice of the eighth circle, the most complex of all the circles, are those of the she-wolf (*la lupa*), the third beast of canto 1.

The image of the city is everywhere in these last three circles. Violence is swift, a flaring up of the human spirit for the purpose of destruction. Fraud is a longer, slower process of deceit, a deliberate undermining of someone else's will. The treachery or betrayal of the ninth circle is treated as the most serious of all sins because in that act all human values between individuals are destroyed. Thus canto 11 provides us with a plan of the devil's city. Virgil and Dante have just seen a few of the first inhabitants, those of the sixth circle, but heresy in the Dantean sense seems to be more related to incontinence than to violence. It stands midway between the first half of Hell and the second half.

Variously called the "scholastic canto" or the "Aristotelean canto," it is a review of the criminal or moral code of behavior. It contains no picture or character that stimulates the reader's imagination, no Charon, no Furies, no Ciacco, but it presents a scheme that holds the reader's mind, and it names in line 80 the philosophical treatise that is the principal source of the moral framework of Dante's *Inferno*. Virgil, the principal speaker and teacher of the canto, calls the book *la tua Etica*, "your Ethics," which is the *Nicomachean Ethics* of Aristotle, listing

le tre disposizion che 'l ciel non vole

[11:81]

[the three dispositions that Heaven does not allow]

Virgil then names them in the following two verses: incontinence, malice and bestiality:

incontenenza, malizia e la matta
bestialitade

[11:82-83]

These three categories are in Aristotle and are usually translated by the terms "vice, incontinence, and bestiality (*Nicomachean Ethics* 7:1). The most likely translation of "bestiality" in Dante would be the violence of the seventh circle. Incontinence, then, would be contained in the first through sixth circles, and fraud and malice would be found in the eighth and ninth circles. Aristotle's ethical system is anthropocentric, but when Dante says that the three dispositions are not allowed by Heaven, he moves into the realm of Christian doctrine.

In the unfolding of the canto, these general definitions are prompted by a leading question asked by Dante in lines 73 and 74:

> perchè non dentro da la città roggia
>   sono ei puniti?
> [Why are not the sins of incontinence punished in the red city?]

The question is full and explicit because in it Dante refers to the four leading circles of incontinence: the marsh of the wrathful (*la palude*) in the fifth circle, the windy second circle of the lustful (*il vento*), the rainy third circle of gluttony (*la pioggia*), and the sharp tongues of the hoarders and spenders in the fourth circle. Virgil explains that God feels less anger toward those outside the city of Dis, a divine distinction which, of course, is not in Aristotle.

Much earlier in the canto, when Virgil advises a brief pause so that the travelers may become accustomed to the strong stench rising up from the abyss, he points out that there are three similar circles (*tre cerchietti*, 11:17) in gradation that lie ahead and that are the continuation of the wider circles they have already passed through. Then the word "malice" (*malizia*) is isolated in the text as the word most applicable to the sins of the seventh, eighth, and ninth circles. "The end of all malice," Virgil says, "is injury" (11:22-23). And immediately he names the two main kinds of malice: "force" (*forza*) and "fraud" (*frode*, 11:24). These are the two terms used by Cicero in *De officiis* I, 13. *Forza* would mean "violence," although today it usually means "strength" or "power"; "fraud" would apply to the eighth circle. Whereas violence characterizes animals as well as men, fraud is peculiar to man and is therefore more displeasing to God and is placed lower in Hell. Since a person may perpetrate violence against God, against himself, or against his neighbor, it is punished in three distinct "rounds" (*gironi*) in the seventh circle.

Dante's system of sins is really twofold: the sins of incontinence, punished in upper Hell or the region outside of Dis, and the sins of malice, punished in lower Hell or Dis. Dante then divides malice into violence and fraud. In omitting any reference to the *ignavi* or neutrals in the vestibule, to the unbaptized in the first circle or limbo, and to the archheretics of the sixth circle, Dante implies that those sinners are not guilty of incontinence or malice. They merely held wrong beliefs; they were not guilty of sinful acts.

Dante, like the scholastic philosophers just prior to his time, drew upon Aristotle's system of ethics. Aristotle had before him the example of the Greek myths, stories incorporating ethical problems which spoke to the people in the guise of narratives through actions and characters and symbols. The lucid philosophical language of Aristotle is vastly different from that of myth, and in his *Commedia* Dante retranslated the language of Aristotle and Aquinas back into stories, the circles of his *Inferno* where characters and situations, punishments and dramas illustrate abstract laws governing human behavior. In his *Poetics* Aristotle claims that the richest source of myths is Homer. Dante the Christian poet adds to the myths of Homer's epics the myths of the Bible. In such a canto as 11, which is an exception in that it is strategically placed just before the descent into Dis begins, he defines the ethical terms of his poem's conception as a philosopher might.

Thus the background of the *Inferno* is a combination of the mythical and the ethical. The myths in the narrative poems of Homer, reworked in Virgil's *Aeneid*, and the myths in sacred scripture, merge with the pagan rules of morality in Aristotle and Cicero and the scholastic version of those rules in Aquinas. The concept of Hell undergoes a considerable change as it moves from the Hellenistic age to the Christian age. Whereas Aristotle condemns a man for an immoral act, Dante damns and punishes him eternally only if there is no repentance. By violating the divine order of God, the sinners themselves create their own Hell.

Immorality for the Greek mind is unwise. It is considered an offense against prudence. For the Roman mind, it is looked upon as illegal, an offense against the law. Dante looks upon it as sinful or infernal, an offense against the law of God.

The end of the canto (11:91-115) is abrupt. Dante expresses his gratitude to Virgil, whom he calls the "sun" healing all troubled visions, and then asks a final question about the sin of usury. In what way, he asks, does usury offend God? This time Virgil alludes by name to the *Physics* of Aristotle, and probably to the remark in that work that "art imitates nature" (2:2). Nature would then be the connecting link between God and man's art. The function of man in his daily life is to labor, to toil. "In the sweat of thy brow shalt thou eat bread" (Genesis 1:28), we read at the beginning of the Bible. Usury is interest on money, and this is contrary to God's plan for the activity of man during his life on earth. The usurer is an exploiter of man's labor. It should be remembered here that usury in Dante's clay was so excessive that it was close to being a form of plunder. For Dante it was the sin of an individual. Today it would be under a monopoly, when industries seize control over public conveniences, that returns from investments of capital could be called usurious.

The first round (*girone*) of the violent is for the sin of blasphemy, that is, violence done to God. The second is for violence perpetrated on other men. The third, referred to in lines 49 and 50, bears the mark of Sodom and Cahors. The sodomites violate nature, and the inhabitants of Cahors violate the art of God's world (the city of Cahors in southern France was famous for usury in the Middle Ages). It would appear that the word *Caorsino* in Italian was synonymous with usurer.

The relationship between Virgil and Dante throughout canto 11 is that of teacher and student. An eagerness to learn is a strong motive in the questions Dante asks as he and Virgil pause before moving on. Neither student nor teacher wishes to waste time. Previously in his journey Dante has learned by what he has seen, by examples. In this circle he learns by listening to doctrine. At the end of the lesson, in his use of the word "sun" (11:91), he pays supreme homage to Virgil, the illuminating master. In canto 1, at the time of his meeting with Virgil, Dante had called him the honor and light of other poets:

O de li altri poeti onore e lume.

[1:82]

Principal Signs and Symbols

Divisions of sin (wrong behavior):

(a) Aristotle: incontinence, bestiality, malice (or vice);

(b) Cicero: violence, fraud;

(c) Dante: incontinence, violence (or bestiality), fraud (or malice).

The nine circles:

1. limbo (unbelief)
2.
3.
4. } incontinence (leopard)
5.

6. heresy

7. violence (lion)

8.
9. } fraud (she-wolf)

The vestibule (canto 3): the "neutrals" constitute a tenth division.

Selected Bibliography

Italian Editions of "The Divine Comedy"

Alighieri, Dante, *La divina commedia*. Testo critico della Società dantesca italiana; riveduto col commento scartazziniano; rifatto da Giuseppe Vandelli. Milan: 1957 (seventeenth edition).

Alighieri, Dante, *La divina commedia*. Edited and annotated by C. H. Grandgent. D. C. Heath: 1913.

Alighieri, Dante, *La divina commedia*. Edited and annotated by C. H. Grandgent. Revised by Charles S. Singleton. Harvard University Press: 1972.

Bilingual Editions with Commentary

Singleton, Charles S., *Inferno*. Vol. 1 text, vol. 2 commentary. Princeton: 1970.

The Inferno. Translated by J. A. Carlyle. Revised by H. Oelsner. The Temple Classics: 1970.

Dante's Inferno. Translated by John D. Sinclair. Oxford: 1974.

English Translations

The Comedy of Dante Alighieri. Cantica 1, *Hell*. Translated by Dorothy L. Sayers. Penguin Books: 1974.

Dante's Inferno. Translated by John Ciardi. Rutgers University Press: 1954.

Dante's Inferno. Translated by Mark Musa. Indiana University Press: 1971.

Commentary and Criticism in English

Auerbach, Erich, *Dante: Poet of the Secular World*. Translated by R. Manheim. University of Chicago Press: 1974.

Auerbach, Erich, *Mimesis*. Translated by W. Trask. Doubleday-Anchor: 1957. (See chapter 8, "Farinata and Cavalcante.")

Barbi, Michele, *Life of Dante*. Translated by P. Ruggiers. Cambridge University Press: 1955.

Bergin, Thomas G., *Dante*. Orion Press: 1965.

Brandeis, Irma, editor. *Discussions of The Divine Comedy*. D. C. Heath: 1961.

Brandeis, Irma, *The Ladder of Vision*. Chatto and Windus: 1960.

Charity, A. C., *Events and Their Afterlife: The Dialectics of Typology in the Bible and Dante*. Cambridge: 1966.

Eliot, T. S., "Dante" in *Selected Essays*. Harcourt, Brace: 1932.

Fergusson, Francis, *Dante*. Macmillan: 1966.

Freccero, John, editor. *Dante, A Collection of Critical Essays*. Prentice-Hall: 1965.

Musa, Mark, editor. *Essays on Dante*. Indiana University Press: 1964.

Snider, Denton J., *Dante's Inferno, A Commentary*. William H. Miner: 1892.

Strauss, Walter A., "Proust, Giotto, Dante." *Dante Studies* 96: 163-185.

Williams, Charles, *The Figure of Beatrice*. Noonday Press: 1961.

Aids to Reading the "Inferno"

Bodkin, Maud, *Archetypal Patterns in Poetry*. Vintage Books: 1958.

Dunbar, H. F., *Symbolism in Medieval Thought*. Oxford: 1929.

Vossler, Karl, *Medieval Culture: An Introduction to Dante and His Times*. Vols. 1 and 2. Harcourt, Brace: 1929.

The Harvest of Reading:
Inferno 20, 24, 26 _____

Alison Cornish

Celestial phenomena are almost totally muted in Dante's *Inferno*, because Hell affords no view of the sky. Yet Virgil, Dante's guide, continues to be aware of the movements of the planets and is able to track the passage of time with surprising accuracy from under the ground. This uncanny ability smacks of the supernatural or necromantic powers with which the Latin poet was often credited in the Middle Ages.[1] There is also, however, a much humbler sort of reader of the stars foregrounded in the *Inferno*. Deep in the regions of fraud, we find three farmers set in relation to the legible heavens and marked as symbolic alternatives to rash sailors, deluded soothsayers, and even a certain perplexed classical poet. Farming is comparable to reading in that it requires the interpretation of signs with the goal of bringing forth fruit. The agricultural use of astronomical knowledge might be said to lie behind Hugh of St. Victor's metaphor of one's studies as a "field of labor," which, "well cultivated by your plough, will bear you a manifold harvest."[2] The star-gazing farmers of Dante's Hell establish the status of the *Commedia*'s astronomy as fruitful reading material, even in the blind prison of the *Inferno*, where the sweet light no longer strikes our eyes.

Dante could find a literary model for useful scrutiny of the visible heavens in the *Georgics*, Virgil's poem about farming. The Roman agricultural song begins by announcing its intention to discuss "under what star to turn the earth." The "bright lights of the world" that "lead the year sliding through the sky" give "sure signs" to the experienced husbandman and to the competent navigator, as to when to plough and when to set sail.[3] Michael Putnam notes that in the *Georgics* the Zodiac "offers crucial stability" in the "sustained parallel between the farmer and the seafarer."[4] These two professions are traditionally linked through their shared reliance on fundamental astronomical learning.

Indeed, they provide examples of the honest uses of a discipline often suspect for its futility or fraud. Cassiodorus remarked that astronomy was not to be despised if from it we learn "the proper season for navigation, the time for ploughing, the date of the summer's heat and of the autumn's suspected rains."[5] Farmers and sailors are not only the original astronomers but also model readers of many other natural signs, upon which their lives depend.

Reading the stars is, of course, also the occupation of professional astrologers, with which Italy was well furnished in Dante's time. Despite some inconsistency in terminology, there was always an acknowledged distinction between the study of the stars' order and motion (*ratio stellarum*) and the science of the stars' significance (*significatio stellarum*). Dante uses the same word, *astrologia*, both for what we would call astronomy and for what is sometimes specified as "judicial" astrology, because it involves judging propitious or inauspicious occasions. There is no question that Dante, like most educated people of his time, believed that the stars influenced the earth, had various effects on the growth and decay of plant and animal life, and could even incline human temperaments one way or another.[6] Although human reason is, to be sure, above the stars, the success of much astrological prognostication can nevertheless be explained by the fact that most people simply follow their passions, as Thomas Aquinas pointed out.[7]

In the *Convivio*, Dante blithely asserts that our life and every living thing here below is caused by heaven, and that nature's seemingly infinite variety is due to the constantly changing disposition of the constellations. He even goes so far as to say that our minds, inasmuch as they are grounded in our bodies, are differently disposed depending on the circulation of heaven.[8] The length of a human life can be compared to an arc, because the shape describes the path from rising to setting of the planets that influence the whole of it.[9] Love is undoubtedly aroused by the revolutions of the heaven of Venus, as the ancients rightly inferred—although the pagans mistook the planet for a deity.[10] So, too, Dante repeatedly implies, his own literary and intellectual talent derived from his being born under the constellation of Gemini (*gloriose stelle, o lume pregno/ di gran virtú*), probably to be identified with the personal star (*tua stella*) that Brunetto Latini implies might lead him to literary glory, and with the good star (*stella bona*) that might aid his careful genius, as the poet himself implies in the canto of Ulysses.[11]

Moreover, Dante seems to have believed that major events involving large numbers of people would be brought about and also presaged by particular planetary conjunctions. Just as the perfect disposition of the heavens mirrored the optimal terrestrial government at the time of Christ's birth, so untoward planetary configurations are associated with the degradation of present-day customs.[12] In "Poscia ch'Amor," the poet laments that grace and courtesy have swerved away from the world because of the state of the heavens (*Ancor che ciel con cielo in punto sia,/ che leggiadria/ disvia cotanto*), and in "Tre donne intorno al cor mi son venute" the virtues have been reduced to begging because men have encountered the rays of such a sky (*che sono a'raggi di cotal ciel giunti*).[13] In his epistolary invectives, Dante forecast upcoming revolutions in store for the contemporary world, which he claimed to know through "truth-telling signs" (*signis veridicis*), because "through the movement of heaven, the human intellect is able to understand its mover and His will."[14] Many of Dante's early commentators were convinced that the prophetic utterances scattered through the *Commedia*, such as the cryptic *veltro* and the *cinquecento diece a cinque*, referred to an imminent great conjunction of Saturn and Jupiter—*già stelle propinque*.[15] In the *Purgatorio*, Dante exhorts the heavens to hasten the arrival of the mysterious individual who will chase off the ancient she-wolf:

> O ciel, nel cui girar, par che si creda
> le condizion di qua giù trasmutarsi,
> quando verrà per cui questa disceda?
> (*Purgatorio* 20.13-15)

[O heaven, through whose turning it appears to be believed that conditions down here are transformed, when will come the one before whom she will flee?]

Beatrice, moreover, encourages us to expect prodigious political vicissitudes to "rain down" from the supernal wheels:

> raggeran sì questi cerchi superni,
> che la fortuna che tanto s'aspetta,
> le poppe volgerà u' son le prore,
> sì che la classe correrà diretta;
> e vero frutto verrà dopo 'l fiore.
> (*Paradiso* 27.144-148)

[These supernal wheels will irradiate such that the fortune that is so long awaited will turn the sterns to where the prows are now, so that the fleet will run straight; and true fruit will follow upon the flower.]

Her mixed metaphor of ships and fruit-bearing flowers follows inevitably from the double role of the stars—as guides and as causes. Stars steer attentive sailors to port, but they also bring forth fruit from well-tended plants, as farmers well know.

The Farmer Among the Soothsayers

Belief in the impact of the stars on human affairs cannot therefore be the criterion on which such astrologers as Michael Scot and Guido Bonatti are condemned to the fourth subcategory of fraud.[16] Their punishment seems instead to be motivated by their concerted, and usually well-paid, efforts to avert or avoid the predicted effects of planetary motion. To put it in the most general terms, the soothsayers are in Hell not for trying to read nature's signs, but rather for reading them perversely—in much the same way, perhaps, that Francesca's eternal predicament is caused not so much by the book that she curses in canto 5, but rather by her uncircumspect use of it. The whole canto of the sooth-sayers has recently come to be seen as a meditation on correct and incorrect ways of reading, particularly as regards classical literature.[17] Indeed, Dante's epic predecessors contribute four of the seers of antiquity named in the *bolgia*—Tiresias from Ovid's *Metamorphoses*, Amphiaraus from Statius' *Thebaid*, Arruns from Lucan's *Pharsalia*, and Manto from Virgil's *Aeneid*. Virgil's text comes under particular scrutiny, as he is made to recant at length the account of Mantua's origins he gave in his epic. Dante's conspicuous re-reading of the *Aeneid* in the context of supernatural divination not only serves to contrast Virgil's *alta tragedía* with his own *comedía*, but also to differentiate the Italian poet's prophetic role from Virgil's vocation as *vates*, or prophet.[18]

Among the various pagan prophets and diviners of note, Dante has Virgil point out the aged seer Arruns, who discerned terrifying omens of civil war at the start of Lucan's *Pharsalia*. In the Roman epic, Arruns' expertise is primarily in the Etruscan arts of extispicy (the inspection of animals' entrails), augury, and the interpretation of lightning bolts, leaving the "secrets of heaven" and astrological prediction to the learned Figulus:[19]

> So they decided to follow the ancient custom and summon
> Seers from Etruria: the eldest of these, named Arruns,
> Lived in the otherwise abandoned city of Luca.
> This was a man well schooled in interpretation of omens—
> Motions of thunderbolts and veins, still throbbing, of entrails,
> Also the warnings of birds by special flight or behavior.[20]

Whereas Lucan imagined Arruns holed up within the walls of a deserted Etruscan city, Dante depicts his dwelling as a cave in the mountains. The tight, dark ditch, or bolgia, around which the seer now trudges, with his head contorted over his rear end, contrasts with the magnificent panorama of sea and sky he once had from up there:

Aronta è quel ch'al ventre li s'atterga,

    che ne' monti di Luni, dove ronca

    lo Carrarese che di sotto alberga,

ebbe tra' bianchi marmi la spelonca

    per sua dimora; onde a guardar le stelle

    e 'l mar non li era la veduta tronca.

(Inferno 20.46-51)

[Arruns is that one who backs up against the other's belly, who in the hills of Luni, where the Carrarese who lives below does his weeding, had a cave for his lodging among the white marble, from where his view of stars and sea was never impeded.]

Omitting the examination of entrails, Dante prefers to characterize Arruns' divinatory activity as a prolonged gaze into the stars and over the sea. His topographical positioning of the seer's cave, high above the fields, introduces the figure of a peasant, totally alien to Lucan's text, that serves to make a marked moral contrast. The simple peasant of Carrara is intent on working the earth (*ronca*) with the hope of making it bring forth fruit, while the famous augur has his attention fixed on the signs and portents visible in the sky and over the horizon.

This incidental farmer inserted into the canto of the soothsayers actually has a common analogue in various indictments of astrology and other arts of divination. In his discussion of the value of astronomy as a liberal art, Cassiodorus differentiated its advantageous uses for navigation, ploughing, planting, and harvesting from its investigation in order to know one's fate, which is contrary to faith. He recommended that passages treating astrological prediction not only should not be read, but should be ignored as if they had never been written.[21] On the same theme, John of Salisbury invokes a farmer's proverb taken from Horace, saying that "he who puts his faith in dreams and augury will never be free of worry," but goes on to vouch for the "authenticity and value of those signs which have been conceded by divine ordinance for the guidance of man."[22] These are signs learned not through books but through experience, and are to the help of working men rather than philosophers: "Consequently farmer and sailors, as the result of certain familiar experiences, infer what ought to be done at any particular time by conjecturing the state of the weather to come from that which has preceded."[23]

A common source for both Cassiodorus and John of Salisbury would have been Augustine's belittling assessment of astronomy in the *De doctrina christiana*, where the profit of this science in the reading of Scripture is reduced to calculating the phases of the moon in order to celebrate the Lord's Passion: "Although the course of the moon, which is relevant to the celebration of the anniversary of the Passion of Our Lord, is known to many, there are only a few who know well the rising or setting or other movements of the rest of the stars without error. Knowledge of this kind in itself, although it is not allied with any superstition, is of very little use in the treatment of Divine Scriptures and even impedes it through fruitless study [*infructuosa intentione*]; and since it is associated with the most pernicious error of vain prediction it is more appropriate and virtuous to condemn it."[24] As we saw in the previous chapter, Augustine was at pains to defend the special coincidence of astronomical events in the commemoration of the Passion as significant parts of God's eloquence, while distancing himself from astrological prognostication in general. In his letter to Januarius, he explicitly differentiates the "fruitless study" of astronomy from its valuable use by husbandmen and navigators. "Who cannot perceive the difference," he asks, between the "useful observation of the heavenly bodies in connection with the weather, such as farmers or sailors make; or in order to mark the part of the world in which they are and the course which they should follow—and prying into the future?"[25] Dante's juxtaposition of Lucan's seer, Arruns, with the simple Carrarese peasant is therefore not wholly without precedent, as farmers are traditionally cited as fruitful readers of the stars in contrast with immoderate seekers of hidden things.

In terms that recall Hugh of St. Victor's agrarian metaphor cited at the beginning of this chapter (*o lector . . . tibi fructum referet*), Dante explicitly likens his reader's task in the canto of the soothsayers to the art of husbandry. He admonishes us to ponder for ourselves how, if God lets us "take harvest from our reading," he could have looked dry-eyed on such deformations of "our image":

> Se Dio ti lasci, lettor, *prender frutto*
> *di tua lezione*, or pensa per te stesso
> com' io potea tener lo visa asciutto,
> quando la nostra imagine di presso
> vidi sì torta, che 'l pianto de li occhi
> le natiche bagnava per lo fesso.
> (*Inferno* 20.19-24)

[If God lets you, reader, *take harvest from your reading*, now think for yourself how I could have kept my face dry when I saw up close our image so twisted that the tears of the eyes bathed the cheeks of the buttocks down the crack.] (emphasis added)

The punishment, or *contrapasso*, of the fourth bolgia consists in a severe form of infernal palsy that has turned the heads of the damned all the way around toward their backs. Looking ahead is now denied them because of their excessive desire to see into the future while alive:

> perché volse veder troppo davante
> di retro guarda e fa retroso calle.
> (*Inferno* 20.38-39)

[Because he wanted to see too far ahead, he looks behind and makes a backward path.]

The sinners rotate eternally around their circular ditch with a monstrous retrograde motion, "backing up" against the belly of their neighbor (*quel ch'al ventre li s'atterga*), the way the concave celestial spheres fit closely one inside the other, or, as one early commentator remarked, the way one student of divination follows closely on the books of his predecessor.[26] Virgil's emphatic scorn in canto 20 for Dante's tears of pity at seeing the weeping of the horribly deformed soothsaying sinners wash down their buttocks (*Qui vive la pietà quand'è ben morta* [*Inferno* 20.87-93]) has been taken as a marked rejection of the popular medieval legends that had transformed the Roman poet into an occultist wiseman and sorcerer.[27]

An extirpation of supernatural ambitions also seems to be the purpose of his long digression, taking up more than a third of the canto, on the origin of his native city, Mantua, in which he directly contradicts the account given in his own "high tragedy." In the *Aeneid*, Ocnus, "son of prophesying Manto," is said to have founded Mantua, giving it walls and his mother's name. As Teodolinda Barolini reminds us, he appears as a hero coming to the aid of Aeneas in the war against Turnus, with the image of Mincius, the river god and son of Lake Benacus, on the prows of his ships.[28] The essential difference between this version of Mantua's founding and its emendation in *Inferno* 20, aside from the elimination of the prophetess' son, is the removal of all taint of the supernatural. Mincio is no longer a river god but simply a river, not born of Lake Garda but formed by its overflow. The city's founders gather together along the swamp where Tiresias' daughter had "left her empty body" and called it Mantua "without further augury" (*senz'altra sorte*).

If the story of the city's founding by Manto's son in the *Aeneid* served to imbue Virgil's birthplace with a heritage of divination, prophecy, or *vaticinatio*, closely associated with his claim to poetic inspiration, as Robert Hollander has argued, here in Hell Dante has him give a purely naturalistic history of the place, consisting primarily of a description of the waterways that descend from Lago di Garda to form the Mantuan marsh. Indeed, the description of the lake they both call Benaco is perhaps derived not from the heroic epic but from the agricultural poem the *Georgics*.[29] Virgil's digression in canto 20 is a lesson on geography as he traces the natural hydraulic system of northern *Italia bella* at the foot of the Alps, a system that feeds the lake from, Virgil thinks (*credo*), more than a thousand springs. He focuses on the variability of names as the water spills out from Lake Benaco to become the river that is called Mincio until it falls in with the Po. Mantua is located in a flat area not far down the river's course, where the water spreads out to form a marsh that smells bad in the summertime.[30]

The prolonged river-narrative is not only nonheroic; it borders on the unpleasant. It provides a demystified reading of the landscape in a canto that is all about reading. This becomes evident from Virgil's striking insistence on the truth of this account, which might otherwise seem unremarkable and even off the subject. With considerable irony, Dante has his teacher instruct him to reject a passage in the *Aeneid*, a poem that he knows by heart (*che la sai tutta quanta*), and which he may well have regarded as divinely inspired and even prophetic. Dante declares that all other stories of Mantua's founding (presumably also and especially the one in the *Aeneid*) will henceforth be for him reduced to "spent coals," not unlike the extinguished power of the sorceress in the revised story of Mantua's origins, who left of herself only her "empty body" by the swamp where the city subsequently rose.[31] Dante's obedience to Virgil in the canto thus requires his repudiation of Virgil's own poem; his faith in what he says here in the fourth bolgia of fraud inside Dante's *comedía* requires that he treats what he said in the *alta tragedía* as a "lie that defrauds the truth." In this literary competition, if that is what it is, the focus on water in the ancient poet's amended etiology of his city may also be particularly significant because of the association of rivers and their sources with literary originality and eloquence.[32] By reducing the *Aeneid*'s mythologized and mantic personifications to indifferent topographical facts (a lake, a river, a marsh), Virgil's lengthy correction of his own text might be seen as a kind of antidote to the sin punished in this bolgia, which involves "reading too much into" natural phenomena.

If the relevance of Virgil's dull geographical digression to the sin of divination is that Dante wants to distance the Roman poet from his medieval reputation as supernaturally inspired *vates*, it is all the more striking that this canto in particular should close with one of his intuitive, and to that extent mantic, readings of the stars:

> Ma vienne omai, ché già tiene il confine
> d'ambedue gli emisferi e tocca l'onda
> sotto Sibilla Caino e le spine;
> e già iernotte fu la luna tonda . . .
> (*Inferno* 20.124-127)

[But come now, because Cain with his thorns (the moon) already holds the border of both hemispheres and touches the waves beneath Seville—and just the other night was the moon full.]

This is a time-reference of the infernal sort; it uses the moon instead of the sun, and moreover implies sunrise by speaking of moonset. From the perspective of Jerusalem, which shares Hell's chronological standard, when the moon is full the sun rises just as the moon sets in the west (here indicated by Seville). In the days that follow, it sets steadily later in the morning. At this point in the journey the setting of the moon would indicate an hour of about half past seven in the morning.

Commentators have contrasted Virgil's popular, even superstitious anthropomorphization of the moon as Cain with Beatrice's scholastic disputation on the qualities of the same planet in *Paradiso* 2. Yet, because the temporal indication is accurate, according to the fictional astronomy of the journey Virgil speaks the truth about the stars even without seeing them, presumably by the light of reason alone. The moon itself, here said to have been of some help to Dante during the night of his solitary travails in the dark wood, might be associated with just the kind of limited, secular knowledge Virgil represents. Augustine linked the moon with knowledge, in contrast with the sun of wisdom in a reformulation of Psalm 18 (*Caeli enarrant gloriam Dei*): "Shine ye over all the earth; and let the day enlightened by the sun utter unto day a speech of wisdom; and night, enlightened by the moon, show unto night a word of knowledge. The moon and stars shine in the night, yet doth not the night obscure them; seeing they give that light unto it, in its degree."[33] In Purgatory, in fact, Virgil will conspicuously defer to the guiding authority of the sun itself, which at the start of the *Inferno* was defined as leading people aright by every path (*che mena diritto altrui per ogni calle* [*Inferno* 1.18]):

> 'O dolce lume a cui fidanza i' entro
>> per lo novo cammin, tu ne conduci'
>> dicea 'come condur si vuol quinc'entro.
> Tu scaldi il mondo, tu sovr'esso luci:
>> s'altra ragione in contrario non ponta,
>> esser dien sempre li tuoi raggi duci . . .'
>>> (*Purgatorio* 13.16-21)

["O sweet light, whom I trust as I enter on the new road, you guide us," he said, "as one ought to be guided through this place. You warm the world and give it light: if no other reason contradicts them, your rays should always be guides."]

In conclusion, the canto of the soothsayers contrasts straightforward and useful interpretations of visible phenomena with the sin of divination, or perverse reading of natural signs. Virgil is pivotal to this issue, as poet (of nature and agriculture as well as of history and myth), as renowned necromancer, and as sage. As always, Dante characterizes Virgil as an immensely knowledgeable but often limited reader. Just because he avoids being condemned to this very bolgia for his popularly supposed occult powers does not mean that in his observation of the world he did not make mistakes, or miss out on the big picture. This is the characterization of Virgil, and of the best of classical antiquity in general, that will develop over the course of the *Commedia*. In the *Inferno*, it is the unassisted gaze of the pagan mind that seems to be the target of its few astronomical references, to each of which is attached the figure of a farmer.

The Farmer in Winter

As in the canto of the soothsayers, Virgil himself also seems to be the specific target of the long rustic comparison at the start of *Inferno* 24. The astronomical opening of this simile, which Robert Hollander has gone so far as to dub Dante's Georgic, takes inspiration from Virgil's advice to shepherds to feed their goats with leafy plants in midwinter, "at the time when the cold Waterbearer (Aquarius) is now setting, sprinkling the departing year" (*iam cadit extremoque inrorat Acquarius anno*).[34] Whereas for the Romans the sign of Aquarius marked the end of the agricultural calendar (*extremo . . . anno*), as Hollander points out, Dante turns it around to presage the approaching end of winter, a time when the sun "tempers its locks," in the early part of the liturgical year (*giovanetto anno*):

> In quella parte del giovanetto anno
>   che 'l sole i crin sotto l'Aquario tempra
>   e già le notti al mezzo dì sen vanno . . .
>   (*Inferno* 24.1-3)

[In that part of the young year when the sun tempers its locks beneath Aquarius and nights head toward the south . . .]

Dante calls attention, moreover, to the lengthening of the days after the winter solstice as the nights "head south" and the sun wends its way back toward the north.[35]

The opening lines of Dante's simile cast the near dead of winter in hopeful language, altering not the season, but the way it is viewed. The rest of the simile that the astronomical periphrasis introduces goes on to stage a parallel reassessment of the hibernal landscape. In early February a shepherd who has no stock of hay is distressed to see the ground all white, as if it were covered with snow:

> quando la brina in su la terra assempra
>> l'imagine di sua sorella bianca,
>> ma poco dura a la sua penna tempra
> lo villanello a cui la roba manca,
>> si leva, e guarda, e vede la campagna
>> biancheggiar tutta; ond'ei si batte l'anca,
> ritorna in casa, e qua e là si lagna,
>> come 'l tapin che non sa che si faccia.
>> *(Inferno* 24.4-11)

[When hoarfrost copies on the earth the image of his white sister—but not for long does his pen stay sharp—the farmer who is short of provisions rises and looks and sees the countryside all whitened; at which he slaps his thigh, turns back into the house, and here and there complains like some poor wretch who knows not what to do.]

When the hoarfrost (which was only impersonating its white sister) soon melts and the world alters its appearance, the simile's agrarian protagonist then gathers back his hope and, taking up his staff, drives his sheep out to pasture:

> poi riede, e la speranza ringavagna,
>> veggendo 'l mondo aver cangiata faccia
> in poco d'ora, e prende suo vincastro
>> e fuor le pecorelle a pascer caccia.
>> *(Inferno* 24.12-15)

[. . . and then goes out again and gathers up new hope on seeing that the world has changed his face in so short a time, and he takes his staff and drives out his flock to pasture.]

The passage narrates an extended parable of misreading, or double take, beginning with the winter constellation from Virgil's *Georgics* now being read as a sign of imminent spring. The peasant misinterprets not only the pattern in the sky, but the pattern on the ground—hoarfrost's counterfeit of snow—and then completely alters his mood, regarnering hope, when he sees that the world has "changed its face." Even the simile's use of equivocal rhyme, words that look the same but mean different things (*tempra*, *tempra*; *faccia*, *faccia*), is a formal reflection of the deceptive appearances central to the region of fraud.[36]

The explicit tenor of the simile is Dante's initial distress at seeing the perturbation of his master upon discovering in the last canto the duplicity of devils (*elli è bugiardo e padre di menzogna*). As Margherita Frankel has noted, the revelation that devils do not always mean what they say comes on the heels of Virgil's stunned amazement at the body of Caiaphas crucified on the ground. Caiaphas' verdict sealing Christ's fate, to let one man suffer for the sake of the people (*porre un uomo per lo popolo a' martiri*), is expressed in a clear echo of Virgil's own *Aeneid*, where Jupiter concedes to let just one Trojan die in place of many: *unum pro multis dabitur caput*. This shocking twist to what must have seemed in the context of the Roman epic a positive trade-off, followed by the apparently astonishing discovery that the devil is "the father of lies," upsets Virgil to the point that he stalks off.[37] This is the perturbation that occasions the agrarian simile of canto 24. It is a crisis provoked not just by fraud, but by Virgil's apparent inexperience with black cherubim and tricksters of the sort he encountered in the circle of barratry, and by his amazement that even his own words might have been deceptive, or at least subject to a radically different interpretation.

Dante's shepherd in the simile may not be a good reader of Virgil's *Georgics*, because he failed to stock up on leafy plants in winter and has a curious way of interpreting the constellations (why shouldn't a farmer expect snow in early February?). Nonetheless, he does not give up hope. Virgil, in contrast, as a virtuous pagan assigned to Limbo, is defined as someone who lives "without hope" (*che sanza speme vivemo in disio*).[38] Because Dante's pastoral image, unlike Virgil's in the *Georgics*, is inevitably charged with the spiritual resonances of Christ's words to Peter ("feed my sheep") as well as with Abraham's unwavering trust that "the Lord will provide," it constitutes an implicit criticism of Virgil's pastoral abilities, following on his rather embarrassing incompetence in dealing with some mischievous devils.[39] The farmer is better, the simile would seem to imply, than the poet of farming; not because he is better equipped or skilled or more experienced, but because he reads the signs of nature hopefully rather than astutely. It is a critique not of Virgil's know-how but of his attitude, which colors all he sees.

The Farmer in Summer

In the canto of the soothsayers, the sinister clairvoyance of an Etruscan magus is contrasted with the simple diligence of the Carrarese who works the land below. In canto 24, it is Virgil, the great sage, who is implicitly held up for comparison with a mere peasant. A third such contrast is apparent in canto 26, in the simile of the *villano* that introduces Dante's first glimpse of Ulysses.[40] In this passage, the two famous Greek heroes of the Trojan war now burning in the gullet of the eighth ditch are reduced to the status of bugs, or fireflies, seen from a great height by a farmer resting on a hillside:

> Quante il villan ch'al poggio si riposa,
> nel tempo che colui che 'l mondo schiara
> la faccia sua a noi tien meno ascosa,

come la mosca cede a la zanzara,
　　vede lucciole giù per la vallea,
　　forse colà dov' e' vendemmia e ara:
di tante fiamme tutta risplendea
　　l'ottava bolgia, sì com'io m'accorsi
　　tosto che fui là've 'l fondo parea.

(Inferno 26.25-33)

[Just as the farmer, resting on the hillside in the season when he who lights the world hides his face from us the least, when the fly yields to the mosquito, sees fireflies down in the valley where he perhaps harvests and ploughs—with as many flames was the eighth ditch resplendent, as I realized as soon as I was where I could see the bottom.]

In this simile, the farmer's complete repose on a summer evening as he rests from his labors (the spring ploughing and the autumn harvest) could not be further removed from the damned sailor's impetuous rush across the ocean (*de' remi facemmo ali al folle volo*).[41] As commentators, beginning with the poet's son Pietro, have noticed, Ulysses' mad dash to the other side of the globe, resulting in the infernal torment of a tongue of fire, recalls the comparison, in the Epistle of James, of unrestrained speech to unguided ships and horses:

If anyone does not offend in word, he is a perfect man, able also to lead round by a bridle the whole body. For if we put bits into horses' mouths that they may obey us, we control their whole body also. Behold, even the ships, great as they are, and driven by boisterous winds, are steered by a small rudder wherever the touch of the steersman pleases. So the tongue is also a little member, but it boasts mightily. Behold, how small a fire—how great a forest it kindles! And the tongue is a fire, the very world of iniquity. The tongue is placed among our members, defiling the whole body and setting on fire the course of our life, being itself set on fire from hell.[42]

Because Dante emphatically associates the virtue of hope with James's epistle when he meets the apostle in Paradise, its presence in *Inferno* 26 underscores Ulysses' presumption as a failure of hope.[43] The only portion of this New Testament text that was conventionally interpreted as indicative of hope is the image of the farmer's patience in the epistle's final exhortation, which Dante had translated in his *Convivio*: "Behold the farmer who awaits the precious fruit of the earth, patiently holding out until it has received both the early and the late" (*Onde dice santo Iacopo apostolo nella sua Pistola: "Ecco lo agricola aspetta lo prezioso frutto de la terra pazientemente sostenendo infino che riceva lo temporaneo e lo serotino"*).[44] Hence Dante's *villano*, awaiting the fruit of his land in the summertime between the early (spring ploughing) and the late (fall harvest) labors, is surely a figure of hope analogous to James's *agricola*. This agrarian figure who introduces the all-important encounter with Ulysses, tragic alter-ego of the poet, exemplifies that virtue of certain expectation (*attender certo*), as Dante defines hope to Saint James in *Paradiso* 25, that the presumptuous Ulysses totally lacks.[45]

The two figures are also opposed in the very different ways they are depicted as viewing the stars. While the farmer's existence is regulated by the seasons of the year, determined by the movements of the sun—the summer heat, the autumn harvest, the spring ploughing—the Greek sailor, despite his intention to circle the globe in pursuit of the sun (*dietro al sol*), marks time by the lunar phases:

> Cinque volte racceso e tante casso
> lo lume era di sotto dalla luna
> poi ch'entrati eravam nell'alto passo. . . .
> *(Inferno* 26.130-132)

[Five times was kindled and five times snuffed the light under the moon since we had entered on the deep way. . . .]

Moreover, Ulysses makes the fatal navigational mistake of abandoning his pole star by crossing over into the southern hemisphere from which it can no longer be seen:

> Tutte le stelle già dell'altro polo
> vedea la notte e il nostro tanto basso
> che non surgea fuor del marin suolo.
> *(Inferno* 26.127-129)

[The night already saw all the stars of the other pole, while our own was so low that it never rose above the surface of the sea.]

The symbolic tenor of Ulysses' lost polar star is articulated in the exchange between a ship's governor and a failed leader in book 8 of Lucan's *Pharsalia*. In his nocturnal flight from the scene of the lost battle, Pompey distractedly consults the boat's helmsman on the navigational use of the stars. The pilot explains: "We do not follow those sliding stars that course over the starry heaven and that, because of their continual motion, deceive poor sailors: but rather that pole that never sets and never submerges itself in the waves, illumined by the two Bears, is the one that guides our prows."[46] The sailor's nighttime disquisition on the stars is clearly less about astronomy or navigation than about governance. Unlike the sure pilot following his single pole, Pompey is wavering and indecisive, hovering, as in Lucan's description of the sun on that same evening, between two hemispheres "neither entirely in the region from whom he was hiding his light, nor in one to which he was showing it."[47] Dante's farmer, by contrast, is troubled by no such uncertain celestial displays, as he enjoys the sun at its maximum, even at dusk, in the season when it least "hides its face."

Dante's relaxed agrarian spectator may also owe something to the three humble witnesses to Icarus' ill-advised flight across the sky described in Ovid's *Metamorphoses*: "Some fisher, perhaps, plying his quivering rod, some shepherd leaning on his staff, or a peasant bent over his plough handle caught sight of them as they flew past and took stock still in astonishment, believing that these creatures who could fly through the air must be gods."[48] Like Ovid's fisherman, shepherd, or farmer, Dante's *villano* is an implicit observer, from a safe distance, of Ulysses' tragic fate, which, like Icarus' mad flight, also ends in flames. Ovid's observers look up in amazed admiration at creatures that resemble gods, whereas what Dante compares to the farmer's fireflies surveyed way down in the valley are in fact damned souls who in life were very close to gods. Explicitly compared with the eager pilgrim (*sì com'io*), the farmer's posture of illumined patience in fact contrasts with Dante's precipitous desire to see Ulysses inside the flame, and serves instead as a warning to the poet as he writes (to restrain the impetus of his genius so that it will not run where virtue does not guide it), as well as to the inevitably curious reader as he reads.[49]

* * *

All three of Dante's farmers encountered in the region of fraud in some way constitute a critique of the classical world. Yet the choice of an agrarian figure to counter the strained vision of the diviners, the shortcomings of Virgil as pastor, and the insane flight of Ulysses to the other side of the world might well derive inspiration from Virgil's own poem on agriculture, which explicitly defines the restful life of the farmer as ignorant of fraud (*at secura quies et nescia fallere vita*).[50] In the *Georgics*, commonly cited as an authority in such astronomical handbooks as Sacrobosco's *Sphere* and Macrobius' commentary on Cicero's *Dream of Scipio*, the farmer is exalted to the status of someone whose knowledge of natural phenomena gives him power over nature. The ostensibly humble subject of the poem thereby becomes cognate with the poet's own aspirations, as Philip Hardie has observed. When, at the end of the second book, the poet declares blessed those who have "been able to win knowledge of the causes of things" and asks the "sweet Muses" to show him "heaven's pathways, the stars, the sun's many lapses, the moon's many labours," this request for information about celestial movement can also be read as a prayer to know not just the path *of* heaven, but the path *to* it.[51] All quests for knowledge translate into journeys; and some, like Ulysses', fail.

Like the canto of Ulysses, the first book of Virgil's agricultural poem also leads from a peaceful portrait of rural life into a violently contrasting image of headlong, precipitous disaster. From a discussion of "sure signs" given by the sun and stars for farming and navigation, the poet shifts to a recollection of the terrible portents announcing disastrous political events in recent Roman history. At Caesar's assassination, witnesses observed an eclipse of the sun, barking dogs, howling wolves, ominous birds, eruptions of volcanoes, bloated rivers, horrifying entrails, freakish lightning, and comets. Virgil magnificently juxtaposes the peace of rural life with the rage of these past wars by imagining a future time "when in those lands, as the farmer toils at the soil with crooked plough, he shall find javelins eaten up with rusty mould, or with his heavy hoes shall strike on empty helms, and marvel at the giant bones in the upturned graves."[52] An appeal for an end to bloodshed concludes the book, depicting contemporary strife as a chariot run wild, not unlike Dante's image of Phaeton (*quando Fetòn abbandonò li freni*) or, for that matter, of Ulysses (*de' remi facemmo ali al folle volo*): "Impious Mars rages over the entire globe, just as when chariots burst from the starting gates. They pick up speed and, uselessly holding the reins, the driver is carried along by his horses; the chariot does not respond to his commands."[53]

In Dante's *Inferno* astronomical knowledge is presented under the humblest possible aspect, exalting the farmer as a fruitful reader of the stars, of which Hell's damned have totally lost sight. A correct understanding of nature's signs, most vividly legible in the pattern of the heavens, was for Dante, as for Virgil, a powerful symbol of poetic aims. Virgil in his *Georgics* exhorts the Muses to give him the kind of knowledge of nature possessed by happy husbandmen, ignorant of their blessings but far from the clash of arms, bearing the last trace of Justice since she altogether left the earth.[54] But it is only as Dante's guide that he emerges temporarily from his permanent prison to see the stars again. In the *Inferno*, Dante's peasants, tied to the land but with a view of the heavens, provide a counterpoint to those whose excessive curiosity leads them to interrogate the stars and navigate uncharted seas, rather than to wait and hope. Ironically enough, the poet whose praise of rural life would have been a fundamental model for Dante's agrarian figures, is himself cut off from the celestial panorama and, from a Christian point of view, from the farmer's essential virtue: hope. The journey to the stars narrated in the *Commedia* is accomplished not by straining toward them, but by descending in the opposite direction, into the very earth.

Notes

1. John Webster Spargo, *Virgil the Necromancer* (Cambridge: Harvard University Press, 1934); Domenico Comparetti, *Vergil in the Middle Ages* (London: S. Sonnenschein, 1895).

2. "Hoc ergo, o lector, quod tibi proponimus: hic campus tui laboris vomere bene sulcatus, multiplicem tibi fructum referet." Hugh of St. Victor, *Didascalicon* 6.3, *PL* 176.801; cf. 808. English translation from Hugh of St. Victor, *Didascalicon*, trans. Jerome Taylor (New York: Columbia University Press, 1981), p. 138. Augustine also uses agricultural metaphor in his interpretation of the literal sense of Genesis, suggesting that to stick to the meaning of the author and never deviate from the rule of piety is to have fruit from one's reading. Augustine, *De Genesi* 1.21, *PL* 34.262: "Aliud est enim quid potissimum scriptor senserit non dignoscere, aliud autem a regula pietatis errare. Si utrumque vitetur, perfecte se habet fructus legentis."

3. Virgil, *Georgics* 1.1-2, 1.5-6, 1.204-207, 1.252-258, 1.302-304. Text and translation from Virgil, *Eclogues. Georgics. Aeneid*, 1-6, trans. H. R. Fairclough (Cambridge: Harvard University Press, 1916).

4. Michael Putnam, *Virgil's Poem of the Earth: Studies in the Georgics* (Princeton: Princeton University Press: 1979), p. 24.

5. Cassiodorus, *Institutiones* 2.4, ed. R. Mynors (Oxford: Clarendon Press, 1963), p. 156: "Est alla quoque de talibus non despicienda commoditas, si oportunitatem navigationis, si tempus arantium, si aestatis caniculam, si autumni suspectos imbres inde discamus." English translation adapted from Cassiodorus Senator, *An Introduction to Divine and Human Readings*, trans. L. W. Jones (New York: Columbia University Press, 1946), p. 156.

6. Dominicus Gundissalinus, in *De divisione philosophiae*, ed. L. Baur, in *Beiträge zur Geschichte der Philosophie des Mittelalters*, vol. 4 (Münster, Germany: Aschendorff, 1903), pp. 119-120, expressed the difference this way: "Alfarabius dicit, quod astronomia est sciencia de significacione stellarum, quid scilicet stelle significent de eo, quod futurum est, et de pluribus presentibus et de pluribus preteris." See Cesare Vasoli's commentary to *Convivio* 2.13.28, in Dante, *Opere minori*, vol. 1, part 2, ed. C. Vasoli and D. De Robertis (Milan: Ricciardi, 1985), p. 241. See also Richard Kay, "Astronomy and Astrology," in *The "Divine Comedy" and the Encyclopedia of Arts and Sciences*, ed. G. Di Scipio and A. Scaglione (Amsterdam: John Benjamins, 1988), pp. 147-162; Richard Kay, *Dante's Christian Astrology* (Philadelphia: University of Pennsylvania Press, 1994), esp. pp. 1-9; Richard Lemay, "The True Place of Astrology in Medieval Science and Philosophy: Towards a Definition," in *Astrology, Science, and Society*, ed. Patrick Curry (Woodbridge, England: Boydell, 1987); Bruno Nardi, "Dante e Pietro d'Abano," in *Saggi di filosofia dantesca* (Florence: La Nuova Italia, 1967), pp. 60-62; I. Capasso and G. Tabarroni, "Astrologia," in *ED*, vol. 1, pp. 427-431; J. D. North, "Celestial Influence—The Major Premiss of Astrology," in *"Astrologi hallucinati": Stars and the End of the World in Luther's Time*, ed. Paola Zambelli (Berlin: Walter de Gruyter, 1986); Edward Grant, "Medieval and Renaissance Scholastic Conceptions of the Influence of the Celestial Region on the Terrestrial," *Journal of Medieval and Renaissance Studies* 17.1 (Spring 1987): 1-23; Paola Zambelli, *The Speculum Astronomiae and Its Enigma: Astrology, Theology and Science in Albertus Magnus and His Contemporaries* (Dordrecht: Kluwer Academic, 1992).

7. *ST* 1.115.4 ad 3, vol. 15 (New York: McGraw-Hill, 1970), p. 106: "Plures hominum sequuntur passiones, quae sunt motus sensitivi appetitus, ad quas cooperari possunt corpora caelesti." For an analysis of Aquinas' view on astrology, see Thomas Litt, *Les corps célestes dans l'univers de saint Thomas d'Aquin*, chaps. 6, 7, and 8 (Louvain: Publications Universitaires, 1963).

8. *Convivio* 4.2.7: "E così la nostra mente in quanto ella è fondata sopra la complessione del corpo, che [ha] a seguitare la circulazione del cielo, altrimenti è disposta in un tempo e altrimenti un altro"; 4.21.7: "E però che . . . la disposizione del Cielo a questo effetto puote essere buona, migliore e ottima (la quale si varia [per] le constellazioni, che continuamente si transmutano), incontra che dell'umano seme e di queste vertudi più pura [e men pura] anima si produce; e secondo la sua puritate, discende in essa la vertude intellettuale possible." In *Convivio* 2.14.16-17, he lists all the things that would not exist without the movement of the crystalline heaven.

9. *Convivio* 4.23.6: "Onde, con ciò sia cosa che la nostra vita, sì come detto è, ed ancora d'ogni vivente qua giù, sia causata dal cielo e lo cielo a tutti questi cotali effetti, non per cerchio compiuto ma per parte di quello a loro si scuopra; e così conviene che

'l suo movimento sia sopra essi come uno arco quasi, [e] tutte le terrene vite (e dico terrene, sì delli [uomini] come delli altri viventi), montando e volgendo, convengono essere quasi ad imagine d'arco asimiglianti."

10. Such seems to be the sense of the opening lines of *Paradiso* 8: "Solea creder lo mondo in suo periclo/ che la bella Ciprigna il folle amore/ raggiasse, volta nel terzo epiciclo." That it is not an indictment of belief in celestial influence is easily proved by Cunizza's happily confessing that she was conquered by the light of this planet ("perché mi vinse il lume d'esta stella" [*Paradiso* 9.33]) and by a similar admission by the Provençal poet Folquet de Marseilles ("questo cielo/ di me s'imprenta, com'io fe' di lui" [*Paradiso* 9.95-96]). Cf. *Convivio* 2.5.15: "E perché li antichi s'accorsero che quello cielo era qua giù cagione d'amore, dissero Amore essere figlio di Venere"; and 2.6.5: "L'operazione vostra, cioè la vostra circulazione, è quella che m'ha tratto nella presente condizione."

11. *Inferno* 15.55; *Inferno* 26.2.3-24; *Paradiso* 22.112-115.

12. *Convivio* 4.5.7: "Poi che esso cielo cominciò a girare, in migliore disposizione non fu che allora quando di là su discese Colui che l'ha fatto e che 'l governa: sì come ancora per virtù di loro arti li matematici possono ritrovare. Né 'l mondo mai non fu né sarà sì perfettamente disposto come allora."

13. "Poscia ch'Amor," lines 58-60; "Tre donne," lines 66-67.

14. *Epistole* 6.4: "Et si presaga mens mea non fallitur, sic signis veridicis sicut inexpugnabilibus argumentis instructa prenuntians;" *Epistole* 5.8: "Et si ex notioribus nobis innotiora; si simpliciter interest humane apprehensioni ut per motum celi Motorem intelligamus et eius velle; facile predestinatio hec etiam leviter intuentibus innotescet." In *Monarchia* 3.15, Dante also argued that only God, who had a full and total view of the disposition of heaven, on which the disposition of earth depends, could be qualified to elect a world governor: "Cumque dispositio mundi huius dispositionem inherentem celorum circulationi sequatur, necesse est ad hoc ut utilia documenta libertatis et pacis commode locis et temporibus applicentur, de curatore isto dispensari ab Illo qui totalem celorum dispositionem presentialiter intuetur."

15. *Inferno* 1.100-102; *Purgatorio* 33.41-45. Francesco da Buti interpreted Virgil's prophecy of the *veltro* as referring to "una influenzia di corpi celesti, che in processo di tempo verrà secondo il movimento de' cieli, che tutto il mondo si disporrà a sapienzia, virtù e amore . . . e questo era noto all'autore secondo la ragione dell'astrologo, et in ciò si manifesta ch'elli fosse astrologo." *Commento di Francesco da Buti sopra la Divina comedia di Dante Alighieri*, ed. C. Giannini (Pisa: Nistri, 1858), p. 46. Pietro, the poet's son, in the earlier drafts of his own commentary, believed that his father predicted that the longed-for political change would come about in the great conjunction due to occur in 1345. See Kennerly M. Woody, "Dante and the Doctrine of the Great Conjunctions," *Dante Studies* 95 (1977): 119-134; Leo Olschki, *The Myth of Felt* (Berkeley: University of California Press, 1949); Bruno Nardi, "Influenze celesti sugli avvenimenti di storia umana," in *Saggi*, pp. 55-61; Lemay, "The True Place," p. 22.

16. Kay, "Astrology and Astronomy," p. 158; "The Spare Ribs of Michael Scot," *Dante Studies* 103 (1985): 1-14; and "Dante's Double Damnation of Manto," in *Res publica litterarum* 1 (1978): 113-128.

17. Teodolinda Barolini ("True and False See-ers in *Inferno* XX," *Lectura Dantis* 4 [1989]: 42-54) declares that this canto "deals with the validity and legitimacy of the acts of writing and reading" because "prophecy is in fact a textual issue . . . essentially a matter of correct and incorrect reading." Zygmunt Barański, "The Poetics of Meter: Terza Rima, 'Canto,' 'Canzon,' 'Cantica,'" in *Dante Now*, ed. Theodore Cachey (Notre Dame: University of Notre Dame Press, 1995), p. 17: "As is now widely recognized, the *canto* of the soothsayers stands as one of Dante's major statements on classical literature."

18. This is the argument of Robert Hollander, "The Tragedy of Divination in *Inferno* XX," in *Studies in Dante* (Ravenna, Italy: Longo, 1980), pp. 131-218.

19. Lucan, *Pharsalia* 1.639. Cicero provides the classical definitions of the various arts of divination in his *De Divinatione*. See "Divination" in *Oxford Classical Dictionary*, ed. N. Hammond and H. Scullard (Oxford: Clarendon Press, 1970), pp. 356-357.

20. Lucan, *Pharsalia* 2.584-587: "Haec propter placuit Tuscos de more vetusto/ acciri vates. Quorum qui maximus aevo/ Arruns incoluit desertae moenia Lucae,/ fibrarum et monitus errantis in aere pinnae." Latin text of the *Pharsalia* from *Lucan* (Cambridge: Harvard University Press, 1957). Translation by P. F. Widdows, ed., *Lucan's "Civil War"* (Bloomington: Indiana University Press, 1988).

21. Cassiodorus, *Institutiones* 2.7.4: "Est alia quoque de talibus non despicienda commoditas, si oportunitatem navigationis, si tempus arantium, si aestatis caniculam, si autumni suspectos imbres inde discamus. Dedit enim Dominus unicuique creaturae suae aliquam virtutem, [quam] tamen innoxie de propria qualitate [noscamus]. Cetera vero quae se ad cognitionem siderum coniungunt, id est ad notitiam fatorum, et fidei nostrae sine dubitatione contraria sunt, sic ignorari [debent], ut nec scripta esse videantur."

22. *Ioannis Saresberiensis episcopi Carnotensis Policratici* 2.1 and 2.2, ed. C. Webb (New York: Arno, 1979), pp. 65, 68: "Rusticanum et forte Offelli proverbium est: Qui sompniis et auguriis credit, numquam fore securum"; "Futuras itaque tempestates aut serenitates signa quaedam antecedentia praeloquuntur, ut homo, qui ad laborem natus est, ex his possit exercitia sua temperare. Hinc agricolae hinc nautae familiaribus quibusdam experimentis." Translation from John of Salisbury, *Frivolities of Courtiers and Footprints of Philosophers*, trans. Joseph B. Pike (Minneapolis: University of Minnesota Press, 1938), pp. 55-56.

23. Ibid.: "Ad laborem natus est, ex his possit exercitia sua temperare. Hinc agricolae hinc naturae familiaribus quibusdam experimentis quid quo tempore geri oporteat colligunt, qualitatem temporis futuri ex eo quod praeteriit metientes."

24. Augustine, *De doctrina christiana* 2.46, *PL* 34.57: "Sicut autem plurimis notus est lunae cursus, qui etiam ad passionem Domini anniversarie celebrandam solemniter adhibetur; sic paucissimis caeterorum quoque siderum vel ortus, vel occasus, vel alia quaelibet momenta sine ullo sunt errore notissima. Que per seipsam cognitio, quanquam superstitione non alliget, non multum tamen ac prope nihil adjuvat tractationem divinarum Scripturarum, et infructuosa intentione plus impedit; et qui familiaris est perniciosissimo errori fatua fata cantantium, commodius honestiusque contemnitur." English translation from Augustine, *On Christian Doctrine*, trans. D. W. Robertson (New York: Liberal Arts, 1958), p. 65.

25. Augustine, Epistle 55.8.15; *PL* 33.211: "Sed quantum intersit inter siderum observations ad aerias qualitates accomodatas, sicut agricolae vel nautae observant; aut ad notandas partes mundi cursumque aliquo et alicunde dirigendum, quod gubernatores navium faciunt, et ii qui per solitudines arenosas in interiora Austri nulla semita certa vel recta gradiuntur; aut cum ad aliquid in doctrina utili figurate significandum, fit nonnullorum siderum aliqua commemoratio; quantum ergo intersit inter has utilitates, et vanitates hominum ob hoc observantium sidera, ut nec aeris qualitates, nec regionum vias, nec solos temporum numeros, nec spiritualium similitudines, sed quasi fatalia rerum jam eventa perquirant, quis non intelligat?" On the skills of prognostication and prophecy necessary to peasants and herdsmen, see also Piero Camporesi, *The Anatomy of the Senses: Natural Symbols in Medieval and Early Modern Italy*, trans. Allan Cameron (Cambridge: Polity Press, 1994), pp. 186-196.

26. Anonimo Fiorentino, *Commento alla Divina commedia*, vol. 1, ed. P. Fanfani (Bologna: Romagnoli, 1866), p. 446.

27. Francesco D'Ovidio, "Dante e la Magia," *Nuova antologia* (1892): 213f.; and "Esposizione del canto XX dell' *Inferno*," in *Nuovo volume di studi danteschi* (Caserta, Italy: A. P. E., 1926); Comparetti, *Vergil in the Middle Ages*.

28. Barolini, "True and False See-ers," p. 50.

29. Hollander, "The Tragedy of Divination." Aristide Marigo ("Le 'Georgiche' di Virgilio fonte di Dante," *Giornale dantesco* 17 [1909]: 31-44) suggested *Georgics* 2.159 as a source: "Teque/ Fluctibus et fremitu assurgens, Benace, marino." Edward Moore (*Studies in Dante*, 1st ser. [Oxford: Clarendon Press, 1896], p. 178) thought that Dante knew the *Georgics* only through passages found in florilegia, such as the episode of Orpheus' head rolling down the river and calling the name of Eurydice (*Georgics* 4.523). But Marigo notes that virtually all Virgilian codices, including those of the thirteenth and fourteenth centuries, contain the *Bucolics* and the *Georgics* in addition to the *Aeneid*.

30. *Inferno* 20.61-81: "Suso in Italia bella giace un laco,/ a piè de l'Alpe che serra Lamagna/ sovra Tiralli, c'ha nome Benaco./ Per mille fonti, credo, e piú si bagna/ tra Garda e Val Camonica, Apennino/ de l'acqua che nel detto taco stagna . . ./ Ivi convien che tutto quanto caschi/ ciò che 'n grembo a Benaco star non può,/ e fassi fiume giú per verdi paschi./ Tosto che l'acqua a correr mette co,/ non piú Benaco, ma Mencio si chiama/ fino a Governol, dove cade in Po./ Non molto ha corso, ch'el trova una lama,/ ne la quai si distende e la 'mpaluda;/ e suol di state talor esser grama."

31. *Inferno* 20.97-102: "'Però t'assenno che, se tu mai odi/ originar la mia terra altrimenti,/ la verità nulla menzogna frodi.'/ E io: 'Maestro, i tuoi ragionamenti/ mi son si certi e prendon si mia fede,/ che li altri mi sarien carboni spenti. '"

32. Hollander notes Dante's "watery" sense of Virgil in "Tragedy," p. 192. David Quint ("The Virgilian Source," in *Origin and Originality in Renaissance Literature* [New Haven: Yale University Press, 1983], pp. 32-42), has identified the episode at the end of Virgil's own *Georgics* involving a visit to the source of all rivers as an allegorical topos of poetic originality and inspiration, much copied in the Renaissance.

33. Augustine, *Confessions* 13.19: "Lucete supra omnen terram, et dies sole candens eructet diei verbum sapientiae, et nox, luna lucens, annuntiet nocti verbus scientiae. Luna et stellae nocti lucent, sed nox non obscurat eas, quoniam ipsae

inluminant eam pro modulo eius." Text and translation from *St. Augustine's Confessions*, trans. William Watts (Cambridge: Harvard University Press, 1912). This observation was made by Albert E. Wingell, in "Dante, St. Augustine, and Astronomy," *Quaderni d'italianistica* 2, no. 2 (1981): 123-142.

34. Virgil, *Georgics* 3.304. Robert Hollander, "Dante's 'Georgic' (*Inferno* XXIV, 1-18)," *Dante Studies* 102 (1984): 111-121. He credits Pietro di Dante (1340) with having first pointed out this Virgilian echo. Also noting the presence of the *Georgics* is David Baker, "The Winter Simile in *Inferno* XXIV," *Dante Studies* 92 (1974): 77-91.

35. This line can be interpreted to mean either that the nights are headed toward becoming half the length of the days or that "night," as the point directly opposite the sun, is now headed toward the south (*mezzogiorno*) just as the sun is headed north.

36. Margherita Frankel ("Dante's Anti-Virgilian *Villanello*," *Dante Studies* 102 [1984]: 81-109) notes that the *rime equivoche* "raise the contrast of their dynamic differentiation" and participate in the whole issue of appearance versus reality. See also Richard Lansing, *From Image to Idea: A Study of the Simile in Dante's "Commedia"* (Ravenna, Italy: Longo, 1977), p. 75: "The equivocal rhymes point up the problem of perception."

37. *Inferno* 23.145-146: "Appresso il duca a gran passi sen gì,/ turbato un poco d'ira nel sembiante."

38. *Inferno* 4.42. Robert Durling and Ronald Martinez call attention to the affinities between this simile and the *rime petrose* and to its hopeful tendency, against those who would see it as a "paralyzed poetics." Robert M. Durling and Ronald L. Martinez, *Time and the Crystal* (Berkeley: University of California Press, 1990), p. 215.

39. See Frankel, "Dante's Anti-Virgilian *Villanello*," and Robert J. Ellrich, "Envy, Identity, and Creativity: *Inferno* XXIV-XXV," *Dante Studies* 102 (1984): 61-79, in which Ellrich notes the simile's christological meaning, as "caring for the flock" relates the scene to the image of Christ as Good Shepherd. See also Warren Ginsberg, "Dante, Ovid, and the Transformation of Metamorphosis," *Traditio* 46 (1991); Peter Hawkins, "Virtuosity and Virtue: Poetic Self-Reflection in the *Commedia*," *Dante Studies* 98 (1980): 1-18; Lawrence Baldassaro, "Metamorphosis as Punishment and Redemption in *Inferno* XXIV," *Dante Studies* 99 (1981): 89-112.

40. Durling and Martinez also link the summer pastoral simile of *Inferno* 26 to the hibernal one of two cantos earlier. *Time and the Crystal*, p. 217.

41. *Inferno* 26.125.

42. James 3:2-7: "Si quis in verbo non offendit hic perfectus est vir. Potens etiam freno circumducere totum corpus. Si autem equorum frenos in ora mittimus ad consentiendum nobis et omne corpus illorum circumferimus. Ecce et naves, cum magnae sint, et a ventis validis minentur, circumferuntur a modico gubernaculo ubi impetus dirigentis voluerit. Ita et lingua modicum quidem membrum est, et magna exaltat. Ecce quantus ignis quam magnam silvam incendit. Et lingua ignis est, universitas iniquitatis. Lingua constituitur in membris nostris, quae maculat totum corpus, et inflammat rotam nativitatis nostrae infiammata a gehenna." See Alison Cornish, "The Epistle of James in *Inferno* 26," *Traditio* 45 (1989-1990): 367-379; Richard Bates and Thomas Rendall, "Dante's Ulysses and the Epistle of James," *Dante Studies* 107 (1989): 33-44; and Maria Corti, "On the Metaphors of Sailing,

Flight, and Tongues of Fire in the Episode of Ulysses (*Inferno* 26)," *Stanford Italian Review* 9, nos. 1-2 (1990): 33-47.

43. *Paradiso* 25.76-77: "Tu mi stillasti, con lo stillar suo,/ ne la pistola poi; sì ch'io son pieno."

44. *Convivio* 4.2.10. James 5:7: "Ecce agricola expectat pretiosum fructum terrae, patienter ferens donec accipiat temporivum et serotinum." In his discussion of the fruits of the Virgin's womb in *Sermones de B. V. M.* 3.3, in *Opera omnia*, vol. 9 (Quaracchi, 1882-1902), p. 670, of the *fructus spei*, Bonaventure writes: "'Debet in spe qui arat arare; et qui triturat, in spe fructus percipiendi' [Cor 9.10] Ista autem spes non permittit hominem fatigari, secundum illud Iacobi ultimo: 'Ecce, agricola . . .'" [James 5.7]. See Cornish, "The Epistle," pp. 378-379.

45. For the definition of hope as the sure expectation of the glory to come, see *Paradiso* 25.67-68: "'Spene,' diss'io, 'è uno attender certo/ de la gloria futura.'" Teodolinda Barolini has reconciled the debate over Ulysses' fate, which has fueled a vast bibliography, by suggesting that the Greek hero so closely represents the poet's own ambitions that he is damned "for Dante's sins." Barolini, "Dante's Ulysses: Narrative and Transgression," in *Dante: Contemporary Perspectives*, ed. Amilcare Iannucci (Toronto: University of Toronto Press, 1997), p. 132.

46. Lucan, *Pharsalia* 8.172-176: "Signifero quaecumque fluunt labentia caelo,/ numquam stante polo miseros fallentia nautas,/ sidera non sequimur; sed qui non mergitur undis/ axis inocciduus gemina clarissimus arcto,/ ille regit puppes."

47. Lucan, *Pharsalia* 8.159-161: "Iam pelago medios Titan demissus ad ignes/ nec quibus abscondit nec si quibus exerit orbem/ totus erat."

48. Ovid, *Metamorphoses* 8.217-220: "Hos aliquis tremula dum captat harundine pisces,/ aut pastor baculo stivave innixus arator/ vidit et obstipuit, quique aethera carpere possent,/ credidit esse deos."

49. *Inferno* 26.21-22: "E più lo'ngegno affreno ch'i' non soglio,/ perché non corra che virtù nol guidi."

50. Virgil, *Georgics* 2.467.

51. Virgil, *Georgics* 2.475-478, 575-579: "Me vero primum dulces ante omnia Musae,/ quarum sacra fero ingenti percussus amore,/ accipiant caelique vias et sidera monstrent,/ defectus solis varios lunaeque labores;" lines 481-82 are repeated in *Aeneid* 1.745. Philip Hardie, *Virgil's "Aeneid": Cosmos and Imperium* (Oxford: Clarendon Press, 1986), p. 37: "On the surface this is an appeal for the communication of information on matters astronomical, but, given the underlying tendency in this whole passage to identify the landscape of the poet with that of his subject-matter, it is easy to read this as a request for directions on literal 'paths to the sky' (rather than 'the paths of heavenly bodies')."

52. Virgil, *Georgics* 1.493-497: "Scilicet et tempos veniet, cum finibus illis/ agricola incurvo terram molitus aratro/ exesa inveniet scabra robigine pila,/ aut gravibus rastris galeas pulsabit inanis,/ grandiaque effossis mirabitur ossa sepulcris."

53. Virgil, *Georgics* 1.511-513: "Saevit toto Mars impius orbe:/ ut cum carceribus sese effudere quadrigae,/ addunt in spatia, et frustra retinacula tendens/ fertur equis auriga neque audit currus habenas." English translation from Gary B. Miles, *Virgil's "Georgics": A New Interpretation* (Berkeley: University of California Press, 1988), p.

108. On this passage in the *Georgics*, see Putnam, *Virgil's Poem of the Earth*, p. 79. See also David O. Ross, *Virgil's Elements: Physics and Poetry in the "Georgics"* (Princeton: Princeton University Press, 1987); and Giuseppe Mazzotta, *Worlds of Petrarch* (Durham, N.C.: Duke University Press, 1993), p. 276. Dante's depiction of Phaeton abandoning the reins is in *Inferno* 17.107.

54. Virgil, *Georgics* 2.458-460: "O fortunatos nimium, sua si bona norint,/ agricolas! quibus ipsa, procul discordibus armis,/ fundit humo facilem victum iustissima tellus"; 2.473-475: "Extrema per illos/ Iustitia excedens terris vestigia fecit."

Submerged Meanings in Dante's Similes (*Inf.* XXVII)

Richard H. Lansing

T. S. Eliot distinguished between Dante's and Shakespeare's characteristic use of the simile by asserting that the former sought merely to make the reader visualize more clearly the scene before him, whereas the latter attempted to add to what the reader saw.[1] Dante's images were explanatory, while Shakespeare's were expansive and intensive. Although Eliot's observation is valid for a number of similes, it fails to account for those whose manifest function extends beyond presenting visual correlations to human experience. Irma Brandeis has noted this, and in her book *The Ladder of Vision* she provides the necessary corrective by emphasizing the changing nature of Dante's images, as the pilgrim, and with him the reader, moves through the three realms of the otherworld.[2] But even Miss Brandeis' thesis, that the images become increasingly less visual and more abstract the higher the pilgrim ascends, so that in Paradise concrete reference to earthly entities is almost wholly absent, seems to me flawed in part. Her assertion that in the *Inferno* similes are structured to make us see more definitely the scene "because to see the scene was precisely all the pilgrim in his condition of mortal ignorance could do" presumes that the similes invariably serve as an index of the pilgrim's, and not Dante the poet's, visual, and hence, moral perspective.[3] This is not the case throughout the *Inferno*, and the substance of my remarks will be directed toward an analysis of two similes whose artistic function ranges well beyond the limitations imposed by the definitions of both T. S. Eliot and Irma Brandeis. Both similes appear in the Guido da Montefeltro episode in Canto XXVII of the *Inferno*: the first is the famous Sicilian bull simile; the second, the comparison of Boniface VIII and Guido da Montefeltro to Emperor Constantine and Pope Sylvester. Neither simile serves primarily to promote a visual clarification of the infernal experience. Each, on the other hand, possesses a remarkable power to suggest conceptual associations that extend beyond the expressed point of analogy between the tenor and vehicle. In particular they share with a number of other similes in the *Commedia* the capacity to introduce and integrate the themes of an episode, and to characterize the conceptual identity of a soul or a group of souls in the otherworld. Unlike other medieval poets who, bowing to the fashion of the day, ignore the artistic possibilities of comparisons, Dante achieves in his similes an unparalleled complexity and subtlety of expression.[4]

The Sicilian bull simile appears at the very beginning of Canto XXVII and introduces Guido da Montefeltro, the famous Ghibelline military leader known as "the Fox," a sinner guilty of "consiglio frodolente," punished, we recall, within a flame of fire in the eighth *bolgia*.

> Come 'l bue cicilian che mugghiò prima
> col pianto di colui, e ciò fu dritto,
> che l'avea temperato con sua lima,
>
> mugghiava con la voce dell'afflitto,
> sí che, con tutto che fosse di rame,
> pur el parea dal dolor trafitto;
>
> così, per non aver via né forame
> dal principio nel foco, in suo linguaggio
> si convertian le parole grame.
>
> (vv. 7-15)

[As the Sicilian bull—which bellowed loud

For the first time when he who gave it shape
    With his file's art was forced to give it his voice,
    Justly—would use a victim's cries, sealed up

Inside its body, to bellow, so that, through brass,

    It seemed transfixed with pain when it was heated;

    So, having at first having no passage or egress

From fire, the melancholy words were transmuted

    Into fire's language. (Pinsky)]

The historical reference is clear: instructed by Phalaris, the tyrant of Agrigento, to construct a machine of torture, Perillus invented the Sicilian bull for the purpose of roasting humans alive. The cries of victims were to issue from the mouth of the brass device, to create the illusion that the bull itself was bellowing. Possessed by the same cruel sense of humor that induced Perillus to invent such an instrument, Phalaris first tried out the device on Perillus. As is characteristic of a number of similes containing historical references, the comparison introduces a very briefly stated but complete narrative sequence. Dante's allusion to the "bue cicilian" requires the reader to call to mind the entire story, even though it is, rather than retold, merely adumbrated.

On the surface of the simile we find an expression of analogy between the bovine sound of the victim's cries and the muffled and inarticulate lamentations of Guido da Montefeltro, the sinner hidden within the flame of fire. The simile serves on a primary level to promote the idea of *contrapasso*: Guido, who once advanced his crafty stratagems by means of subtle articulation of words ("lunga promessa con l'attender corto" ["large promises with scant fulfillments"], v. 110), is now condemned to express himself in confused utterances ("confuso suon," v. 6).[5] His "linguaggio," no longer direct, must translate itself through a flicker of the tip of the flame which swathes him. But beneath this lies a submerged point of analogy that becomes apparent only after Guido has told us the story of his life and revealed the reason for his damnation. The supreme irony of the history of the Sicilian bull is that its maker was himself the first to suffer its torture. It was only appropriate that the inventor of the instrument should suffer the very mode of inhuman punishment that he had fashioned for others. This is the essential point of the story, the irony of Perillus' fate, and both Dante and Ovid, his likely source for the incident, seize on it as the moral of the tale. Dante takes Ovid's lines "neque enim lex aequior ulla,/ quam necis artifices arte perire sua" ["Nor is there a more just law than the murderous maker of artifices should perish by his own art"] and reduces them to a curt and biting expression of the justice of Perillus' fate: "e ciò fu dritto" ["and that was right"].[6] The point of submerged analogy is the following: Guido's fate, his being carried off to Hell by a black angel while expecting to ascend into Heaven with St. Francis, is in the same way ironically just. The motif of justice in the simile intimately relates Guido to Perillus. Both men are inventors, contrivers, artificers: Guido admits this himself: "Li accorgimenti e le coperte vie/ io seppi tutte, e sì *menai lor arte*" ["I was expert in all the stratagems and covert ways and practiced them with so much cunning art"] (vv. 76-77). Moreover, crafty and sly in their inventions, both are judged to have been undone by themselves. Guido, we remember, had repented of his sins and retired from a life of political intrigue, until Pope Boniface VIII called him back and asked him how he might win the war against the Colonna faction. Guido initially refused, but assented when Boniface promised to open the doors of Heaven to him in spite of his sin. With the promise of papal absolution, Guido suggests that Boniface adopt the diplomatic stratagem of making greater promises to his enemy than he intends to keep: "lunga promessa con l'attender corto." Guido believes he can sin by providing counsel with the intent to commit fraud, and still come to Heaven. But ironically Boniface's "lunga promessa" of eternal salvation to Guido is also met with an "attender corto."[7] In spite of the subtlety of his "opera di volpe" ["works of a fox"]—his cunning deeds—the logic of the black angel prevails, and Guido is swept into Hell. Hence the very expression which Guido contrived for Boniface as a means to secure papal victory in his conflict with the Colonnas turns on its maker and aptly characterizes his own predicament. He is, so to speak, hoist by his own petard. Both Guido and Perillus experience the same ironic twist of fate. Both were at the service of a figure of authority and presumed to gain reward for that service: Perillus the continued respect and favor of Phalaris, and Guido the gift of heavenly salvation. In the end, each is rightly undone by his own invention.

The irony is further compounded by the fact that Guido continues to repeat for eternity the same sin, to reenact that moment of ironic "chute" in which his expectations of successful diplomacy are met with categorical failure. As many have noted, Guido's remarks to the pilgrim Dante, predicated on the sinner's false belief that their words are confined to an infernal audience, result ironically in a self-exposition of unforeseen dimensions.[8] Again he is the victim of self-deception. For no other figure in Hell can it be said with such relevance that the sinner damned himself.

Now what I am trying to argue here is that the Sicilian bull simile is not primarily calculated to make the reader visualize the scene, visualize what Guido da Montefeltro looks like tucked away in a flame that shifts back and forth in front of Dante the pilgrim. Rather the simile serves to introduce a major theme of the canto. There is an element of anticipation in the simile, so that the analogy prepares for an event which is presented only later in the narrative.[9] The success of the simile rests on the fact that it introduces the pattern of ironic reversal long before its full significance can be related to the narrative development. The simile is an excellent example of Dante's classical method of composition: the part must mirror and contain the whole. But it is more than this. For by delaying the revelation of the significance of a particular piece of information, the poet can create the impression that the events and phenomena of the otherworld, and by analogy, of this world, have a meaning which must be discovered through a process of education. What we see along the journey is visually clear, to both the pilgrim and the reader, but the meaning will not declare itself: the vision comes first, the meaning follows and must be explained. Thus when we come to comprehend retrospectively the meaning of a particular image, we can be all the more appreciative of the order and perfection of the reality of the otherworld, and again, by analogy, of the present world. Hence the Sicilian bull simile is a kind of sign whose full significance is not immediately available. Dante compels the reader to duplicate, by analogy, the experience of the pilgrim who first perceives phenomena and subsequently learns to comprehend their meaning. For Dante, the sign not only points to the meaning, it contains it. As readers of the poet's text, we understand retrospectively why the story of the Sicilian bull was a fitting choice. We are left with the impression, again, as always, that everything in Dante's vision of the otherworld is ordered and has a purpose.

The second simile, which Guido himself utilizes to describe his relationship to Boniface, appears near the end of the canto and is not epic in style. It lacks the poetic elaboration of the former, and succinctly compares Boniface VIII and Guido da Montefeltro to Emperor Constantine and Pope Sylvester.

> Ma come Costantin chiese Silvestro
> d'entro Siratti a guerir de la lebbre,
> così mi chiese questi per maestro
> a guerir de la sua superba febbre.
>
> (vv. 94-97)

> [As Constantine
> Sought out Sylvester in Soracte, his aim
>
> To have him cure his leprosy, this man
> Came seeking me as one who meant to find
> A cure the fever he was in,
>
> Of pride. (Pinsky)]

Guido adopts the metaphor of the physician as he reveals how Boniface solicited political advice which would enable him to defeat in war the powerful Colonna clan which had challenged the validity of his accession to the papacy. The comparison, like the previous one, abounds in irony. Boniface wants Guido to devise a means to save not his life, but his political power. Moreover, although Guido is able to assuage Boniface's anger at being unable to subdue the Colonnas, the pope's true disease, moral degeneracy, is not to be cured by Guido or anyone. And finally, while Pope Sylvester acts in good faith and saves Constantine, Boniface, acting in bad faith, sends Guido's soul to eternal damnation. It was Guido, ironically, who had need of a physician. The displacement of a parallel between a pope and another pope, Boniface and Sylvester, to one between a pope and an emperor, Boniface and Constantine, only underscores sarcastically the inversion of Boniface's role: he, as Christ's vicar on earth, ought to have been the physician, ought to have healed the spiritually infirm, ought to have saved Guido's soul.

All this is apparent on the surface of the simile. But I suggest that there is more here. If we but extend the analogy between Boniface and Constantine and recall what transpired as a result of Sylvester's healing of the emperor, we shall discover a further significance in the comparison. In gratitude for having been restored to health by Sylvester, Constantine makes his donation of temporal authority to the pope, an authority which Dante believed the emperor had no right to transfer. In the *De Monarchia*, and repeatedly elsewhere, Dante asserts vehemently that to the pope is reserved ecclesiastical authority, and to the emperor temporal jurisdiction, and that neither potentate has the right to assume, usurp or be invested with legal control over the dominion of the other.

Hanc ego minorem interimo et, cum probant, dico quod sua probatio nulla est quia Constantinus alienare non poterat Imperii dignitatem, nec Ecclesia recipere. Et cum pertinaciter instant, quod dico sic ostendi potest: nemini licet ea facere per officium sibi deputatum que sunt contra illud officium; quia sic idem, in quantum idem, esset contrarium sibi ipsi: quod est impossibile; sed contra officium deputatum Imperatori est scindere Imperium, cum officium eius sit humanum genus uni velle et uni nolle tenere subiectum, ut in primo huius de facili videri potest; ergo scindere Imperium Imperatori non licet.[10]

[This minor premise, then, I deny. Their proof is no proof, for Constantine had not the power to alienate the imperial dignity, nor had the Church power to receive it. Their insistent objection to what I say can be met thus. No one is free to do through an office assigned him anything contrary to the office, for thereby the same thing, in virtue of being the same, would be contrary to itself, which is impossible. But to divide the Empire would be contrary to the office assigned the Emperor, for as is easily seen from the first book of the treatise, his office is to hold the human race subject to one will in all things. Therefore, division of his Empire is not allowed an Emperor.]

In the eyes of God, Dante believed the Donation of Constantine to be a travesty of justice: the gift was illegitimate, improper, and unjust. Boniface's gift of absolution to Guido was likewise illegitimate, improper, and unjust: a pope has no right, and no power, to excuse an act of sin before it has been committed, nor a sinner a right to absolution without having repented ("ch' assolver non si può chi non si pente" ["for no one has absolution without repenting"], v. 118). Thus a secondary, and submerged, point of analogy is evident when one extends the logic of the initial point of similitude. The simile functions artistically to relate Boniface to Constantine in more ways than one, ultimately in order to suggest a conceptual link between Boniface's false gift and the Emperor's illegitimate donation, and to focus on the abuse of authority inherent in each action. The comparison is especially apt, we discover, because the pope in his wars with the Colonnas, whom he finally scatters at the battle of Palestrina, is functioning in a temporal, not an ecclesiastic, capacity. The simile emphasizes with trenchant sarcasm the state and nature of degeneracy into which the pontificate has been plunged. It was, after all, Emperor Constantine's very donation of temporal authority over the western provinces of the Roman Empire which was the source of Pope Boniface's justification for his temporal enterprises, one of which was his campaign against the Colonnas.[11] As Guido says, the pope's wars were not with infidels, but against innocent Christians:

> Lo principe d'i novi Farisei,
> avendo guerra presso a Laterano,
> e non con Saracin né con Giudei,
>   ché ciascun suo nimico era Cristiano,
> e nessun era stato a vincer Acri
> né mercatante in terra di Soldano. . . .
>   (vv. 85-90)

>   [The Prince of new Pharisees
>   Nearby the Lateran was making war,
>
> And not against Saracens, not against Jews,
>   His enemies all being Christians: and none
>   Had been at Acre's conquest, nor one of those
>
> Who went as merchants to the Sultan's domain; . . . (Pinsky)]

And still ringing in our ears, from Canto XIX, is Dante's invective against papal corruption, against simony, in words spoken to Nicholas III, but indirectly meant for Boniface:

> Ahi, Costantin, di quanto mal fu matre,
> non la tua conversion, ma quella dote
> che da te prese il primo ricco patre!
>   (XIX, 115-117)

[Ah, Constantine, what measure of wickedness

Stems from that mother—not your conversion I mean:
Rather the dowry that the first rich Father
Accepted from you! (Pinsky)]

With masterly simplicity of expression, Dante has characterized in the simile the ills of the papacy, pointed to their origin, and set Boniface in true perspective as a morally corrupt imperial figure.

The two similes from the Guido da Montefeltro episode under analysis share a similar function. That function is not to make us see more clearly the topography of Hell, or the manner in which sinners suffer physically, although I agree that the Sicilian bull comparison, while ostensibly emphasizing an auditory parallel, does provide us also with a visual analogue to Guido's predicament, since both Guido and Perillus suffer incineration and are contained inside the instrument of their death. The visual here gives way to the conceptual. Dante employs these similes to reveal the conceptual identity and exemplificative character of an otherworld figure. Guido like Perillus is the trickster tricked; and Boniface, like Constantine, is the example of one who bears false gifts. Dante uses his similes in this way not to restrict our attention to a single facet of a figure's otherworld identity, but to focus it on the central dramatic aspect; not to diminish our sense of the complexity of a poetic figure, but to categorize our response to it. If we are conscious of the extraordinary power of the Dantean simile to convey a multiplicity of correspondences, both superficial and submerged, our reading of the *Commedia* is enriched.[12]

From *Dante Studies* 94 (1976): 61-69. Copyright © 1976 by the Dante Society of America. Reprinted with permission of the Dante Society of America.

Notes

[*Editor's Note:* All translations citing Pinsky are from *The Inferno of Dante*, translated by Robert Pinsky (New York: Farrar, Straus and Giroux, 1994). Other translations in brackets are provided by the volume editor, unless otherwise noted.]

1. T. S. Eliot, *Selected Essays* (New York: Harcourt, Brace, 1932), p. 205.

2. Irma Brandeis, *The Ladder of Vision: A Study of Dante's Comedy* (Garden City, New York: Doubleday, 1962), pp. 143-164.

3. Brandeis (who is indebted to Francis Fergusson for the observation), p. 145.

4. Medieval rhetoricians enjoined poets from deploying the "per collationem" simile (a simile with separate and syntactically parallel vehicle and tenor) but permitted the use of the "per brevitatem" simile (which collapsed the parallel structure, as in the example "white as snow"). See the remarks of E. Faral, *Les arts poétiques du XIIe et du XIIIe siècle* (Paris: Champion, 1924), pp. 68-69.

5. The idea of *contrapasso* in the simile is interpreted variously by the critics. B. Terracini, in *Letture dantesche*, [a cura di G. Getto], Vol. I (Firenze: Sansoni, 1964), emphasizes the nature of fraud: "come la frode ha fasciato i loro ben artefatti consigli, così il fuoco ora li traveste" (p. 519); J. Truscott, "Ulysses and Guido, *Inf.* XXVI-XXVII," in *Dante Studies*, XCI (1973), pp. 47-72, shows, more perceptively, that both Guido and Perillus "are punished by the symbol of the art by which they hoped to deceive and harm others" (p. 57).

6. Ovid, *Ars amatoria*, I, 655-656.

7. Truscott makes the same observation (see p. 60).

8. See, in particular, Guido's opening remarks to Dante the pilgrim (vv. 61-66).

9. The function of anticipation in the Dantean simile has been noted in several isolated instances by critics, though none has discussed it systematically. J. Applewhite, "The Extended Simile in the *Inferno*," in *Italica*, XLI (1964), pp. 294-309, observes that the "villanello" simile (*Inf.* XXIV, 1) serves as a prelude to the transformations of the Thieves (p. 301); Leo Spitzer, "Two Dante Notes," in *Romanic Review*, XXXIV (1943), pp. 248-256, suggests that the simile of the baptismal fonts (*Inf.* XIX, 16) introduces anticipatory evidence regarding the fate of the Simonists. See also E. Sanguineti's discussion of the simile (*Inf.* XXVIII, 7) in imitation of the Bertran de Born canzone, in *Interpretazione di Malebolge* (Firenze: Olschki, 1961), p. 287, and A. Pagliaro's remarks on the topic, in *Ulisse: ricerche semantiche sulla Divina Commedia*, Vol. II (Messina-Firenze: D'Anna, 1966), p. 652.

10. *De Monarchia*, III, x, 4-5. [English translation from *The De Monarchia of Dante Alighieri*, edited and translated by A. H. Reinhardt (Boston: Houghton Mifflin, 1904).]

11. Not only the justification of papal assertion of temporal political authority, but, in Dante's vision, of papal claim to rightful possession of worldly wealth. In this connection, it is perhaps worth noting that the immediate cause of Boniface's attack on the Colonnas was Sciarra Colonna's theft of a part of the papal treasure (see Villani, *Cronica*, VIII, 21).

12. This paper was read in slightly different form at the 79th annual meeting of the Michigan Academy of Science, Arts and Letters held in Ann Arbor, April 1975. I am grateful to the Mabelle McLeod Lewis Memorial Fund of Stanford, California, for a grant in aid.

Inferno 27 and the Perversions of Pentecost_____

Glending Olson

Several commentators on *Inferno* 19 have argued that the flames playing over the soles of the simonists parody the tongues of fire that alighted upon the apostles at Pentecost to signify the descent of the Holy Spirit (Acts 2:1-4).[1] This association contributes to the canto in various ways: as an indication that simoniac clergy have turned the powers and purposes of the gift of the Spirit upside down, as part of the *contrapasso* in that the sinners are tormented by a fire that evokes ironically the consolations of the Holy Spirit, and as a particularly apt punishment for simoniac popes, who define their authority with reference to the apostle Peter. The other citations of the Acts of the Apostles in Canto 19 make this parodic evocation all the more apparent: first Dante's apostrophe on Simon Magus and his followers (1-6), and later his appeal to the selection of Matthias in order to illustrate to Pope Nicholas that the apostles did not make spiritual decisions on the basis of financial motives (93-95). True apostolic behavior—that evoked by the references to Peter (91, 94), Matthias, and "li altri" (94)—stands as a judgment on the false apostolicism of Simon, of the three popes who are or will be "pursed" in this bolgia, and of Judas, the "anima ria" (96) who is the worst of all betrayers of apostolic ideals and who lies but one circle lower.[2]

Inferno 27 is most obviously connected with its preceding canto; both Guido da Montefeltro and Ulysses are judged guilty of the same sin (whether identified as false counselling or as some less precisely defined misuse of intellect), and Dante's paired treatment has received much close comparative analysis. The bolgia of Cantos 26-27 is linked to that of the simonists through the appearance of punishment by fire and through their structural symmetry within the ten *malebolge*, one the third and the other the third-to-last.[3] More specifically and forcefully, Canto 27 calls *Inferno* 19 to mind through Guido's account of his meeting with Boniface VIII, who in the earlier is named as a future occupant of Nicholas's hole, and by repetition of two important religious and political themes. At nearly identical points in each canto Dante refers to the power of the two "chiavi": in Canto 19 his reverence for them tempers his "parole . . . gravi" condemning simoniac popes, and in Canto 27 Boniface invokes them as part of what Guido considers the "argomenti gravi" that led him to sin (19:100-105; 27:104-107). The two passages, linked by content and rhyme, form a counterpoint of honorable and dishonorable rhetorical use of a central text in theological-political controversy. Both cantos also allude to the Donation of Constantine, concerning which Dante distinguishes between pious Christian motive and disastrous social effect (19:115-117) and Guido bitterly delineates an ironic analogy between Constantine's calling on Pope Sylvester and Boniface's calling on him (27:94-97). Given these obvious parallels, it is worth exploring ways in which the evocation of Pentecost in *Inferno* 19 may figure as well in *Inferno* 27. While some critics have noted that the speaking fires of the eighth bolgia allude to the descent of the Spirit,[4] I think that the echoes of Pentecost in 27 are more extensive and that the canto gains resonance when perceived in light of some common medieval interpretations of Acts 2. From this perspective many of Dante's references to speech—including Boniface's drunken words and invalid absolution, and Guido's confused sound and counsel of unfulfilled promise—cohere as a perverse replaying of an episode in which fire, tongues, confusion, and counsel all work to heavenly rather than hellish ends.

Acts 2 begins with sound and fire—first a noise like that of a vehement wind, and then parted tongues as of fire, phenomena that signal the descent of the Holy Spirit upon the apostles, which gives them the power to speak in many languages.[5] Medieval commentary on Acts 2:1-4 is not uniform in its assessment of the significance of the mighty sound and the tongues of fire, but either could be seen as a symbol of the apostles' gift of tongues, that is, their gift of universal communication; and the "linguae tanquam ignis" are most often explained as an image of newly acquired affective and intellectual strengths, the fire

---

signifying spiritual fervor, the tongues indicating powers of articulate-ness.[6] *Inferno* 27 also begins with sound and fire—a "confuso suon" emanating from the tip of "un'altra [fiamma]" (4-6). Dante's oft-explored comparison of the first sound Guido makes to that emanating from the Sicilian bull draws an analogy between the conversion of cries of human pain into the bellowing of an animal and the conversion of Guido's "parole grame" into the "linguaggio" of fire (7-15). In both cases human expression is reduced to nonhuman noise. Only when Guido's words reach the very tip of the flame does it act in concert with his "lingua" and allow comprehensible language out (16-18). Here, along with the briefer association of "fiamma" and "lingua" in Canto 26 (85-90), is the *Commedia*'s most direct allusion to the "linguae tanquam ignis" at Pentecost, an infernally ironic version in which the divine gift of speech made comprehensible to all is reversed by an im-age of human speech rendered (until the very end of its venting) in-comprehensibly subhuman, only the crackle and roar that fire itself speaks. In contrast to the spiration that animates Christian speech in Acts 2, Guido's breath is merely a "fiato" (60), which elsewhere in the *Inferno* describes only hellish winds and blasts (cf. 5:42; 11:12; 33:108). Some medieval commentary on Acts also points out that the Pentecostal fire is of a special kind—it illuminates or stimulates but does not consume or destroy. Virgil's observation in Canto 26 that "Dentro dai fuochi son li spirti;/ catun si fascia di quel ch'elli è inceso" (47-48) establishes the antithesis: the visible flame at Pentecost, which was merely a symbol of the inward filling of the apostles with the di-vine *spiritus*, now literally and exteriorly wraps around the sinners' spirits, which are punished without being enlightened. The apostles burned spiritually; Guido, like Ulysses, burned psychologically in worldly ambition and thus burns painfully in hell.[7]

The canto will explain shortly what kinds of speech have led to Guido's "confuso suon," and we will see the Pentecostal allusiveness of that phrase later. While it certainly points psychologically to his baf-flement at how his plans for salvation went awry,[8] it points as well to the spiritual distance between what he did with his tongue and what was done by those his tonguelike fire evokes. The ironic contrast between his sound and the sounds of Pentecost—both the noise of the Spirit's arrival and the preaching in various languages which that arrival inspires—is furthered by his own claim that he used his fox-like abilities so skillfully "ch'al fine de la terra il suono uscie" (78). This line is a condensed translation of Psalms 18:5—"In omnem terram exivit sonus eorum,/ Et in fines orbis terrae verba eorum" [Their sound hath gone forth into all the earth: and their words unto the ends of the world]. However, in Guido's case that sound concerns his "accorgimenti" and "coperte vie" (76), the fame of his worldly cleverness, not the glory of God. Medieval readings of Psalm 18 take it as a prophecy of Christ, and interpret its fourth and fifth verses in particular as referring to the sound of the apostles (and other preachers) spreading the Christian word, sometimes with specific reference to the Pentecostal gift of tongues. This connection, established early and often by Augustine, is a crucial element in the Pentecostal subtext of *Inferno* 27.[9] It sharpens the irony of Guido's claim to a universal reputation, a fame as extensive as that provided by the travels and preaching of the apostles—this from a soul whose concerns have already been revealed as limited to "Romagnuoli" (30).[10]

Further, Guido's implicit comparison of his reputation as trickster to Christ's fame manifests a pride that suggests another contrast between the false counsellor and the true preachers of Acts 2. Pentecost, according to a common medieval interpretation, reversed Babel—the confusion of tongues sent by God to thwart human pride was undone by humble men given the gift of speaking in all tongues.[11] As part of the degeneration of language in *Inferno* explored by Joan Ferrante, Guido's "confuso suon" is a step along the way to the unintelligible sounds of Nimrod, an "anima confusa," the builder of the tower of Babel, whose arrogance is the cause of the world's not speaking a single language (31:74-78). His *contrapasso* is to be isolated linguistically from all other beings: "così è a lui ciascun linguaggio/ come 'l suo ad altrui, ch'a nullo è noto" (80-81). That condition is the precise opposite of the powers of speech granted to the apostles by the descent of the Spirit, which rendered them able to speak in a way knowable by all others.[12] Viewed retrospectively, the linking of Guido's confused sound with the confusion of speech wrought by Nimrod reinforces the portrait in Canto 27 of his pride and the implied, humble remedy to such arrogance that took place on Pentecost.

Guido the military leader, line 78 establishes, was the subject of a certain kind of earthly apostolicism; and not even in Hell has he come to understand the irony of his grandiose allusion: that, as Augustine says, Psalm 18:4-5 proclaims God's glory, not one's own.[13] Presumably becoming a Franciscan friar should have helped him recognize the difference; the Franciscans held their general meetings at Pentecost and, given the ideals of their founder, naturally viewed their religious condition as like that of the apostles.[14] Still, the person in Canto 27 who ought best to understand the significance of Pentecost is the man who occupies Peter's "alto seggio" (111). Boniface's behavior, however, is an equally perverse and more detailed parody of its meaning, as Guido, for his own purposes, makes clear. Boniface practices "guerra" (86) against Christians, in contrast to the peaceful unity of the apostles on Pentecost.[15] He reveals "superba" (97) rather than humility. And when he asks counsel, "le sue parole parver ebbre" (99). Typically "ebbre" is glossed here, if at all, as referring to a loss of reason or sense, certainly consistent with the standard medieval characterization of drunkenness as an abandonment of the human faculty of reason; critical attention has tended to focus on the preceding comparison of Boniface and Guido to Constantine and Sylvester. However, in the context of Pentecost, Boniface's drunken words are no less allusive. His speech shocks Guido into silence, and a reader conscious of the canto's evocations of Acts 2 will think of another audience stunned at certain words—those devout Jews ("viri religiosi") who became "confounded in mind" when they heard the apostles speaking in various tongues (Acts 2:6: "et mente confusa est"), unable at first to understand how they could have such powers. Some of the listeners mockingly said that the apostles "were full of new wine" ("musto pleni sunt" [2:13]), but Peter stood up and asserted the contrary: "these are not drunk, as you suppose" ("Non enim, sicut vos aestimatis, hi ebrii sunt . . ." [2:15]), explaining that instead they were filled with the divine *spiritus* prophesied in Joel.

On a literal level the accusation of drunkenness is wrong. But allegorically, much medieval commentary argues, it turns out to be correct, for the apostles are inebriated spiritually. Filled, as Augustine and others say, with the new wine of grace, they become on Pentecost the new wine in new bottles of which Jesus speaks in the synoptic gospels (Matt. 9:17, Mark 2:22, Luke 5:37-38).[16] And the old wine in old bottles, in context and in commentary, could mean the scribes and Pharisees, so that Guido's reference to Boniface as "[l]o principe d'i novi Farisei" (85) becomes part of the canto's network of allusions to true and false apostolicism.[17] Boniface's sinful misuse of power renders his words "ebbre" not just because they are irrational or shocking but also because they travesty what is simultaneously the literal sobriety and the spiritual inebriation of the apostles, out of which plenitude of Spirit came words that brought conversion to the faith. For what happens subsequently between Boniface and Friar Guido is the reverse of what happens between Peter and his audience of religious men. Peter's words, though they first appear "ebrii" to some, ultimately lead all his hearers to "compunction," "penance," and baptism, a fulfillment of the "promise" made to anyone who calls on the Lord.[18] In sum, he provides profitable spiritual counsel. Boniface's words appear "ebbre" to Guido, but unlike Peter's they do not prove salvific—just the opposite. They invert the only valid sequence of movement from sin to salvation by promising absolution before and thus without compunction and penitence. Boniface is portrayed in this scene as a kind of anti-Peter: asking for "consiglio" (98) rather than speaking out of the "spiritus consilii" (spirit of counsel) that is one of the traditional gifts of the Holy Spirit (Is. 11:2), and expecting Guido to act as his "maestro" (96) rather than being the "doctus magister" (learned teacher) that Bede says Peter was to the assembled throng at Pentecost.[19] Peter's audience starts "confusa," hears him speak, reflects, performs penitence, and ends baptized and saved; Boniface's audience starts—at least Guido so claims—"pentuto e confesso" (83), hears him speak, acts then as one who "non si pente," and ends "confuso" and damned. It is thus particularly fitting that in *Paradiso* 27 Peter should have the *Commedia*'s last word on Boniface, as he pronounces him unworthy of being among "nostri successor" (47), evoking both *Inferno* 19 in condemning his use of the church "ad acquisto d'oro" (42) and *Inferno* 27 in condemning his use of the "chiavi" to fight "contra battezzati" (49-51).

While this perversion of apostolic behavior speaks to the spiritual state of the canto's protagonists, it also has a political resonance. Dante's well-known views on church/state relations are vigorously opposed to papal claims of power in the temporal sphere, and Gordon Leff has argued that for him and other thinkers of similar conviction the apostolic ideal became a touchstone. Invoking a primitive church uncorrupted by the Donation of Constantine, a church of poverty and community rather than wealth and hierarchy, served to justify criticism of the worldly entanglements and authoritarian claims of the contemporary church.[20] Recognizing echoes of Pentecost in *Inferno* 27 enables us to see more fully another instance in the *Commedia* of a political argument—the limits of papal power—rendered through dramatic means. Boniface's claim to be able to absolve Guido in advance asserts something that Dante flatly denies in the *Monarchia*: not even God, let alone the pope, can save a person who has not repented.[21] The Pope's coercive use of the keys to achieve his worldly goals takes place against an allusively evoked backdrop that suggests an alternative image of the relationship between the church and the world, the apostolic community of "Pier [e] li altri" (19:94). In *Monarchia* Dante cites passages from Acts to support his position that the early church recognized the legitimate temporal authority of the empire, and he mentions the apostles' charity to the poor as a proper ecclesiastical disposition of material goods from the secular power, goods that the vicar of God should hold not as owner but as distributor.[22] Pentecost was a day of unity and inclusiveness; the Holy Spirit filled first all the apostles and then all the people they converted. Peter appears more as *primus inter pares* than as the special recipient of divine power that papalists contended in their reading of Matthew 16:18-19. Similarly in *Monarchia* Dante notes that according to Matt. 16:19 and other passages Jesus bestowed the power of binding and loosing on all the apostles, not just Peter, and in *Paradiso* he presents Peter in the circle of the fixed stars along with James and John.[23] The infusion of the Spirit that extends to all provides an image of Christian community against which the present condition of the church, inaugurated long ago by the Donation of Constantine and currently represented by the simoniac Boniface, can be seen as an historical degeneration, a degeneration later played out allegorically in *Purgatorio* 32.

In the depths of Hell sinfulness often takes shape as parody of goodness—Satan is a grotesque and impotent Trinity, and the wind from his wings a frigid echo of the divine *spiritus*; Ugolino is a stony recipient of his children's self-sacrifice. I would argue that in a similar parodic strain Boniface VIII and Guido da Montefeltro play out a perverted version of the early church on the day of Pentecost: the gift of tongues is transformed into drunken words reflecting the inebriation of pride, not the gifts of the Spirit; Peter's preaching and counsel become a wicked request that leads not to penitence, unity in the Spirit, and ultimately salvation but rather to an invalid absolution, an act of war against Christians, and, for his audience of one, confusion and damnation. In the context of this set of contrasts, Guido's advice to his Pope—"lunga promessa con l'attender corto" (110)—provides a final ironic echo, for Pentecost is about the *fulfillment* of promises: first of Christ's promise ("promissionem") to the apostles that they will be baptized with the Spirit (Acts 1:4-5) and then the more general "promise" ("repromissio"), spoken by Peter, of salvation to anyone who will repent and be baptized (Acts 2:39).[24] As often noted, the betrayal of promise that Guido counsels ensures a fulfillment that he was

---

hardly expecting, one that exposes the exceptionally short validity of Boniface's own promise of absolution, and one that leaves his "dolorando" tongue of fire "torcendo e dibattendo 'l corno aguto" (131-132) in eternal grief and befuddlement. His counsel *not* to fulfill a promise marks the point at which he cuts himself off from the spiritual fulfillment promised and delivered in Acts 2 to those truly penitent; and the final image of his twisting flame contrasts not only psychologically with Ulysses's "dritta . . . fiamma" (1) but spiritually with the joy and peace of those who followed Peter's true counsel and received the Spirit.

For the classical hero who has let his intellect run where virtue does not guide, Canto 26 establishes as its dominant metaphorical backdrop the philosophical journey, evoked by images of sailing and flight, to which, as Corti has argued, the metaphor of the tongue as fire is assimilated.[25] In Canto 27, for the supposedly penitent Franciscan, while he too knows that his sails should be lowered, it is appropriate that the principal subtext be an episode from Christian history rather than a philosophical metaphor. A network of references—to tongue-like fire, sound going to the ends of the earth, confusion, drunken speech, penitence, promise and fulfillment—evokes a narrative whose story of inspiration and conversion adds both depth and light to Dante's portrait of the wrecked souls of the simonist and the false counselor. Further, against the Spirit-denying speech of Guido da Montefeltro[26] stands ultimately, if we attend to its own self-dramatized poetics, the Spirit-receptive speaking/writing of the entire *Commedia*. This is surely the implication of Dante's theologically resonant response, "quando/ Amor mi spira, noto" (*Purg.* 24:52-53), in the famous exchange on the "dolce stil novo."[27] And during his examination on faith in *Paradiso* 24, Dante explicitly mentions Pentecost in referring to Peter and other apostles as "voi che scriveste/ poi che l'ardente Spirto vi fé almi" (137-138), thus linking the descent of the Spirit not only with the apostolic preaching in Acts but also with all the apostolic writing in the New Testament. When a few lines later "l'appostolico lume" (153) bestows a blessing on the poet, it would seem to extend as well to the writing that will come from one of similar apostolic zeal and faith. The Pentecostal gift subtly evoked in *Inferno* 27, even as it helps condemn Guido and Boniface, also helps underwrite the possibility of inspired and spiritually profitable communication. And such a possibility— whatever the *Commedia*'s level of self-consciousness about appealing to it—ultimately provides a foundation for the poetics of this fiction that claims not to be a fiction.

Notes

1. The point is argued most fully in Reginald French, "Simony and Pentecost," *Annual Report of the Dante Society*, 82 (1964), 3-17. See also Ronald B. Herzman and William A. Stephany, "'O miseri seguaci': Sacramental Inversion in *Inferno* XIX," *Dante Studies*, 96 (1978), 39-65 at 40-41; Joan M. Ferrante, "The Relation of Speech to Sin in the *Inferno*," *Dante Studies*, 87 (1969), 33-46 at 40-42; Robert Hollander, *Allegory in Dante's "Commedia"* (Princeton, New Jersey: Princeton University Press, 1969), 118 n. 12; Mark Musa, *Advent at the Gates: Dante's Comedy* (Bloomington: Indiana University Press, 1974), 143 n. 8; Kenelm Foster, *The Two Dantes* (Berkeley: University of California Press, 1977), 94. Influential here is André Pézard's larger argument: that in several cantos of *Inferno* sins classified as those against the Holy Spirit are punished by a fire alluding to the fire in which the Spirit manifested itself on Pentecost (*Dante sous la pluie de feu* [Paris: J. Vrin, 1950], 283-293).

2. All Dante citations will be to canto and line numbers of the Petrocchi text as it appears in *The Divine Comedy*, tr. and comm. Charles S. Singleton, 3 vols. (Princeton, New Jersey: Princeton University Press, 1977).

3. Edoardo Sanguineti, *Interpretazione di Malebolge* (Firenze: Leo S. Olschki, 1961), 44.

4. Ferrante, 40-41; Maria Corti, "On the Metaphors of Sailing, Flight, and Tongues of Fire in the Episode of Ulysses (*Inferno* 26)," *Stanford Italian Review*, 9 (1990), 33-47 at 44-46; Giorgio Bàrberi Squarotti, "La voce di Guido da Montefeltro," *Forum Italicum*, 21 (1987), 165-196 at 166-167; Giuseppe Mazzotta, "The Light of Venus and the Poetry of Dante: 'Vita Nuova' and 'Inferno' XXVII," in *Modern Critical Views: Dante*, ed. Harold Bloom (New York: Chelsea House, 1986), 189-204 at 200-201.

5. Acts 2:2-4: "et factus est repente de caelo sonus, tanquam advenientis spiritus

vehementis. . . . Et apparuerunt illis dispertitae linguae tanquam ignis, seditque supra singulos eorum: et repleti sunt omnes Spiritu sancto, et coeperunt loqui variis linguis, prout Spiritus sanctus dabat eloqui illis." [And suddenly there came a sound from heaven, as of a mighty wind coming. . . . And there appeared to them parted tongues, as it were of fire, and it sat upon every one of them. And they were all filled with the Holy Ghost; and they began to speak with divers tongues, according as the Holy Ghost gave them to speak.] Biblical citations are to *Biblia Sacra iuxta Vulgatam Clementinam nova editio*, ed. Alberto Colunga and Laurentio Turrado, 7th ed. (Madrid: Biblioteca de Autores Cristianos, 1985); translations follow the Douay version.

6. Some examples: Bede, in his influential commentary on Acts, cites Gregory's *Moralia* on the tongues of fire as symbols that God had made the apostles "zelo succensos et uerbo eruditos" [inflamed with zeal and skilled with words]. *Expositio Actuum Apostolorum* 2.2, ed. M. L. W. Laistner, in *Opera omnia*, pars II, 4, CCSL 121 (Turnhout: Brepols, 1983), 16; tr. Lawrence T. Martin, *Commentary on the Acts of the Apostles* (Kalamazoo, Michigan: Cistercian Publications, 1989), p. 28. The continuation of Peter Comestor's *Historia scholastica* says that the appearance of fire shows that the Spirit gave the apostles vigor ("robur"), the tongues that they were given knowledge ("scientiam"). *PL* 198, 1652; repeated in Vincent of Beauvais, *Speculum historiale* 7.66, in *Speculum quadruplex*, 4 vols. (1624; rpt. Graz: Akademische Druck—u. Verlagsanstalt, 1964), 4.245. See also John Beleth, *Rationale divinorum officiorum*, *PL* 202, 136; Hildebert of Lavardin, Sermon 52, *PL* 171, 593; Peter Abelard, Sermon 18, *PL* 178, 510; Hugh Ripelin of Strasbourg, *Compendium theologicae veritatis* 1.9, printed as part of Albert the Great's *Opera omnia*, vol. 34, ed. Auguste Borgnet (Paris: Vivés, 1895), 11. The great sound is more often taken as a manifestation of the Spirit itself than as a bestowal of power on the apostles, although the *Glossa ordinaria* indicates that the sound of Acts 2:2 can be read as signifying the apostles' gift of tongues (*PL* 114, 430), and both Hildebert and Abelard associate it with apostolic preaching (*PL* 171, 593; *PL* 178, 510). In medieval art the tongues of fire are sometimes given quite literal depiction atop the heads of the apostles; see the examples *passim* in the generous selection of representations of Pentecost, medieval through baroque, in Gertrud Schiller, *Ikonographie der christlichen Kunst* 4.1 (Gütersloh: Gerd Mohn, 1981), plates 1-79. Such efforts at visualizing the scene could have contributed to Dante's fiery inventions in *Inferno* 19 and 26-27.

7. On the Pentecostal fire: Augustine, Sermon 269 (*PL* 38, 1234): "ignis ille non cremavit, sed excitavit" [That fire did not consume; rather it stimulated]. Pseudo-Augustine, Sermon 186 (*PL* 39, 2094): "Advenit ignis divinus, non comburens, sed illuminans; non consumens, sed lucens" [The divine fire came not consuming but illuminating, not destroying but clarifying]. Thomas of Chobham, after delineating a three-part *distinctio* on fire, defines the fire in Acts 2 as "non comburens sed illuminans et inflammans" [not consuming but illuminating and rousing]; Sermon 14 in *Sermones*, ed. Franco Morenzoni, CCCM 82A (Turnhout: Brepols, 1993), 148. On the fire in Cantos 26-27 as a contrapasso representing the sinners' internal burnings, see Mario Trovato, "Il contrapasso nell'ottava bolgia," *Dante Studies*, 94 (1976), 47-60 at 56, though I do not agree with his interpretation of the issues here as essentially secular, directed toward Ulysses's and Guido's failures within the realm of political activity.

8. Judith Davies, "Inferno XXVII," in *Cambridge Readings in Dante's Comedy*, ed. Kenelm Foster and Patrick Boyde (Cambridge: Cambridge University Press, 1981), 49-69.

9. See Sermon 269 (*PL* 38, 1234); *De Trinitate* 4.20.29, ed. W. J. Mountain, CCSL 50 (Turnhout: Brepols, 1968), 201, where Augustine discusses the sending of the Holy Spirit as fulfilling ("ut impleretur") the prophecy of Psalm 18:4-5; and especially the second *enarratio* on Psalm 18 in *Enarrationes in Psalmos* I-L, ed. D. E. Dekkers and J. Fraipont, CCSL 38 (Turnhout: Brepols, 1956), 108-109, where in explaining the fourth and fifth verses he tells the reader to consult Acts 2 and says that the apostolic *sonus* extends through every land, and to present listeners, to make salvation possible. Cassiodorus reads the opening verses of Psalm 18 as praise of "God's preachers" and most fruitfully applied to "apostles . . . and prophets," citing specifically in regard to the fourth and fifth verses the apostolic gift of tongues, and reading "calore" in the seventh ("there is no one that can hide himself from his heat") as referring to the Holy Spirit, since it came to the apostles in fire on Pentecost. *Expositio Psalmorum* I-LXX, ed. M. Adriaen, CCSL 97 (Turnhout: Brepols, 1958), 169-172. Both Augustine and Cassiodorus are cited in the *Glossa ordinaria*'s reading of the early verses (*PL* 113, 870-871); see also the Psalms commentary once attributed to Bede (*PL* 93, 581); the *Breviarium in Psalmos* printed among Jerome's works in *PL* 26, 925; Peter Abelard, Sermon 18 (*PL* 178, 510); Peter Lombard, *Commentarium in Psalmos* (*PL* 191, 208). The connection between the sound of Psalm 18:5 and the sound of Acts 2:2 is made most succinctly in Rupert of Deutz, *Liber de divinis officiis* X.13: "*Sonus*, qui adueniente Spiritu sancto *repente factus est de caelo*, signum fuit soni, qui *in omnem terrain exiturus* erat. . . ." [The *sound* which *suddenly came from heaven* with the arrival of the Holy Spirit was a sign of the sound which had *gone forth into all the world*.] Ed. H. Haacke, CCCM 7 (Turnhout: Brepols, 1967), 348.

Guido's allusion to Psalm 18 has further ironic significance for him: in its last section the speaker, as Cassiodorus says, returns "ad memoriam fragilitatis suae" [to the recollection of his own weakness] and prays for help in cleansing himself of sins (*Expositio*, ed. Adriaen, 175-176). Augustine's second *enarratio* interprets the *delictum maximum* [the greatest sin] of Psalm 18:14 as pride. "Who can understand sins?" (18:13). Clearly not Guido. We will see shortly that Acts 2, as well as Psalm 18, comes to have a penitential meaning mocked by both pope and friar.

10. On Guido's constricted regional vision here, in contrast to Ulysses's broader one, see Bàrberi Squarotti, 169-171.

11. E.g., Augustine, Sermon 271 (*PL* 38, 1245); Ambrose, Sermon 36 (*PL* 17, 698); Arator, *De Actibus Apostolorum* 1.129-138, ed. Arthur P. McKinlay, CSEL 72 (Vienna: Hoelder-Pichler-Tempsky, 1951), 18-19; Bede, *Expositio* 2.4, ed. Laistner, 16, expanded in his *Retractatio in Actus Apostolorum* 4.32, ed. Laistner, 127; Honorius of Autun, *Speculum ecclesiae* (*PL* 172, 964). The *Glossa ordinaria* (*PL* 114, 431) points up the antithesis between the confusion of tongues at Babel and the confusion of Acts 2:6: "Confusio ista confusion linguarum opponitur, a qua Babel vocabulum sortita est. Sic humilitas apostolorum humanae superbiae respondet" [This confusion is opposed to the confusion of tongues from which the name Babel comes. Thus apostolic humility answers human pride].

12. On the echo of the biblical confusion of tongues in Dante's reference to Nimrod as "confusa," see Singleton's notes to lines 74 and 77. On Nimrod's appearances in the *Commedia* see Teodolinda Barolini, *The Undivine Comedy: Detheologizing Dante* (Princeton, New Jersey: Princeton University Press, 1992), 51 and n. 13. His pride and his resultant bemusement are stressed in *Purgatorio* 12:34-36; Dante develops the association of Babel with pride and confusion in *De vulgari eloquentia* 1.6-7. On Nimrod's five unintelligible words as a parody of the apostolic gift of tongues, see Robert Hollander, *Dante and Paul's Five Words with Understanding*, Center for Medieval & Early Renaissance Studies, Occasional Papers 1 (Binghamton: Medieval & Renaissance Texts and Studies, 1992), 17-19 and n. 25.

13. *Ennaratio* II.2: "Haec est, inquam, gloria Dei, non tua." Ed. Adriaen, 106.

14. Mazzotta, 200-201. See further Penn R. Szittya, *The Antifraternal Tradition in Medieval Literature* (Princeton, New Jersey: Princeton University Press, 1986), 236-238 and *passim* on antifraternal satire attacking friars' apostolic claims, particularly Chaucer's *Summoner's Tale*.

15. A commonplace of interpretation and very important in Augustine's sermons on Pentecost, particularly Sermon 268 (*PL* 38, 1231-1234). Hildebert (*PL* 171, 593) says of the apostles: "quod congregati erant, unitatem Ecclesiae significat" [that they had gathered together signifies the unity of the Church]. Raoul Ardent treats their "pax et concordia" [peace and harmony] as a model for Christians who desire the Spirit in their lives. He says that where discord and hatred arise among those who should be unified (as in the cloister or in marriage), there Satan has entered rather than the Holy Spirit (*PL* 155, 1937-1938). Although he does not mention Pentecost, Guido da Pisa, commenting on *Inferno* 27:91-92, gives particular weight to Boniface's request for counsel as an insult to the peace that Christ's life, death, and resurrection were meant to bring: "Et in hoc actu non habuit respectum ad se, qui erat vicarius illius regis pacifici qui pacem in mundum portavit, pacem nascendo adnuntiavit, vivendo predicavit, moriendo in testamento sue familie dereliquit, et resurgendo eisdem pacem obtulit atque dedit." [And in committing this act he showed no regard for himself as vicar of that peaceful king who brought peace into the world, made peace known through his birth, preached it while alive, in dying left it as a legacy to his followers, and in rising again brought and gave peace to them.] *Expositiones et Glose super Comediam Dantis*, ed. Vincenzo Cioffari (Albany: State University of New York Press, 1974), 559.

16. Augustine, Sermon 266 (*PL* 38, 1225): "Dicebant enim: *Hi ebrii sunt et musto pleni.* Quam stulta et calumniosa reprehensio! Homo ebrius non alienam linguam discit, sed suam perdit. Verumtamen per ignorantes et calumniantes veritas loquebatur. Jam quippe illi pleni erant vino novo, quia facti erant utres novi." [They said, "These are drunk and full of new wine." What a stupid and malicious insult! A person who is drunk does not acquire another language but loses his own. Yet truth spoke even through the ignorant and the malicious, for indeed they had been filled with new wine, because they had become new bottles.] Similarly Pseudo-Augustine, Sermon 182 (*PL,* 39, 2090) and Sermon 186 (*PL* 39, 2094); Arator, I, 148-155, ed. McKinlay, 20; Bede, *Expositio* 2.13, ed. Laistner, 18; Rupert of Deutz, *De divinis officiis*, X, 19, ed. Haacke, 354. Recognizing the play on "ebbre" here would be facilitated by the familiar medi-

eval "distinzion" (to borrow Aquinas's term from *Par.* 13:109) between *in bono* and *in malo* meanings of drunkenness. See, e.g., *Allegoriae in sacram scripturam*, s. v. *ebrietas* (misattributed to Rabanus Maurus in *PL* 112, 914). Petrus Cantor, *Distinctiones Abel*, divides *ebrietas* into bodily and spiritual meanings (British Library MS Royal 10 A. xvi, fol. 33). Maurice of Provins, *Distinctiones Mauricii*, cites "multiplex" biblical meanings of *ebrietas* from the earthly and the damnable to the devotional and the eternally joyful (Bibliothèque Nationale MS lat. 3270, fol. 120v). On sober drunkenness (*sobria ebrietas*) as a Christian commonplace for spiritual elevation beyond the rational, see the list of references in Isaac of Stella, *Sermons*, vol. 1, ed. Anselm Hoste, trans. Gaston Salet, Sources Chrétiennes 130 (Paris: Editions du Cerf, 1967), 336-337.

17. Thus Jerome, *Commentarionum in Matheum Libri IV* on Matt. 9:16-17: "Veteres [uestimenti et utrium] debemus intellegere scribas et Pharisaeos." (We should understand the old garments and bottles to be the scribes and Pharisees.) Ed. D. Hurst and M. Adriaen, CCSL 77 (Turnhout: Brepols, 1969), 58. The *Glossa ordinaria* offers "scribae et Pharisaei" as one of the possible meanings of the "old bottles" of Luke 5:37 (*PL* 114, 259). Line 85 also has a distinct political resonance—the *supercilium Pharisaeorum* of contemporary anti-papal thought—on which see J. A. Watt, "Dante, Boniface VIII and the Pharisees," in *Post Scripta: Essays on Medieval Law and the Emergence of the European State in Honor of Gaines Post*, ed. Joseph R. Strayer and Donald E. Queller, Studia Gratiana XV (Rome: Ateneo Salesiano, 1972), 203-215.

18. Acts 2:37-41. To emphasize the movement toward repentance and salvation at the end of Acts 2 Augustine (Sermon 266; *PL* 38, 1225) uses a rhetorical *gradatio* to describe the conversion of even the skeptical Jews: ". . . audiendo compuncti sunt, compunctione mutati sunt, mutati crediderunt; credentes, hoc quod in aliis mirabantur, accipere meruerunt." [Through listening they were stung, through stinging transformed, through transformation brought to belief, and, believing, they deserved to receive what they were marvelling at in others.] See also the sermon for Pentecost by the Franciscan Anthony of Padua, which contains substantial material on its penitential implications; *Sermones Dominicales et Festivi*, ed. B. Costa, L. Frasson, and J. Luisetto, vol. 1 (Padova: Messaggero, 1979), 367-385, esp. 377-381, 385.

19. Bede, *Expositio* 2.22-23, ed. Laistner, 20. That Peter is providing counsel ("consilium") to his audience is stressed in Hugh of St. Cher's exposition of Acts 2; see *Opera omnia in universum Vetus et Novum Testamentum*, 8 vols. (Lyons, 1668-1669), 7:280v and 282v. He divides the chapter into three parts, the third treating the compunction of those who hear Peter ("de compunctione auditorum"). Hugh's divisions of this part include the audience's seeking Peter's counsel ("consilium") [Acts 2:37], Peter then giving his "consilium" [2:38-40], three thousand taking satisfaction in it ("acquiescunt consilio eius") [2:41] and as a result advancing spiritually [2:42-47]. I owe this reference to John Alford.

20. Leff, "The Apostolic Ideal in Later Medieval Ecclesiology," *Journal of Theological Studies*, n.s. 18 (1967), 58-82. For a convenient survey of the controversy over papal power in the age of Dante see Joan Ferrante, *The Political Vision of the "Divine Comedy"* (Princeton, New Jersey: Princeton University Press, 1984), 3-43; and for an overview of greater chronological scope, J. A. Watt, "Spiritual and Temporal Powers,"

in *The Cambridge History of Medieval Political Thought c. 350-c. 1450*, ed. J. H. Burns (Cambridge: Cambridge University Press, 1988), 367-423. On the politics of Canto 27 see Ferrante, *passim*, and of Dante's evocation of apostolic poverty in *Par.* 21:127-129, see Ferrante, 95.

21. *Monarchia* 3.8.7, ed. Pier Georgio Ricci (Milano: Arnoldo Mondadori, 1965), 250: "Posset etiam solvere me non penitentem: quod etiam facere ipse Deus non posset."

22. Respectively *Mon.* 3.13.5 and 3.10.17 (". . . non tanquam possessor, sed . . . dispensator").

23. *Mon.* 3.8.1-2, invoking Matt. 18:18 and John 20:23. Hollander, *Allegory*, 318, notes that in *Paradiso* the three apostles are "representative of the communal accomplishments of the twelve."

24. For the language of promise and fulfillment in medieval thinking about Pentecost, see e.g. Augustine, Sermon 267 (*PL* 38, 1230), on what the day celebrates: "Dominus enim Spiritum sanctum de coelo misit, quem in terra promisit. . . . passus est, mortuus est, resurrexit, ascendit; restabat ut impleret quod promisit." [God sent the Holy Spirit from heaven, which he had promised on earth. . . . He suffered, died, rose again, and ascended; it remained for him to fulfill what he promised.]

25. Corti, 44-46, developing the idea of philosophical presumption argued in John Freccero, "Dante's Prologue Scene," *Dante Studies*, 84 (1966), 1-25 at 12-19. She observes that the association of the tongue with fire, evoked by the punishment in the eighth bolgia, has both *in bono* and *in malo* interpretations in Christian exegesis, and that in Ulysses's case the dominant evocation is of the sins of the tongue. The central text for such *in malo* meanings is James 3:6: "Et lingua ignis est, universitas iniquitatis."

26. Long before Pézard's more encompassing reading, Benvenuto da Imola interpreted the devil's speech at the end of Canto 27 as indicating to Guido that his decision to act according to Boniface's wishes and invalid promise rather than his own conscience constitutes a sin against the Holy Spirit, because he sinned in the expectation of grace to come: "tu peccasti sub spe futurae veniae, quod est peccare in spiritum sanctum." *Comentum super Dantis Aldigherij Comoediam*, ed. J. P. Lacaita (Firenze: Barbèra, 1887), 2:329.

27. Here I follow Giuseppe Mazzotta, *Dante, Poet of the Desert* (Princeton, New Jersey: Princeton University Press, 1979), 192-210, and R. L. Martinez, "The Pilgrim's Answer to Bonagiunta and the Poetics of the Spirit," *Stanford Italian Review*, 3 (1983), 37-63. Barolini, discussing Dante's own awareness of the risks of such a claim, notes that one early perspective on the *Commedia*, citing these lines, imputes the poem's authorship to the Holy Spirit rather than to Dante; *The Undivine Comedy*, 52-53 and 284 n. 20.

RESOURCES

1265	Dante Alighieri is born in Florence (in what is now Italy), probably in late May or early June, to Alighiero di Bellincione and Bella degli Abati.
1274	Dante encounters Beatrice Portinari for the first time.
1274-1275	Dante's mother dies.
1278	Dante enters into a marriage contract with Gemma di Manetto Donati.
1283	Dante's father dies.
c.1283	Dante begins his initial formative Florentine education with Guido Cavalcanti and Brunetto Latini and others of the *dolce stil nuovo* (sweet new style).
1285	Dante marries Gemma Donati.
1287	Beatrice marries banker Simone dei Bardi.
1289	Dante participates, probably as a cavalry officer, in the Battle of Campaldino.
1290	Beatrice dies.
1291-1293	Dante engages in further study with Dominican and Franciscan schools in Florence at Santa Maria Novella and Santa Croce, respectively.
1293-1294	Dante writes *La vita nuova*.
1294	In Florence, Dante meets Charles Martel, king of Hungary and heir to the kingdom of Naples.
1295-1297	Dante joins the guild of apothecaries and physicians and begins his political life as a Florentine council member.

1300	Dante turns thirty-five ("midlife") and sets the fictive symbolic date for the *Inferno* (and the whole of *The Divine Comedy*) as Easter weekend. Dante is elected as a prior of Florence. Black and White Guelfs divide into splinter factions in Florence. Pope Boniface VIII declares a jubilee year for Rome.
1301	Dante is sent on a trip to Rome from Florence to meet with Pope Boniface VIII after Charles of Valois marches on Florence as a papal representative. Black Guelfs overthrow White Guelfs as they sack Florence. Pope Boniface orders Dante detained.
1302	Dante, in Siena, is exiled from Florence in January as a White Guelf and fined five thousand florins; his exile is made permanent in March.
1303	Dante travels to Treviso, Arezzo, north of Lucca and Valdichiana. He becomes a long-term guest of Bartolomeo della Scala in Verona.
1303-1305	Dante begins to write *De vulgari eloquentia* and *Il convivio*.
1304-1309	Dante writes *Inferno*.
1309	The papacy moves from Rome to Avignon.
1310	Dante possibly writes *De monarchia*.
1312-1318	Dante is a guest of Cangrande della Scala in Ravenna.
1314	Dante publishes *Inferno*.
1315	Dante is offered the opportunity to return to Florence from exile if he admits to being guilty of barratry, but he refuses. Dante publishes *Purgatorio*.
1319	Dante becomes a guest of Guido Novello da Polenta in Ravenna. He corresponds in Latin with Giovanni del Virgilio in Bologna.
1320	Dante lectures on *Quaestio de aqua et terra* in Verona.

| 1321 | Dante finishes *Paradiso*. He engages in diplomatic missions for Ravenna in Venice, where he contracts malaria in the marshes. Dante dies in Ravenna. |

Works by Dante

Poetry

La vita nuova, c. 1292 (*Vita Nuova*, 1861; better known as *The New Life*)
La divina commedia, c. 1320 (*The Divine Comedy*, 1802)

Nonfiction

Epistolae, c. 1300-1321 (English translation, 1902)
De vulgari eloquentia, c. 1306 (English translation, 1890)
Il convivio, c. 1307 (*The Banquet*, 1887)
De monarchia, c. 1313 (English translation, 1890; also known as *Monarchy*, 1954; better known as *On World Government*, 1957)
"Epistola X," c. 1316 (English translation, 1902)
Eclogae, 1319 (*Eclogues*, 1902)
Quaestio de aqua et terra, 1320 (English translation, 1902)
Translation of the Latin Works of Dante Alighieri, 1904
Literary Criticism of Dante Alighieri, 1973

Bibliography

Anderson, William. *Dante the Maker*. Boston: Routledge & Kegan Paul, 1980.

Ascoli, Albert Russell. *Dante and the Making of a Modern Author*. New York: Cambridge University Press, 2008.

Auerbach, Erich. *Dante: Poet of the Secular World*. New York: New York Review of Books, 2006.

_____. *Mimesis: The Representation of Reality in Western Literature*. Trans. William R. Trask. 1953. Princeton, NJ: Princeton University Press, 2003.

_____. *Scenes from the Drama of European Literature: Six Essays*. Trans. Ralph Manheim. 1959. Minneapolis: University of Minnesota Press, 1984.

Barański, Zygmunt G. *Dante e i segni: Saggi per una storia intellettuale di Dante Alighieri*. Naples: Liguori, 2000.

_____. "Reflecting on Dante in America, 1949-1990." *Annali d'Italianistica* 8 (1990): 58-87.

Barolini, Teodolinda. *Dante and the Origins of Italian Literary Culture*. New York: Fordham University Press, 2006.

_____. *Dante's Poets: Textuality and Truth in the "Comedy."* Princeton, NJ: Princeton University Press, 1984.

_____. *The Undivine Comedy: Detheologizing Dante*. Princeton, NJ: Princeton University Press, 1992.

Becker, Christopher Bennett. "Dante's Motley Cord: Art and Apocalypse in *Inferno* XVI." *Modern Language Notes* 106.1 [Italian issue] (1991): 179-83.

Boccaccio, Giovanni. *Boccaccio's Expositions on Dante's "Comedy."* Trans. Michael Papio. Toronto: University of Toronto Press, 2009.

_____. *The Life of Dante*. Trans. Vincenzo Zin Bollettino. New York: Garland, 1990.

Boswell, John E. "Dante and the Sodomites." *Dante Studies* 112 (1994): 63-76.

Boyde, Patrick. "Inferno XIII." *Cambridge Readings in Dante's "Comedy."* Ed. Kenelm Foster and Patrick Boyde. New York: Cambridge University Press, 1981. 1-22.

Caputo, Rino. *Per far segno: La critica dantesca americana da Singleton a oggi*. Rome: Il Calamo, 1993.

Cervigni, Dino S. "Dante and Modern American Criticism: An Introductory Essay." *Annali d'Italianistica* 8 (1990): 5-28.

Cestaro, Gary P. *Dante and the Grammar of the Nursing Body*. Notre Dame, IN: University of Notre Dame Press, 2003.

Cioffari, Vincenzo. "Guido da Pisa's Basic Interpretation." *Dante Studies* 93 (1975) 1-25.

Compagni, Dino. *Chronicle of Florence*. Trans. Daniel E. Bornstein. Philadelphia: University of Pennsylvania Press, 1986.

Contini, Gianfranco. *Un'idea di Dante*. Turin: Einaudi, 1976.

Croce, Benedetto. *The Poetry of Dante*. Trans. Douglas Ainslie. New York: Henry Holt, 1922.

Curtius, Ernst Robert. "Dante." *European Literature and the Latin Middle Ages*. Trans. W. R. Trask. 1953. Princeton, NJ: Princeton University Press, 1990. 348-79.

Dante. *Dante's Inferno*. Adapted by Sandow Birk and Marcus Sanders. Illustrated by Sandow Birk. San Francisco: Chronicle Books, 2004.

_____. *Dantis Alagherii Epistolae: The Letters of Dante*. Ed. and trans. Paget Toynbee. 1920. New York: Oxford University Press, 1966.

_____. *The Divine Comedy of Dante Alighieri*. Trans. Robert M. Durling. Intro. and notes by Ronald L. Martinez and Robert M. Durling. 3 vols. New York: Oxford University Press, 1996, 2003, 2010.

_____. *The Divine Comedy of Dante Alighieri: Inferno*. Trans. Allen Mandelbaum. New York: Bantam Books, 1980.

_____. *The Divine Comedy of Dante Alighieri: Paradiso*. Trans. Allen Mandelbaum. New York: Bantam Books, 1984.

_____. *The Divine Comedy of Dante Alighieri: Purgatorio*. Trans. Allen Mandelbaum. New York: Bantam Books, 1982.

_____. *The Divine Comedy: 1. Inferno*. Trans. John D. Sinclair. New York: Oxford University Press, 1961.

_____. *The Inferno*. Trans. Robert Hollander and Jean Hollander. New York: Anchor, 2002.

_____. *Rime giovanili e della "Vita Nuova."* Ed. Teodolinda Barolini. Milan: Rizzoli, 2009.

De Sanctis, Francesco. *De Sanctis on Dante*. Ed. and trans. Joseph Rossi and Alfred Galpin. Madison: University of Wisconsin Press, 1957.

Ferrante, Joan M. *The Political Vision of the "Divine Comedy."* Princeton, NJ: Princeton University Press, 1984.

Frayling, Christopher. *Strange Landscape: A Journey Through the Middle Ages*. London: Penguin Books, 1995.

Freccero, John. *Dante: The Poetics of Conversion*. Ed. Rachel Jacoff. Cambridge, MA: Harvard University Press, 1988.

_____. Foreword. *The Inferno of Dante*. Trans. Robert Pinsky. New York: Farrar, Straus and Giroux, 1994.

Gilson, Simon. "Historicism, Philology and the Text. An Interview with Teodolinda Barolini." *Italian Studies* 63.1 (Spring 2008): 141-52.

Girard, René. "The Mimetic Desire of Paolo and Francesca." *To Double Business Bound: Essays on Literature, Mimesis, and Anthropology*. Baltimore: Johns Hopkins University Press, 1988.

Gragnolati, Manuele. *Experiencing the Afterlife*. Notre Dame, IN: University of Notre Dame Press, 2005.

Guido da Pisa. *Expositiones et glose super Comediam Dantis*. Ed. Vincenzo Ciioffari. Albany: State University of New York Press, 1974.

Harrison, Robert Pogue. *The Body of Beatrice*. Baltimore: Johns Hopkins University Press, 1988.

_____. "Comedy and Modernity: Dante's Hell." *Modern Language Notes* 102.5 (1987) 1043-61.

Hawkins, Peter S. *Dante's Testaments: Essays on Scriptural Imagination*. Stanford, CA: Stanford University Press, 2001.

Hawkins, Peter S., and Rachel Jacoff, eds. *The Poets' Dante: Twentieth-Century Responses*. New York: Farrar, Straus and Giroux, 2002.

Hollander, Robert. *Dante: A Life in Works*. New Haven, CT: Yale University Press, 2001.

_____. "Dante's Harmonious Homosexuals (*Inferno* 16.7-90)." *Electronic Bulletin of the Dante Society of America* 27 June 1996.

_____. "Dante's Use of *Aeneid* I in *Inferno* I and II." *Comparative Literature* 20.2 (1968): 142-56.

_____. *Virgilio dantesco: Tragedia nella "Commedia."* Florence: Olschki, 1983.

Holmes, George. *Dante*. New York: Farrar, Straus and Giroux, 1980.

Honess, Claire E. *From Florence to the Heavenly City: The Poetry of Citizenship in Dante*. London: Legenda, 2006.

Jacoff, Rachel. "Transgression and Transcendence: Figures of Female Desire in Dante's *Commedia*." *Dante*. Ed. Jeremy Tambling. New York: Longman, 1999. 51-67.

_____, ed. *The Cambridge Companion to Dante*. 2d ed. New York: Cambridge University Press, 2007.

Jacoff, Rachel, and Jeffrey T. Schnapp, eds. *The Poetry of Allusion: Virgil and Ovid in Dante's "Commedia."* Stanford, CA: Stanford University Press, 1991.

Kirkpatrick, Robin. *Dante's Inferno: Difficulty and Dead Poetry*. New York: Cambridge University Press, 2008.

Kleinhenz, Christopher. "Notes on Dante's Use of Classical Myths and the Mythological Tradition." *Romance Quarterly* 33 (1986): 477-84.

Landino, Cristoforo. *Comento sopra la "Comedia."* 4 vols. Ed. Paolo Procaccioli. Rome: Salerno, 2001.

Lansing, Richard, ed. *The Dante Encyclopedia*. New York: Garland, 2000.

Leigh, Gertrude. *New Light on the Youth of Dante: The Course of Dante's Life Prior to 1290 Traced in the "Inferno," Cantos 3-13*. London: Kenikat Press, 1969.

Lewis, R. W. B. *Dante: A Life*. 2001. New York: Penguin, 2009.

Mazzotta, Giuseppe. "The American Criticism of Charles Singleton." *Dante Studies* 104 (1986): 27-44.

_____. *Dante, Poet of the Desert: History and Allegory in the "Divine Comedy."* Princeton, NJ: Princeton University Press, 1979.

_____. *Dante's Vision and the Circle of Knowledge*. Princeton, NJ: Princeton University Press, 1993.

_____. "Reflections on Dante Studies in America." *Dante Studies* 118 (2000): 323-30.

_____, ed. *Critical Essays on Dante*. Boston: G. K. Hall, 1991.

Minnis, A. J., and A. B. Scott, eds. *Medieval Literary Theory and Criticism, c. 1100-c. 1375: The Commentary Tradition*. Oxford: Clarendon Press, 1988.

Moevs, Christian. *The Metaphysics of Dante's "Comedy."* New York: Oxford University Press, 2005.

Pequigney, Joseph. "Sodomy in Dante's *Inferno* and *Purgatorio*." *Representations* 36 (Fall 1991): 22-42.

Raffa, Guy P. "Dante's Mocking Poetic Muse." *Dante Studies* 114 (1996): 271-91.

_____. *Danteworlds: A Reader's Guide to the "Inferno."* Chicago: University of Chicago Press, 2007.

Scott, John A. *Understanding Dante*. Notre Dame, IN: University of Notre Dame Press, 2004.

Singleton, Charles S. *Dante Studies 1: Commedia. Elements of Structure*. Cambridge, MA: Harvard University Press, 1954.

_____. *Dante Studies 2: Journey to Beatrice*. Cambridge, MA: Harvard University Press, 1958.

_____. *Essay on the "Vita Nuova."* Cambridge, MA: Harvard University Press, 1949.

_____. "The Irreducible Dove." *Comparative Literature* 9 (1957): 129-35.

_____. "The Poet's Number at the Center." *Modern Language Notes* 80.1 [Italian issue] (Jan. 1965): 1-10.

Stone, Gregory B. *Dante's Pluralism and the Islamic Philosophy of Religion*. New York: Palgrave Macmillan, 2006.

Toynbee, Paget. *A Dictionary of Proper Names and Notable Matters in the Works of Dante*. 1898. Revised by Charles S. Singleton. Oxford: Clarendon Press, 1968.

Wilkins, Ernest Hatch, and Thomas Goddard Bergin. *A Concordance to the "Divine Comedy" of Dante Alighieri*. Cambridge, MA: Belknap Press of Harvard University Press, 1965.

CRITICAL INSIGHTS

About the Editor

Patrick Hunt received his Ph.D. from University College London (1991) and has taught in the humanities at Stanford University since 1993. He has been a postdoctoral Research Fellow at the University of California, Berkeley, and he is currently an Associate at the University of California, Los Angeles, Center for Medieval and Renaissance Studies. As a poet, he has published work in *Poet Lore*, *The Penguin Book of Classical Myths*, *Classical Outlook*, *Amphora* (American Philological Association), *Akoué* (American School of Classical Studies, Athens), and many others. His poetry has also been published by the Classical Association of the United Kingdom and in several collections, including *House of the Muse* (2005) and *Cloud Shadows of Olympus* (2009). He has authored ten other books, including several on classical mythology, literary analysis, and art historical biography, such as *Caravaggio* (2004), as well as *Ten Discoveries That Rewrote History* (2007).

Several of Dr. Hunt's articles on Dante have been published in Stanford's *Philolog*, as have his articles on Carolingian reuse of Roman spolia inscriptions, the medieval contexts of the Grand Saint Bernard monastery in the Alps, and the medieval reuse of Celtic sword history sourcing the Lady of the Lake in Arthurian tradition. He has authored more than fifty peer-reviewed articles, including reviews of mythology studies in *Renaissance Quarterly*, and has written many entries for Salem Press encyclopedias and other reference works, including on the medieval scientist Roger Bacon.

About *The Paris Review*

The Paris Review is America's preeminent literary quarterly, dedicated to discovering and publishing the best new voices in fiction, nonfiction, and poetry. The magazine was founded in Paris in 1953 by the young American writers Peter Matthiessen and Doc Humes, and edited there and in New York for its first fifty years by George Plimpton. Over the decades, the *Review* has introduced readers to the earliest writings of Jack Kerouac, Philip Roth, T. C. Boyle, V. S. Naipaul, Ha Jin, Ann Patchett, Jay McInerney, Mona Simpson, and Edward P. Jones, and published numerous now-classic works, including Roth's *Goodbye, Columbus*, Donald Barthelme's *Alice*, Jim Carroll's *Basketball Diaries*, and selections from Samuel Beckett's *Molloy* (his first publication in English). The first chapter of Jeffrey Eugenides's *The Virgin Suicides* appeared in the *Review*'s pages, as have stories by Rick Moody, David Foster Wallace, Denis Johnson, Jim Crace, Lorrie Moore, and Jeanette Winterson.

The Paris Review's renowned Writers at Work series of interviews, whose early installments include legendary conversations with E. M. Forster, William Faulkner, and Ernest Hemingway, is one of the landmarks of world literature. The interviews received a George Polk Award and were nominated for a Pulitzer Prize. Among the more than three hundred interviewees are Robert Frost, Marianne Moore, W. H. Auden, Elizabeth Bishop, Susan Sontag, and Toni Morrison. Recent issues feature conversations with Jonathan Franzen, Norman Rush, Louise Erdrich, Joan Didion, Norman Mailer, R. Crumb, Michel Houellebecq, Marilynne Robinson, David Mitchell, Annie Proulx, and Gay Talese. In November 2009, Picador published the final volume of a four-volume series of anthologies of *Paris Review* interviews. The *New York Times* called the Writers at Work series "the most remarkable and extensive interviewing project we possess."

The Paris Review is edited by Lorin Stein, who was named to the post in 2010. The editorial team has published fiction by Lydia Davis, André Aciman, Sam Lipsyte, Damon Galgut, Mohsin Hamid, Uzodinma Iweala, James Lasdun, Padgett Powell, Richard Price, and Sam Shepard. Recent poetry selections include work by Frederick Seidel, Carol Muske-Dukes, John Ashbery, Kay Ryan, Mary Jo Bang, Sharon Olds, Charles Wright, and Mary Karr. Writing published in the magazine has been anthologized in *Best American Short Stories* (2006, 2007, and 2008), *Best American Poetry*, *Best Creative Non-Fiction*, the Pushcart Prize anthology, and *O. Henry Prize Stories*.

The magazine presents three annual awards. The Hadada Award for lifelong contribution to literature has recently been given to Joan Didion, Norman Mailer, Peter Matthiessen, John Ashbery, and, in 2010, Philip Roth. The Plimpton Prize for Fiction, awarded to a debut or emerging writer brought to national attention in the pages of *The Paris Review*, was presented in 2007 to Benjamin Percy, to Jesse Ball in 2008, and to Alistair Morgan in 2009. In 2011, the magazine inaugurated the Terry Southern Prize for Humor.

The Paris Review was a finalist for the 2008 and 2009 National Magazine Awards in fiction and won the 2007 National Magazine Award in photojournalism. The *Los Angeles Times* recently called *The Paris Review* "an American treasure with true international reach," and the *New York Times* designated it "a thing of sober beauty."

Since 1999 *The Paris Review* has been published by The Paris Review Foundation, Inc., a not-for-profit 501(c)(3) organization.

The Paris Review is available in digital form to libraries worldwide in selected academic databases exclusively from EBSCO Publishing. Libraries can contact EBSCO at 1-800-653-2726 for details. For more information on *The Paris Review* or to subscribe, please visit: www.theparisreview.org.

_____

Patrick Hunt received his Ph.D. from University College London (1991), and he has taught humanities at Stanford University since 1993. He is also an Associate at the University of California, Los Angeles, Center for Medieval and Renaissance Studies. He is the author of ten books, including *Caravaggio* (2004), *Ten Discoveries That Rewrote History* (2007), *Cloud Shadows of Olympus* (2009), and *Myth and Art in Ekphrasis* (2010), and he has published several articles on Dante in Stanford's *Philolog* and in *Electrum Magazine*. He has published many articles in venues such as *Renaissance Quarterly* and the *Wiley-Blackwell Encyclopedia of Ancient History*, and he is a frequent contributor to the encyclopedias and other reference works published by Salem Press.

Nicole Rudick is Managing Editor of *The Paris Review*. She received her graduate education at Columbia University, and she has been an editor at *BookForum* and *Artforum*. She has authored many professional articles on art and literature. In addition to her ongoing work in *The Paris Review*, she has been published in the *Los Angeles Times*, *Arts & Letters*, *McSweeney's*, *The Millions*, and *Aperture* and has written for the National Book Critics Circle, among others.

Robert Pogue Harrison is Rosina Pierotti Professor of Italian Literature at Stanford University. He received his Ph.D. in romance studies at Cornell University, where he wrote his dissertation on Dante. He is the author of *The Body of Beatrice* (1989), which deals with Dante's early work *Vita Nuova*; *Forests: The Shadow of Civilization* (1992); *The Dominion of the Dead* (2003); and *Gardens: An Essay on the Human Condition* (2008). Each of his books discusses Dante's *Divine Comedy* in depth. He has also published essays on Dante, including on *Inferno* 27; one titled "Comedy and Modernity: Dante's Hell" appeared in *Modern Language Notes* (1987).

Heather Webb is Associate Professor of Italian at the Ohio State University. She is the author of *The Medieval Heart* (2010) as well as articles on Dante's *rime petrose*, Catherine of Siena's typology of tears as related to Dante's thought, late medieval notions of sensory function in religious and secular writings, Catherine of Siena's ideas of heart function, and a *lectura dantis* of *Paradiso* 25.

David Lummus is Assistant Professor of Italian at Yale University. He received his Ph.D. in Italian from Stanford University in 2008 with a dissertation on Giovanni Boccaccio's *Genealogie deorum gentilium*. His research focuses on fourteenth-century Italian poetry and humanism. He has published reviews in *Italian Culture* and *The Medieval Review*, and among his forthcoming publications are essays on Albertino Mussato, Boccaccio's *Buccolicum carmen*, and Italian poet Edoardo Sanguineti's criticism on Dante. He is currently working on a book about the politics of poetry in fourteenth-century Italy.

Elizabeth Coggeshall is a Ph.D. candidate in Italian at Stanford University, specializing in Dante studies and medieval Italian poetry. Her dissertation, titled "Dante's Friends," analyzes the shifting valence of friendship and community in Dante's life and works. She has also written on vision and the imagination in medieval literature and has previously published articles on Dante's relationship to Islam in the journals *Telos* and *La Fusta*.

Robert Hollander is Professor in European Literature (Emeritus) at Princeton University. He has authored or edited more than a dozen books, including *Allegory in Dante's "Commedia"* (1969), *Studies in Dante* (1980), *Dante: A Life in Works* (2002), and his translation of *Dante: Inferno* (2002). He has also published more than one hundred articles on Dante or Boccaccio. He is founding director of the Princeton Dante Project, and in 2007 he became the first American to be elected to the Council of the Società Dantesca Italiana.

Wallace Fowlie (1908-98) was Professor of French Literature at Duke University. He authored more than twenty books, including *A Reading of Dante's "Inferno"* (1981), *The Clown's Grail: A Study of Love in Its Literary Expression* (1947), *Rimbaud: The Myth of Childhood* (1946), *Age of Surrealism* (1950), *Mallarme* (1953), *André Gide: His Life and Art* (1965), and *Poem and Symbol: A Brief History of French Symbolism* (1990).

David Thompson has authored several books, including *Dante's Epic Journeys* (1974), and has coauthored and translated Italian texts in *The Humanism of Leonardo Bruni* (1987). His work has also been published in various journals, including *Dante Studies*, *Viator*, and *Neophilologus*.

John C. Barnes is Professor of Italian Studies at University College Dublin. Among other books, he is coeditor of *Dante and His Literary Precursors* (2007) and *Dante and the Human Body* (2007). He has also authored many entries in *The Dante Encyclopedia* (2000) and the *Oxford Companion to Italian Literature* (2002) as well as in *Medieval Italy: An Encyclopedia* (2004).

Francesca Guerra D'Antoni received her Ph.D. in Italian and comparative literature from the University of Illinois at Urbana-Champaign. She has taught at the University of Kansas and the University of Colorado. She is the author of *Dante's Burning Sands: Some New Perspectives* (1991) and of articles on Italian art and literature published in such journals as *Romance Philology*.

John Freccero is Professor of Italian Studies and Comparative Literature at New York University. His many books include *Dante: A Collection of Critical Essays* (1965), *Dante: The Poetics of Conversion* (1988), and *Dante's Cosmos* (1998). He has also written forewords to several books, including Robert Pinsky's translation *The Inferno of Dante*, as well as many seminal articles on Dante.

Joseph Luzzi is Professor of Italian and Director of the Italian Program at Bard College. He received his Ph.D. from Yale University, and he has been awarded numerous prizes for writing and teaching. His publications include *Romantic Europe and the Ghost of Italy* (2008) and many articles that have appeared in such journals as *Dante*

Studies, Italica, and *Yale Italian Poetry.* He has been a guest editor of *Modern Language Quarterly* and *Yale Journal of Criticism.*

Gabrielle Lesperance did her doctoral studies at the University of California, Los Angeles. She has coedited the *Atti del XVI Congresso of AISLLI* (International Association of Italian Studies) and has written for *Carte Italiane* and for the collection *Dante, Cinema, and Television* (2004). She has taught at the University of Southern California and at the University of California, Santa Barbara, as well as at the University of California, Los Angeles.

Alison Cornish is Associate Professor of Italian at the University of Michigan. Her many Dante publications include articles in *Dante Studies, Lectura Dantis, Studi Danteschi,* and *Traditio* and two books, *Vernacular Translation in Dante's Italy: Illiterate Literature* (2010) and *Reading Dante's Stars* (2000). She also coedited the volume *Sparks and Seeds: Medieval Italian Literature and Its Afterlife—Essays in Honor of John Freccero* (2000).

Richard H. Lansing is Professor of Italian Studies and Comparative Literature at Brandeis University. He received his Ph.D. from the University of California, Berkeley. He has been editor in chief of *Dante Studies* since 2008. He is editor of *The Dante Encyclopedia* (2002) and of the eight volumes that make up *Dante: The Critical Complex* (2003), as well as coeditor of *Medieval Italy: An Encyclopedia* (2004). His other publications include *From Image to Idea: A Study of the Simile in Dante's "Commedia"* (1977) and many articles on Dante.

Glending Olson is Professor at Cleveland State University, Emeritus. He is the author of *Literature as Recreation in the Later Middle Ages* (1982) and coeditor of a volume of Chaucer's *Canterbury Tales* (1989); he has also published on Dante and related topics in *The Cambridge History of Literary Criticism* and *The Chaucer Review,* among others.

Acknowledgments

"The *Paris Review* Perspective" by Nicole Rudick. Copyright© 2012 by Nicole Rudick. Special appreciation goes to Christopher Cox, Nathaniel Rich, and David Wallace-Wells, editors at *The Paris Review*.

"The Moral System of the *Commedia* and the Seven Capital Sins" by Robert Hollander. From *Allegory in Dante's "Commedia"* (Princeton University Press, 1969) by Robert Hollander. Copyright © 1969 by Robert Hollander. Reprinted with permission of Robert Hollander.

"Canto 1: The Dark Wood" by Wallace Fowlie. From *A Reading of Dante's "Inferno"* (1981) by Wallace Fowlie. Copyright © 1981 by The University of Chicago Press. All rights reserved. Reprinted with permission of The University of Chicago Press.

"Aeneas and Dante" by David Thompson. From *Dante's Epic Journeys* (1974) by David Thompson. Copyright © 1974 by The Johns Hopkins University Press. Reprinted with permission of The Johns Hopkins University Press.

"Dante's Knowledge of Florentine History" by John C. Barnes. From *Dante and His Literary Precursors: Twelve Essays* (2007) edited by John C. Barnes and Jennifer Petrie. Copyright © 2007 by the University College Dublin Foundation for Italian Studies. Reprinted with permission of the University College Dublin Foundation for Italian Studies.

"Nature's Revenge" by Francesca Guerra D'Antoni. From *Dante's Burning Sands: Some New Perspectives* (1991) by Francesca Guerra D'Antoni. Copyright © 1991 by Peter Lang Publishing, Inc. Reprinted with permission of Peter Lang Publishing, Inc.

"Canto 4: Limbo (First Circle)" by Wallace Fowlie. From *A Reading of Dante's "Inferno"* (1981) by Wallace Fowlie. Copyright © 1981 by The University of Chicago Press. All rights reserved. Reprinted with permission of The University of Chicago Press.

"The Portrait of Francesca: *Inferno* V" by John Freccero. From *MLN* 124.5 Supplement (December 2009): S7-S38. Copyright © 2010 by The Johns Hopkins University Press. Reprinted with permission of The Johns Hopkins University Press.

"Echoes of Andromache in *Inferno* X" by Joseph Luzzi. From *Dante Studies* 122 (2004): 27-43. Copyright © 2004 by the Dante Society of America. Reprinted with permission of the Dante Society of America.

"Beginning to Think about *Salò*" by Gabrielle Lesperance. From *Dante, Cinema, and Television* (2004) edited by Amilcare A. Iannucci. Copyright © 2004 by the University of Toronto Press. Reprinted with permission of the publisher.

"Dante's Monsters in the *Inferno*: Reimagining Classical to Christian Judgment" by Patrick Hunt. From *Philolog* 3 April 2010. Copyright © 2009 by Patrick Hunt. Reprinted with permission of Patrick Hunt.

"Canto 11: The Plan of Hell" by Wallace Fowlie. From *A Reading of Dante's "Inferno"* (1981) by Wallace Fowlie. Copyright © 1981 by The University of Chicago Press. All rights reserved. Reprinted with permission of The University of Chicago Press.

"The Harvest of Reading: *Inferno* 20, 24, 26" by Alison Cornish. From *Reading Dante's Stars* (2000) by Alison Cornish. Copyright © 2000 by Yale University Press. Reprinted with permission of Yale University Press.

"Submerged Meanings in Dante's Similes (*Inf.* XXVII)" by Richard H. Lansing. From *Dante Studies* 94 (1976): 61-69. Copyright © 1976 by the Dante Society of America. Reprinted with permission of the Dante Society of America.

"*Inferno* 27 and the Perversions of Pentecost" by Glending Olson. From *Dante Studies* 117 (1999): 21-33. Copyright © 1999 by the Dante Society of America. Reprinted with permission of the Dante Society of America.

Index

Guido da Montefeltro (*Inferno*), 44, 301-302, 305, 312, 314, 316, 319

Hardie, Colin, 171
Hardie, Philip, 291, 299
Harpies, 248
Harrison, Robert Pogue, viii, 14, 341
Hell; as a city, 83; depiction in *Inferno*, 6, 11, 44, 172, 184-185, 203; harrowing of, 174, 257; medieval conceptions of, 5, 55, 247; structure in *Inferno*, 11-14, 29, 101, 260, 265-269, 310; structure in *Nicomachean Ethics* (Aristotle), 176
Henry VII, 24, 95, 137
Hollander, John, 216
Hollander, Robert, 249, 280, 284, 326, 342
Homer, 173, 268; Augustine on, 208; in *Inferno*, 175
Hunt, Patrick, 339

Incontinence, 176, 265, 267
Inferno (Dante); critical responses, 63; language of, 8, 65-66, 73, 315; sources, 5; structure, 102; time frame, 23, 45, 172

Jewell, Keala, 246
Jewiss, Virginia, 247
Justice, 11, 16, 29, 64, 185, 235, 246, 256, 260, 304, 312

Kay, Richard, 168

Landino, Cristoforo, 66
Lansing, Richard H., 298, 343
Latini, Brunetto. *See* Brunetto Latini
Leff, Gordon, 318
Lesperance, Gabrielle, 343
Letter to Can Grande (Dante). *See* Epistle to Cangrande della Scala
Limbo, 7, 12, 172-176; poets in, 175

Love, 47, 51, 54-55, 60, 165, 179-180, 185, 190, 194-195, 197, 201, 205, 217, 273; contrasted with lust, 53, 59, 187, 197; courtly, 192
Lukács, György, 183
Lummus, David, 341
Lust, 14, 44, 50, 53-57, 59, 105, 187
Luzzi, Joseph, 342

Malice, 267
Martinez, Ronald L., 298
Mazzotta, Giuseppe, 75
Medusa (*Inferno*), 249
Metamorphoses (Ovid), 161, 175, 193, 199, 290
Metempsychosis, 7, 158, 169
Migliorini, Bruno, 160
Minotaur (*Inferno*), 103, 252
Monarchia (Dante). *See* De monarchia
Monsters; as allegories in *Inferno*, 245; in classical myth, 246
Montaperti, Battle of, 20, 87, 143, 145, 150
Montefeltro, Guido da. *See* Guido da Montefeltro
Motifs. *See* Themes and motifs

Najemy, John M., 86, 93
Nicomachean Ethics (Aristotle), 176
Nuova cronica (Villani), 27, 134, 151, 156

Odyssey (Homer), 169, 173
Olson, Glending, 343
Ovid, 161, 175, 193, 199, 245, 290, 304

Paolo and Francesca episode, 16, 44, 49, 51-52, 165, 179-182, 187, 192, 194, 202-203, 205-207, 209-210, 217-218
Paradiso (Dante), 47, 49-50, 60, 63, 106, 190; Florence in, 130, 139, 148; love in, 60; structure, 101

Pasolini, Pier Paolo, 235
Peripety, 8, 11, 13
Phaedrus (Plato), 179, 198, 206
Poggioli, Renato, 195
Portinari, Beatrice. *See* Beatrice Protinari
Pound, Ezra, 69
Pride, 50, 103, 110, 163, 315
Prologue Scene, 11, 35-37, 45, 70, 113-
    119; beasts, 14, 114; Vergil's
    appearance, 114, 119
Purgatorio (Dante), 49-50, 52, 56, 58,
    145; correlations with *Inferno*, 102
Purgatory, 58, 116, 242; contrasted with
    Hell, 46, 50, 101, 181
Pézard, André, 168, 321

Rhyme scheme of *Inferno*, 10, 41-42, 75
Rudick, Nicole, 341

Salò o le 120 giornate di Sodoma (film),
    connections with *The Divine
    Comedy*, 235-242
Sanders, Marcus, 67
Scalla, Cangrande della. *See* Cangrande
    della Scala
Schwartz, David, 236
Sicilian School, 21
Similes, 301; agrarian, 284-287; avian,
    186, 188; Boniface VIII and Guido
    compared with Constantine and Pope
    Sylvester, 306-307; Sicilian bull,
    302-303, 305
Simon Magus (*Inferno*), 15, 191, 312
Simony, 15, 110
Singleton, Charles S., 73, 78, 96, 126, 233
Sins; avarice, 105, 107, 164; bestial, 14,
    59, 159, 265; blasphemy, 164, 166,
    269; envy, 103, 109; fraud, 29, 103,
    110, 165, 256, 265, 268, 272, 275;
    gluttony, 106, 254; incontinence, 176,
    265, 267; lust, 14, 44, 50, 53-57, 59,

105, 187; malice, 267; pride, 50, 103,
    110, 163, 315; punishments, 11, 16,
    29, 43-44, 55, 64, 176, 235, 260, 268,
    275, 279, 312; simony, 15, 110; sloth,
    102, 107-108; sodomy, 58, 161, 167,
    269; usury, 162, 166-167, 269; wrath,
    102, 109
Sloth, 102, 107-108
Sodomy, 58, 161, 167, 269
Spiral movement, 12, 38, 46, 74, 259
Spitzer, Leo, 187, 311
Storms, 49-51
Swing, T. K., 101-102, 104

Terza rima, 10, 42, 75
Themes and motifs; ascent through
    descent, 14, 18, 38, 46, 293; circles,
    12, 14, 29, 38, 41, 46-47, 166, 190,
    280; corruption, 9, 17, 66, 83, 89, 95,
    106, 109, 309; desire, 16, 43, 54, 56,
    59, 174, 179, 182, 185, 188-191, 196,
    198, 202; estrangement from God,
    114, 119; greed, 14, 89, 105, 107,
    158, 163-164; journey of the poet,
    30, 36, 47, 66, 74, 113, 305, 320;
    justice, 11, 16, 29, 64, 185, 235, 246,
    256, 260, 304, 312; love, 47, 51, 53-
    55, 60, 165, 179-180, 185, 187, 190,
    192, 194-195, 197, 201, 205, 217,
    273; protest, 174; sleep, 172-173;
    storms, 49-51
Thomas Aquinas, 17, 74, 126, 265, 273
Thompson, David, 342
Translations of *Inferno* into English, 48,
    68, 181, 193
Trinity (Christian), 10, 42, 255; Satan as
    parody of, 319

Ulysses (*Inferno*), 44, 70, 122, 287, 290-
    291, 299, 312
Usury, 162, 166-167, 269

Vergil, 39, 131, 171, 188, 221, 292; Dante's imitations of, 246, 255

Vergil (*Inferno*), 36, 115-116, 173, 176, 269, 276, 281; as authority figure, 38-39, 115, 119; knowledge of, 265, 272, 283; on love, 54; as symbol of human reason, 30, 39; as virtuous pagan, 287

Vestibule of the neutrals, 176, 268

Vico, Giambattista, 67

Villani, Giovanni, 27, 84, 86, 134, 140, 151

Virgil. *See* Vergil

Vita nuova, La (Dante), 23, 30, 218

Waste Land, The (Eliot), allusions to *Inferno*, 71

Webb, Heather, 341

Wordplay, 8, 196-197, 202, 243

Wrath, 102, 109